CALIFORNIA AFTER ARNOLD

CALIFORNIA AFTER ARNOLD

Stephen D. Cummings
Patrick B. Reddy

Algora Publishing
New York

Library of Congress Cataloging-in-Publication Data —

Cummings, Stephen D., 1947-
  California after Arnold / Stephen D. Cummings, Patrick B. Reddy.
    p. cm.
  Includes bibliographical references and index.
  ISBN 978-0-87586-738-0 (trade paper : alk. paper) — ISBN 978-0-87586-739-7 (hard
cover: alk. paper) 1. California—Politics and government—1951- 2. Schwarzenegger,
Arnold. I. Reddy, Patrick B., 1960- II. Title.
  JK8716.C86 2009
  320.794—dc22
                        2009032347

Front Cover: Governor Schwarzenegger Speaks at the AltaMed Health Services
Corporation Policy Forum held at the Beverly Hilton Hotel in Beverly Hills. May 01, 2009
© Axel Koester/Corbis

Printed in the United States

Table of Contents

INTRODUCTION

This book is about two global phenomena — Arnold Schwarzenegger and California — and their interaction with each other. Both are stars in their own right.

Arnold — as he is known around the world — is a bigger-than-life, top box office, Hollywood movie star. His every move is watched by legions of fans and movie star groupies everywhere. Two incidents that occurred during the writing of this book illustrate the scale of his notoriety. The first occurred on the grounds of the State Capitol in Sacramento. A group of young people was posing for photos at the bottom of the stairs, when one asked in Russian-accented English, "Is this where Arnold works?" It is a jarring question when one realizes that these people probably lived thousands of miles away on another continent and were now standing in front of a building that most Californians never visit. The second incident was even more amazing — "Schwarzenegger" is in MS Word spell-check. Can anyone conceive of the idea that such an agglomeration of consonants and vowels would be in spell-check? Arnold is everywhere. Foreign newspapers track every burp and belch of the California state budget crisis because of him. Many of them asked the question "has Arnold's legacy been tarnished" when his budget propositions failed in the May 2009 special election. While the impact of California's financial crisis on the national and global economy would be significant by the very size of California's economy, no doubt Arnold's role in the drama has added to the stories and additional circulation to newspapers.

California is equally a star and has been one since long before Arnold. It is not only the most populous state in the United States; it is a state of mind. Indeed California, as the home of Hollywood and the movie industry, made Arnold, not the other way around. California has been many things to many people. Its geographic diversity is remarkable. Just about any geographic area that you can find elsewhere in the United States, you can find in California. California has in the space of 85 miles the highest point in the lower forty-eight states and the lowest point in North America.

In addition to great mountain ranges and vast deserts, it has huge metropolitan areas like Los Angeles County, the San Francisco Bay Area, and the suburban counties of Southern California, each of which would be among the largest states in the union. California's extensive farmlands, the largest and most valuable in the nation, are peppered by metropolitan areas of half a million people, dwarfing farming communities in other states. California has extensive forests containing the largest, tallest, and oldest trees on the planet. It has deltas and marshes. All of these geographic wonders are fronted by over 700 miles of some of the most spectacular coastline in America.

California's people are as remarkable as its geography. As the Mecca for gold rush prospectors, adventurers, movie starlets, Dust Bowl refugees, New Age gurus, and ordinary people from across the country and around the world seeking a better life, California boasts a diversity of people that is astonishing. More than one commentator has viewed this aggregation of social and ethnic groups, cults, and personalities as the "land of fruits and nuts." Nevertheless, the people living here have built the fifth, sixth, seventh or eighth largest economy in the world, depending on how one crunches the numbers.

California's politics is as remarkable as California's personality. Since Governor Hiram Johnson revolutionized California's government with the initiation of the initiative, referendum, and recall in 1911, California has practiced a form of direct ballot box democracy unlike any other state. The combination of Arnold Schwarzenegger, California, and its unique politics came together in its gaudiest form with the 2003 recall election of Governor Gray Davis. The recall was part direct democracy, part voter outrage and revenge, part media circus and Hollywood glamour. With 135 of the most bizarre candidates ever to run for major public office, the result was an election that installed as governor an ex-bodybuilder who made his early success in Hollywood running around nearly naked in various films and who was a Republican who married into the Kennedy family. In one evening in October 2003, Arnold was transformed into Governor Schwarzenegger of California.

The "Arnold Show" has been going on for six years now and has another year and a half to run. It has been quite a ride from the highs of 2004, to the crash of the special election of 2005, to re-election in 2006, to the current battle over the California budget and the ongoing battle with the global financial crisis that is pounding the state and is guaranteed to make the governor's remaining term in office a difficult one. Likewise, the upcoming 2010 election to select Schwarzenegger's successor as governor is clouded by the state's fiscal mess, and the fact that previous governors faced economic crises with the specter of Hiram Johnson's recall provision hanging over them like a guillotine or the Sword of Damocles. The question one has to ask, then, is what happens to California after Arnold?

That is the question that this book attempts to answer. It attempts to do so in three parts. The first part is the Arnold factor, with Chapter 1 about the 2003 recall, Chapter 2 covering Arnold's years as governor, and Chapter 3 his ultimate legacy as governor.

Part 2 is about California. Chapter 4 is a brief history of California politics from 1911 to the present and shows the historical forces that affect the upcoming 2010 election. It covers the legacy of Hiram Johnson's reforms, describes the rise of the

Democratic Party, and culminates in the election of Pat Brown in 1958, followed by the conservative era of the Reagan Coalition from the 1960s through the 1980s when working class Democrats were firmly in the Republican camp based on social issues, and the break-up of that coalition, starting in 1992, into the current Democratic Coalition based on the return of those working class Democrats and the rising electoral strength of minority voters. Chapter 5 discusses the institutional structures such as the initiative and the Two–Thirds Budget rule, term limits, and other forces that affect how politics is run in California. Chapter 6 covers the issues that the next governor will be facing.

Part 3 is about California in 2010 and the 2010 election. Chapter 7 tracks the demographic, economic and political changes from 1958 and how they will impact 2010 and future elections. It breaks California down by regions, race and ethnicity, class and ideology. Chapter 8 is about the governorship, with profiles and characteristics of past governors, and biographical sketches of the candidates. The last chapter is an assessment of who most likely will be the party nominees and who will be elected the next Governor of California.

Following the text is an extensive statistical appendix covering the demographics of California from 1960 to the present, the geographic and ethnic breakouts of the governor and U.S. Senate races from 1958 to 2008, and the geographic and ethnic breakouts for key ballot propositions from 1958 to 2008. We greatly appreciate this data base and also Mr. Schneider's tutoring on both California and national politics. The appendix is the most detailed collection of California election data of its kind in one source.

California and its people continue to fascinate observers of all kinds. Its sheer size, diversity and economic power mean that it has the ability to influence events in the United States and around the world. It directly impacted two presidential elections in 1916 and 1968. Californians were elected four times between 1968 and 1984. Today, the current battle regarding Governor Schwarzenegger, the California legislature, and the California budget makes headlines in the foreign press as well as this country. The next governor of California will not only have to deal with the current financial crisis, but will be making decisions that will affect the nation and the world. It is for this reason that books like this one are written.

The credit for the concept of this book must go to Roger Carrick, whom both authors met on the Kathleen Brown Campaign of 1994. Some of the data were compiled by Mr. Reddy two decades ago when he was a research assistant for Bill Schneider at CNN and the American Enterprise Institute. For the data collected in 2009, numerous persons were indispensable, including: the crack staff at the California State Archives, Keating Holland of CNN, Sarah Dutton at CBS, Jim Barnes, Karlyn Bowman, Dennis Kelly in San Francisco's Chinatown, David Cismowski, Dan Mitchell and the rest of the staff at the California State Library, Mark DiCamillo, and Mervin Field and Jennifer Turley at the Census Bureau. At the UC Data Archive at Berkeley, Jon Stiles and the lovely and charming Susan Grand performed above and beyond the call of duty. Generous financial assistance was provided by Jack and Sue Reddy, Martha Reddy Lehman, Bill Schneider, Darry Sragow, Ed Stevens, Alan Anderson, Robert Hertzberg, Antonio Villaraigosa, Herb Wesson, Steve Soboroff, Charles McKittrick and the late Mark Smith. Mike Witherow, Mike Wagaman and John Connally delivered needed technical assistance.

Over the past 20 years, numerous pundits, scholars, observers and consultants have shared their insights about California with the authors, particularly Mr. Reddy: Lynn Montgomery, Bill Cavala, Tim Reardon, Tony Quinn, Greg Schmidt, Roger Carrick, Bob Vogel, Alex Parr, Ed Mitchell, Lorena Fajardo, Greg Wickstrom, Xandra Kayden, Carlota Gutierrez, Tim Douglas, Barbara Guido, Joe Scott, Brenda Coleman, Debbie Van Ness, John Fairbank, Paul Goodwin, Richard Maullin, Larry Sokol, John Kim, Ed Stevens, Richard Murray, Kam Kuwata, Bruce Cain, Don Stone, Delilah & Bob Schelen, Janice Berman, Howard Elinson, Martha Felix, Jim Wisley, Trent Hager, the late Mike Gordon, Darry Sragow, Bill Mashburn, Bernd Schwieren, Don Levin, Ray Sotero, Susan Pinkus, Claudia Vaughn, the late Bud Lewis, Maggie Linden, Chris Wagaman, Sherry & Doug Jeffe, Howard Cohen, Henry Sheinkopf, Steve Sailer, Kim Nethercutt, Shawn Cook, Tom Jakubek, Bob Mulholland, Claudia Piston and the late Wade Piston. Kimberly, Rosemary and, of course, Vickie and Elizabeth provided much-needed inspiration.

Finally, many thanks to Martin, Andrea and all the people at Algora Publishing for their support and assistance in making this book possible.

Steve Cummings
Ventura, California
Patrick Reddy
Santa Monica, California
September, 2009

PART I. THE ARNOLD CHRONICLES

CHAPTER 1. ARNOLD AND THE RECALL

> "When one has money, one day it becomes less interesting. And when one is the best in film, what can be more interesting? Perhaps power. Then one moves into politics and becomes governor or president or something." — Champion bodybuilder Arnold Schwarzenegger at the start of his film career in 1978 on his future plans. [1]

Since Arnold Schwarzenegger was once the world's most popular movie star, let us begin with a pitch in Hollywood for a script about California politics:

> [T]he story begins with a couple of street thugs sitting in a Cleveland prison after being arrested on suspicion of car theft. While there, the two Lebanese-American brothers decide that stealing cars is too risky a business and perhaps there is money to be made in preventing car theft with an alarm system. So they start a new business, the brothers' car alarm company is a wild success, and they make millions.
>
> One brother moves to California and gets involved in Republican politics, using his wealth to win a seat in the House of Representatives in 2000. A few years later, he notices that the Democratic Governor of California is quite unpopular and there is an embryonic movement to recall him. The Congressman gives crucial financial support for the recall — almost $2 million — allowing it to qualify for the ballot. In doing so, he clears the way for the election of a man who spent the first 35 years of his life pumping weights and popping steroids, before segueing into a career as an actor who was most famous for running around half-naked killing people while cracking silly one-liners. A man who apologized for groping women on "rowdy movie sets," bragged about attending orgies in Venice Beach and admitted using various drugs...

A studio executive might reject this script too preposterous for either the critics or the public to believe — even on HBO. However, this was pretty much the story of the 2003 California recall election.

---

1 Wendy Leigh, *Arnold: An Unauthorized Biography*, (Chicago: Congdon & Weed, 1990), 178.

The cast of characters for this story include Darryl Issa as the car thief-turned-Congressman who funded the recall, Gray Davis as the embattled Governor and Arnold the actor-turned-candidate. (A word about the Arnold Brand Name: When a producer in the 1970s advised him to change his last name, Schwarzenegger replied that one day he would be so famous, the entire world would know him by his first name alone. Thus it has been — the name Arnold evokes just one person, just as the names Hillary, Madonna, and now Barack do.) Here is a brief history of how it all happened.

THE DAVIS DEBACLE

Background

> "The missing ingredient has been the lack of political rapport with major political figures in his party." — Gray Davis, Chief of Staff to Governor Jerry Brown on his boss's mistakes in 1980. [1]

In 1998, Democrat Gray Davis was elected governor of California by a 20-point landslide, a bigger margin than Ronald Reagan ever won by here. Coming after 16 years of Republican governors, including the last eight under Pete Wilson who had gained a well-deserved national reputation for divisiveness, Davis seemed to offer a calm unifying competence. Wilson had promoted Proposition 187 to cut off state services to illegal immigrants and their children (even to those kids who were American-born) plus Proposition 209 to end all affirmative action in state government operations. Both passed but also sparked ferocious battles with the black, Hispanic, and Asian communities. Just as in 1958, the Republican rightwing took on organized labor 40 years later with Proposition 226, which sought to curtail labor's participation in campaigns. Just as in 1958, labor beat back this challenge. (The Assembly Democrats' "1998 Blueprint for Victory" campaign manual said "the defeat of Prop 226 has given new strength to our allies in labor.") Labor's mobilization, combined with a high minority turnout eager to end the Wilson years (the forceful slogan in East Los Angeles was "Adios Pete Wilson") gave a tremendous boost to Davis. Arguing that the time for division was over and presenting himself as a candidate of cool competence (his ads called him, "California's most qualified governor in waiting" who had "experience money can't buy"), Davis overwhelmed Republican Dan Lundgren by over 1.6 million votes and carried in huge Democratic majorities in both Houses of the State Legislature (see Appendix 1D). It was the broadest Democratic sweep since Pat Brown in 1958.

For the first two years of his tenure, Davis was widely popular, earning a 61–21% positive job rating from the Field Poll in June of 2000. And why not? The state's high-tech boom produced a $12 billion surplus in the spring of 2000, which Governor Davis happily spent on both social programs for the Democrats and tax cuts for the Republicans. Sure, a few curmudgeons like Tom McClintock pointed out that money does not grow on trees, but they were a distinct minority. The boom had also eased the state's social tensions by providing jobs for the poor and immigrants and he was starting to build more schools, just as the public wanted. Davis was perhaps, a little

---

1 Lou Cannon, "Jerry Brown: A Back to Basics," *Washington Post*, August 13, 1980.
2 Antonio Villaraigosa, Assembly Democrats 1998 Blueprint for Victory, Campaign Manual.

bland and cautious, but overall, quite an acceptable governor for the times. After recovering from a devastating bust in the 1990s due to reduced defense spending, California could have borrowed the phrase: "Let the Good Times Roll."

And the good economic times meant political rewards for all Democrats. Al Gore carried the state by over 1 million votes despite hardly campaigning there and the Democrats picked up a few more seats in the Legislature. After the November 2000 triumph, California Democrats even felt confident enough to invade the Republican stronghold of Orange County by holding their state convention there for the first time in party history.

But beginning in the winter of 2000–01, a series of events — energy shortages, rolling blackouts, dubbed "Gray-outs" by his critics, a high-tech economic slowdown and chronic budget problems (that $12 billion surplus had turned into a $30 billion-plus deficit) that led to tax/fee increases — slowly undermined Davis' political base. And surprisingly, Davis repeated Jerry Brown's mistakes of becoming isolated from both his party and the people, preferring to spend much of his time raising money. "Davis' standing with Californians has plummeted. Majorities of voters oppose his re-election," screamed the headline in the May 2001 Field Poll press release just after the energy crisis hit. That same Field Poll revealed that Davis' job rating had gone from 57–34% positive in December 2000 to 36–55 negative, a stunning 42-point reversal in less than six months (See Table 1–1). By 2002, the voters had grudgingly re-elected Davis over Republican Bill Simon despite the fact the *L.A. Times* exit poll gave him only a 39% job approval rating. In his victory speech, Davis acknowledged that he was surprised by his small margin and admitted that it was a "wake-up call." Pat Caddell, an advisor to Jerry Brown's 1992 presidential campaign pointed out on MSNBC Election Night that a majority of Californians had rejected Davis and speculated that there might be a recall election in Davis' future. Republicans, including Simon's former campaign manager Sal Russo, announced their recall effort shortly after Davis was inaugurated for his second term, but the public appeared uninterested at that time; only 39% supported recalling Governor Davis in the March *Los Angeles Times* Poll, while 51% were opposed.

At the 2003 California State Democratic Party Convention shortly after the recall effort was announced, a co-author of this book Patrick Reddy ran into Davis' pollster John Fairbank, whom Reddy had worked for in the early 1990s, and asked him about the possible recall, given Davis' dismal 27% job rating in the same *Times* Poll. He replied that he did not think it would qualify for the ballot. When asked, what if it does? He repeated that he did not think it would make it and moved on.

For a while, it looked like Mr. Fairbank was right. Less than 10% of the required 900,000 registered voters had signed the recall petition by the end of winter, the drive simply lacked money and oomph. Gray Davis himself ridiculed the recall as being led by "rich, rightwing sore losers." And there was an institutional conservatism that could help save any governor. As the *San Diego Union–Tribune* commented:

> "This editorial page endorsed Davis' opponent for governor. But we see no legitimate grounds for his recall from office. Even to attempt Davis' recall strikes us as a reckless and unwarranted use of the recall provision."[2]

1 Patrick Caddell commentary on MSNBC, November 5, 2002
2 Editorial, "No Recall," *San Diego Union–Tribune*, February 18, 2003.

Polls also showed that voters were not engaged yet on this issue. Since California Republicans were only about 35% of the state's registered voters, they would need more than the base to succeed. As Bill Cavala, the state's top consultant in legislative campaigns put it: "unless Democrats and Independents join the lynch mob, the effort would fail."[1]

TABLE 1–1. JOB APPROVAL RATINGS FOR GOVERNOR DAVIS

Poll	Date	%Approve	% Disapprove
Field	August 2000	56%	28%
Field	January 2001	57%	34%
Field	May 2001	36%	55%
Field	December 2001	38%a	51%
Field	January 2002	39%	53%
Field	April 2002	39%	54%
Field	July 2002	41%	49%
Field	September 2002	39%	49%
Field	April 2003	24%	65%
Field	July 2003	23%	66%
Field	August 2003	22%	70%
L.A. Times	October 2000	59%	26%
L.A. Times	January 2001	51%	39%
L.A. Times	June 2001	43%	46%
L.A. Times	February 2002	47%	47%
L.A. Times	October 2002	46%	49%
L.A. Times	November Exit Poll	39%	61%
L.A. Times	March 2003	27%	64%
L.A. Times	July 2003	22%	67%
L.A. Times	August 2003	26%	72%
L.A. Times	October Exit Poll	25%	75%

But the disappointment with Davis and the constant harangues of local conservative talk radio hosts caused the recall effort to stick around like an iceberg just below the surface threatening Davis' governorship. The Governor's popularity had been bleeding consistently since the energy crisis of 2001 and as Republican analyst Tony Quinn commented: "Sometimes recalls, like propositions, can take on a life of their own."[2] At the end of March 2003, George Skelton wrote in the *Los Angeles Times*, "The

---

1 Patrick Reddy conversation with Bill Cavala in Speaker's Office.
2 Patrick Reddy, Private conversation with Tony Quinn, spring of 2003.

recall-Gray Davis movement seems dead in the water. But this governor is so disliked and disrespected, nobody but a fool would count out the freebooters gunning for him."[1] Reddy wrote in a United Press International column that was prepared in late April and published on May 6, 2003, that for Davis to be recalled, everything would have to go wrong: the economy would have to get worse, his own party would have to turn against him, and there would have to be a credible replacement.[2] It simply did not look probable in early May.

The Issa Intervention

However, on May 6, Republican Congressman Darryl Issa, the multi-millionaire car alarm salesman, announced that he would donate $1.7 million of his own money to hire professional signature-gatherers. It seems that Congressman Issa was also interested in running for governor himself and apparently was encouraged to fund the recall by a famous Hollywood action star with a Teutonic accent. The movement immediately picked up momentum, getting over half the necessary 900,000 signatures by Memorial Day. By the July Fourth weekend, the *Los Angeles Times* Poll was reporting that 70% of Californians were "following the recall story closely" and even most importantly, now 51% favored recalling Davis compared to just 39% in March (See Table 1-2). The wire services reported that the signatures were continuing to come in rapidly and the only question became whether the recall election would be held in the fall of 2003 or the regularly-scheduled primary in the winter of 2004.

TABLE 1–2. TRENDS IN THE RECALL QUESTION:
SHOULD GOVERNOR DAVIS BE RECALLED?

Poll	Date	% Yes	% No
L.A. Times	March 2003	39%	51%
L.A. Times	July 2003	51%	42%
L.A. Times	August 2003	50%	45%
L.A. Times	September 2003	56%	42%
Field	April 2003	46%	43%
Field	July 2003	51%	43%
Field	August 2003	58%	37%
Field	September 2003	55%	40%
Field	October 2003	57%	39%
Election Day Result	October 2003	55%	45%

---

1 George Skelton, "Governor Has Reason to Worry Over the Dump-Davis Effort, *Los Angeles Times*, March 13, 2003, http://8.12.42.31/2003/mar/13/me-cap13.
2 Patrick Reddy, "Will California Recall Governor Davis?," *United Press International*, May 6, 2003

What are the legal standards for recalling a public official in California? The federal constitutional standard for impeaching a federal official is "high crimes and misdemeanors." Merely being unpopular is not enough, there has to be some violation of the law. However, the California State Constitution reads, "All political power is inherent in the people. Government is instituted for their protection, security, and benefit and they have the right to alter or reform it when the public good may require"; or as former Republican presidential nominee Bob Dole might say, the recall standard in California is "whatever."

The surge of interest reflected in the July *Los Angeles Times* Poll was confirmed on July 23 when California Secretary of State Kevin Shelley made the dramatic announcement that the recall forces had turned in 175% of the required signatures and that he had no choice but to certify them as valid, thus paving the legal road for a recall election. As required by law, Lt. Governor Cruz Bustamante the next day scheduled the recall election for October 7, 2003. The most intriguing campaign of the new millennium was on.

As Bill Cavala noted, the public dismay over the Davis Administration kept growing all through 2003 and he commented: "the voters were mad about the state budget, mad about the car tax, mad about the recession, mad about the Davis–Simon choice in 2002. They said to themselves, the Constitution permits a 'do-over,' so let's have another election." [1] Gray Davis simply became the symbol of hard times and budget mistakes.

The recall ballot would contain two questions: Should Davis be recalled, and if he is recalled, who should replace him? A simple majority decided the first question: If 50% plus one of the total votes was cast to keep the governor in office, the process is over. However, if a majority votes to recall the governor, the second question would be a nonpartisan "winner-take-all" election. There is no need to obtain a majority, whoever got the most votes that day would be the new governor-elect.

Almost immediately, public speculation began of who would seek to replace Davis if he was recalled. Mr. Reddy was attending a Convention of the National Conference of State Legislators in San Francisco the week the election was called and all everyone wanted to talk about was whether Dianne Feinstein, the most popular leader in the state would clear the field or celebrities like Arnold Schwarzenegger, Rob Reiner or Warren Beatty would run. At a forum on state legislative redistricting, Professor Bruce Cain of Berkeley joked that he had not been brought there to "discuss the political prospects of Austrian weightlifters." However, that is what the forum ended up being about.

With the election set for October 7, the 60-day deadline for entering the contest was August 7. From the moment the signatures were certified on July 23, candidates and leaders of both parties began to maneuver. The strategy of Gray Davis and California Democratic Party Chair Art Torres was to keep all big-name Democrats from entering the race, thus hoping to convince the state's Democratic majority that it was only a choice between Davis the Democrat (warts and all) or a new Republican Governor. That strategy got off to a good start as Democratic statewide officers Senator Barbara Boxer, Attorney General Bill Lockyer, Treasurer Phil Angelides, Controller

---

1 Patrick Reddy, conversation with Bill Cavala in Speaker's Office.

Steve Westly, Secretary of State Shelly and Superintendent of Public Education Jack O'Connell all immediately said they wouldn't run, while Bustamante and Insurance Commissioner John Garamendi hinted they wouldn't. Senator Feinstein sharply denounced the recall, having been the target of such a campaign in 1983 when she was Mayor of San Francisco. On the Republican side, Bill Simon and Issa jumped in and former L.A. Mayor Richard Riordan planned for a campaign where there would a much larger pool of moderates to appeal to than a typical GOP primary. Among the Hollywood celebrities, Beatty and Reiner quickly dropped out, presumably out of loyalty to Davis. All eyes moved to Arnold — would he take the plunge?

Arnold's H-Bomb

> A cool, shrewd and boyish charmer, he exudes the easy confidence of a man who has always known he will be a star of some kind (and who could, if this movie takes off, become a multimedia presence of some force). — *Time Magazine* on Arnold in *Pumping Iron*. (1977).[1]

Arnold had been a politically active celebrity for many years. When he became an American citizen in 1983, he immediately registered as a Republican. He often used his celebrity to raise money for Republicans like the Bush family, Phil Gramm and Pete Wilson. Arnold also has supported his Kennedy in-laws, Ted and Joe, in their Massachusetts campaigns. He, of course, famously married into the most famous Democratic family in America, winning the heart of JFK's favorite niece Maria Shriver. Even so, he claimed that his inspiration for becoming a Republican was the Kennedys' arch foe, Richard Nixon. In 1989, rumors first surfaced that he was considering running for Governor in 1990. However, Arnold deferred to Pete Wilson and made movies like *Total Recall* and *Terminator 2* instead. He joked that he enjoyed arguing politics with his in-law Ted Kennedy, who replied that Arnold was very persuasive, "especially when he's holding you upside down by the ankles!"[2] In 2002, Arnold successfully sponsored Proposition 49 to fund after-school programs for teenagers; a campaign that some observers predicted was a trial run for office. Observers noted that a recall election would be a quick hit on the political system without a divisive Republican primary.

However, leaks from the Arnold Camp indicated that his wife Maria Shriver had strong reservations about him running. Several pundits, including CNN's Jeff Greenfield predicted he would not run in the end. Building up the suspense like a good showman, Arnold scheduled an appearance on his friend Jay Leno's show the night before the filing deadline. On the afternoon of the show's taping, Internet gossip columnist Matt Drudge reported that Arnold had decided to skip the race and would dramatically introduce his chosen candidate Riordan on the "Tonight Show." That same morning, Dianne Feinstein definitively withdrew and said she would not support a replacement candidate. Perhaps Maria would change her mind.

The "Tonight Show" was taped at about 5pm Pacific Time and Arnold put on a bravura performance. He joked that running for governor was the toughest decision he had since getting a bikini wax in 1978. He said that "California is in a very disas-

---

1 Richard Schickel, "A Delicate Beefcake Ballet," *Time*, January 24, 1977.
2 Ted Kennedy interview with CNBC, August, 2003.

trous situation right now" and while the people were doing the right thing, working hard, taking care of their children, paying their taxes,

> "[T]he politicians are fiddling, fumbling, and failing! And the man that is failing the people more than anyone is Gray Davis. He's failing them terribly and this is why he needs to be recalled and this is why I am going to run for governor of the state..." [1]

The studio audience went crazy and the assembled multitude of reporters who been sitting there looking bored while waiting for Arnold's anticipated withdrawal, jumped on their phones to call headquarters. The announcement was a media sensation as Arnold simultaneously appeared on the cover of *Time* and *Newsweek*, the latter dubbing it the "California Circus." CNN interrupted their regularly scheduled newscast with the news and Schwarzenegger consultant George Gorton told the press that he was surprised as they were. Richard Riordan huffed that he had been snookered and slid out of the campaign, endorsing Arnold.

Perhaps the press should have seen this coming; Arnold had always been politically active, had tested the waters for a potential gubernatorial run in 2001–02, and told *Talk Magazine* in a 1999 interview: "I think about it many times. The possibility is there, because I feel it inside." [2] The titles of his movies also provided clues — his most famous role was *The Terminator*. His second highest-earning role was in *Total Recall* and he starred in *The Running Man, Eraser, and End of Days*. Arnold's entry electrified the Recall. There was plenty of criticism of Arnold and the recall process from various sources, but California voters seemed happy about the process.

The Schwarzenegger Persona

> "He arrived in America a penniless bodybuilder, born in an obscure Austrian village, armed only with the immigrant's time-honored weapons of hope, ambition and an almost supernatural belief in the great American Dream. Arnold Schwarzenegger has become a Hollywood legend, a latter-day Jay Gatsby, a self-created man whose unwavering belief in himself has led him to scale undreamed-of heights in quest of his chosen destiny.... What, in fact, does Arnold still want?" — Wendy Leigh in *Arnold: An Unauthorized Biography*. [3]

Who and what was Arnold about? Schwarzenegger seemed a bundle of contradictions — an outspoken Republican who is married to Democratic stalwart Sen. Ted Kennedy's niece, Maria Shriver, the daughter of George McGovern's running mate. A man who proclaims his life story to be a triumph of individual will, yet often reaches out to people less successful than he. An actor who has regularly been roughed up by critics (Stanley Kauffman in *The New Republic* labeled him "a lumbering actor", while *Time* called Conan "stupid and stupefying"), yet who won a Golden Globe Award for Best Acting debut for *Stay Hungry*. A dedicated "jock" that spent years in the weight

---

1 Joe Mathews, *The People's Machine: Arnold Schwarzenegger and the Rise of Blockbuster Democracy* (New York: Public Affairs, 2006), 140.
2 Wikipedia, s.v. "Arnold Schwarzenegger," http://en.wikipedia.org/wiki/Arnold_Schwarzenegger
3 Leigh, *Arnold*, 265.

---

room, but also has a master of business administration degree. A brutally tough business negotiator who also gave away millions to charity. An aggressive bachelor in his younger days who also helped advance women's bodybuilding. A "health nut" who had also taken massive doses of steroids. A man whose father was literally a Nazi in occupied Austria, but whose career has been immeasurably helped by Jewish promoters and producers and who calls himself an "honorary Jew." A top-notch athlete whose first charitable work was with handicapped children.[1]

Schwarzenegger became the most famous bodybuilder ever. The book and film *Pumping Iron* brought the sport into the mainstream and helped spark the fitness boom of the 1970s. The film *Conan the Barbarian* made Schwarzenegger a worldwide star in 1982. Over the next two decades, he starred in a dozen blockbusters. His second *Terminator* film was the last pure action movie to lead the box office totals for the year. Since *Twins* in 1988, he has shifted to a mix of family-oriented comedies alternating with action films. After an early 50s career slump, Arnold came back bigger than ever with *Terminator 3*, which took in more than $130 million just a few weeks before he jumped into the Governor's race.

Wendy Leigh's controversial profile — the book sparked a lawsuit — depicts a complex, fiercely proud, ferociously ambitious, totally driven, shrewd, strong-willed man who is a fast learner, a ruthless competitor, fanatically loyal to benefactors, surprisingly generous, and a world-class charmer. As *Pumping Iron* demonstrated, he can be competitive to the point of outright meanness, with a history of ugly practical jokes — he said that he enjoyed using "psychological warfare" against body-building rivals.

His marriage to Shriver in 1986 and maturity changed Schwarzenegger for the better. Undoubtedly his mother-in-law, Eunice Shriver, President Kennedy's younger sister, who has devoted her life to the handicapped and underprivileged, influenced him. After scoring a hit playing a killing machine in the original *Terminator*, he shifted his screen persona to the Father/Brother/Protector roles of *Twins*, *Kindergarten Cop*, the *Terminator* sequels, *Eraser* and *End of Days*. He often starred with minority actresses — Grace Jones, Vanessa Williams, Rachel Ticotin, Tia Carrera, Elpidia Carrillo, Maria Conchita Alonzo, and Cassandra Gava — who later supported his campaigns, thus broadening his appeal. Ms. Williams, the first black Miss America, sang at his Inaugural.

Schwarzenegger faced up to his father's Nazi past, reaching out to the Jewish community and donating part of his salary (more than $1 million) from *Terminator 2* to the Holocaust Museum. Since he met Shriver, he has been the weight-lifting coach for the Special Olympics. He's also a leading sponsor of the Inner City Games. His first independent foray in California politics was his championing of Proposition 49 in 2002 to create after-school programs for kids. He both financed the campaign and starred in the TV ads. Like Maria's uncle, Robert Kennedy, he has tremendous rap-

---

1   Much of this Arnold background is taken from Reddy's coverage of the recall for *UPI*. See "Analysis: California recall election coming," *United Press International*, July 10, 2003; "Commentary: Arnold in Total Recall2?" *United Press International*, July 28, 2003; "The Arnold Factor," *Buffalo News*, August 10, 2003

port with children — if the voting age were lowered to five, he'd be a sure bet to win any election.

Schwarzenegger's politics also changed as he aged. A Reagan Republican and a staunch conservative in the 1980s, he moderated his politics in the last decade. Schwarzenegger said he was pro-choice, supports gay rights, and endorses "reasonable" gun controls and environmental regulation. During the Clinton impeachment drama, Schwarzenegger said he was "embarrassed" by Ken Starr's investigation of the president's private life. While his fellow national Republicans appear to be tilting right, he followed the recent leftward drift of California politics. He ended up being a lot closer to Clinton than Newt Gingrich.

As someone who'd never held office, he was free to create an ideological profile. Schwarzenegger seemed a fiscal conservative and social liberal, very much in the mainstream of California politics. Dan Weintraub of the *Sacramento Bee* calls him a "pragmatic libertarian," who believes in both the merit principle and "providing the opportunity for every child to fulfill his dreams."[1]

From the beginning, Arnold shrewdly cast himself as non-partisan "citizen" reformer, trying to put together a coalition of moderate Republicans, independents and ethnic Democrats. In short, he was a more personable and sane version of Ross Perot, a wealthy populist reformer who might buy an office, but would do so "for the people."

In a standard two-way partisan match-up against say, Feinstein, he would have been at a disadvantage because California has more Democrats than Republicans, more female voters than males and more moderate & liberals than conservatives. The initial Field Poll showed that a majority of Californians had a positive impression of Schwarzenegger, but were also "not inclined" to vote for him. Under normal conditions, he would likely struggle to win statewide office.

But the circumstances of 2003 were anything but normal. Both the *Times* and Field polls showed that more than two thirds of voters thought the state was going in the wrong direction. And both parties in the state legislature got even worse marks than Davis, thus creating a classic "throw-the-bums-out" mood. Who better to play the "man on horseback" role riding to the state's rescue than the cinematic successor to John Wayne and Clint Eastwood? In a July 28 column for *UPI*, Mr. Reddy wrote that, "Democrats underestimate this man at their peril: Schwarzenegger will be the toughest opponent they've faced since Reagan."[2] Arnold apparently likes being underestimated.

Arnold's first ad was a "talking head" shot that struck all the "outsider" themes and put Arnold firmly in the reform camp: "I am running for governor to lead a movement for change and give California back its future. I want to be the people's governor. I will work honestly, without fear or favor, to do what is right for all Californians."[3]

Hiram Johnson himself might have said the same thing.

---

1 Patrick Reddy, "The Arnold Factor," *Buffalo News*, August 10, 2003
2 Patrick Reddy, "Commentary: Arnold in Total Recall?," *United Press International*, July 28, 2003.
3 Mathews, *The People's Machine* p. 149.

That's Entertainment!

> "All That's Missing Is the Popcorn. Come one, come all to the greatest political show of the fall...." — *Time's* Cover Story on the recall.[1]

The recall was dubbed a "circus" by the Eastern media and a "carnival" by Gray Davis.[2] While in the end, this election was deadly serious for Gray Davis, there can be no doubt it provided plenty of amusement for ordinary voters and much material for late-night comedians. Once Arnold jumped in, the recall was a 62-day thrill ride of a campaign with wild charges of lying, corruption, sexual harassment, Hitler admiration, murder charges, and anti-Semitism. Even looking back today, it still seems really weird — and unbelievable.

While the most notable of the 135 candidates on the ballot were Arnold, Cruz Bustamante, conservative Republican State Sen. Tom McClintock and Independent Arianna Huffington, there were many other famous names in the race. For example — California got to choose from candidates named Adams, Burton, Davis, Dole, Edwards, Feinstein, Issa, Jackson, Kennedy, McCarthy, Newman, Quinn, Simmons and Walton. However, they were just not the folks we would expect.

Democrat Edward Kennedy was running for California governor. No, not Massachusetts Sen. Ted Kennedy, but Weaverville businessman Ed Kennedy, who's a former union member and proclaims that he, not Arnold, was "the real Kennedy."

Republican Congressman Darryl Issa put up the money to qualify this recall in July. Rep. Issa tearfully withdrew from the race when Arnold got in. But Saab Issa, an immigrant from Kuwait and computer engineer, also ran as a Republican. His program included a 36-hour workweek to spread out job opportunities and having the Feds bail California out of its debt.

Republican Robert Dole also wanted the job. Not the 1996 GOP presidential nominee and elder statesman, but "Butch" Dole, a former Marine who promised to whip the Golden State into shape with the slogan: "No excuses, no sniveling!"

The next California leader could have been a member of the Adams family — 25-year-old Independent Brooke Adams. As far as we know, she is not related to Presidents John and John Quincy Adams. The 1995 Huntington Beach homecoming queen and public relations executive asserted that it is time for a new generation of Californians to take charge. Her rallying cry was "Lead, follow or get out of the way."

Many Democrats wanted the state's most popular pol, Sen. Dianne Feinstein, to run in the replacement election. She steadfastly refused, but her nephew Dan Feinstein took her place. He is a "visual effects artist" in the film industry, and he insisted that people "should vote for the ideas, not the name." Dan Feinstein was yet another "citizen-politician" running "for the people."

Independent Scott Davis was running to replace Gray Davis. However, he withdrew from the race after it was revealed that he was once arrested in connection with the murder of a man involved with his ex-wife in Georgia seven years ago. He was subsequently convicted.

---

1 *Time*, August 16, 2003.
2 Rene Sanchez and Dan Balz, "More than 125 File in Calif. Recall Election; Davis Criticizes Effort as A Dangerous Carnival," *Washington Post*, August 10, 2003.

California had two Democratic governors named Brown in the last century — Pat and his son Jerry. In 2003, Democratic director Art Brown was running to promote his latest short film, which he describes as portraying all the various ways to say a certain four-letter expletive.

John Burton was the President Pro Tem of the State Senate in 2003 and California's leading liberal. Sen. Burton had just pushed a health care reform bill through both Houses of the California Legislature that opponents denounce as "socialized medicine." Senator Burton did not run, but Independent civil rights lawyer John Christopher Burton did, promoting "a socialist solution" to the Golden State's problems. Republicans probably would not support either John Burton.

Joseph McCarthy became a national sensation in the 1950s for his charges that Communist spies had infiltrated the government. Sen. Eugene McCarthy became a national figure in the 1960s for his anti-Vietnam War crusade. The McCarthy in this race was Mike McCarthy, a used car salesman from the Santa Barbara area. He said his profession "has many negative connotations, not unlike our elected officials."

Basketball fans certainly remember star UCLA center and NBA Hall of Famer Bill Walton. He certainly fit into the "Left Coast" as he traveled with the Grateful Dead on tour and raised his children with the values of "peace, social activism, and justice." His son, Nathan "Whitecloud" Walton, played college basketball at Princeton and professionally in Europe. Nate was running as an Independent and staunch environmentalist.

There's perhaps another basketball connection — Sacramento Kings All-Star Chris Webber was known as "C.Webb." Well, union member and state employee C.T. Weber of Sacramento ran under the Peace and Freedom Party banner seeking to redistribute income and abolish the death penalty.

Nate Walton wasn't the only athlete running: There was sumo wrestler Kurt "Tachikaze" Rightmyer, whose nickname means "Wind from a sword stroke." This Independent candidate pledged to "attack the 800-pound gorilla of big government from every angle."

There was former World Boxing Federation welterweight champ Paul Nave, whose ring moniker was the "Marin County Assassin." Nave was running as a conservative pro-business Democrat and wanted to cut taxes.

Libertarian Ned Roscoe was running to vindicate the rights of what he calls the "most oppressed minority" in California — smokers. He figured if almost all of the state's 5 million smokers voted for him, he would win by a landslide.

Native Americans rose to wealth and power through Indian casinos in the last decade. Naturally, there were several Native Americans running. Among them was Trek "Thunder" Kelly, who is part black, part Irish and part Indian. This Venice native asks people to vote for him, "thus breaking the Seventh Seal and incurring Armageddon." He wants to legalize drugs, gambling, and prostitution to create more tax revenue. He sounds like a real Venice guy.

Of course, Arnold was not the only actor or entertainer in the race. Gary Coleman, the 4-foot-8-inch actor who won fame playing Arnold Jackson on "Different Strokes," ran as a gag. In addition, real-life fruit-smashing comedian Leo Gallagher threw both his hat and a few watermelons into the ring. He had a couple of terrific slogans: "Insanity that makes sense" and "Why settle for amateurs? California deserves a professional comedian."

Michael Jackson also ran as a Republican. Not the rock superstar who died young in the summer of 2009, but an engineer from Long Beach. Speaking of namesakes, Richard Simmons also wanted to lead California. Not the flamboyant exercise guru, but Independent pension attorney Richard J. Simmons who said the key to reviving California was reforming the workers compensation system.

Then there was Angelyne, the pink-clad blonde model and B-movie star who has been on the Hollywood scene since the 1970s with her pink Corvette and ubiquitous billboards around Southern California. In fact, her billboards have appeared in more films than she has. She is a living definition of someone who's "famous for being famous." As she said on her Web site, "I don't do — I am!" She actually ran as a reformer with the one-word platform "Honesty," and she wanted to raise revenue by conducting personal tours of the State Capitol at $10,000 a pop.

The candidates also included several entertainers who had, shall we say, "interesting" acts. Adult film star and stripper Mary Carey was an Independent who wanted to raise revenue by taxing breast implants and making lap dances tax deductible to spur the entertainment economy. She also supports a "porn for pistols" trade-in program to get guns off the streets. Her Web site may be the only political platform statement that includes nude pictures of a candidate doing jumping jacks.

Finally, there was Hustler magazine publisher Larry Flynt. The billionaire pornographer may have had the most original slogan in American political history, "the smut peddler who cares."

The California recall/replacement election had candidates who were Democrats, Republicans, Independents, socialists, capitalists, men, women, young, old, middle-aged, gays, Asians, Latinos, African Americans, Native Americans, entertainers, athletes and radicals of both the right and left. Also in the running were a railroad brakeman, several teachers, numerous small business people, a few writer/directors, some students, and a marijuana legalization attorney. Who says politics is dull?[1]

Down the Stretch

> "I knew I was a winner. I knew I was destined for great things. People will say that kind of thinking is totally immodest. I agree. Modesty is not a word that applies to me in any way — I hope it never will." — Arnold in his autobiography.[2]

Those novelty candidates would eventually shrink to less than 10% of the vote as attention shifted to the more plausible aspirants. Millionaire writer Arianna Huffington and former Major League Baseball Commissioner Peter Ueberroth were thought to be strong contenders. But after the first debate and Arnold's advertising campaign took hold, they both faded and dropped out shortly before the voting. The race soon narrowed to three major candidates — two Republicans and one Democrat. Although the replacement election was legally non-partisan, meaning any number of candidates could run, the major parties could support anyone based on free-speech

---

1 Patrick Reddy, "Wild and Crazy Candidates," *Buffalo News*, September 28, 2003.
2 Arnold Schwarzenegger with Douglas Hall, *Arnold: The Education of a Bodybuilder* (New York: Simon & Schuster, 1977), p.66.

principles. Cruz Bustamante was officially endorsed by the California Democratic Party, while Arnold and the staunchly conservative Republican State Senator Tom McClintock vied for GOP backing.

In many ways, McClintock was the biggest threat to Arnold. If he took half of the 36% of voters who were registered Republicans away from Arnold, then Schwarzenegger would need nearly all of the independents and a third of the Democrats to get to even 30% of the vote. No Republican, not even Reagan, had been able to do that since 1958. McClintock was a down-the-line conservative on taxes and social issues, compared to Arnold's support for gay rights, abortion and some gun control measures. Fortunately for Arnold, McClintock rarely attacked him personally and couched his disagreements with the actor in terms of policy.

From the beginning, the Schwarzenegger team realized that in a large field, having a strong base would be the key to victory. The first Field Poll after Arnold got in showed that he did best with Republicans and Independents — plus younger voters and Hispanics. The latter two groups were presumably his film fans. Arnold's handlers decided to build a base among Republicans and then reach out from there.[1] The last two GOP gubernatorial nominees had averaged 40%, mainly because voters were turned off by hardliner conservative positions on social issues like guns, gay rights, and women's rights. So Arnold staked out positions as a moderate Republican — tolerant on social issues (for domestic partnerships for gays, but not gay marriage), pro-environment (against offshore oil drilling and for a "hydrogen highway"), but against tax increases and the "big spenders in Sacramento." Arnold sought to take enough conservatives away from McClintock and unite Republicans behind by stressing fiscal conservatism: cutting taxes and balancing the budget. To do so, Arnold reached back to 1978, to the greatest triumph of populist conservatism, Proposition 13. On the *Tonight Show*, he quoted the Oscar-winning film *Network*: "we're mad as hell and we're not going to take it anymore," a line that Howard Jarvis had used to such great effect in the Proposition 13 drive.[2] Arnold then openly endorsed Proposition 13 and won the support of Jarvis' widow. Using Reaganite language, he drove home his anti-tax message:

> The people of California have been punished enough. From the time they get up in the morning and flush the toilet, they're taxed. Then they go in and get a coffee, they're taxed. They get into their car, they're taxed....This goes on all day long. Tax, tax, tax, tax, tax....[3]

When Schwarzenegger advisor Warren Buffet questioned the fairness of Proposition 13, Arnold said he'd make him do 500 sit-ups if he mentioned it again. To dramatize his opposition to the car tax increase, he destroyed several old cars while gleefully shouting that he wanted to "terminate" high taxes.

At the State GOP Convention in mid-September, Arnold killed McClintock with kindness, borrowing his conservative message on taxes, while making the standard argument in a three-way race: "A vote for McClintock is a vote for Bustamante." State Republicans swallowed their doubts about Arnold's social moderation and decided

---

1 Mathews, *The People's Machine*, 171–174.
2 Ibid., 141
3 Ibid., 155.

to go with a more likely winner.[1] (McClintock actually made long-term gains from the recall effort. He ended the campaign with a 55% approval rating, four points higher than Arnold, and his conservative base helped him win a Congressional seat in the suburbs of Sacramento five years later, one of the few new GOP wins in the Democratic year of 2008).

Cruz Bustamante's candidacy started out with great potential to win with a minority of roughly 40% in a split field and become California's first elected Hispanic governor, but was a major misfire. On paper, it all looked good. As the Lt. Governor and the most prominent Democrat in the race, all he had to do was come close to the state Democratic registration number (about 45% of voters) and capitalize on Arnold and McClintock dividing Republicans and Independents. It was expected that Cruz could run as the Governor-in-waiting and practical Central Valley Democrats that he was. With the usual bloc votes from the black (6% of all voters) and Hispanic (18%) communities, plus a 25–30% showing among white and Asian voters, a highly respectable state total in the 40% range seemed doable. [2]

But the effort seemed ill-fated from the start, quickly getting sidetracked by accusations that he took illegal contributions from Indian casinos (he had; the simpler approach would have been to let the casino owners run an independent TV ad campaign on his behalf), which Arnold turned into one of his sharpest attacks on "special interests."[3] Bustamante's campaign manager, Richie Ross, a former counsel to the United Farm Workers, must have thought this was a Democratic primary in East Los Angeles because he focused almost exclusively on minority concerns with very little outreach to moderate white Democrats and Independents. One issue Bustamante repeatedly raised was a bill signed by Davis and opposed by Arnold that would have granted undocumented immigrant's drivers' licenses and discounted college tuition. Exit polls showed that over two-thirds of voters opposed that bill. Bustamante simply never gained momentum, never rising above a third of the vote in any public poll. Coupled with lackluster performances in the debates (as Joe Mathews wrote, "Bustamante managed the self-defeating combination of sounding both tired and condescending"[4]), Cruz suffered massive defections from Democrats and fell to just 31% of the total vote, the worst performance for a Democratic candidate in 70 years.

Meanwhile, as Cruz was sinking, Arnold was steadily rising. As Table 1–3 shows, backed by increasing Republican and independent support, and fortified by a huge ad buy of nearly $10 million per month, Arnold advanced toward victory just as surely as The Terminator had closed in on his targets. In both the Field and L.A. Times Polls, voters were skeptical at first, but Arnold won them over with the slogan "Join Arnold" and the message of reform. He skipped the first debate on September 3, but gained in the Field Poll anyway.

Arnold's message was taking hold. In early August, he had gone into seclusion to study state issues, what his aides called "Schwarzenegger University."[5] He slowly

---

1 Ibid., 171–174.

2 Patrick Reddy, "Analysis: Cruz Bustamante's American Dream," *United Press International*, September 3, 2003.

3 Mathews, *The People's Machine*, 176–179.

4 Ibid., 182.

5 Ibid., 152–153.

began to unveil his political profile: Arnold hated tax increases, wanted to cut wasteful spending, end "special interest" control of Sacramento and above all, clean up what he termed the "Gray Davis' mess." He was running as both a reformer like Hiram Johnson and as a "citizen politician" in the mode of Ronald Reagan.

The turning point probably came in the September 24 debate in Sacramento, which was broadcast worldwide by CNN. Like his fellow former actor Reagan, Arnold blew away the competition on TV. The debate allowed Arnold to showcase his energy and wit, while meeting the basic minimum requirements of policy knowledge. McClintock was polite, serious and substantive, Bustamante was bland, Arianna Huffington was outspoken and aggressive, providing the perfect foil for Arnold's cleverness and humor. It was a verbal smackdown that caused the moderator to complain, "This is not Comedy Central!" When Ms. Huffington complained that Arnold was interrupting her too often and slapped him down with the attack, "we know this is how you treat women," Arnold was given the chance to respond. He did not disappoint, getting off the zinger: "I just realized Arianna, that I have the perfect role for you in *Terminator 4*."[1] The audience howled with laughter and Arnold was on his way.

Once Arnold demonstrated he was smart as well as tough, the voters, who were so mad at Davis and so desiring of change, decided to balance off the liberal Legislature with a moderate Republican. Arnold's momentum seems to be unstoppable.

TABLE 1–3. POLLING TRENDS IN THE 2003 REPLACEMENT ELECTION

Poll	Date	Arnold	Bustamante	McClintock	Others	Undecided
Field	August	22%	25%	9%	25%	19%
Field	Sept. 7	27%	32%	14%	9%	18%
Field	Sept. 28	30%	31%	19%	7%	13%
Field	October	36%	26%	16%	9%	13%
L.A. Times	August	22%	35%	12%	22%	9%
L.A. Times	Sept. 3	25%	30%	18%	22%	5%
L.A. Times	Sept. 29	40%	32%	15%	9%	4%
	Election Day Results	49%	31%	14%	6%	

There was only one issue left that still had the potential to trip Arnold up — rumors about his personal life. Arnold's team had polled on this subject in 2001 when he first explored entering politics and found out the public did not really care. Moreover, there was ample precedence for this. Former California Republican governors

---

1 Ibid., 179–183.

Ronald Reagan and Pete Wilson were divorced. In his announcement on the "Tonight Show," Arnold had launched a pre-emptive strike against the Davis camp attempting to attack his character: "I know that they're going to throw everything at me and they're going to, you know, to say that I have no experience and I'm a womanizer and that I'm a terrible guy..."[1]

Then on October 2, another H-bomb was tossed into the campaign. In an "October surprise," the *Los Angeles Times* reported five days before the election that 15 women over the previous three decades had accused Schwarzenegger of "groping and humiliating" them. Although he denounced the accusations as politically-motivated "trash politics," Arnold then did something surprising and very rare for a candidate — he admitted it and apologized.

> Wherever there is smoke, there is fire. Yes, I have behaved badly sometimes...I was on rowdy movie sets and I have done things that were not right, but now I recognize that I have offended people. And to those people that I have offended, I want to say that I'm deeply sorry....Now, let's go from the dirty politics back to the future of California.[2]

Perhaps appropriate for the generally unique and perhaps weird circumstances of the recall, the *Times* H-bomb set off a media feeding frenzy. Several other women came forward to complain about Arnold's behavior and rumors swirled that he had fathered an out-of-wedlock child with an actress in the 1980s. ABC News also reported that while filming the documentary Pumping Iron, Schwarzenegger had allegedly expressed admiration for Nazi leader Adolf Hitler's public speaking skills. Arnold said that the full transcript would reveal where he immediately added, "But I didn't admire him for what he did with it." George Butler, the director of the film, confirmed Arnold's account. "Well, there goes the Jewish women's vote," wisecracked Maureen Dowd in the *New York Times*.[3]

Maria Shriver leapt to her husband's assistance, defending him every bit as vigorously as Hillary Clinton defended Bill in Monica-gate, calling the stories "gutter politics." Meanwhile, the feeding frenzy had an unexpected positive affect on the Schwarzenegger Camp — it rallied Republicans and conservatives to his banner. Since 1964, when the media demolished Republican nominee Barry Goldwater for allegedly being a racist mad bomber, conservatives have been very suspicious of the Establishment Press, charging them with liberal bias. Susan Estrich, a Democrat who was supporting Arnold, predicted that the *L.A. Times* story would backfire: "This attack, coming as late as it does, from a newspaper that has been acting more like a cheerleader for Gray Davis than an objective source of information, will be dismissed by most people as more Davis-like dirty politics." Republicans saw the Times story as more mischief by the "Liberal Media" and voting for Arnold became a way to stick it to the media. As conservative Bay Area talk radio host Melanie Morgan said, "It became a rally point for our audience. It made it acceptable for people to vote for Arnold."[4] Some Republicans and Independents decided not to "waste" their vote on

---

1 Ibid.,141.
2 Reddy, "Wild and Crazy Candidates"
3 Maureen Dowd, "Win One for the Groper," *New York Times*, October 5, 2003.
4 Mathews, *The People's Machine*, 187–188.

McClintock and broke for Arnold. Most Californians were not fazed by this issue. The Field Poll showed that 80% of voters agreed with the statement that Arnold's alleged affairs "were not relevant to his abilities to carry out his duties as Governor." Californians were being consistent here: they did not care about Bill Clinton's personal life and opposed Republican attempts to impeach him and they did not care about Arnold's personal life either.

Total Recall 2: Judgment Day for Gray Davis

As Table 1-1 shows, the "Yes" vote on the recall never dropped below the necessary 50% in public polls after Arnold got in. From August until the final Field Poll of October 1, huge majorities of two-to-one and even three-to-one believed that Davis would be recalled.[1] Richard Scammon and Ben Wattenberg once described political realignments as like plastic snapping, that "under stress, plastic breaks suddenly, swiftly and cleanly." [2] In the summer of 2003, Gray Davis' lifeline of support snapped and he simply never recovered. Like the old Chinese saying about certain emperors, he had "lost the mandate of heaven."

Nothing Governor Davis tried during the recall campaign worked. He brought in popular national Democrats like Bill Clinton and Al Gore, but voters were not moved. He held public forums to help explain his actions as governor and ran over $100 million in ads quoting editorials from newspapers of all ideological stripes opposing it, but voters were having none of it. He issued a modest apology for not reacting quickly enough to the energy crisis. About the only thing he did not do was cry or faint publicly. Like a spouse who had already filed for divorce, the electorate had had enough and was not going to change its mind.

Although the media's feeding frenzy caused a slight drop in support for the recall on the day after the *Times* groping story, the basic pro-recall structure of public opinion soon re-asserted itself. Team Arnold helped by pounding Davis in a last-weekend million-dollar ad buy featuring white males — Arnold's base — railing against the car tax increase and complaining that Gray wasn't "competent to do the job." Davis would need a miracle to survive on October 7 and his prayers were not answered.

On October 7, California voters made history in perhaps the ultimate fulfillment of Hiram Johnson's vision of direct democracy. As predicted by both the *L.A. Times* and Field Polls, the voters were decisive, recalling Gray Davis by 55–45%, nearly a million-vote margin. There would be no recounts or doubts here. The election itself was legitimate as 61% of registered voters turned out, a higher figure than in either of the years when Gray Davis was elected governor.

In his book *The People's Machine*, Joe Mathews of the *Los Angeles Times* argued that Arnold was creating something entirely new in California with the recall — "blockbuster democracy." With this concept, Arnold was combining movie-star charisma and popularity, big money raised by his celebrity & message and Hiram Johnson's tools of direct democracy (recall, referendum, and propositions) to bypass the politi-

---

1 Field Poll, http://field.com/fieldpollonline/subscribers/RLS2095.pdf
2 Richard Scammon & Ben Wattenberg, "Is It the End of An Era?," *Public Opinion*, October, 1980.

cians in Sacramento and fundamentally change state government. [1] For a while, Arnold and Mathews were right.

As expected, voters in the Bay Area went heavily (63% No) against the recall. But in the Democratic stronghold of Los Angeles County where Gore beat Bush by 63–32% in 2000, only 51% voted against the recall. The pro-Davis votes in the Bay Area and L.A. County were buried by landslides in favor of the recall in the Southern California suburbs and Rural California (both 69% Yes), plus the Central Valley (64% Yes). As shown immediately below, the ethnic vote on the recall had some big surprises. Democrats had hoped that a big minority vote would save Governor Davis, but Asians and Hispanics lacked enthusiasm for the Governor. When Democrats win statewide elections in California, they usually win at least 40% of the white vote, bloc votes of 70–85% among blacks & Hispanics, and a majority of Asians. Democrats had hoped Davis could use this formula to turn back the recall. He got the minimum "No" vote from blacks and whites, but Asians and Hispanics — immigrants and their children — were the missing links. A 20-point gain in support for Davis among Hispanics and Asians would have saved him. (In fact, Davis reached these goals in his 1998 landslide victory. See Appendix 2 for the full data set). As for why these two groups defected from Davis, the *L.A. Times* exit poll offered clues — 70% of Asians and 60% of Hispanics disapproved of the way Davis was handling his job. And Asian-American political activists have told us that their community also resented the fact that Davis raised millions of dollars from Asian businesspeople, but showed little gratitude or respect in return. ("He treats us like an ATM," complained one Asian-American activist). And of course, all the minorities liked Arnold more than a typical Republican.

TABLE 1–4. ETHNIC BREAKDOWN /SOCIAL GROUP
VOTING OF THE RECALL QUESTION,
"SHALL GRAY DAVIS BE RECALLED AS GOVERNOR OF CALIFORNIA?"

Group	No%	Yes%	% of State Voters
Asians	53%	47%	6%
Blacks	79%	21%	6%
Hispanics	55%	45%	15%
Whites	40%	60%	73%
Statewide	45%	55%	

AFTER THE RECALL

What Kind of Election Was the Recall?

"Davis is on a near-certain course of removal...." — Republican Analyst Tony Quinn.[2]

1 Mathews, *The People's Machine*, xvi, xxiii.
2 Tony Quinn, "Davis Strategy," *Los Angeles Times*, September, 2003

The *Times* exit poll also showed that the basis of the recall was substance-, not personality-driven. They allowed voters who pulled the Yes lever to cite their two main reasons for why they voted to recall Davis. [1] Here were the results:

TABLE 1–5. REASONS FOR RECALL OF GRAY DAVIS

He mismanaged the state	64%
His handling of the energy crisis	32%
The budget crisis/shortfall	22%
He's beholden to special interests	12%
Davis is not honest	10%
Not a good governor	9%
Not a good leader	8%
Mismanaged education	4%
I want a Republican governor	4%
Weak economy	3%
Other/Nothing in particular/don't like him	5%

As Table 1-5 shows, the "personality-driven" factors like "he's not a good leader" and "don't like him" were a tiny fraction of the Yes voters. The top choices — "he mismanaged the state, the energy crisis and budget" — sounded like policy, not personal reasons. Most people based their decision on how they viewed the Governor in his job. This was obviously true — Davis' lack of charisma did not prevent him from winning in 1998 or 2002. There were no personal scandals that would cause voters to radically re-appraise his character. His wife had not divorced him; he had not abused any children or animals, nor cheated on his taxes. No Cabinet members had been indicted. We could say that this was the most famous negative "job performance review" in California history.

Since this was the first statewide recall in California history, no one was sure how the voters would react to it. The whole shooting match may have come down to this question: Was it a "no confidence" vote in the Governor like in European parliamentary systems or just another campaign where "back-and-forth" arguments could sway the voters? The handlers for Governor Davis clearly believed it was the latter, comparing it to the proposition/initiative campaigns that are so common in California. His pollsters, Paul Maslin and Ben Tulchin, argued in a campaign memo that, "Initiatives that start out at around 50% nearly always lose...we firmly believe that the recall is eminently beatable."[2]

The strategy of raising doubts about a hot new idea is how opponents usually seek to defeat initiatives. Over the past generation in California, numerous policy initiatives — a big income tax cut in 1980, handgun control in 1982, a massive environmental regulation scheme called "Big Green" in 1990, "right-to-die" laws in 1992, an upper-bracket income tax increase in 1996, labor law changes in 1998 — have all

---

1 *LA Times* exit poll, October 7, 2003
2 Maslin press release, August 2003.

started out ahead, but ended up losing when opponents succeeded in raising doubts about the end results of these ideas. As Democratic consultant Darry Sragow has observed, the best way to defeat an initiative is to say that is too flawed to accomplish its announced goals.[1]

The Davis camp was clearly using this tactic all the way. Their TV ads quoted editorials from every major big-city newspaper in the state about how the recall was a huge waste of time and money and that it diverted attention from the state's real problems. Davis consultants Maslin and Tulchin recommended a sound bite that the Davis Campaign used repeatedly — "The recall will cost taxpayers an additional $60 million and is a partisan effort by Republicans to pursue their right-wing conservative agenda."

In dramatic contrast to Gray Davis' consultants, Republican Analyst Tony Quinn argued that it was virtually impossible for Davis to survive. When people are unhappy, the greatest slogan is "it's time for a change" and that was the best idea recall advocates had going for them. Davis critics started out with the concept that most Californians just did not like their governor as evidenced by his record-low approval ratings and by the stark fact that a majority of voters (53%) did not support him when he ran for re-election the year before. Quinn's thinking implied that voters had already decided that they intensely disliked Davis and would almost "mechanically" march to the polls to oust him just as they overwhelmingly voted for Proposition 13 in 1978 when they were upset by high taxes.

On the other hand, Davis strategists Maslin and Tulchin believe that once voters realized the cost of the election and saw the potential for chaos, recall supporters would eventually dip below 50%. By this light, the recall would have been just another intriguing, trendy West Coast idea that would not stand up to serious scrutiny.

Who was right? The lessons of the results are that the combination of a quick recall campaign along with some reasonably attractive alternative will be devastating to an unpopular incumbent. Pete Wilson was able to come back from 20 points behind in 1994, but that was partly because he had two years to recover from the GOP crash of 1992. Since recall election campaigns, by law, last less than 90 days, Gray Davis simply did not have the time he needed to soothe voters' anger. In simple terms, the recall was a landslide vote of no confidence in Gray Davis' leadership. In their own way, Issa and Arnold had brought European-style democracy to California — short campaigns and no-confidence votes.

The New Governor: Arnold as Reagan 2?

> "Of all the would-be fathers that came over the years, this thing, this machine, was the only thing that measured up. In an insane world, it was the sanest choice." — Sarah Connor on hooking up with Arnold in *Terminator 2: Judgment Day.* [2]

As for the replacement election, the voters were equally decisive, choosing Arnold as the replacement Governor by nearly 1.5 million votes or 18 points. By region, Ar-

---

1 Patrick Reddy, Conversation with Darry Sragow, Fall, 1998.
2 Internet Movie Data Base, "Memorable Quotes from 'Terminator 2: Judgment Day,'" http://www.imdb.com/title/tt0103064/quotes

nold lost only the Bay Area and even there, the combined Arnold–McClintock vote almost equaled that of Bustamante. Arnold carried L.A. County by a surprising 8 points, Rural California by over two-to-one and the Southern California suburbs by nearly three-to-one. It was the biggest victory for a Republican since the glory days of the Reagan Era in the 1980s. Among social groups, Arnold carried Asians by 12 points and won the white vote by 54–25%. He also gathered 18% of black voters and won a stunning 32% of the Hispanic vote — against the first Hispanic elected to statewide office. Arnold scored the best performance for a Republican among the minority communities since Goodwin Knight in 1954. He also demolished Cruz among white voters, sweeping the Central Valley, the North & Central Coast and the white working class in L.A. County. Arnold even won 36% in white liberal areas, compared to 47% for Bustamante. In a two-way race, Arnold would have won by at least a 60–40 margin. By winning big among white suburban Republicans and the L.A. County white working class Democrats and cutting into the Democratic bloc votes with upwardly mobile minorities, Arnold essentially revived and updated the Reagan Coalition.

In a high turnout election where 98% of the voters told the *Times* Poll that they were interested in the process, voters chose for the new Governor a man who 96% of voters knew enough about to have an opinion. Grassroots direct democracy does not get more organic and real than that.

2. The Four Phases (Faces?) of Arnold

> "That is a message that is from California all the way to the East Coast for Republicans and Democrats alike to say to them: 'Do your job for the people and do it well or otherwise you are *hasta la vista*, baby!'" — Arnold, on the meaning of the recall.[1]

Based on Arnold Schwarzenegger's extraordinarily successful life story, one would have guessed that his governorship would have either been a smashing success or a spectacular failure. He would be either a terrific actor-turned-candidate like Reagan or a historical curiosity like Jesse Ventura in Minnesota, who did not even bother to run for re-election. Instead, the Arnold phenomenon has been a bit of both, soaring triumphs combined with baffling failure.

In Act 1, in 2003 and 2004, Arnold replicates the Ronald Reagan role of the "Citizen Politician" sent by voters to "clean up the mess in Sacramento." He wins big and gets off to a great start, proving wise, competent, and broadly popular.

In Act 2 in 2005, he seems to tire of the mundane details of governing, gets impatient at the slow pace of change, and misses the "juice" of campaigning and winning. Therefore, he calls a special election to force his reform agenda. He seems to be channeling the spirit of Pete Wilson — the most divisive California Governor ever — and ends up fighting with unions, women, minorities and the poor. His popularity collapses and he suffers a humiliating rebuke from the same grassroots voters who elected him a few years earlier.

In Act 3 in 2006, he quickly changes course, morphing into the type of moderate Republican governors from the 1940s and 1950s (Earl Warren, Goodwin Knight) with an emphasis on building infrastructure for the future — while still supporting reform measures. This phase of Arnold worked brilliantly as he is easily re-elected,

---

1 Joe Mathews, *The People's Machine: Arnold Schwarzenegger and the Rise of Blockbuster Democracy* (New York: Public Affairs, 2006), 141.

one of the few Republican victories in a Democratic landslide year and has a generally successful 2007.

In Act 4 in 2008 and 2009, the national economy tanks, dragging California's budget back into a deep deficit. Through no fault of his own, he now appears to be close to becoming George W. Bush — a Republican executive struggling with huge economic problems and sliding out of office a disappointment. The second half of 2009 and 2010 will be his last chance to straighten out the budget and leave a solvent fiscal legacy, a task made infinitely harder by the defeat of a budget deal, including a tax increase, by the voters in May 2009. As of the summer of 2009, he is locked in battle with the Democratic state legislature in a battle of financial chicken as the state pays its bills with IOUs and is rapidly running out of money.

ACT ONE: ARNOLD, CONAN THE CONQUEROR

> "The future has not been written; there is no fate but what we make for ourselves."
> — The opening line of *Terminator 3*.

The Arnold landslide sent shock waves through the political class in Sacramento. Two veteran Democratic legislative consultants went on the record as saying that if the entire Legislature had been on the ballot, the Democrats would have lost their huge majorities.[1] The public was that fed up.

In his Inaugural Address, Arnold stated that he was "an idealist without illusions," like his wife's uncle, former President John Kennedy. He thanked Governor Davis for assisting with a "smooth transition" and then quickly went back to his reform message:

> To the thousands of you who came here today, I took this oath to serve you. To others all across this state — Democrats, Republicans, Independents — it makes no difference. I took this oath to serve you.
>
> To those who have no power, to those who have dropped out — too weary or disappointed with politics as usual — I took the oath to serve you.
>
> I say to everyone here today and to all Californians, I will not forget my oath and I will not forget you...
>
> My fellow citizens: Today is a new day in California. I did not seek this office to do things the way they've always been done. What I care about is restoring your confidence in your government...
>
> What I learned — and I've never forgotten — is sovereignty rests with the people, not the government.
>
> In recent years, Californians have lost confidence. They've felt that the actions of their government did not represent the will of the people.
>
> This election was not about replacing one man; it was not replacing one party. It was about changing the entire political climate of our state.
>
> Everywhere I went during my campaign, I could feel the public hunger for our elected officials to work together, to work openly and to work for the greater good.

---

1 Conversation with Bill Cavala and Trent Hager.

The election was the people's veto — for politics as usual.

With the eyes of the world upon us, we did the dramatic. Now we must put the rancor of the past behind us and do the extraordinary.

It's no secret I'm a newcomer to politics. I realize I was elected on faith and hope. And I feel a great responsibility — not to let the people down...

There's a massive weight we must lift off our state.

Alone, I cannot lift it. But together, we can.

It's true; things may get harder before they get better. But I've never been afraid of the struggle. I've never been afraid of the fight and I have never been afraid of the hard work.

I will not rest until our fiscal house is in order.

I will not rest until California is a competitive job-creating machine.

I will not rest until the people of California come to see their government as a partner in their lives, not a roadblock to their dreams.[1]

In interviews, Arnold set out an ambitious agenda for his first year with seven major goals: 1) repeal of the 300% car tax increase; 2) repealing the law that gave driver's licenses to undocumented immigrants; 3) improving California's business climate by curbing excessive regulation and reforming workers' compensation; 4) making state government more "user-friendly" with better computer access and improved service; 5) getting state employee unions to make concessions; 6) reaching agreements with Indian tribes to pay higher taxes on their casino profits; and 7) reducing the state's massive budget deficit without a tax increase. Immediately after his Inaugural, Governor Schwarzenegger went right to work.[2]

A veteran of many action films, Arnold promised that "action, action, action" would be the hallmark of his administration — and so it was in his first year. In a performance Theodore Roosevelt (Progressive Party Vice Presidential nominee Hiram Johnson's presidential running mate in 1912) would have applauded, Arnold used the "bully pulpit" to force his goals into the public's mind. Within hours of being sworn, he was already threatening go over the heads of legislators via the initiative process if necessary. He certainly got everyone's attention: for the first time since the Jerry Brown era in the 1970s, the statewide and even national media covered Sacramento again. Almost like a presidential candidate, his early speeches pre-empted local television and his Inaugural speech was carried live on worldwide TV. He earned a new nickname "the Governator," a combination of his new title and famous "Terminator" role. His office web site was headlined, "The People's Governor." A majority of voters in early polls liked his leadership style and saw him as a distinct improvement over Gray Davis.

He got off to a strong start in 2003–04, achieving five of his seven original goals completely and had partial success in the remaining two. The car tax increase was repealed minutes after he took office via executive order in his first official act and

1 "The Text of Gov. Arnold Schwarzenegger's Inaugural Address," *sfgate.com*, November 18, 2003, http://www.sfgate.com/cgi-bin/article.cgi?f=/c/a/2003/11/18/MNGHA34EEM1.DTL
2 Patrick Reddy, "Arnold's First 100 days," *United Press International*, March 5, 2004

the Legislature voluntarily repealed the driver's license rule a few weeks later. Reforming the workers comp system took nearly six months, but the new law he signed delivered a 50% reduction in business costs, while sharply curtailing fraud (though labor advocates complained loudly that it was shortchanging injured workers). His attempts to make government more "user-friendly" produced a few modest successes in the area of updating technology. Arnold's negotiations with California's Indian Casino owners took even longer, but eventually bore modest fruit. During the recall campaign, Arnold had stated that he would demand that tribes pay a 25% tax on casino profits, as did the Foxwood Casino in Connecticut. After marathon negotiations and two initiatives, the Governor settled for 12.5%, doubling the amount of revenue for state coffers that the Gray Davis Administration had received. The teachers unions agreed to a spending freeze in his first year, but all the other unions begin trench warfare against his budgets. Finally, on the issue that had bedeviled nearly every governor the past 50 years, making ends meet, Arnold was frustrated by intractable problems — pretty much like the other 49 governors.

By far, the biggest issue Arnold faced in his first year was the budget mess with an immediate deficit of over $20 billion. State Legislative Analyst Elizabeth Hill estimates that even with the new budget cuts and borrowing, California still would face a "structural" deficit of $5–7 billion for many years. Under California's budget rules, continuing spending programs will get automatic "cost-of-living-adjustments" (COLAs) that will increase their costs every year. Unlike a one-time expenditure like repairing a bridge after an earthquake, the $10 billion-plus spending increase on education and health care programs signed by Gray Davis in 2000 would cost another $300 million the next year and even more the year after. And so on. To get California through his first year shortfall, Arnold sponsored his first Propositions, Numbers 57 and 58 in the winter of 2004. Number 57 borrowed $15 billion for the 2004 deficit, which was exacerbated by the governor's car tax cut. Number 58 imposed a modest spending cap on the state budget until it was balanced and required creation of a reserve fund equal to 5% of the total budget.

If Arnold had proven one thing in the early days, it's that he was able to win the voters' trust. When the budget propositions were first announced, they were behind by four to eight points. After a vigorous TV ad campaign that also featured Democrats Dianne Feinstein and State Controller Steve Westly, public opinion was turned around in less than six weeks. Proposition 57 won with 63% and Proposition 58 with 71%. Each won across-the-board support from all ethnic groups. Arnold was particularly effective in bringing along his fellow Republicans. In January, less than 40% supported his budget propositions. On Election Day, March 2, 2004, over 70% of California Republicans did. Voters clearly understood the concept of re-financing debt, because almost every family does so these days with second mortgages and low-interest credit cards.

Arnold's failure to cure the budget's structural deficit was eased by the fact that the beginning of the housing boom was adding unexpected revenue to state coffers. He did not even have to use the entire new $15 billion bond due to the new money coming in and got through the summer of 2004 without a debilitating budget stalemate that had done so much damage to Davis.

Arnold had brought former Democratic Speaker of the Assembly Robert Hertz- berg as an informal advisor. Hertzberg recommended what he called an "inside–out- side" strategy where the Governor would fire up public support for his policies and at the same time, negotiate new legislation with the same lawmakers and interest groups he was threatening with initiatives. This strategy worked brilliantly for the first year — Arnold wielded his popularity and the levers of direct democracy just like Conan wielded his sword. Just the possibility of facing Arnold in an initiative contest frankly intimidated labor to cave on workers' comp reform, the Legislature to repeal laws like the driver's license bill and the Indians to compromise on revenue- sharing. Moreover, Arnold kept in his back pocket the threat that if he did not get his way, he would be back with another dose of direct democracy.

Comparisons soon arose to another "citizen-politician" and actor-turned-gover- nor, Ronald Reagan. Arnold seemed smarter, more focused, more moderate; and polls showed that he was more popular with minorities than Reagan. Unlike the Gipper, who had a strong fixed conservative ideology on almost all issues, Arnold was more practical. Arnold's two absolutes were government reform and Proposition 13. For example, when told that his new budget would cut aid to severely handicapped chil- dren, the man whose favorite charity was the Special Olympics simply reversed course. Even Senator John Burton, the veteran San Francisco liberal Democrat was impressed — "I go all the way back to Gov. Pat Brown, and the only one secure enough to change his mind was Gov. Schwarzenegger." Because of Reagan's outspoken conservatism, a third of California voters always despised his administration. Being closer to the center, Arnold's early disapproval ratings were lower than Reagan's were in their first years. Tables 2–1 and 2–2 detail how both Arnold's approval ratings and California's "right track" numbers soared in his first year.

TABLE 2–1. JOB APPROVAL RATINGS FOR GOVERNOR SCHWARZENEGGER

Poll	Date	% Approve	% Disapprove
Field	January 2004	52%	27%
Field	February 2004	56%	26%
Field	May 2004	65%	23%
Field	September 2004	65%	22%
L.A. Times	February 2004	61%	22%
L.A. Times	April 2004	64%	26%
L.A. Times	October 2004	69%	22%
CNN	November Exit Poll	71%	25%

TABLE 2–2. OVERALL DIRECTION OF CALIFORNIA

Poll	Date	% Wrong Track	% Right Direction
Field	August 2003	76%	16%
Field	February 2004	54%	35%
Field	May 2004	51%	37%
L.A. *Times*	August 2003	76%	14%
L.A. Times	October 2003	73%	27%
L.A. *Times*	February 2004	53%	34%
L.A. *Times*	April 2004	56%	36%
L.A. *Times*	October 2004	45%	45%

Arnold would soar to even greater heights of popularity in the summer and fall of 2004. A solid majority of 54% told the Field Poll that he was doing "better job than expected," while only 13% said he was doing "worse than expected." As a popular and practical Governor, he felt free to break with conservative dogma, endorsing stem cell research, which the Bush Administration opposed. His staff produced a colorful brochure, "Governor Arnold Schwarzenegger's Ballot Proposition Voter Guide" and mailed it to 5 million households. Arnold's late-breaking campaigning produced come-from-behind victories on two Propositions that conservatives really wanted to see defeated. On Proposition 72, which was a referendum, voters narrowly rejected a proposal by State Senate Democratic Leader John Burton to require business to provide health insurance for employees. In late September, Proposition 72 led by 45–29. After Arnold attacked it as too costly for business, it lost by 49–51% on Election Day. The most dramatic turnaround came on Proposition 66. In 1994, voters had passed a "3-strikes and you're out" law that required a life sentence for anyone convicted of three felonies, even a non-violent crime like passing bad checks. A decade later, Proposition 66 sought to change this law by mandating a life sentence only if the third felony was a violent crime. In early October, the Field Poll gave Proposition 66 a 65–18% lead. But after a dramatic meeting with the families of crime victims, Arnold charged into the anti-66 fight. He spent over $2 million on late ads that featured mug shots of career criminals and ended with the Terminator himself shouting, "Keep them behind bars."[1] The voters agreed with Arnold by a 53–47% margin. This represented a 50-point turnaround in the last month, the greatest last-minute shift in the history of the Field Poll. Overall, the voters agreed with Arnold's endorsement on 10 of the 12 initiatives. The CNN exit poll gave Arnold an astonishing 71–25% approval rating — on a day when Californians voted for Democrat John Kerry by 10 points.

---

1 Mathews, *The People's Machine*, 297-306.

In addition, his popularity went well beyond California's borders: he gave a well-received nationally televised speech to the Republican National Convention where he ridiculed "economic girlie-men." Moreover, his vigorous last minute stumping in Ohio for George W. Bush[1] may well have tipped the balance in that state, thus saving the president's one-state majority in the Electoral College. In *The Terminator*, the film that cemented his superstar status, Arnold plays a robot sent back in time to prevent the birth of its enemy by killing his mother. California Democrats must have felt like Linda Hamilton's character in the first *Terminator* film when she was told about the monstrous machine coming after her:

> "That terminator is out there. It can't be bargained with. It can't be reasoned with. It doesn't feel pity, or remorse, or fear. And it absolutely will not stop, ever..."[2]

If the primary election in the winter of 2004 had hinted at Arnold's power to sway public opinion, the fall campaign removed all doubt. In doing so, "Arnold" became the best brand name in California politics since Reagan. Ordinary voters are often too busy to pay much attention to politics, so listening to the Governor became a shortcut. Arnold's opinion on an initiative was decisive back then, his endorsement was golden in the suburbs and cut across party lines, while his opposition would be fatal for most ideas.

Act Two: 2005, Pride, Over-Reaching, and A Sophomore Slump

The 2005 Special Election

> "You moved too soon. Now the first rule of a crisis situation is you negotiate first and you attack last." — Arnold in *Twins*.

> "Everything I have ever done in my life has always stayed with me. I've just added to it...but I will not change. Because when you are successful and you change, you are an idiot." — Arnold on his career strategy.[3]

Fresh from using the tools of direct democracy to fuel his stunning triumphs of 2004, Team Arnold began to consider more propositions for 2005. However, before that, in the winter of 2004–05, Arnold was savoring popularity rare for politicians and usually reserved for sports heroes or entertainers. Arnold had restored the state's confidence and avoided a budget meltdown. And the people loved him for it. Soon, numerous opinion movers and shakers began to envision a national future for the Governor.

Fans of science fiction films may remember the scene from the 1993 movie "Demolition Man" where Sandra Bullock drives Sylvester Stallone past the "Schwarzenegger Presidential Library." As Stallone stares on in disbelief, it is explained that Arnold's popularity caused the US Constitution to be amended in the twenty-first century and he was elected president in a landslide. The movie was meant for laughs, but

---

1 Ibid., 302.

2 Internet Movie Data Base, "Memorable Quotes from 'The Terminator,'" http://www.imdb. com/title/tt0088247/quotes

3 Internet Movie Data Base, "Biography of Arnold Schwarzenegger," http://www.imdb.com/ name/nm0000216/bio

for Senator Orrin Hatch (R-Utah), it was no joke. Senator Hatch co-sponsored an amendment that would have changed the Constitution to allow immigrants to run for President. (The 12th Amendment also makes immigrants ineligible to be Vice President). Hatch held Senate hearings on his bill in 2004 and Arnold's name quickly came up. In 2005, the New York Times speculated whether the Constitution could be amended in time for Arnold to enter the 2008 New Hampshire primary. Arnold referred to the issue as a "distraction," but that did not stop him from endorsing it.

So Arnold was popular locally and nationally. Of course, there were skeptics. Some veterans of California politics noted that former Governors Goodwin Knight, Pat Brown, Jerry Brown, Pete Wilson, and Gray Davis were all initially popular before being ridden out of town on a rail. While the public was definitely giving Arnold an extended honeymoon, there was some criticism in the press.

"Lights! Camera! Ego!" sneered the *Fresno Bee* in an editorial after Arnold endorsed amending the Constitution to benefit himself. After watching Arnold campaign for his budget proposals, veteran *L.A. Times* columnist George Skelton wrote: "Schwarzenegger does have this tendency — let's put it gently — to stretch the truth, to not let facts get in the way of a good sales pitch."[1]

However, they were in the minority. In early 2005, Arnold was the most powerful and popular governor since Earl Warren won both the Republican and Democratic parties' nominations in 1946 and was re-elected with 92% of the vote. Not only was changing California's Constitution repeatedly through propositions an ongoing option, but even "reforming" the law of the land to allow him to run for national office was a possibility. Everything seemed to be going Arnold's way — and therein lay the problem. Overconfidence led to over-reaching and Arnold's most embarrassing flop in over a decade. As Joe Mathews wrote,

> It was when Schwarzenegger combined his ability to attract the limelight with a good message (and money to broadcast it) that he was most difficult to beat....

> The aftermath of victory can be a dangerous time for politicians. Overwhelming triumphs breed over-reaching policies. Schwarzenegger would not prove immune.[2]

In his 2004 State of the State Address, the new Governor said that while every governor promises to move around the boxes of government, he wanted "to blow them up." A year later, the Legislature discovered that "blowing up the boxes," meant a massive campaign of reforming the state. Arnold saw the 2005 "Year of Reform" as a sequel to the recall. Moreover, he had terrific experience with follow-ups; Terminator 2 was the most successful sequel ever, with its take five times as large as the original. However, the special election of 2005 would prove to be a bomb that almost wrecked Arnold's Administration.

While enjoying the highest ratings for any California governor in the last generation, Team Arnold decided to strike while the iron was hot. In the winter of 2004–05,

---

1 Patrick Reddy, "President Schwarzenegger?," *Buffalo News*, 1/30/2005.
2 Mathews, *The People's Machine*, 306.

the Governator ordered his staff to draft proposals that would become ballot propositions for a special election, either in June or the fall. But while this planning for new
wave of elections began, the Administration missed a major opportunity to get the
budget under control. Arnold came very close to taming the structural deficit that
had plagued Gray Davis. According to Joe Mathews, the real deficit was down to just
$6 billion.[1]

Arnold also had another tool available in the budget struggle; the California Constitution gives every Governor the right to veto any or all budget items. The Legislature can override a veto with a two-thirds vote. The point is, through the veto process
Arnold could have frozen total spending at, say, $100 billion for 2004 and 2005. The
natural growth of revenue would have ended the structural deficit by 2006, the year
he was scheduled to run for re-election. A more experienced governor would have
seen that he had the veto power to control spending instead of reflexively reaching
for the Special Election weapon.

Don Perata had succeeded John Burton as the Senate Democratic Leader, and
out of respect for Arnold's soaring popularity he expressed hope that a compromise
could be reached with the Administration on easing the structural deficit. There were
several options. The new Governor's "California Performance Review" had identified
over 100 boards and agencies that could be consolidated with savings allegedly in
the billions. That was probably an exaggeration, but even saving $100–200 million
would have helped. There are numerous spending formulas in the budget to give "pre-
miums" to certain groups and regions. For example, Medi-Cal reimburses doctors
in San Francisco at over 200% the rate for other counties due to the City's higher
costs. Many of these "goodies" were written under the direction of former Assembly
Speaker Willie Brown, which raised the cost of services by several hundred million
dollars. (San Francisco deserves perhaps a 125% premium, but not 280%).[2] Why not
work with former Willie Brown staffers to eliminate these imbalances? Better yet,
why not hire Mr. Brown himself to do so, since he was out of office.

There were other chances to increase state revenues — without raising income
taxes. Arnold could have allowed the Indian Casinos to operate games like craps and
roulette in exchange for a higher share of their profits, adding $1 billion per year in
state revenues. He could have agreed to a 1 penny-per-gallon increase in state gas
"fees." He could have put a "severance tax" on natural resources leaving the state as
Texas does. A 25-cent surcharge on movies shipped out of state would have raised
nearly $100 million. He could have extended the sales tax to lawyers (most corporate
law fees/taxes are applied to businesses with headquarters out of state and besides,
lawyers are unpopular). At that point, there were numerous options.

In retrospect — and hindsight is always 20/20 — the outlines of a "Grand Bargain"
to curb the structural deficit was there. A temporary freeze on state worker costs
in exchange for a "no-layoffs" pledge, more revenues from Indian gaming, and some
modest cuts in spending including the dismantling of patronage jobs on state boards
that were once known as "Willie Brown Incorporated." However, Arnold decided
that the people wanted reform and that he was going to lead a "people's army" on

---

1 Ibid., 315.
2 Patrick Reddy, Interview with Senate Budget Staffers.

a crusade. Therefore, he put on his armor and picked up his sword, charging ahead into battle, only to find out that the people were not sure they wanted to follow him.

If the Governor's team had paid attention to the Field Poll in February 2005, several trends would have stood out. First, his approval rating had dropped to 54–35% positive, compared to 65–22% positive the previous fall. The drop was caused almost exclusively by losses among Democrats and Independents who were concerned about his alleged cuts to education and other services. Second, the percentage of voters who believed that Arnold "catered to a few special interests" rose from 27 to 38%. Third, the approval ratings for his chief adversaries — the State Legislature — had risen from a low of 19% in July 2003 to 36% in 2005. Fourth, a majority of voters once again thought the state was on the wrong track. Fifth, and most importantly, when told it would cost an extra $50 million, voters opposed calling a special election by the astonishing margin of 67–30%. Even 45% of Republicans opposed a 2005 election after learning of the cost.[1] *Sacramento Bee* columnist Dan Weintraub argued that voters would get over the costs once they had the opportunity to shape public policy through the ballot box. He — and Team Arnold — could not have been more wrong.

In his January 2005 "State of the State" Address, the Governor left no doubt that he would be going all out for reform in 2005 — with or without the Legislature. Arnold started out paying tribute to those he called "the greatest rescuers of the state... the people of California." He added,

> "Last year we stopped the bleeding. This year we must heal the patient.

> "To continue California's recovery, this year we must do two things.

> "To solve the budget's continuing structural deficit, we must reform the way the government spends its money. And to restore the trust of the people, we must reform the way the government operates.

> "My friends, this is a time for choosing....

> "I'm going to tell you something that you know in your hearts to be true.

> "In every meeting I attend in Sacramento, there's an elephant in the room. In public, we often act like it's not there. But, in private, you come up to me — Republican and Democrat alike — and you tell me the same thing, "Arnold, if only we could change the budget system. But the politics are just too dangerous."

> "The elephant in the room is a budget system that has removed our ability to make the best decisions for California. It has taken away the freedom and the responsibility of legislating. We can change that..."[2]

For his second full year in office, the Governor proposed major changes in the budget's "autopilot" spending that caused funds for education and health care to grow with the economy and the cost of living (nearly three fourths of the budget is

1 Field Press Release #2153, http://field.com/fieldpollonline/subscribers/RLS2153.pdf

2 Office of the Governor of the State of California, *Governor Schwarzenegger's State of the State Address*, 01/05/2005, http://gov.ca.gov/speech/2408/

subject to these automatic increases). He also proposed merit pay for teachers and raising the time it takes public school teachers to earn tenure (i.e., a near-permanent job guarantee) from to two to five years. The Governor said public pensions were "another financial train on track to disaster" and proposed ending guaranteed "defined benefits" for future public employees. Lastly, he endorsed taking away the power to draw legislative lines from the State Legislature and giving it to a panel of retired judges. The Governor was immediately calling a Special Session of the Legislature and demanding action: "If we here in this chamber don't work together to reform the government, the people will rise up and reform it themselves. And I will fight with them."

Arnold returned to Jay Leno's show to pitch his ideas as "Recover, Reform, and Rebuild." The 2004 budget deal was the beginning of the recovery, so in 2005, Reform would take center stage.

In the abstract, some of the Governor's ideas made sense and some of his concrete proposals like eliminating boards where appointees made $100,000 per year for doing tasks of dubious value would have been wildly popular. However, Arnold overestimated the public's tolerance for more political noise and turmoil. He also united his labor/liberal opposition, leading to disaster.

As all film buffs know, in the original *Terminator* Arnold was the villain, a robot sent back in time by computers attempting to exterminate the human race by killing the woman's son. But the *Terminator's* human rivals also sent back a soldier named Reese to protect Sarah Connor and her son John Connor, who would go on to lead the human resistance in the twenty-first century. Reese tells Sarah that the machines had almost won — "we were so close to being wiped out" — but that her son John rallied the people and eventually destroyed the computer network. Reese helps Sarah Conner survive the Terminator's extremely vigorous onslaughts and allows her unborn son to survive and grow up.

Many Democrats and labor leaders no doubt saw the Special Election in 2005 as similar to the script for the first *Terminator*. In this reading, a monstrous villain menaces women and children (California Teachers' Association President Barbara Kerr stands in for Sarah Connor) until a noble warrior teaches them to fight back and win. Under this scenario, Dean Tipps of the Service Employees International Union, who spurred the labor drive that defeated Arnold in the special election, plays the role of John Connor. (Reese was probably John Mockler of the Teachers' union). Just as in the movies, Sarah Connor and Reese eventually terminate The Terminator and save the planet.

The California Teachers Association fired the first shot in labor's war against Arnold. In 2004, the union had agreed to delay $2 billion in assistance that they were entitled under Proposition 98. A year later, Arnold was trying to avoid restoring these funds to help ease the structural deficit. CTA began airing radio and TV ads featuring, Liane Cismowski, a charming and down-to-earth classroom teacher, scoring the Governor for his "broken promise" to the schools.[1] The California Nurses Association soon followed with protests and pickets. They also set up billboards along

---

1 Daniel Weintraub, *Party of One: Arnold Schwarzenegger and the Rise of the Independent Voter* (Sausalito: PoliPointPress, 2007), 80.

every major highway in the state featuring Arnold's image on a successively smaller set of TV screens that eventually faded out. This was the start of a carpet-bombing campaign that would eventually see organized labor spend over $100 million on TV and radio ads. By the time it was over, Arnold's image had taken a severe battering with Field showing a majority of Californians believed that the Governor had called the Special Election in order "to strengthen his own political position" rather than pursue reforms. Field also showed that by a 64-27% margin, people believed that he should "scale back his confrontational style with the legislature and rely more on negotiation and compromise". In what was probably the unkindest cut, the same Field Poll revealed that by a 50-26% margin, voters agreed that although the Governor "talked about reducing the power of special interests, he is taking as much money if not more from them than previous Governors."[1]

The Governor's reform project was so rushed and so poorly thought out that the initiatives his allies wrote created one public relations problem after another. For example, his proposed spending cap also included giving any governor the unilateral power to cut spending without either the voters' or legislative approval. In 1992, voters had rejected Proposition 165, which contained this exact provision, by 53-47%. His spending cap also could lead to education funds being cut below the 40% requirement that voters approved with Proposition 98, something that scared off women voters. His pension reform proposal, which sought to ban future guaranteed pensions, could possibly be interpreted as forbidding survivor benefits being paid to families of police officers killed in the line of duty. As Republican Consultant Bernd Schwieren observed, instead of consolidating support for his reforms, he ended up uniting the Democratic opposition.[2]

The opposition ads painted Arnold as a rich, obnoxious, arrogant, sexist bully who was trying to take food out of the mouths of poor children, books away from classroom teachers, and even benefits from the widows of policeman and firefighters. Arnold reacted with bewildered hurt (the special interests were running "TV ads calling me cruel and heartless.") He also had a substantive reply; his budgets were spending literally billions and billions on programs to help the poor and the main reason he withheld the $2 billion in Proposition 98 money from the schools was to protect funding for health services for the poor. However, this was a classic example of political haste making policy waste, thus allowing his opponents to capitalize on his errors.

Although the idea of the special election was originally Arnold's, he was clearly egged on by former Governor Pete Wilson and his staff (who would collect fat consulting fees). From seeking unilateral executive power to cut the budget to attacking immigrants to fighting with organized labor, they seemed to be recycling every Wilson battle from the 1990s. The last successful campaign many of the Wilsonites had run was the great GOP sweep of 1994. In that year, Republicans and Democrats had an almost equal share of the electorate. A decade later however, thanks in part to the Hispanic mobilization provoked by Wilson's immigrant bashing, Democrats had a solid 45-37% advantage. The Wilson Team apparently thought they were running

1 Field Poll, http://field.com/fieldpollonline/subscribers/RLS2167.pdf
2 Patrick Reddy, Interview of Bernd Schwiern, Fall of 2005.

a campaign in only suburbia, like in Orange County or San Diego. They were simply facing a different electorate — more ethnically diverse, poorer, more unionized — and were unprepared. Team Arnold performed poorly across the board in 2005. Like Pete Wilson, they got Arnold into huge fights with unions, immigrants, and public employees with the same negative impact on his popularity. Republican Analyst Tony Quinn called them "Arnold's Keystone Kops."[1]

The Governor's previously sure political touch also was missing in 2005. He bragged (probably in humor) that he had "kicked the Nurses' Association's butts" in the previous budget fight, thus offending some women. He mused aloud about having the US Army close the Mexican border, thus offending Hispanics. He repeatedly accused union members — including rank-and-file police officers and firefighters — of betraying the public trust, thus hurting him with his base of white men. In acting as he did with them, Schwarzenegger came across as a bully, not a reformer. In the summer of 2005, it was revealed that he had a contract with some bodybuilding magazine that would pay him over $1 million while he was governor. Although he ended the deal, it was embarrassing and dinged his reform image. Arnold once joked that if he could sell tickets to *Red Sonia* and *The Last Action Hero*, he could sell anything. But his memory was simply incorrect there; those movies lost millions of dollars. To borrow terms from the 1960s, 2005 was a "bad scene, a bummer all the way" for Arnold.

Coming on the heels of the gubernatorial election of 2002, the recall of 2003, the presidential election of 2004, having a 2005 Special would mean the fourth consecutive year of heavy politics, meaning ordinary voters would be bombarded once again by TV and radio ads, phone calls, emails, strangers knocking on their doors and a tide of direct mail. As Tony Quinn said, "the voters hired Arnold to clean up Gray's budget mess, not to conduct a permanent campaign." People were simply burned out on politics and that probably doomed Arnold's effort from the start.

All of this began take a severe toll on Arnold's standing. In the Field Poll, his job approval rating dropped steadily from 54% in February 2005 to just 37% in October 2005 with Democrats and Independents leading the way down. Forty-seven percent of voters thought he was doing a "worse than expected" job compared to just 13% a year before. The immediate source of his problem was the special election; 49% thought it was "bad thing" for the state and by a solid 57–34% margin, voters believed that he should call it off. Fully 46% of voters said the special election made it less likely they would vote for him and only 36% were inclined to support him. Democratic frontrunners Phil Angelides and Steve Westly opened up 6-point leads against Arnold while Rob "Meathead" Reiner led him by 45–43%. [2]

In the fall, Arnold strongly endorsed four main Propositions: Number 74 to delay teacher tenure, Number 75 to curtail the political participation of public employee unions, Number 76 to implement a spending cap and Number 77 to reform the redistricting process. The Field Poll showed a steady erosion of support for all four from when they were announced in June to late October.[3]

---

1 Tony Quinn, "Arnold's Keystone Kops," *Sacramento Bee*, July 26, 2005.
2 Field Poll, http://field.com/fieldpollonline/subscribers/RLS2167.pdf
3 Field Poll #s 2159, 2160,2168, 2174, http://field.com /fieldpollonline/subscribers/.

On Election Day, November 8, 2005, the Governator's reform crusade was solidly rebuffed: Proposition 74 received 45%, Proposition 75 came closest to passing with 47%, Proposition 76, the spending cap, got crushed with only 38% and Proposition 77 also got clobbered with just 40%.

The classic definition of a political disaster is when someone ends up with the worst of all worlds. In 2005, Arnold took all the abuse for the alleged flaws of his reform proposals, angered the voters for disregarding their wish that he cancel the Special Election, temporarily damaged his reform credentials, hurt his own power and influence and then to top it all off, lost every issue in the election. It was a text-book disaster.

While some blamed Arnold's impulsive character for this mistake, the fact is numerous other American leaders had done the same thing. Successful politicians tend to be "alpha" males or females with a strong tendency to forge ahead and take risks. That is why they ran for office in the first place. For example, the best president of the nineteenth century (Lincoln) and the best president of the twentieth century (Franklin Roosevelt) both got into big trouble with schemes to pack the Supreme Court. Lyndon Johnson overreached disastrously with a land war in Southeast Asia, while George W. Bush did the same with a land war in Southwest Asia four decades later. Bill Clinton overreached with his health care proposal and Pat Brown made a terrible blunder in going for a third term. Politicians usually run the same campaign playbook until they lose. Even California's greatest reformer, Hiram Johnson, overdid it when he called another special election in 1915 and lost on every issue.[1] It is human nature.

The special election disaster of 2005 holds the key to the budget meltdown in Arnold's second term. In his 2005 State of the State Address, Arnold had denounced the idea of raising taxes, saying, "We don't have a revenue problem. We have a spending problem."[2] True enough, but his detour into the Special Election interfered with his chance to mend the spending problem. If the Governor had been more patient in the winter of 2005 and worked on the budget instead preparing for another campaign battle, the increasing revenues reported in May (after the April tax collections) would have allowed him to reach an accommodation with the education lobby — and pretty much end the structural deficit. Just think how much better 2005 would have been for Arnold and the state if in the spring he had a press conference with Legislative and labor leaders announcing a "historic budget deal that ended crazy deficit spending once and for all." When he was dealing with the legislature from a position of great strength in his first year, he could force them to make big concessions on issues like workers comp reform and repealing the immigrant license bill. But by losing the special election and severely damaging his popularity, the Governor was now in a position of almost complete weakness. He had no choice but to make peace with the Legislature if he wanted to get re-elected. Assembly Speaker Fabian Nuñez's price of peace was that the Governor surrender on the budget and let the Assembly spend virtually all the new revenues that the national economic recovery and California housing boom were bringing in. Conan caved on the budget and as a result, total spending

---

1 Mathews, *The People's Machine*, 10.

2 Office of the Governor of the State of California, *Governor Schwarzenegger's State of the State Address 01/05/2005*, http://gov.ca.gov/index.php?/print-version/speech/2408/.

went up by $20 billion in 2006 and 2007, similar to the spending increases under Gray Davis. This would have huge policy implications in a few years. By spending the temporary housing boom windfall in 2005–07, there would be no money for much more worthwhile projects like universal health and infrastructure building. And when the national economy tanked in 2008, the Golden State ended up back where it was when the recall began in 2003 — dead broke and with very few good options.

Thus, the twin goats of the 2008–09 budget crisis are the Republican consultants who helped push Arnold into the Special Election and the Democratic Legislative leaders who busted the budget with new spending after the Special Election debacle had brought Arnold to his knees.

A Flawed Theory of the "People's Machine?"

> "That's my style. As soon as I grasp something, I take control." — Arnold's autobiography. [1]

While the Governor's tactical errors contributed hugely to the 2005 defeat, the fact is the whole concept of a "peoples' machine" is fatally flawed. Political machines are usually government bureaucracies composed of mostly like-minded individuals who have one permanent goal — to hold onto power. The individual candidates will change over time, tactics and appeals may also change, but the goal remains the same, winning. By contrast, "The People" are the anti-thesis of machine politics. They are not an organization; they are millions of individual voters. The people have various interests that change all the time and they will want different factions to win at different times. Sometimes they will elect candidates who come from a "regular" party structure like John Burton. Sometimes they will elect persons who are completely independent of any party organization (like Hiram Johnson or Richard Riordan). However, "the people" will remain apart from the permanent government bureaucracy.

There were other flaws in Arnold's concept of "blockbuster democracy," including style and culture. While Hiram Johnson was a civil servant and upper-middle class prosecutor, Arnold was the world's most famous star, married into one of the most famous families in American history and worth a peak net worth of $800 million. Johnson was truly one of the people, while Arnold saw himself as working for the people.

Beyond style, the other fatal flaw of the "People's Machine" was it needed a lot of money to keep running. Former Assembly Speaker Jess Unruh famously observed that, "money is the mother's milk of politics." To run constant statewide propositions would require Arnold to keep milking wealthy contributors for millions of dollars, thus severely compromising his reform image. Arnold could put in over $10 million of his own to fund his race in 2003, but he would need Other People's Money to have the Special Election of 2005, the taxpayers' money to administer the election and business money to run his campaigns. As the Field Poll data showed, there is a vast contradiction between railing against certain "special interests" and raising megabucks from them.

---

1 Arnold Schwarzenegger with Douglas Hall, *Education of a Bodybuilder* (New York: Simon and Schuster, 1977), 59.

Arnold's Apocalypse Now?

> "They were sick of campaigns and probably sick of the campaigner....As soon as one election was over, long-range campaigning for the next one will begin. This sort of political endless chain is not alluring." — Hiram Johnson on why all 11 of his measures lost in the 1915 Special Election.[1]

Like almost everything Arnold does, his special election defeat drew national attention. "Arnold Schwarzenegger got his 'a_ _' handed to him," gleefully laughed Stephen Colbert on the Comedy Channel. However, it was no laughing matter; the 2005 defeat ended Arnold's winning streak on propositions, cost him precious opportunities to fix the budget mess and temporarily stalled his reform express. It raised serious question about whether his career would end in ignominious failure. State Controller Steve Westly, the billionaire co-founder of eBay, announced that he was willing to spend whatever it would take to become Governor. And State Treasurer Phil Angelides, the self-proclaimed "anti-Arnold," who had opposed the Governator from Day One, also jumped in. The Field Poll gave both small leads over Arnold. However, Arnold being Arnold, he did not give up. After all, he always said he would be back.

ACT THREE: 2006 & 2007, CONAN THE COMEBACK KID

Picking Up the Pieces

> "He always taught to fight." — The final line of Terminator 3.

Arnold quickly realized that he had misfired badly and told the *L.A. Times,* "The buck stops with me." One of the first principles of good leadership is that if the ship is heading for the rocks, you change course. As John Burton noted, Arnold has not had trouble admitting mistakes and switching direction. That is why voters liked him. There were no complaints from him about the media being unfair or not having enough money to get his message out. In his previous careers as an athlete and actor, whenever Arnold had a disappointment, he would sit down with his advisors to figure out what had gone wrong and how to prevent it from happening again. He used the same concept in 2005 and almost immediately began to get his ship back on course. A few days after the election defeat, he said at a press conference, "If I would do another Terminator movie, I would have the Terminator travel back in time and tell Arnold not to have a special election."[2] He also said that he would listen to his wife more often because she had correctly advised him to cancel the special election. Action followed words as he quickly retooled his Administration and reshaped his message.

After *The Last Action Hero* bombed, the satirical magazine *Spy* ran a cartoon of Arnold sitting at home in workout clothes watching Steven Spielberg accept his Oscar for *Schindler's List.* An annoyed Arnold writes the names of those responsible for his failed movie, whom he wants to get back at, on a notepad. The cartoon's caption

---

1 Mathews, *The People's Machine,* 10.
2 Ibid., 394.

was "Schwarzenegger's List."[1] After November of 2005, Arnold would have had a list of political consultants to get rid of — and he did so. He replaced virtually all of the Pete Wilson team that had helped push him into the special election. He replaced them mostly with Democrats, including making Susan Kennedy, former Gray Davis cabinet official and open lesbian, his new Chief of Staff. In a 2007 interview, she said that the first task was stop the Administration from "fighting with every stakeholder in the state," from organized labor to law enforcement. To borrow once again from his movies, Arnold went from being the villain in *The Terminator* to the likeable big brother in *Twins*.

The new influence of Susan Kennedy was quickly apparent in the 2006 State of the State speech. As he often did, the Governator opened with a quip, in reference to Texas upsetting Southern California in the Rose Bowl. "Now, what a difference a year makes — a year ago USC and I were #1; what happened?" and then turned to more serious matters. Arnold did not mince words when looking back at the Special Election debacle:

> "I've thought a lot about the last year and the mistakes I made and the lessons I've learned. What I feel good about is that I led from my heart.

> "Now it's true that I was in too much of a hurry. I didn't hear the majority of Californians when they were telling me they didn't like the special election. I barreled ahead anyway when I should have listened...

> "I have absorbed my defeat and I have learned my lesson. And the people, who always have the last word, sent a clear message — cut the warfare, cool the rhetoric, find common ground and fix the problems together. So to my fellow Californians, I say — message received..."

Arnold said that he still believed in his "fundamental agenda" of reform and fiscal discipline, but he now wanted to achieve them in partnership with the Legislators. He then proudly went over his accomplishments — workers comp reform, reducing the deficit, economic recovery, increased education funding and new "green energy" regulations, before pivoting to the main thrust of the speech.

Arnold started out by praising the Governors of the past who built California. He noted that the Golden State's population had doubled twice in his lifetime and would double again in the next generation ("A new California is coming whether you plan for it or not.")

He described all the current and upcoming needs in transportation, housing, pollution control, schools, flood protection, prisons and courts, and ended with the tag line — "I say, build it." Arnold was proposing $70 billion worth of new bonds to build all this, the largest infrastructure investment done by any state ever. In another nod to Democrats, he endorsed the importing of low-cost Canadian drugs and added, "If we work together, there is literally no problem we cannot solve."[2] In fact, a few weeks

---

1 "Schwarzenegger's List," *Spy*, February, 1994.

2 Office of the Governor of the State of California, *Governor Schwarzenegger's 2006 State of the State Address, Thursday, 01/05/2006 05:05pm As Delivered*, http://gov.ca.gov/index.php?/print-version/speech/358/.

later, the Legislature and Administration acted quickly to plug the gaps for California senior citizens in the new Medicare prescription drug program.

While tacking to the center, Arnold also threw a few bones to conservatives, telling the Legislature to "bring me your innovative ideas" on fixing the structural deficit and strongly endorsed a strict new law to track sex offenders. But on the whole, the tone of the speech was "Reaching Out." In making these changes, Arnold, in effect, left the Republican Party and became more of an independent. "Party of One" was the title of Dan Weintraub's favorable biography of Arnold and it was a highly accurate assessment of the New Arnold in 2006. In the Capitol Morning Report, Tony Quinn wrote that Arnold was imitating Goodwin Knight, California's "last non-partisan" governor:

> He's jettisoned his hardcore Republican image as well as the partisan nincompoops who ran his special election campaign; his profuse apologies last night are proof of that. Now we have a new Arnold, the political independent, the great empire builder, and the man who's going to pour concrete and build it all.[1]

In 2005, Arnold had described to Jay Leno his "3-R plan: Recovery, Reform and then Rebuild." The economic recovery had taken hold, the voters had rejected some of his reforms (but he still hoped they would pass in the future), so it was time to move on to rebuilding California's infrastructure. And he might have added a fourth R: re-election.

TABLE 2–3. JOB APPROVAL RATINGS FOR GOVERNOR SCHWARZENEGGER

Poll	Date	% Approve	% Disapprove
Field	October 2005	37%	56%
Field	February 2006	40%	49%
Field	July 2006	49%	40%
Field	September 2006	48%	37%
L.A. Times	October 2005	40%	57%
L.A. Times	April 2006	44%	53%
L.A. Times	May 2006	44%	51%
L.A. Times	October 2006	59%	40%
L.A. Times	November Exit Poll	59%	41%
CNN	November Exit Poll	65%	34%

---

1 Quinn, *California Morning Report*, January 6, 2006.

Conservatives were obviously very unhappy about the new Arnold 3.0 version. Of course, these conservatives were perhaps forgetting that their two previous candidates for Governor — Lundgren and Simon — averaged barely 40% of the vote. On the other hand, Arnold apparently subscribed to the Davis Principle. Not Gray Davis, but Oakland Raider Owner Al Davis, whose motto was "Just win, baby!"

Beyond the rightwing pundits, ordinary voters responded well to Arnold's new tone of bi-partisanship. The reason was simple: People liked Arnold in the beginning — both as a person and as a moderate reformist leader. Once the irritation of the Special Election was removed, they were free to go back to liking him — and so they did. Table 2–3 shows the steady recovery of his job approval ratings. The voters' perception about the condition of the state in Table 2–4 was similar to the Governor's job ratings. Even at his nadir in the fall of 2005, there was a glimmer of hope for the Governator; a majority of voters (by 52–41%) told the *L.A. Times* Poll that Arnold had "shown decisive leadership in his two years as governor." Reddy attended a labor celebration on the night of the 2005 Special Election and asked veteran Democratic/labor consultant Jim Alford if Phil Angelides could beat Arnold, Alford's reply was "gut feeling, no."[1]

TABLE 2–4. OVERALL DIRECTION OF CALIFORNIA

Poll	Date	% Wrong Track	% Right Direction
Field	October 2005	63%	30%
Field	February 2006	55%	31%
Field	July 2006	41%	47%
Field	September 2006	36%	49%
L.A. Times	October 2005	64%	26%
L.A. Times	May 2006	55%	34%
L.A. Times	October 2006	46%	41%
L.A. Times	November Exit Poll	38%	62%

The Arnold comeback was based on substance, as well as style. He negotiated a popular bi-partisan deal with the Legislature, putting his bonds on the November 2006 ballot. Both Field and the *L.A. Times* Poll consistently showed the bonds ahead. He supported an increase in the minimum wage. The state had its first on-time budget in six years, with the funds lost in 2003–04 fully restored to the schools and modest increases for health care for the poor due to the soaring revenues from the mid-decade housing boom. Perhaps more importantly, he agreed to sign landmark

---

1 Patrick Reddy, Interview with Jim Alford, November 2005.

environmental legislation, sponsored by his Assemblywoman Fran Pavley of Agoura Hills, to reduce "greenhouse gases" by 25% by 2020. Assembly Bill 32 would make California the first state to require an active plan to reduce carbon emissions and won Arnold plaudits from California to Europe to the United Nations. Nancy Ryan of the group Environmental Defense called Arnold "a real-life climate action hero" for signing AB32.[1] HBO talk show host Bill Maher endorsed Arnold specifically because of AB32. Arnold also began building a "hydrogen highway" for cars and issued executive orders to make state buildings greener and more energy-efficient. The Governator also went on the show "Pimp My Ride" to demonstrate his Hummer S.U.V. being retrofitted with Green technology. The Field Poll data shows that Arnold's first lead beyond the 5% margin of error came about in May 2006.

TABLE 2–5. POLLING TRENDS IN THE 2006 GOVERNOR'S RACE

Poll	Date	Arnold	Angelides	Others	Undecided
Field	October 2005	41%	47%	N/A	12%
Field	February 2006	39%	39%	2%	20%
Field	April 2006	44%	40%	3%	13%
Field	May 2006	46%	39%	4%	11%
Field	July 2006	45%	37%	3%	15%
Field	September 2006	44%	34%	7%	15%
Field	October 2006	49%	33%	6%	12%
L.A. Times	October 2005	34%	37%	2%	27%
L.A. Times	April 2006	43%	43%	1%	13%
L.A. Times	May 2006	45%	46%	1%	8%
L.A. Times	October 2006	50%	33%	8%	9%
Election Day		56%	39%	5%	

Meanwhile, the Democrats had a typical primary brawl where Phil Angelides, the former State Democratic Party Chair, ran as the candidate of the party regulars and Steve Westly as the new face. Angelides won the party endorsement at the Convention and then won the primary narrowly (48–43%) with much help from organized labor, especially in the black and Hispanic neighborhoods.

The fall campaign was essentially a bore as Arnold quickly tagged Angelides as too partisan and too eager to raise taxes. With Arnold claiming the center, his opponent simply failed to gain any traction. Arnold told the press that he and the Legislature "had found their groove" in 2006. The state's two most famous newspapers, the *L.A. Times* and *San Francisco Chronicle*, both of whom had heatedly opposed the recall, endorsed Arnold for re-election. The result was another across-the-board Arnold sweep as he won 60% of Asian voters, 63% from whites and highly impressive shares

---

1 Weintraub, *Party of One*, 117.

of 39% among Hispanics and 27% from blacks. Arnold won nearly half the vote in middle class Hispanic precincts in places like Whittier, Azusa, and Santa Ana. His performance in the minority communities was the best for a California Republican since Goodwin Knight in 1954.

Normally, issues usually matter more than personalities and the "Personality/ Charisma" School of politics. However, 2006 would appear to be an exception. When a Republican governor overcomes a million-vote Democratic registration edge to win a landslide in a year when California Democrats win almost all the state races and national Democrats re-take both Houses of Congress, it can only be called a personal triumph. Perhaps the best clue was in the October *L.A. Times* Poll that asked voters who they thought had the stronger leadership qualities. The result was Arnold 60%, Angelides 20%.[1]

Successful Second Term Start-up

"The worst I can be is the same as everybody else. I hate that." — Arnold[2]

The new bi-partisan "Make-Nice" Arnold was no mere campaign ploy. In his second Inaugural Address, he re-affirmed his commitment to moderation and reform. He claimed that the 2005 special election defeat was "an experience that opened his eyes," like St. Paul on the road to Damascus:

> "I saw that people, not just in California, but across the nation, were hungry for a new kind of politics, a politics that looks beyond the old labels, the old ways, the old arguments...

> "The people are disgusted with a mindset that would rather get nothing done than accomplish something through compromise. I want to thank the Legislature for taking action this past year on behalf of the people, not politics. I thank them for taking that risk...

> "But this is a dynamic center that is not held captive by either the left or the right or the past. Centrist does not mean weak. It does not mean watered down or warmed over. It means well-balanced and well-grounded..."

> "So as I begin this new term as your governor, governor, I make this simple pledge to the people of California. I will look to the future. I will look to the center. And I will look to the dreams of the people."[3]

In his next State of the State Address, Arnold outlined his agenda for his second term: prison reform, more infrastructure, a deal on universal health care, "clean" energy, improved vocational training, and of course, another attempt at redistricting reform. He also emphasized the need for co-operation:

---

1 Michael Finnegan, "The Times Poll: As Vote Nears, Schwarzenegger Surges Ahead; Survey find Republican governor leading Democratic challenger Angelides 50% to 33%. Most see the incumbent as a stronger leader," *Los Angeles Times*, October 1, 2006.
2 Internet Movie Data Base, "Biography of Arnold Schwarzenegger," http://www.imdb.com/name/nm0000216/bio.
3 Office of the Governor of the State of California, *Transcript of Governor Schwarzenegger's Second Inaugural Address*, 01/05/2007, http://gov.ca.gov/index.php?/press-release/5049/

"So I have asked myself, what must we do in this chamber to help fulfill this future? It starts very simply. We can start by all of us working
together."[1]

How did the Governor do in completing this second-term agenda? On prison reform, California was dealing with the fact that in the 1980s and 1990s, both voters and
the Legislators passed numerous laws to "crack down" on crime with tougher mandatory sentences. As a result, the number of inmates soared from 22,000 to 160,000
by the time Arnold was elected, becoming the third-largest item in the budget (after
education and human services), and a significant drain on state resources. In addition, over 70% of California prisoners ended up going back to prison within a few
years, the highest recidivism rate in the nation. In 2004, Arnold appointed a commission chaired by former Governor George Deukmejian that recommended changing
the state's automatic sentencing laws, putting emphasis on rehabilitating the small
fraction of prisoners who could be helped, providing for more vocational training
and drug treatment. In 2005, Arnold endorsed these proposals as part of his "Year
of Reform." Like most things that year, they got sidetracked by the Special Election
controversy. In the summer of 2005, a federal judge declared state prison conditions,
particularly in health care, to be so bad as to violate the constitutional standard of
"cruel and inhumane" punishment. After much feuding between Arnold and the Prison Guards' Union, a reform proposal that adopted much of the Deukmejian Commission's program passed the Legislature. More prisons would be built and millions
would be spent on improving inmate health care, drug treatment and parole centers.
It was some progress, but the state prison system remains under a federal court order
to spend billions more on expanding facilities.

On infrastructure, the situation is that although Arnold's bonds were passed by
voters with great fanfare in November of 2006, the pace of building got off to a very
slow start. It was not until 2009 that a single project began. His legacy here will
largely lay in future governors' hands.

With regard to clean energy and global warming, the regulations implementing
AB32 are still being discussed as this is written. As one can imagine, environmentalists
want to make them as strict as possible, while business wants them to be voluntary
guidelines. Arnold supports a "cap and trade" approach where industries that pollute
less can sell "pollution credits" to heavy industries with the goal a gradual reduction
of pollution every year. This policy will also be dependent on future Administrations.

On health care, Arnold endorsed a "hybrid" approach of the Republican principle
of requiring individuals who could afford health insurance to purchase it in the private sector, while using the Democratic idea of providing subsidies to help lower-
income families. The comparison was to car insurance: it would not pay for normal
maintenance like a brake job or oil change, but would provide coverage for big problems like accidents or theft. This reform would be financed by higher taxes on smokers and having both small business and hospitals pay a "flat fee" based on their total
revenues. His plan passed the Assembly with only Democratic votes and was sent to

---

1 Office of the Governor of the State of California, *Transcript of Governor Arnold Schwarzenegger's
State of the State Address*, 01/09/2007, http://gov.ca.gov/index.php?/press-release/5089/

the State Senate for consideration in 2008. Meanwhile, significant action on vocational education and redistricting reform would wait for another year.[1]

Not only was the press happy with the Governor, so were California voters. The Field Poll gave Arnold positive job ratings in the 56–60% range all through 2007, with even majorities of Democrats giving him thumbs up[2]. The Governator passed much of 2007 in a holding pattern. There were no great controversies, the economy created decent revenue, he passed a few mild reform measures, and his popularity was maintained. However, there were no great new accomplishments either.

ACT FOUR: FADING AWAY, ARNOLD W. BUSH?

> "Nooooooo!!!" — *Twins* co-star Danny DeVito, when asked by David Letterman if Arnold could fix California's problems.

Both the California housing bust and Wall Street Crash made 2008 a tough year for all incumbents. Arnold was no exception. By the end of 2008, his job approval rating would be below 40% and over two thirds of voters would see the state as going in the wrong direction.[3] Little of this was the Governor of California's fault, but it did not matter.

In 2008, the State Senate Health Committee buried the Administration's health care plan because the declining number of smokers simply would not provide enough revenue. Also by that time, the recession was beginning to hit California hard, shrinking tax revenue and increasing the demand for social services. There was a tidal wave of foreclosures in California, thus depressing real estate revenue and eliminating thousands of construction jobs. The net result was an even worse budget crunch with the deficit approaching Gray Davis levels. The Legislature stalemated between Republicans who would not raise revenue and Democrats who would not curb spending. The final budget, which essentially delayed the problem until the next year in hopes of a miracle economic recovery, broke the 2002 record set under the Davis Administration for being late.

In early 2009, the economy had gotten even worse and the Legislature was already running out of the money that was supposed to last until June 2009. The deficit surged to a record $42 billion, $4 million greater than the deficit when Davis was recalled in 2003. Therefore, the Governor reversed himself and was forced to break his "no new taxes" pledge. Most of his reduction in the car tax was revoked, a temporary sales tax increase was approved and various schemes to borrow from future lottery proceeds and dedicated special funds like the Mental Health and Tobacco Tax were signed by the Governor. A Special Election was scheduled on May 19, 2009 to allow voters to approve these changes.

Only a few Republicans in the Legislature supported the new tax plan and two of them were immediately targeted for recall elections. Some anti-tax zealots even began circulating a petition to recall Arnold in May 2009. (They would need to collect roughly 200,000 valid signatures per month to qualify it by October. If they were to succeed, the actual recall election would be scheduled sometime in the spring of

---

1 Weintraub, *Party of One*, Chapters 9, 11, and 13.
2 Field Poll, http://field.com/fieldpollonline/subscribers/Rls2257.pdf
3 Field Poll, http://field.com/fieldpollonline/subscribers/Rls2297.pdf

2010). Even with the new budget deal, the State Controller's Office reported that revenues were running behind estimates to the tune of at least $2 billion per month, thus making the deal already "upside-down" in banking terms.

As expected, conservative activists and pundits were upset, turning on Arnold with a fury previously reserved for the likes of Hillary Clinton. In light of Arnold signing the tax increase, the State Republican Convention passed a resolution actually apologizing to Gray Davis for helping to recall him. Conservatives were further angered with the Administration for agreeing to a modest and temporary tax increase in the winter of 2009. The new budget was a combination of spending cuts, increased "fees" on gas purchases and user fees, plus a two-year temporary sales tax increase. A Special Election was scheduled in May to give voters the opportunity to extend the sales tax hike by another two years and to protect education funding. The Administration and Legislature were also asking voters' permission to borrow from future lottery winnings and from special funds previously dedicated to mental health and anti-smoking efforts.

On May 19, 2009, voters said a resounding "no" to all of the above ideas with not a single budget item getting even 40% of the vote (see Appendix). Just as in the 2005 Special Election, voters were angry and pretty much said "no" to everything. (The one Proposition that did pass, 1F, was also a slap at the Capitol: it prohibited pay raises for elected officials anytime the state was running a deficit. Prop 1F won with over 70% of the vote).

Because of the failure of the May 19 special election, it is back to the drawing board for the Governor. Will there be another "New Arnold, an Arnold 4.0?" Would he become a budget-slasher like Deukmejian or would he raise taxes like his GOP predecessors, Reagan and Wilson? As it turned out, the May 19 defeat gave Arnold and the Republicans a huge opportunity. The voters clearly rejected new taxes, so Arnold could accurately say the only way to a balanced budget was massive spending cuts. Given the two-thirds requirement to pass a budget, combined with his veto powers, Arnold has huge advantages in the next round of budget negotiations. His budget negotiators quickly went to work, coming up with deep cuts to various social programs. Arnold really will be the Terminator Governor. He is not merely proposing "decreases in the rate of increases" or even 10–30% cuts in real spending, but the actual elimination of programs like Cal-Works (basic welfare assistance) or the Healthy Families program. The budget approved in September 2008 had a General Fund of roughly $101 billion. The February 2009 budget deal, which also raised taxes, cut that spending by 11% and Arnold wants to subtract another $6 billion in General Fund spending by June 30, 2009. His State Finance Director Mike Genest candidly said that the cuts would hit the poor hardest because "If you look at what the government does, the government doesn't provide services to rich people. We don't provide many services even to the middle class. . .You have to cut where the money is."[1]

For years, conservatives like Reagan and Gingrich have dreamed about sharply reducing social spending. Due to the Golden State's impending bankruptcy and two-thirds rule, Arnold may (inadvertently) accomplish much of the Reagan dream.

---

1 Kevin Yamamura, "Governor Says $2.8 Billion More Is Needed," *Sacramento Bee*, May 30, 2009, http://www.sacbee.com/capitolandcalifornia/v-print/story/1903769.html.

In early June, he addressed the Legislature about the grim financial realities of 2009:

> "Now, as I stand here today, we are in the midst of the greatest economic crisis since the Great Depression...[I]n the past 18 months one third of the world's wealth literally evaporated...because of that and because of California's outdated and volatile tax system, our revenues have dropped 27% from last year...We are now back to the same level of revenues we had in 2003 and when you adjust for inflation and population, we are back to the level of the late '90s...
>
> ...
>
> "I know the consequences of those cuts are not just dollars. I see the faces behind those dollars....[O]ur wallet is empty, our bank is closed and our credit is dried up....We are not like Washington. You see, in Washington they print more money. We cannot print more money here. They can run up a trillion-dollar deficit; we cannot do that. We can only spend the money that we have. That is the harsh but simple reality..."[1]

As he pointed out after the Special Election, the people have emphatically spoken against new taxes, so virtually all of the deficit reduction will come from spending sacrifices. Republican consultant Don Levin points out that Arnold is now becoming the "deficit hawk" fiscal conservatives Republicans expected him to be back when he was first elected. Most Capitol budget insiders expect the vast majority of the deficit reductions to be in the form of cuts, rather than revenue increases. While a federal bailout, similar to what happened to New York City in 1975, remains an outside possibility, the Obama Administration has already said they will not act without Congressional approval, which looks very doubtful at the moment. From the budget deal that was subsequently struck on July 20, 2009, it looks as if Arnold got much of the spending cuts that he wanted. Painful as the budget "root canal" may be, Arnold could yet leave office fulfilling his original promise to end "crazy deficit spending."

---

1 Office of the Governor of the State of California, *Governor Delivers Speech on the Status of State Budget*, June 12, 2009, http://gov.ca.gov/index.php/print-version/speech/12520/.

3. The Schwarzenegger Legacy

> "It is not the critic who counts: not the man who points out how the strong man stumbles or where the doer of deeds could have done better. The credit belongs to the man who is actually in the arena, whose face is marred by dust and sweat and blood, who strives valiantly, who errs and comes up short again and again..." — Theodore Roosevelt.

> "And he not only became president, but as an ex-president he served his country, always in the arena. Sometimes wrong, sometimes right, tempestuous, strong, but he was a man...." — Richard Nixon on Theodore Roosevelt.

> "It is noteworthy that the chief casualties, in both parties in the fall elections in 1960 were governors...largely because of grass-roots tax revolts. It is obviously far more dangerous to be a Governor than a Senator." — Theodore White in *The Making of the President, 1960*.

As this book is going to press, Arnold Schwarzenegger is entering his final months as California Governor. While there will be numerous historical appraisals of his tenure and probably a few revisionist histories, here is an attempt at an early analysis.

A reasonable approach would be to judge any Golden State governor in five areas of policy in no particular order: education/social policy, infrastructure, the environment, financial management/budget, reform measures. A sixth one could be added: the intangible category of "leadership" that every successful executive from Hiram Johnson to Earl Warren to Pat Brown to Reagan had. Governors could be "graded" on an "A, B, C, D, & F" scale with each subject equal in importance. How did Arnold do by these six criteria?

We should remember that his tenure is not complete yet and that perceptions of events can change over time as more information becomes available. Nevertheless, this is the preliminary take on the Schwarzenegger Years.

Education/Social Policy. The best governor in these areas was probably Pat Brown. Arnold's proposed "universal" health care plan was derailed by the state's latest budget crunch in 2008. His bonds will eventually add more classroom capacity and he does get credit for protecting poor children from excessive budget cuts for his first five years. Give him a "Gentleman's C" here.

Infrastructure. The two best governors in terms of building things were Goodwin Knight and Pat Brown. While Arnold began the largest building spree since the Pat Brown years, the start of these projects has been very slow. For getting it all restarted, give him a B.

The Environment. The two best environmental governors, ironically, hated each other, Ronald Reagan and Jerry Brown. Reagan signed landmark laws on auto emissions and clean water, which became national models. Jerry Brown followed up and strengthened these laws. With AB32 and his executive orders on green energy, Arnold earns at least a B here.

Financial management/budget. This is Arnold's worst grade. While he could conceivably yet get a budget deals that improves things, the fact is that he utterly failed in his vow to "terminate crazy deficit spending" with the state in as deep a hole as when he came in. He will almost certainly be leaving a huge fiscal mess for his successor to clean up. This is even more surprising given his record of accomplishment as a hugely profitable businessman. The record is still incomplete but he gets a D, with either a C or an F still possible. The best governors on the budget were Reagan and Wilson, two Republicans who raised taxes that turned deficits into surpluses. The worst were Davis and Deukmejian who left behind record budget messes for their successors to clean up. Pat and Jerry Brown also left deficits.

Reform. The greatest reform governor was obviously Hiram Johnson, followed by Earl Warren. Gray Davis, who was booted out of office early, partly for his obsessive fundraising was probably the worst. Due to his relentless and successful championing of redistricting reform and open primaries, Arnold gets his only A here.

Leadership: This one is especially complicated because Arnold has been a bold leader on reform, very skillful at getting elected, all over the place in terms of dealing with the legislators and a big disappointment in financial matters. His Administration has been as complicated as the man himself. It is an Incomplete for now, but a final grade of B or C seems likely.

SUMMARY

Arnold's best performance has been on reform, his worst on the budget. On the latter, though, he deserves some sympathy. One reason, besides the national economic slowdown, that California is so broke is its vast number of children, especially poor children. Due to the high birthrates of the last two decades, there is currently a "demographic bulge" of children, who are overwhelmingly non-taxpayers and consumers of services. Presumably, a few years down the road these children will become productive citizens and net revenue producers. Another painful reality is there are currently 6 million children from broken homes who also need state assistance. As of 2008, the Golden State had approximately 11 million children, over 30% of who were poor and another 30% who were eligible for state assistance of some kind. That is over 6 million children that the state had committed to educate, feed, house and provide health care for. To his credit, Arnold did his best, particularly for a Republican, to fund these programs. As it turned out, until 2009, Arnold was a big softie when it comes to spending on kids. That scene in *Terminator 2* where his robot picks up a Mexican baby and lovingly examines him was really a reflection of the man himself. In the six years that he was governor, California spent at least $30 billion per year on poor and working class children, over $200 billion total. Arnold essentially had the harsh choice of neglecting these children or raising taxes on the middle class. There was no easy way out and he chose to muddle through with borrowing, gimmicks and hoping things would get better.

The preliminary assessment is that Arnold is on the edge of either a B-minus or C-plus. His biggest positives were his reforms, his biggest disappointment the budget mess. In historical terms, he figures to fit in somewhere near Jerry Brown and Ronald Reagan. From the authors' standpoint, the best California governors of the last 100 years were 1) Earl Warren; 2) Pat Brown; 3) Hiram Johnson; 4) Goodwin Knight; and 5 tie) Ronald Reagan and Jerry Brown. Warren, Brown, and Knight are listed because of the vital role they played in the growth of the state during its golden era of the 1940s to the 1960s. Johnson is up there because of his ground-breaking reforms, some of which were positive and some which were negative. Reagan and Jerry Brown were strong governors in an era of decline for the state. Reagan signed laws on therapeutic abortion, clean air, welfare reform benefits, and state parks, but was also responsible for putting mentally ill homeless on the streets. Brown made advances for agricultural workers, minority and women appointments in state government and environmental issues, but perpetuated Reagan's slow growth in other areas such as University of California and California State University campuses. The Reagan and Brown records, however, were more positive than the records of stagnation by their successors. If Arnold finishes strong, he could yet pass some on the list, but he will definitely be in the top 10. It is relatively safe, however, to label Arnold as the best governor since Reagan and Brown. In historical terms, he'll benefit from the fact that his three predecessors — George Deukmejian, Pete Wilson, and Gray Davis respectively — had none of the other governors' ground breaking reforms or policy and program achievements that advanced the state. Arnold looks very good in comparison to the recent occupants of the governor's mansion.

PART II. CALIFORNIA POLITICS

4. THE STRUCTURE OF CALIFORNIA POLITICS — FROM HIRAM JOHNSON TO THE PRESENT

August 6, 1945, was a defining day in world history. At approximately 8:15 in the morning Japan time, the American bomber *Enola Gay* dropped the first atomic bomb on the Japanese city of Hiroshima. August 6 also turned out to be a defining day in California politics, for a few hours later after the dropping of the bomb, California's senior U.S. Senator Hiram Warren Johnson died of a stroke in Bethesda Naval Hospital in Washington. He was 78.

HIRAM JOHNSON AND THE PROGRESSIVE ERA (1910–1930)

Johnson had been the dominant politician in California in the first half of the twentieth century. He had been senator for 28 years, the longest term of service by any Californian, and had come to Washington in March 1917, after his election in 1916. More importantly, prior to that, he had been governor of California from January 1911, having won election in 1910 and again in 1914. Johnson's election in 1910 was part of the larger Progressive Movement that had been sweeping across the country for over a decade. In the case of California, this movement was in response to ending the dominance in state politics by the Southern Pacific railroad. (Ironically, Johnson's father had once been a lobbyist for the railroad and broke bitterly with his son over reform issues). The result of Johnson's election in 1910 was a tidal wave of political reform that to this day has a profound effect on the political structure of this state. Indeed, Arnold Schwarzenegger would not be governor of this state without Johnson's innovation of the recall. Other governors, such as Earl Warren and Pat Brown may have left a more lasting legacy in terms of their physical impact on California. But no one has had a greater impact on the political structure than Hiram Johnson.

Johnson's inauguration in January 1911 set off a whirlwind of political reform, much like Franklin Roosevelt's 100 days in the 1933 Congress would do. In the 1911 session of the legislature, just about every election vehicle that affects us today was passed in the few weeks that the legislature was in session that year. Most important of these reforms were the initiative, referendum, and recall. All three of these ballot processes are now used in one form or another across the country. But in 1911, they were in the vanguard of the Progressive movement.

The initiative, referendum, and recall were forms of political action that ended on the ballot. The initiative is the most widely known as it is the most used. It provided that a statute with sufficient signatures from eligible voters could be placed on a ballot, whether it would be a local or state ballot. In the case of a state ballot, a statue or a constitutional amendment could be placed on the ballot depending on the number of qualifying signatures that were for presented the measure. The idea for the initiative was to allow the public to pass legislation blocked by special interests in the legislature. Modern use of the initiative process by professional political activists has radically changed its use from the original intent, but in its original form, it was a procedure that was designed to be used by the voting public.

The referendum is a version of the initiative. It is also a ballot measure, but unlike the initiative, it is not an attempt to pass new legislation but a means by which voters could directly approve or disapprove a law passed by the legislature. It is most familiar use is when the legislature placed items on the ballot, such as a bond issue. But it occasionally shows up as a voter-inspired measure, such as the measure put on the ballot by business groups in 2004 to repeal SB2, the legislation that required businesses above a certain size to provide healthcare for their employees. In general, referendums have not been as controversial as initiatives, and have not generated the same public interest.

The recall process is another matter. Recall allows voters to decide to remove (or recall) elected officials by getting enough signatures to place the issue on the ballot. The most famous recall measure, of course, was the successful recall of Governor Gray Davis in 2003, who was replaced by Arnold Schwarzenegger in the same action. Only two other recall attempts of a governor, that of James Rolf in the 1930s and Culbert Olson in the early 1940s, have even been attempted. (Some conservative activists filed a recall petition against Schwarzenegger after he signed a tax hike in 2009). Where the recall has been most widely used has been in elected offices below the statewide constitutional officers, in many cases with strong political overtones. The most recent attempt on a state legislator that made it to the ballot was the failed attempt in 2008 by Senate President Pro Tem Don Perata (D-Oakland) to recall Senator Jeff Denham (R-Merced) because he would not support certain state budget proposals. The recall is most often used in local elections, where its occurrence is common.

The referendum and recall, and in particular the initiative, have had a major impact on the way California has been governed, and various ballot measures have had significant impact on individual elections. One only has to look at California's lengthy and convoluted state constitution to see that. This will be discussed in the next chapter. But the initiative, referendum, and recall were only the first shots by Hiram Johnson and his Progressives in that epic legislative session of 1911. Johnson's next target was the political patronage system of the political parties and the political party structure as well. This covered a number of acts promulgated by the 1911 legislature.

One attack was on the political parties themselves. Prior to 1911, the political parties acted like they currently do in most states of this country. The state party appointed or heavily influenced who could sit on the county central committees; then, from these county committees, people were selected to sit on the state committee. The 1911 legislature demolished this arrangement. The legislature required that the county committee members be elected in the party primary and barred the appoint- ment to the committee by the state party. Since the county committees had to reorga- nize themselves between the primary and the general election and the state party had no control over them, this severely weakened the party at all levels to run elections. The state party had minimal representation from the county level and most of its members were elected officials and their appointees. The result was that candidates had to organize their own campaigns and could not rely on the party. It also meant elected officials were also the most influential people in the state party structure. While a great deal of change has occurred in California political parties in the past 50 years (in the case of the California Democratic Party, only one third of the state committee members are elected officials and their appointees), the party structure in California is still relatively weaker than is the case of most other state parties.

In addition to the weak party structure, the 1911 legislature further damaged the parties by making all elected office below the state legislature, non-partisan races. Today, if you pick up a ballot for mayor, judge, city council, school board, county su- pervisor, and the like, all of the names listed for those offices on the ballot do not show their party registration. This results in some interesting alliances between Republi- cans, Democrats, Decline to State (California's term for Independent candidates), and other minor parties. It also emphasized the need for candidates to run independent campaigns beyond the crippled party structure.

The final piece of the 1911 governmental reform structure was a merit system for government employment. This eliminated political patronage, which was a source of power for political parties, as it still is in many states. So in addition to severing the county party structures from the state, the patronage pipeline, which was a major source for securing manpower for political parties, was eliminated.

In addition to governmental reforms, there were a number of other progressive pieces of legislation that had been fostered by the Progressive movement in other states, such as women suffrage, the direct election of U.S. Senators, the presidential primary, and the like. The governmental reforms were just part of a larger progressive agenda.

All of these ideas eventually were put in the form of some twenty-three consti- tutional amendments, which were voted on and passed by the public in a special election held in November 1911.[1] The sheer volume of activity was astonishing. It was nothing less than a complete social upheaval in one legislative session.

But there were sound political reasons for engaging in such energy. Unlike to- day's California legislature and in fact until Assembly Speaker's Jesse Unruh's reform in the 1960s, the California legislature of Johnson's era met once every two years in January after the previous November election. It was a part-time legislature that met a few months from January to the late spring in the odd numbered years, and un- less called into special session by the governor, closed up shop until the next regu- lar session following the general election roughly 18 months later. That meant that Johnson's Progressive forces in the legislature and in the Republican Party would eventually find renewed opposition from the conservative faction in the party along

---

1 Gladwin Hill, Dancing Bear: An Inside Look at California Politics (Cleveland: World Publish- ing Company, 1968), 53.

with the Democrats, and continued ability to pass Progressive legislation would be in jeopardy. Thus, the need to pass legislation in a hurry in order to entrench the Progressive agenda.[1]

As remarkable as the 1911 session was, one key piece of legislation was passed in the 1913 session, which would have as profound an impact on elections as anything passed in 1911. The item in question was inserted by Johnson in a 1913 election law revision and apparently passed by the legislature and signed by Johnson without much notice at the time. The language inserted was as follows: "nothing in this act contained shall be construed to limit the right of any person to become the candidate of more than one political party for the same office...." This was Johnson's famous cross-filing provision, which was to have enormous ramifications on California partisan elections for the next forty years until the advent of the forces that led to its ultimate repeal in 1959.

Unlike Johnson's classic Progressive reform legislation of 1911, this was a purely crass political power play reflecting the politics of 1913, which in turn were a result of the 1912 presidential election. In 1912, the progressive wing of the Republican Party had tried to nominate former President Theodore Roosevelt in lieu of President William Howard Taft, who was supported by the conservative wing of the party. Johnson led a Progressive delegation from California to the Republican convention, but their efforts failed as Taft was nominated. After the convention the Progressives pulled out and convened their own Progressive Party convention which nominated Roosevelt as president and Johnson as vice president. While the Progressive slate got more popular and electoral votes than Taft, including carrying California, the result was to split the normally Republican vote in the North & West, electing Democrat Woodrow Wilson as president, who also ran on a progressive agenda.

After the 1912 election, several factions of the Progressive Party, including those in California, attempted to maintain the Progressive Party as a viable political operation. Cross-filing was an attempt to do that. The progressives had decided to withdraw from the Republican Party in December 1913 in order to create an official Progressive Party. The Progressive would then be able to nominate their own candidates and have them on the November ballot, but their best chance of getting them elected from a third party would be to have their candidates nominated from *both* the Progressive and Republican parties. This meant that legislation had to be passed that allowed candidates to be able to file in more than one party. As a result cross-filing was created and passed for the benefit of Progressive nominees. As a political strategy for the Progressive Party, however, it ultimately failed. In the 1914 election, Johnson and his progressive allies were able to win re-election as governor and several legislative seats, which gave the progressives control in California for the time being. By 1916, the progressive and conservative wings of the Republican Party had reconciled and the Progressive Party as a viable political entity was gone. It would reappear in 1924 under the candidacy of Senator Robert LaFollette, Sr., but with his death in 1925, it disappeared as a national movement, although it was able to elect people at the state level, such as U.S. Senator Robert LaFollette, Jr. from Wisconsin. Henry Wallace would run under the banner for president in 1948.

---

1 Ibid., 55.

In California, however, cross-filing did not disappear. Johnson did not have it re-pealed, and it stayed on the books. Cross-filing was a unique form of open primary activity in that it technically occurred in a closed primary, meaning that the parties had separate ballots in the primary, rather than having candidates on one single ballot in the primary as is normally the case in an open primary. In short, candidates ran in multiple primaries, rather then in one big primary. Since cross-filing could be used by any candidate in another party's primary, the net result was that voters would see most if not all candidates on their primary ballot. In addition, because of cross-filing, candidates did not show their party registration on the ballot. The only partisan snag in cross-filing was that the candidate had to win the primary of the party he or she was registered in, in order to win the other parties' primary. Since the Progressives expected to win their primary, they saw cross filing as a means of poaching another party nomination. For the Republicans and Democrats, a candidate winning their own primary was much more problematical as there was traditionally more competi-tion in those primaries.[1]

The net result of the 1911 and 1913 legislation was that the Progressive movement was able to secure a solid position in the Republican Party. This had the effect of making the Republican Party the dominant party in California. Even though the Pro-gressive movement had managed to elect a Democrat as president, the net effect in California was to make the Democrats a semi-permanent minority party in the state. There were times where they could align themselves with progressive Republicans and be on the winning side of an election, such as when Wilson barely carried the state in 1916 and won re-election for president by doing so. But at the state level, it meant that they would not win the governorship in the forty-year period between 1898 and 1938, and would not hold it again until 1958. Similarly, the Republicans would control the state legislature for most of that period. A similar situation would occur nationally in the U.S. Congress in the 1920s, where progressive and farm Re-publicans would occasionally align themselves with the Democrats on certain is-sues, particularly farming. The 1920s were a particularly grim time for Democrats in California. At the absolute bottom in 1924, the year the national party took 103 ballots to nominate a presidential candidate; Democrats had only 7 of the 120 seats in the legislature. As future Democratic Attorney General Robert Kenny would say, there were no Democratic politics to speak of in the 1920s and getting the Republican nomination virtually guaranteed election. The combined progressive and conserva-tive Republican bloc outnumbered the Democrats 5 to 1.[2] In 1930, Democrats had just 21.8% of two-party registration.[3]

As a result, the political fight in California from 1911 to the 1930s was not between Republicans and Democrats; it was within the Republican Party. As Johnson and the progressives feared, the conservatives would reorganize and by the 1920s, they dominated the Republican Party with the progressives reduced to a faction within the party. This set the stage for a fundamental split in the Republicans that would last into the 1980s, with events giving one side an advantage over the other and the

---

1 Ibid., 58–60.
2 Ibid., 70–71
3 Ibid., 75.

conservative wing finally pretty much winning for good in the Goldwater and Reagan campaigns of the mid-1960s.

The Great Depression (1930–1942)

Despite the lopsided registration advantage in the 1920s and inter-party bickering among Republicans, one goal of Johnson's progressives continued to operate through the 1920s and later periods — the strong undercurrent of nonpartisanship that ran through California politics. The elevation of Arnold Schwarzenegger to the governorship was the most recent aspect of non-partisanship display in the state, and was facilitated by Johnson's recall provision. Schwarzenegger was only the latest politician to ride the coattails of nonpartisanship to office. Events after the 1920s would make that graphically apparent.

Like the rest of the country, the stock market crash of 1929 and the ensuing Great Depression, would radically alter the political scene in California. The most startling change in California was the tidal wave of Democratic registration. From the 21.8% two-party Democratic registration in 1930, Democrats exploded to 42.6% in 1932.[1] By election day 1934, the Democrats would have a registration advantage that that they have held to this day.[2] The 1932 election showed a new set of political forces at work. Hiram Johnson, having won election to the U.S. in 1916 and having served since that time, endorsed Franklin Delano Roosevelt. The continued explosion in Democratic registration in support of the New Deal had come from Johnson's electoral base, and thus found Johnson gravitating into the Democratic electoral orbit.[3]

More significant for California, however, was the 1934 governor's race, which pitted former Socialist Upton Sinclair, who had won the Democratic Party nomination with his famous EPIC (End Poverty in California) platform against Governor Frank Merriam. This campaign, eventually won by Merriam after a bitter battle and a substantial vote to the Progressive Party gubernatorial candidate, was a landmark campaign in many ways. It is generally considered the first truly modern political campaign in U.S. history, because of its extensive use of media. Sinclair's campaign so frightened the business community that they organized a negative media blitz (in 1934, that meant newspaper, radio, and even newsreels shown before movies) to discourage voters away from Sinclair. The media techniques developed in this campaign would be refined over time to what we see in campaigns today.

But Sinclair's campaign also generated a huge grassroots movement, which resulted in the creation of over 800 Sinclair clubs.[4] This campaign was the forerunner of the Democratic club movement, which two decades later would result in the formation of the California Democratic Council (CDC, itself formed on the foundation of hundreds of Adlai Stevenson clubs in 1952), which would revolutionize California politics in the 1950s.

The Republicans did not stand idly by as the Sinclair clubs organized. While the Democrats would take another twenty years to form their statewide organization,

1   Ibid.
2   Ibid., 85.
3   Richard Coke Lower, *A Bloc of One: The Political Career of Hiram W. Johnson* (Stanford, California: Stanford University Press, 1993), 279.
4   Hill, *Dancing Bear*, 80.

the Republicans, fearing not only the Sinclair campaign, but also the fact that they were suddenly the minority party in the state, formed the California Republican Assembly (CRA), their version of a volunteer grassroots organization to combat the rising Democratic tide. The key activity in the early days of the CRA was to create "fact-finding committees" to screen primary candidates and unite around one.[1] This in effect allowed Republicans to better control their primary, even though Democrats were able to cross-file into it. At the same time, a disorganized Democratic Party was vulnerable to Republican cross-filing in their primary.

The CRA was one of many factors the allowed the Republicans to win more than their share of elections from 1934 right into the 1950s. For starters, since they had controlled the elective offices so completely in the 1920s, Republican candidates had the advantage of name recognition. Under cross-filing, where party affiliation was not listed, name recognition was an enormous advantage. Also in a Democrat majority state, hiding one's Republican registration through cross-filing was similarly a considerable advantage. The Republican financial advantage that showed itself against Upton Sinclair was another major advantage. They had a media advantage in that the vast majority of California newspapers supported Republicans. Finally, having control of the legislature meant that Republicans could gerrymander the legislative and congressional districts to their advantage. Cross-filing, the CRA, gerrymandering and the momentum from incumbency helped keep the Republicans in power long after it should have been a Democratic state.[2]

Despite Republican advantages in 1934, however, they could not stop the gains down ticket. Democrats in the Assembly rose from 25 to 37, and Democrats in the State Senate increased from 5 to 8.[3] Nor could the Republicans stop the flood tide of Democratic registrations, which wrenched up the Democratic lead from a 100,000 to over a million. The result was that by 1938, the Democrats with Culbert Olson as their candidate captured the governor's mansion for the first time since 1898. Olson's tenure as governor was not successful, and in 1942 he was challenged by Attorney General Earl Warren.

EARL WARREN AND THE POST-WAR ERA (1942–1958)

The 1942 election for governor was in its own way, a referendum on the governance ideas of Hiram Johnson. Olson as the incumbent with the registration advantage, tried to run a partisan race. Warren, who was Alameda County District Attorney at the time of 1934 election and Republican Party chairman, had seen the value of a non-partisan vote, and that became his strategy for Attorney General in 1938 and his three successful elections for governor. Warren understood that the Republicans could not win a statewide partisan race in the end as a minority party. He revered Hiram Johnson and his campaigns, and Warren always gave the appearance of non-partisanship even though he was a highly partisan political activist as his party officer

---

1 Ibid., 118.
2 Royce D. Delmatier, Clarence F. McIntosh, and Earl G. Waters, eds., *The Rumble of California Politics 1848–1970* (New York: John Wiley and Sons, 1970), 306. From Henry A. Turner and John A. Vieg, *The Government and Politics of California* (New York: McGraw-Hill, 3rd ed., 1967), 46–48.
3 Hill, *Dancing Bear*, 85.

status indicated. In office, he made quality appointments from both Republicans and Democrats, and he had a reputation for running a well-managed office. His victory in 1942 was the result of these actions.[1]

Earl Warren today, of course, is remembered for his historic and controversial tenure as Chief Justice of the United States Supreme Court from 1953 to 1969. What tends to get lost in his resume is that many political scientists regard him as California's greatest governor (Johnson and Edmund G. "Pat" Brown are the other two main contenders for that distinction). He won three consecutive elections in 1942, 1946 and 1950, the only person to accomplish that feat, and with the advent of the two-term limit in 1990, the only one who ever will. He was governor for over ten years, from January 1943 to October 1953, when President Dwight Eisenhower appointed him Chief Justice. He was Governor Thomas Dewey's vice presidential running mate on the Republican ticket in 1948, and but for President Harry Truman's remarkable upset in that election, might have been vice president and one day president. But the most remarkable achievement of his political career was the 1946 election in which under cross-filing, he won both the Republican and Democratic nominations for governor, the only time for governor it ever occurred. More than any other election, the Warren sweep in 1946 validated his and Hiram Johnson's principle of nonpartisanship campaigning and governing. Much of what one sees today in Governor Schwarzenegger's approach can be seen in Johnson's, Warren's, and their great Democratic counterpart Pat Brown's approach to the governor's office. The main difference between Johnson and the later work of Warren and Brown, was that Johnson's legacy is in terms of government structure; Warren's and Brown's was in the economic development of the state.

While Warren himself reigned as a political colossus across the state, underneath him there was great political ferment. Warren's liberal bipartisanship did not sit well with the conservative elements of his party, but there was little they could do; one, because of Warren himself, and two, it was difficult to ignore the logic of Warren's political argument that a highly partisan and conservative Republican would lose statewide in a heavily Democratic state. To that effect, Warren was able to promote his protégés up the political ladder, the most important of these being Thomas Kuchel, who was first appointed by Warren to be state controller in 1946, and then more importantly, appointed U.S. Senator in 1953 to fill the seat vacated by Richard Nixon when he became Vice President. The conservatives had their own power base in Nixon and William F. Knowland, the son of *Oakland Tribune* publisher and Republican power broker Joseph Knowland. William Knowland was appointed by Warren (reportedly as a favor to his former mentor in Alameda County, Joseph Knowland) in 1945 as U.S. Senator after Hiram Johnson's death. In effect, with Nixon and Knowland on the Right coupled with Warren and Kuchel on the Center–Left, California Republicans had a balanced ticket. These fights became more intense after Warren left for Washington and culminated in the electoral disaster of 1958.

But even more ferment was brewing on the Democratic side. Frustrated at losing election after election to the Republicans even with a million-voter registration advantage, the situation finally boiled over after the 1952 election. In 1950, only one

1 Ibid., 91–103.

Democrat, Pat Brown as Attorney General, had won statewide office in another Republican sweep, including Nixon's win in the U.S. Senate's race. Now in 1952, it was Eisenhower and the Republicans sweeping over Adlai Stevenson and the Democrats. The Republicans still controlled the legislature and had gerrymandered the legislative districts again. Finally, State Senator and Democratic Party Chair George Miller had had enough. Following a scathing open letter entitled "What's Wrong with the Democratic Party?" Miller and a few key Democratic Party officials set up a meeting at the Asilomar Conference Center near Monterey in the last weekend in January 1953 to discuss what needed to be done. The meeting was heavily attended with lively discussions throughout. One of the key participants turned out to be a 39-year-old former journalist by the name of Alan Cranston. The Democrats agreed to form a statewide organization using the recently organized Stevenson clubs as a base. The new organization would not only help organize grassroots clubs and organizations, but would also issue pre-primary endorsements of Democrats to combat cross-filing. Thus out of the Democratic wreckage of the 1952 election came the birth of one of the most dynamic political organizations California had ever seen — the California Democratic Council, more commonly known as CDC.

Coming out of the Asilomar meeting, it was agreed to establish CDC at a convention in Fresno the last weekend in November. At that meeting, CDC's first annual convention, the CDC Constitution was passed and Alan Cranston named as first President. CDC then turned to the 1954 election. In February, in preparation for the June 1954 primary, CDC made its candidate endorsements and then issued over 1.3 million slate mailers to Democrats around the state.[1]

While this was going on, the Democrats were getting some benefit from the one action from the 1952 election that would benefit them in the future. In the 1952 election the Democrats has managed to get an initiative on the ballot to ban cross-filing. The Republicans, seeing an end to a key piece of their political strategy, countered with a proposition to continue cross-filing, but require candidates show their party affiliation. Since the Republicans controlled the Secretary of State's office under Frank Jordan, they managed to get their initiative numbered number 7, while the Democratic ballot measure was pushed down the ballot to number 13, a decided disadvantage. In the end, Proposition 7 won while the 1952 version of "Proposition 13" barely lost. It had appeared that the Republicans had a minor victory in the dual of ballot measures.[2]

However, when analysis of later elections was done, it turned out that cross-filing itself was not the major advantage; the key was not having party affiliation on the ballot. The combination of CDC endorsements and slate mailers, plus the listing of party affiliation in cross filing, had a devastating blow on Republican dominance on the ballot. In the 1954 primary, CDC endorsed candidates won every primary for state and congressional office and ultimately in November picked up six Assembly and five State Senate seats, including the key State Senate seat in Los Angeles County.[3]

---

1   Dr. Reuben Fred Kugler, *Volunteers in Politics: The Twenty-seven year History of the California Democratic Council 1953–1980*, 5th ed. (Ventura, California: CDC Archives, Section IF, 1980), 2.

2   Hill, *Dancing Bear*, 116.

3   Kugler, *Volunteers in Politics*, 2.

And for the first time since cross-filing had been introduced in 1913, Democrats were able to place a full slate of candidates for the statewide offices on the November ballot.[1] The impact of CDC and the new party disclosure was accompanied by a surge of Democratic registrations. Between 1952 and 1958, two of every three new voters joined the Democratic Party, and the registration margin over the Republicans increased from roughly 950,000 to 1.2 million. Total Democratic registration was nearly 4 million. After the 1956 election, the Democrats were dead even in the Senate at twenty seats apiece, and had narrowed the gap in the assembly to 42–38, very different from the 1920s.[2]

THE PAT BROWN ERA (1958–1966)

This set the stage for the historic year of 1958 and the 1958 governor's race. For the Democrats, the nomination was a simple one. Attorney General Pat Brown, the only Democrat to hold statewide office since 1950, was the logical choice. For the Republicans, what should have been a logical choice turned into political intrigue, trickery, and then electoral disaster. The logical choice for governor should have been the incumbent Goodwin Knight, who as Lieutenant Governor in 1953 had assumed the governor's job when Earl Warren went to Washington. Elected in his own right in 1954, he was a popular non-partisan governor with no seeming problems for the nomination and re-election.

The factor neither Knight nor the Republicans had accounted for was the burning Presidential ambitions of their senior U.S. Senator and Senate Minority Leader William F. Knowland. As one of the leading Republicans in the national party, Knowland along with other Republicans was eyeing the 1960 presidential election, which promised to be a wide-open election with President Dwight Eisenhower being forced to leave office under the newly enacted two-term limit of the Twenty-Second Amendment. Positioning himself for the race, and believing that he had a better shot for the nomination as California's governor than as its senator, Knowland announced in late 1957 that he would not be running for re-election to his Senate seat in 1958, and instead run for governor. This brought great consternation to Republican ranks in the state, and set the stage for further political intrigue. For Knowland was not the only Californian looking at the 1960 president's race. There was the small matter of that other leading California politician, Vice President Richard Nixon. As vice president, Nixon was obviously in a very key position to get the nomination. He also had another great advantage over Knowland; he didn't have to run for election in 1958, while Knowland did. Ultimately, in one of the great Machiavellian moves in California state politics, Nixon convinced Knight to run for the Senate so that Knowland could run for governor. With that decision, the Republicans changed what should have been incumbents running for re-election at the top of the ticket to a wide-open race in a year when the Democrats were expected to gain seats nationwide. Ever since Hiram Johnson had ended the power of bosses in "smoke-filled" rooms to choose party nominees, most California voters have distrusted "backroom" politics. This attempted "double-

---

1 Hill, *Dancing Bear*, 152.
2 Ibid., 152–153.

switch" offended key reform-oriented middle class voters and added greatly to the Democratic tide.

Compounding the Republicans problems in California was Knowland's weak campaign. Knowland failed to realize (as many long term incumbents do) that staying in Washington too long tends to make you lose touch with the voters that sent you there. On top of that, he was perceived as using the governor's office as a stepping-stone to the presidency, thereby setting himself up not only as a carpetbagger, but also as an opportunist. In the process, he had alienated voters as well as members of his own party who felt that he had run roughshod over "Goody" Knight. So Knowland's campaign started out with an image problem. He then compounded it, by running a partisan, divisive campaign highlighted by his support of the anti-labor right to work initiative, Proposition 18. This strategy united labor against him and joined them with the independents, moderates, and progressives that had been alienated by his campaign from the beginning.

In contrast, Brown stayed above the fray and ran an essentially non-partisan campaign. In his campaign, he made statements such as the following:

> "I believe that the governor must call on the most able and experienced men and women of our state, without regard to partisanship....I intend to guide our state government in the great tradition of Earl Warren and Hiram Johnson."[1]

Brown also projected a friendly, non-threatening image compared to Knowland.

When the votes were tallied on general election day in November 1958, it was a virtual Democratic sweep. Brown beat Knowland by over a million votes. The popular Northern California Congressman Claire Engle beat Knight for the U.S. Senate seat by some 700,000 votes. The Democrats took every statewide office except Secretary of State (Frank Jordan and his father practically owned the job from 1912 to 1970), took control of the Assembly for the first time since 1942 and the State Senate for the first time since 1890.[2] It was the greatest Democratic victory in California since 1889, some seventy years before in a vastly different state.[3]

One of the big winners in that election was Alan Cranston, who had resigned as CDC's first president in December, 1957 to run and win election as State Controller. CDC had once again proven its strength in the election, having mailed its slate of endorsed candidates to most Democratic voters, and registering voters to increase the Democrats registration lead. Nearly all of CDC's endorsed candidates won their primaries. Pat Brown and other Democrats gave CDC major credit for this victory.[4] CDC had reached a peak that no volunteer political organization had ever approached, and has not been duplicated since.

As for CDC's counterpart the CRA, it had shown itself ineffective in the election, particularly in its former area of strength, which was resolving primary candidate disputes and providing unity to the party. By standing by and allowing Knowland to conduct his power play, it came to be regarded not as an agent of Republican unity,

---

1 Ibid., 154.
2 Ibid., 158–159.
3 Kugler, *Volunteers in Politics*, 2.
4 Ibid.

but as part of the conservative old Republican guard that resented the likes of Warren, Knight and Kuchel and today has serious ideological problems with Schwarzenegger. Over time, it drifted from its more moderate stance, and became more of a right-wing organization.[1] But a right-wing Republican Party was simply not what the voters wanted in 1958. The *San Francisco Chronicle*'s view of the situation was as follows:

> An extreme group in the California Republican party decided...to take California back into the 19th century, away from 'modern Republicanism' that the members of the group so heartily loathe; away from their Progressive tradition...of the great Republican governorships of Hiram Johnson... and Earl Warren: away from Goodwin Knight, whom they hold in contempt of the odd notion that the way for Republican candidates to win is to try to gain support from all elements of the public, including labor.[2]

This conservative brand of Republicanism would win supporters in a few years, but it would take another gubernatorial defeat in 1962 before it would gain any traction.

But in 1958, it was the Democrats' era, as they became the solid majority party. In many ways, the governorship of Pat Brown was an extension of the Warren and Knight years. Like Warren and Knight, Brown understood that the spectacular growth of California needed planning and infrastructure development on a scale that was unprecedented in the state. But unlike Warren and Knight, Brown was able to achieve those plans and complete what his two Republican predecessors had started. Today, fifty years after he entered the governor's mansion, no other governor has had as profound a physical impact on the state as Pat Brown did. The California Aqueduct, the freeway system, and University of California and California State University systems are just some of the projects that are a visible reminder of the Brown Administration.[3] In effect, until Arnold Schwarzenegger's building campaign in 2006, California had been living off the infrastructure investments of Pat Brown.

Brown would go on to win a second term against Richard Nixon on 1962, and be the first Democrat to serve two four-year terms. But by the time he decided to run for a third term in 1966, the political winds had changed. The change occurred in both parties and the political structure of the state. For starters, politics gradually became more partisan with the repeal of cross-filing in 1959. On the Democratic side, the unity that the party had had in the 1950s began to unravel. This was in part due to the successes up to 1958. Politicians that had worked together with Democratic organizations such as CDC decided that they could increasingly campaign on their own without the need for CDC or the party. Some resented a volunteer organization like CDC having influence and thought that CDC had too much power. CDC's own positions on issues were often too far to the left for elected officials to run on. The most celebrated of those were CDC's opposition to the Vietnam War, which triggered the fight to remove CDC president Si Casady by Pat Brown and Alan Cranston in 1966.[4]

---

1 Hill, *Dancing Bear*, 160.
2 Ibid., 159.
3 Ethan Rarick, *California Rising: The Life and Times of Pat Brown* (Berkeley and Los Angeles: University of California Press, 2005), 251.
4 Dr. Reuben Fred Kugler, *The California Democratic Council, Highlights in its Record of Achievements 1953–1972* (Ventura, California: CDC Archives Section IF, 1972), 11–12.

Thus began the conflict between CDC and the Party, which would carry in some form for the next four decades.

There were splits within the Democratic elected officials as well, the most serious of them between Brown and Assembly Speaker Jesse Unruh. This fight flared out in a number of party battles, the most serious being the U.S. Senate race in 1964. Senator Claire Engle was dying from a brain tumor, and this triggered a fight to replace him. Brown and CDC backed Alan Cranston. Unruh and his links with the Kennedys got White House Press Director Pierre Salinger to file at the last minute. This triggered a bitter fight in which Salinger won, handing CDC its first major loss on a pre-primary endorsement. But it created enormous damage to the party. Salinger would have to fight the same "carpet-bagging" accusations that Knowland had had to in 1958. Plus, Salinger and the Democrats had the additional issue of Proposition 14, which was placed on the ballot to repeal the Rumford Fair Housing Act, which banned racial discrimination in housing sales. Also like Knowland, Salinger tied his campaign to a losing proposition, while his opponent, actor George Murphy, stayed clear of the proposition. On election night Murphy beat Salinger by 200,000 votes attracting some 700,000 Democrats. Proposition 14 won by 4.5 million votes to 2.4 million votes (although later it was declared unconstitutional). All this occurred during Lyndon Johnson's presidential landslide that year.[1] In addition to being a stunning defeat for the Democrats and a repeat of carpet bagging and a proposition as issues affecting a race, it was also the first successful win by movie personality in a statewide race, a factor that would have important implications for one or two governors later on.

THE REAGAN AND EARLY CONSERVATIVE COALITION ERA (1966–1974)

The 1964 Senate race marked the beginning of Democratic Party decline in the state. The internal party battles and the impact of external issues such as Vietnam, the student revolt on college campuses, the Watts riots, all contributed to that decline. Other issues were also starting to register with blue-collar Democrats that showed that the Democratic base was eroding. Working people started to show more concern for "crime," "high taxes," "big government," and "open housing." Clearly, these people were becoming more conservative.[2] They would eventually form the base both in California and the nation for the "Reagan Democrats." CDC would have one last triumph in its opposition to the Vietnam War, bringing in Eugene McCarthy into the 1968 primaries, and seeing Lyndon Johnson pull out of the race,[3] but in the process splitting both the party and CDC, and permanently damaging itself as a factor in California politics. The Democratic Party in California came apart at the seams from 1964 to 1968[4] — just as it did nationally. It would take nearly three decades to recover.

For the Republicans, the trend started upward after the 1962 election. It was based on the conservative wing of the party beginning to assert itself. In 1962, the conservatives made a bid to obtain the governor and Senate nominations, but after Nixon's loss, began to make a series of moves to take over their party. It was based on

---

1 Hill, *Dancing Bear*, 189.
2 Ibid., 210–211.
3 Kugler, *Volunteers in Politics*, 3.
4 Delmatier, *Rumble of California Politics*, 390–391.

four key points: (1) to take over the volunteer party organizations, (2) to support conservative candidates, (3) to defeat moderate Republicans elected officials in primaries, and (4) to capture control of the Republican State Central Committee. This plan was started by taking over the Young Republicans in 1963 and then CRA in 1964. Previously, the more conservative members of the CRA had split off to form the United Republicans of California (UROC), so this group was already under the conservatives' control. Once under their control, conservative Republicans denied endorsements to Republican incumbents who did not meet their Republican standards; this meant in turn loss of organizational and financial support. Thus, moderate Republicans were gradually marginalized in the party and the CRA became a right-wing splinter group whose effectiveness in the party was pre-empted by subsequent events.

The subsequent events were the increasing professionalization of the Republican Party's various structures. This included the application of rational planning to politics and development of party organization at all levels. It meant the state party and the county central committees were strengthened and superseded the volunteer organizations. The volunteers would still do endorsements (and still do. Unlike the California Democratic Party, which does endorsements, the California Republican Party does not, leaving that to the CRA and the Howard Jarvis Taxpayers Association), but the party machinery would be focused on organizing, financing, and targeting races. In particular, the Republicans began targeting races where they could pick up seats.[1] The net result was that conservative Republicans were able to become an effective political force, and starting with the 1966 election right through 1998, were able to dominate gubernatorial politics. Only the advent of the Watergate scandal and its impact on the 1974 election nationally as well as the return of a Brown running for governor, kept it from being a clean sweep.

The 1966 governor's race signaled a number of these changes. Pat Brown, running for a third term, was pressing his luck as it was. Only Earl Warren, in a much less partisan time had pulled off the feat and his popularity was still very high by the end of his second term. Brown's popularly was not. He was running a tired administration, where the great infrastructure projects were forgotten, and the public was more concerned about high taxes, and riots on campus and in the streets. And he was confronted by a most formidable politician in former actor Ronald Reagan. Reagan was able to effectively voice the concerns of the voters and come across in the "nice-guy," non-partisan manner that California voters favored. And what was evident from this first campaign as in all his later campaigns was that he was a master communicator. His greatest political masterstroke was in understanding that the Democrats were now weakest where they had once been strongest — the blue-collar workers. Sensing that the Democrats were vulnerable because of the fear, anger, and resentment of these groups, he appealed to them directly. The result was that he made great inroads into this group in 1966. Where Pat Brown had won 78% of the blue-collar vote in 1958, he won just 57% in 1966. In the twelve most working class towns in California, many of them filled with workers from the aeronautics factories, Brown had carried all twelve in 1962; in 1966, he carried just one. This was the first election where the

---

1 Ibid., 387–391.

Reagan Democrats showed up in numbers for the Republican Party, and they have been a mainstay for the party right up through the 1992 election.[1]

Since 1966 has gone down as a landmark election, it is worth an extended examination. In 1962, when Pat Brown beat Nixon, the New Deal Coalition of white workers in the big urban areas, white populists in the Central Valley and inner city minorities was still intact. Table 4-1 shows how that coalition fell apart in just four years, from Pat Brown in 1962 to LBJ and Pierre Salinger in 1964 plus the vote to repeal the Rumford Fair Housing Act (Proposition 14) in 1964 and finally with Pat Brown's landslide loss to Reagan in 1966. Lyndon Johnson won such a massive across-the-board victory that his results do not reveal much, but the defeat of Pierre Salinger and the Rumford Act ("No" on 14) were the real long-term stories of 1964 in California. Both Salinger and No on 14 held all of the black vote and most of the Hispanic vote. But there were massive defections in the Central Valley, the Southern California suburbs and among white workers in both the Bay Area and L.A. County. The defeat of Pat Brown in 1966 was entirely predicted by Salinger's upset loss and the wipeout loss of Fair Housing. Pat Brown's loss among three white populist voting streams — the Central Valley and white worker neighborhoods in both Northern and Southern California — was shocking. In the Central Valley Cities, he dropped from 66% in 1958 to a respectable 56% four years later, to 44% in 1966. Among Bay Area white workers, he dropped from 70% in 1958 to a solid 62% in 1962 and a disappointing 50% in 1966. The biggest changes occurred in the white working class precincts of L.A. County: Pat Brown won 66% there in 1958, a good-enough 54% in 1962 and a disastrous 39% in 1966. In the L.A. County blue-collar neighborhoods, he went from a 32-point lead against Knowland in 1958 to a 22-point loss to Reagan in 1966. That is a net swing of over 50 points and it is what the political scientists call "realignment" (a fancy word for a significant and durable shift in voting trends). These patterns carried over into 1968 and cost Democratic presidential nominee Hubert H. Humphrey dearly: because he lost the white working class, he could not carry the Golden State — and California's 40 electoral votes provided Richard Nixon with his majority in the Electoral College. Just as in 1916, when California elected Woodrow Wilson when much of the East voted against him, the Golden State made history again in 1968 by choosing a president.

In retrospect, the 1966 results set up a pattern that would last for a generation as the so-called "Reagan Democrats" in the suburbs and Central Valley would keep California Republican for president six straight times from 1968 to 1988. The Republicans also held the governorship for a majority of these years. Senator Alan Cranston was the Democrats' only consistent winner from 1968 to 1986. Table 4-2 shows how the state changed politically from the Pat Brown era (1958-64) to the Age of Reagan (1966 to the end of the Cold War in 1991). On average, the Democrats sustained significant losses outside the coastal cities and with Hispanic, Asian and with white voters, especially in the blue-collar suburbs.

---

1 Rarick, *California Rising*, 363.

TABLE 4–1. THE DECLINE OF THE DEMOCRATS, 1964–68

Social Group	Brown	Johnson	Salinger	Fair Housing (Prp14)	Brown	Humphrey
	1962	1964	1964	1964	1966	1968
Blacks	93%	98%	96%	93%	96%	91%
Hispanics	81%	90%	75%	67%	80%	87%
Whites	48%	54%	42%	29%	35%	39%
White Liberals	61%	69%	59%	49%	59%	60%
Conservatives	39%	44%	35%	22%	28%	30%
Central Valley	56%	64%	53%	34%	44%	47%
Bay Area Suburbs	54%	64%	50%		45%	47%
SoCal White Subs.	41%	48%	35%	25%	30%	30%
White Working Class:						
Bay Area	62%	67%	55%	37%	50%	54%
L.A. County	54%	58%	45%	23%	39%	44%
Statewide	52%	59%	48%	35%	42%	45%

Source: All Tables shown in this chapter are from the Patrick Reddy data base and the Appendix.

These trends lasted through 1990. With the loss of white non-intellectual liberal voters, Democrats struggled to win with a coalition of just minorities and white liberals. Without those crucial votes from formerly economic "populists" in the Central Valley cities and big metro areas who had voted for Franklin Roosevelt, Harry Truman and Pat Brown, California Democrats floundered, losing 14 out of 21 races for president, governor and US Senate from Reagan's debut in 1966 to the end of the Cold War in 1991. The basic Reagan Coalition of those who were anti-hippie, anti-black and anti-liberal set the pattern for Richard Nixon's vote in 1968 and beyond.

As governor, however, Reagan would also show the characteristics that were present in abundance in the White House. As the state's first suburban governor, Reagan sought to protect the Anglo middle class from both urban crime and minority & liberal demands for income redistribution. Reagan actually talked more conservative than he governed. While long on political rhetoric, Reagan showed again and again that he was a practical politician. While he would preach against higher taxes, and in his first year in the White House delivered substantial income tax cuts, both as governor and as president he signed numerous tax increases.

TABLE 4–2. CALIFORNIA VOTING PATTERNS

Region	Average Dem %	Average Dem %	Change %
	1958–64	1966–91	
Bay Area	56%	54%	-2%
North/Central Coast	50%	47%	-3%
Central Valley Cities	57%	47%	-10%
Los Angeles County	52%	50%	-2%
Southern California	46%	39%	-7%
Rural California	55%	42%	-13%
Ethnic Breakdown / Social Group Voting			
Asians	61%	51%	-10%
Blacks	89%	90%	+1%
Hispanics	82%	74%	-8%
Whites	48%	42%	-6%
White Sub-Groups:			
White Liberals	59%	60%	+1%
Conservatives	41%	34%	-7%
Bay Area Suburbs	54%	49%	-5
South Cal. Whites	44%	35%	-5
Working Class Whites:			
Bay Area	60%	54%	-6
L.A. County	55%	48%	-7
Statewide	53%	47%	-6

In his first year as governor, Reagan signed the largest tax increase in state history. He also followed Pat Brown in a number of other policies, such as the Therapeutic Abortion Act, increasing benefits in a welfare reform act, expanding the state parks system, signing clean air laws and doubling the state budget.[1] Indeed, many conservative Republicans bemoaned that Reagan's advisors had steered him away on the true conservative path and would not allow "Reagan to be Reagan," whatever that meant. In many ways, Reagan embodied the non-partisan trappings of the old Progressives, but with a conservative slant.

One difference between Reagan and his GOP predecessors like Warren and Knight was that he was an outspoken conservative before he was a reformer. This

---

1 Peter Schrag, *California: America's High-Stakes Experiment* (Berkeley and Los Angeles: University of California Press, 2006), 98-99.

had politically divisive consequences. With his spirited opposition to blacks and (especially) hippies, he polarized the electorate. In his 1970 re-election, Reagan's margin was reduced by almost half. Jess Unruh gave Reagan the toughest battle of his career, making solid gains in the Central Valley cities and L.A. County white working class areas, but he still failed to win a majority from either group. As the Democrats' former Assembly Speaker and leader of the "party regulars," Unruh also simply lacked the "reform" credentials to compete in the suburbs where he ran behind Pat Brown's already disastrous 1966 performance in the Bay Area suburbs. In 1972, George McGovern ran worse than Humphrey among every group in the state with one exception — voters on the smaller city-dominated North & Central Coast who were also helping to pass via initiative the creation of the California Coastal Commission to protect the environment.

THE JERRY BROWN ERA AND PROPOSITION 13 (1974–1982)

Nineteen seventy-four brought the end of the Watergate scandal and an opening for Democrats everywhere. Into this gap, strode the ultimate "New Politics" candidate, Jerry Brown, running on the slogan: "serve the people, protect the earth, explore the universe." He won the Democratic primary against four main opponents largely because of his last name (which attracted bloc votes from the black and Hispanic communities) and of his sponsorship of a major Proposition, the Political Reform Act of 1974 (Proposition 9), which introduced strict ethics rules for legislators, Capitol staff and lobbyists.

Jerry Brown won the governorship against lackluster Establishment Republican Houston Flournoy by winning impressively in the Bay Area and L.A. County and shaving the GOP margin in Southern California for a 50–47% statewide victory. In a sharp break from the patterns of the Reagan Era, Jerry Brown carried the Central Valley cities by 50–48% and won back the white workers in the Bay Area and L.A. who had abandoned his father in 1966. Also crucial to Jerry's success were the bloc votes from the Black and Hispanic communities. As one of the first "New Democrats," Jerry also proved popular in the North and Central Coastal counties, running almost as well there as in the more traditionally Democratic Central Valley cities, the shape of the future Democratic Coalition to come.

Jerry Brown embodied many contradictions. Although the only other Democrat to serve two full terms like his father, in many political aspects, Jerry was not his father's son. At only 36 years of age, Brown represented a new generation coming of age politically. Brown's austere personal style — he refused to live in the governor's mansion and rented a $275 per month apartment, while ditching the gubernatorial limousine for a 1974 Plymouth Satellite with just an AM radio — was a distinct break from gubernatorial tradition. From a fiscal standpoint, Jerry Brown was much more like Ronald Reagan than Pat Brown. He continued Reagan's slowdown of the development of University of California and California State University campuses. It was not until the late 1990s, with UC-Merced, that another University of California campus was built. This conservative fiscal approach disappointed many liberal Democrats who thought he would follow with his father's programs. But Jerry Brown believed that the state government should live within its means because it could not run deficits like the federal government could. But at the same time Brown believed in maintaining the state tax levels to maintain the revenue base because cutting taxes meant cutting services that the public wanted.[1]

Brown's administration was significant for several other activities that developed during this era. One was in the area of labor relations with his ground-breaking agricultural labor relations act, which protected farm workers and he also signed the law that would allow government employees to join unions. Still another was reforming government by appointing numerous women and minorities. Another was his work, begun as Secretary of State, on campaign finance disclosure. Most important, was his support of environmental issues, which had begun with the Coastal Protection Act (Proposition 20) in 1972. Environmental issues neatly dovetailed with Brown's stand on budgetary issues — protecting the earth fit in very well with living within your means. It also reflected a change of attitude with the public from the 1940s and 50s bigger is better, to the 1970s views that the state was too big already. It was in the 1970s that the slow growth movement began its rise to its prominent place in local politics.

The most important issue to impact Jerry's Brown's administration and governments across the state was the passage in June 1978 of the most celebrated proposition in California history — Proposition 13, the Jarvis–Gann initiative capping property taxes. No other proposition in the history of California initiatives is remembered by its ballot number. There have been many other Proposition 13s, but only the Jarvis–Gann initiative of 1978 has stayed in the conscience of California voters and politicians. Proposition 13 has been a true re-aligning issue. No one has been elected to statewide office since 1978 who has favored repealing it. Howard Jarvis, whom no one took seriously prior to 1978, ended up being a visionary equal to Hiram Johnson, and Pat Brown.

Proposition 13 was another landmark conservative "grassroots" initiative that would help re-align state politics for another few decades. Accordingly, its breakdown of voter support is worth a detailed look. A good comparison can be made between the votes for Reagan's tax cut attempt in 1973 (Proposition 1), and for Proposition 13.

Proposition 13 posted double-digit gains compared to Proposition 1 in every California region, with Asians and whites, with suburbanites and especially in white working class neighborhoods where it gained a stunning 33 points in the Bay Area white labor areas. In short, As Bill Schneider pointed out Proposition 13 did best with the property-owning middle class[2] and helped incite a national "tax revolt." Just as the repeal of the Rumford Fair Housing Act in 1964 helped set up Reagan's gubernatorial triumph, so did Proposition 13 help him win the presidency.

1 Robert Pack, *Jerry Brown, the Philosopher Prince* (New York: Stein Day, 1978), 199–201.
2 William Schneider, "An Insiders' View of the Election," *Atlantic*, July 1988.

TABLE 4-3. YES VOTES ON TAX CUTS

Region	Proposition 1	Proposition 13	Change %
	1973	1978	
Bay Area	42%	62%	+20%
North/Central Coast	42%	66%	+24%
Central Valley Cities	39%	57%	+18%
Los Angeles County	48%	67%	+19%
Southern California	52%	66%	+14%
Rural California	44%	72%	+28%
Ethnic Breakdown / Social Group Voting			
Asians	45%	61%	+16%
Blacks	16%	18%	+2%
Hispanics	37%	40%	+3%
Whites	49%	64%	+15%
White Sub-Groups:			
White Liberals	35%	55%	+20%
Conservatives	59%	70%	+11%
Bay Area Suburbs	45%	68%	+23%
South Cal. Whites	52%	68%	+16%
Working Class Whites:			
Bay Area	40%	73%	+33%
L.A. County	50%	73%	+23%
Statewide	46%	65%	+19%

THE POST-PROPOSITION 13 CONSERVATIVE ERA (1980–1992)

The 1980s in California became the "Post-Proposition 13 Reagan Conservative Republican Decade" as his combination of tax cuts for the upper classes and defense spending that provided well-paying jobs for thousands of middle class residents in Greater Los Angeles and San Diego proved a potent force. Using the Reagan method of running up huge margins in the Southern California suburbs while winning over moderate Democrats in the Central Valley with hardball negative campaigns, California Republicans won seven of nine major statewide elections in the 1980s. Suburbanites almost everywhere were the key to GOP victories as they even carried the Bay Area suburbs that had once been Pat Brown strongholds. Only Senator Alan Cranston kept the Democrats from being completely shut out during that decade. Isolated in the inner cities and some white liberal areas in the suburbs like Marin County and Santa Monica, California Democrats were consistently outvoted. Republicans not only began to carry the small Asian-American vote, but also nearly doubled their share among Hispanics as they began to move up to the middle class.

The actual mechanics of Proposition 13 is less important than its political impact on the country. More than any other single action, Proposition 13 initiated the conservative revolt against high taxes and big government, which lasted until the financial crisis thirty years later. It has affected every aspect government in this state since it was enacted. Indeed, some people believe that next to Hiram Johnson's reforms of 1911–1913, it is the most influential piece of legislation in California in the twentieth century. Not only did it have a direct impact on state government, it unleashed the initiative as a formidable weapon in impacting fiscal policy. Numerous initiatives have been passed which impact the state budget, most notably Proposition 98 in 1988, which fixed the percentage of the budget general fund which had to be devoted to K–12 education.[1]

The stream of impact propositions coincided with another change — the radically shifting demographics of the state. Since the 1960s, nearly 80% of California's population growth has been Latino or Asian. By 2005, more than 26% of the population of the state was foreign-born, the highest in recent times.[2] This has led sociologists and political scientists to postulate that there is a connection between increasing immigration and the anti-tax, anti-government mood of the California taxpayer and voter. Alberto Alesina, Reza Baqir and William Easterly noted that public expenditures in U.S. metropolitan areas on such things as education, roads are inversely related the area's ethnic fragmentation.[3] In a 2004 study, economist Peter H. Lindert noted that lower voter turnouts and ethnic diversity tended to reduce social spending. The more that a middle-income voter can identify with the receiver of public funds, the more willing the voter is likely to vote to raise taxes for public spending.[4] Polling since the mid-1990s has shown that there is great hostility in certain segments in the California population who, according to Peter Schrag, "say they'll be damned if they pay one more cent to educate the kids of people who have no right to be in this country in the first place."[5] The most graphic result of these attitudes was the passage of Proposition 187 in 1994, which was to cut such funds. On the federal level, political observers have noted for years that programs such as Social Security and Medicare, where all people are eligible regardless income, are far more popular than welfare programs, which target only certain income groups.

The combination of the Republican's anti-tax, anti-government, and anti-immigration message was facilitated by the difference in the demographics of the state's population base with those of its voters. Although 35% of the population is Latino, only 14% of the voters are Latino; nearly 70% of the voters are non-Hispanic whites. However, since the state legislature is apportioned in equal-sized districts based on

---

1 Schrag, *California*, 130.

2 Ibid., 6.

3 Alberto Alesina, Reza Baqir, and William Easterly, "Public Goods and Ethnic Division," *Quarterly Journal of Economics* 114, no. 4 (November 1999).

4 Peter H. Lindert, *Growing Public: Social Spending and Economic Growth Since the Eighteenth Century* (Cambridge: Cambridge University Press, 2004), 29, 187.

5 Schrag, *California*, 241.

the total population, voter and non-voter, the legislature more accurately reflects the demographics of the state. This has encouraged the more conservative middle-class white voters to support the initiative process. In most recent polls, the public trusts the initiative process more than they trust the legislature or the governor.[1]

The votes to repeal the Fair Housing law in 1964 and for Proposition 13 in 1978 were driven by the same political forces — middle class suburbanites plus white populists in the Central Valley and blue collar neighborhoods. That was the Reagan Coalition at that time. The Republican strategy was an essentially negative strategy aimed at severing white Democrats from their ancestral party. To do so would require campaigns that would often be abrasive, divisive and sometimes racist and sexist — there's generally no polite way to say that your opponent is a financially irresponsible crook who will let guilty criminals run free and give away the middle class' hard-earned tax dollars.

Two of the more famous hardball negative "wedge" campaigns came in success-ful efforts against Tom Bradley, who was seeking to become the nation's first black Governor since the Civil War Era and against Dianne Feinstein, who was seeking to become the state's first female governor. Since these campaigns were the essence of 1980s "Reaganism," they are worth a look back.

In 1982, Los Angeles Mayor Tom Bradley was almost elected governor of Califor-nia. The 1982 campaign, which ended in an excruciating one-point upset loss, set up a pattern in racial politics that lasted over two decades until Obama's big win in 2008. Bradley's candidacy showed that even blacks that go out of their way to reassure white voters would still face racial barriers that are almost impossible to overcome.

In retrospect, Bradley's candidacy in 1982 was a crucial test of racial politics for several reasons. Bradley was the first black major party nominee for governor; he was also the first black Democrat nominated for Governor or US Senator and the first major black candidate to run outside the Northeast. So, in short, there were many unanswered questions going into 1982.

The 1982 and 1986 gubernatorial campaigns showed how racial problems were still very much part of elections. These divisions would wrack American politics for the rest of the twentieth century as the country became increasingly non-Ang-lo. Not surprisingly, they appeared first in multi-ethnic California, where the 1980 Census showed that minorities were much larger a share of the population that the national average (33% in California compared to 21% nationally), and the 2000 Cen-sus showed that Hispanics, Asian–Pacific Islanders and blacks outnumbered non-Hispanic whites.

Tom Bradley had made a name for himself in 1973 by being the first black Mayor of Los Angeles, then only about 20% black. Mayor Bradley set a record for a black mayoral candidate by winning an astounding 43% of the white vote in 1973. By con-trast, the first black mayors of Cleveland, Chicago, Philadelphia, and Detroit had to struggle to win even 20% of the white vote. But Los Angeles and California seemed to indicate a new, non-racial brand of politics as African-Americans Wilson Riles was elected state Superintendent of Public Instruction in 1970, Mervyn Dymally was elected Lt. Governor in 1974 and an Asian woman, March Fong Eu, won five straight

---

1 Ibid., 7.

elections for Secretary of State from 1974 to 1990. California's history as a place for all kinds of people to make a fresh start earned the Golden State a well-deserved reputation for tolerance. That reputation was momentarily rocked in 1982.

Contrary to the charges of his opponent Mayor (1961–1973) Sam Yorty, Bradley's policies as mayor were quite moderate. He made an alliance with businessmen and unions to build up the Downtown area and revive the Harbor. As long as the Southern California economy was booming, there was something for everyone: expansion for business, construction jobs for both white and minority union members, city jobs for the minorities, access and appointments for (mainly Jewish) white liberals. The Bradley Coalition worked. He was re-elected handily in 1977 and carried every city council district in the city in 1981, thus becoming the front-runner for governor in 1982.

Bradley seemed to have everything going for him in 1982. Unemployment hit a post-war high of 11%, the Republicans had a bitter primary between George Deukmejian and Mike Curb, President Reagan was at the depths of his popularity due to the recession, a majority of voters were registered Democrats. The public seemed to approve of Bradley as a moderate, reassuring black candidate with executive experience that exceeded his opponent's. His campaign went out of its way to avoid racial polarization by emphasizing economic issues. In every pre-election poll, he led the Republican nominee.

The Deukmejian campaign said race was not an issue they would bring up. Despite their assertions of a clean campaign, Deukmejian's ads actually used the slogan "A Governor for all the People," which seemed to imply at the very least, that a black man could not fairly represent non-blacks. In early October, the Field Poll showed Bradley 14 points ahead and pulling away. Deukmejian's handlers panicked. They tried to raise their polls by injecting race into the campaign.

From that point on, Deukmejian rallied with white voters. The final tracking polls and exit surveys showed Bradley slightly ahead, but he lost by one percent or roughly 94,000 votes. (This was the only statistically significant error, i.e., more than 4%, by the Field Poll in an election for president, governor, or senator in the last 50 years). Except for Jerry Brown, the rest of the Democratic ticket, consisting of four white men and one Asian woman, all won handily in what was generally a good Democratic year across the nation — Democrats gained 26 House seats and 8 governorships in 1982. In the non-partisan race for School Superintendent, another Black Democrat was defeated by a white Democrat. Numerous pundits weighed in with opinions about how Bradley lost, ranging from the GOP's subtle playing of the race card to a heavy conservative vote against a handgun initiative (Proposition 15) to a low black turnout to Jerry Brown's disastrous loss in a US Senate race that same day.

Regarding the gun control/rural vote theory, the Handgun Registration Initiative did cause the share of the statewide vote cast by rural Californians (i.e., the counties outside of the Los Angeles, San Francisco Bay Area, San Diego and Central Valley metropolitan areas) to increase from 5% in 1978 to 6% in 1982. But even if all of these new rural voters went Republican, that still would not have equaled Bradley's deficit of 94,000. The gun control issue hurt Bradley at the margins, but did not cost him the election by itself. As for Jerry Brown being a drag on Bradley, there can be no doubt: after his failed presidential campaigns, he was catastrophically unpopular with a 28%

approval rating and he ran almost half a million votes behind the top of the ticket in losing by 45–52% to Pete Wilson. But every other Democrat running for statewide office — except the black gubernatorial nominee — overcame the Jerry Brown burden plus the anti-gun control vote and won. Again, Brown's problems contributed to the Bradley loss, but did not solely cause it.

Could a higher black and/or Latino turnout have won the election for Bradley? The answer is definitely yes. The Latino turnout was only about 20% for the governor's race with roughly 70% supporting Bradley. That was the lowest turnout for any group in the country. But the 1982 Latino turnout was consistent with the Latino turnouts from 1978 to 1990, which is to say, extremely low. Latinos simply had a low interest in politics until the recession of 1991–93 and the anti-immigrant Proposition 187 campaign of 1994. The low Latino turnout in 1982 may have been costly to Bradley, but it was the norm back then among Latinos. Similarly, the four most heavily black Assembly Districts, which were on Mayor Bradley's home turf in the South–Central section of Los Angeles County, had a combined turnout rate of 65.7% compared to the 68.1% statewide gubernatorial turnout. However, increasing the Bradley vote by 94,000 votes in South Central would have meant that over 90% of voters there would have had to turn out. That kind of turnout never happened in a statewide election in California during the twentieth century, not even in presidential years, which are usually the high-water marks for participation. So a lower minority turnout did hurt Bradley, but not as much as the last factor, which was the race card.

Surely, all three factors were possibly enough, either alone or (especially) combined, to cause a one-point defeat. But every other Democrat who won that day overcame these same obstacles. The clincher that race made the difference is that there was only one group in the entire state where Jerry Brown ran ahead of Bradley during his loss to Pete Wilson that same day — urban white labor precincts that were in close proximity to black neighborhoods. These voters live in close proximity to urban black populations and compete with minorities for jobs and living space — hence, their racial sensitivity. It was exactly those Democratic defections that sank Bradley's bid to become the first black governor since Reconstruction. The Democratic voters who defected from Bradley were the same ones who would not support the Fair Housing law 18 years earlier. If Tom Bradley had won the vote of every white Democrat who voted for the extremely unpopular Jerry Brown that same day, he would have been governor of the nation's most populous state. There is no explanation for his loss of white working class voters other than race.

Race was not the only reason for Tom Bradley's defeat. In the early 1980s, California was still a "Red" Republican state. The Nixon–Reagan coalition was still intact as Republicans were in the middle of carrying the Golden State six times in a row for president from 1968 to 1988. And in fact, Bradley did run fully 12 points ahead of Democratic President Jimmy Carter in 1980 when Carter lost the state by over 1.5 million votes (53–36%) to Ronald Reagan. But racial prejudice was the "X factor" that tipped the balance in a close election.

After using anti-black (and anti-Jerry Brown) sentiment to undercut Bradley, the Republicans' next gubernatorial triumph was to use wedge issues against the first serious female candidate for governor. In 1988, the bland Democratic nominee Michael

Dukakis, whom few people in California had heard of before he was nominated, had reduced the GOP margin in the Golden State from 18 points in 1984 to just 3 points. Dukakis had scored big gains in every urban and suburban area, but fell just short when he failed to crack the GOP hold on the Southern California suburbs (which provided twice the GOP's state 352,000 vote margin). Change was in the air, and as a woman Dianne Feinstein seemed to symbolize that mood. Knowing that a Democratic governor would sign another Democratic gerrymander (as Pat and Jerry Brown had done before), Republicans were desperate for their nominee Pete Wilson to win despite their misgivings on some of his moderate stands (he was pro-choice on abortion, for instance).

The week after he was nominated, Wilson began a bombardment that kept up until Election Day. When Feinstein said she favored "gender-balanced appointments," Wilson was quick to accuse her of favoring racial quotas. In the Central Valley and the suburbs, Republican sent out mailers linking her to the black Assembly Speaker Willie Brown, who was the state's most unpopular politician. Republicans attacked her for being a "San Francisco liberal" with all the anti-gay sentiment that that label stimulates. Wilson contrasted his fiscal record as Mayor of San Diego with her "tax-and-spend" ways, though he was careful to avoid a "no-new-taxes" pledge. It was a multi-front assault that sought to depress Democratic turnout and separate white male Democrats from her and it worked again. Wilson also benefited from an outside event, when Iraq invaded Kuwait, it helped make older voters yearn for more traditional (i.e., white male) leadership. The Wilson campaign ran an almost flawlessly-executed campaign and won by 49–46% with the Southern California suburbs once again providing all the Republican margin of victory. And Democrats were once again hurt by a low minority turnout.

As noted above, the Deukmejian and Wilson tactics worked like a charm for Republicans in the 1980s and 90s. The only problem was that Deukmejian and Wilson were poor governors and politicians compared to Reagan. There was little to distinguish their governorships beyond their anti-tax, anti-government message. And in Wilson's case, he was forced to abandon the anti-tax message when the devastating 1990 recession and 1994 Northridge Earthquake forced his hand. Without a credible Republican program or strong leaders, the party was vulnerable to the political changes in the 1990s.

The Current Democratic Era (1992–)

The beginning of the end of the conservative Republican era in California came with the presidential election of 1992. In a memo to clients of the polling firm he worked for, a co-author of this book, Patrick Reddy, wrote in June of 1992:

> Under the political realities of the 1980s, Republicans had a slight "structural" edge. Because the GOP could at least break even in the L.A. County suburbs, Democratic strength in the Bay Area and the city of Los Angeles was matched or exceeded by GOP margins in Southern California. This means that close elections were decided by the Central Valley and Rural California, areas that have consistently voted Republican for the last decade. To win, Democrats need to either steal some moderate Republican votes in the suburbs, or to mobilize a huge turnout of minorities in Los

Angeles and the other big cities. They have not been able to do either in the last decade...

But the prediction here is that California will change in 1992. First is that Californians have always liked to be contrarian, even sometimes seeking "change for the sake of change." Second and more importantly, the defense buildup-driven boom of the 1980s is over and California will suffer from above-average unemployment for the next few years. Third is the perception that the GOP has mismanaged the state after the L.A. riots and the recession. Fourth is that George Bush is not at all popular in California. In the last six months, Democratic registration went up slightly, while GOP lost half a point. This is the first positive Democratic trend in registration since the 1970s. The GOP glory days of the 1980s are over. All of the above will override any previous Republican advantages. There will be two Senate races in California this year. In the first race, appointed Senator John Seymour will battle Dianne Feinstein to fill out Pete Wilson's term until 1994. The match-up of an Establishment Republican versus a Centrist Democrat would ordinarily be close. But Seymour has zero charisma and almost no name recognition. Feinstein lost a race for governor she probably should have won and the race will be hers to lose. The other race is for a full six-year term. It will undoubtedly be one of the classic races in the country: Barbara Boxer, an outspoken New Politics Liberal from Marin County against Bruce Herschensohn, an outspoken Reagan Republican from Orange County. The race will be bitter and close, but the votes of moderate GOP women could tip it to Boxer.[1]

California offered probably the most stunning turnaround of any state in 1992. In the afterglow of Bush's amazing popularity in the spring of 1991 after the surprisingly successful (first) Persian Gulf War, conservative Republicans dreamily talked of sweeping both Senate seats with ultra-conservatives Bob Dornan and William Dannemeyer. Instead, the President was reduced to 33% of the vote, Clinton won the state by almost 1.5 million votes — the first Democrat to carry California since LBJ in 1964 — and two Bay Area Jewish women Democrats won the Senate races.

The emergence of Ross Perot as a popular Sun Belt patriot/businessman/fiscal conservative alternative to the GOP in combination with Bill Clinton's appeal as a "New Democrat" with the right mixture of moderation on business issues and social liberalism doomed California Republicans. The fact that Republicans under Bush in Washington and Wilson in Sacramento were in charge when the roof fell in also did maximum damage. In the winter of 1992, with the economy worsening, only a third of California voters told the Field Poll that they were inclined to re-elect President Bush. Immediately after the successful Democratic National Convention when Perot temporarily de-activated his campaign, a poll done by the firm Fairbank, Maullin & Associates gave the Clinton–Gore ticket a 52–26% lead. After that, the Bush Camp gradually withdrew from California to focus key states back East like Florida and Ohio. In effect, like Jimmy Carter in 1980, Bush made an early concession in California.

The Republicans suffered a total debacle here in 1992. The Reagan coalition of white suburbanites, rural voters, white blue collar Democrats and upwardly mobile

---

1 Patrick Reddy Memo, June 1992.

New Minorities may have been completely destroyed in 1992 as Clinton won by 46–33 with 21% for Perot. The Reagan Coalition was based on 3 middle class appeals: 1) anti-communism and a strong defense; 2) tax cuts for the middle class; 3) tough law enforcement to protect middle class lives and property. With the Cold War winding down, defense cuts cost the state thousands of jobs. Bush's surrender of the tax issue in 1990 made it difficult to portray the Democrats as reckless big spenders and lost him the trust of conservatives. And the horrific riots following the Rodney King verdicts in the spring of 1992 lost the issue of public safety for the GOP (After presiding over $5.5 billion in property destruction and having their Republican governor forget to give the National Guard bullets, the voters came to believe that Republican anti-crime rhetoric was just that). The 1992 Rodney King riot played a huge role in driving California beyond the plausible reach of the Bush Campaign. The Reagan Coalition, which was born in the aftermath of the Watts riot, died in an urban uprising that happened under the Republicans' watch.

Clinton carried the Bay Area by 56–25% and Los Angeles County by 53–28%, with Perot polling 18% in both these areas. Only the GOP margin in Orange County saved Bush from the embarrassment of losing the Southern California suburbs. Bush's margin in Southern California, however, dropped from 717,000 in 1988 to 60,000 in 1992. Perot's best area was the sunbelt stronghold of Southern California suburbia with 25% and rural California.

Among social groups, Clinton posted net gains based on the economy, carrying every racial group — the exit polls showed that Clinton beat Bush by 62–8% among those who believed the economy to be in poor condition. Clinton made relative gains among both Asians and Hispanics, turning a 13-point deficit among Asian-Americans in 1988 into a 45–40 lead this time. Hispanic politics may have reached a turning point in 1992. In an economics-driven vote, Clinton ran about the same as Dukakis while Bush dropped 19 points. The Hispanic share of the electorate also hit a record 7% according to exit polls. Republicans had doubled their Hispanic support in the 1980s with a combination of prosperity and evocation of traditional values. But the most important "family value" is having a job and feeding one's family. Bush's Hispanic support dropped to pre-Reagan 1976 levels.

Clinton won a landslide in "Limousine Liberal" Marin County (59–23–18%). Bush suffered a catastrophic decline in Orange County, the classic conservative stronghold. His 68–31% margin in 1988 fell to 43–32 with 24% for Perot. The result was a net loss of 26 points for the President. The story was much the same among white suburbanites in Southern California; they were also Perot's best constituency at 28%. In other regions, Clinton won the Northern/Central Coast by 47–31%, and even won the Central Valley Cities by 41–38%, while Bush barely hung onto Rural California by 39–35%.

In the "short" Senate race to fill the term of Pete Wilson until 1994, Dianne Feinstein buried appointed Sen. John Seymour by 54–38% and 1.76 million votes. With over 5.8 million votes, Sen. Feinstein set all-time records for most votes in a Senate race and most votes garnered in a single state, breaking Reagan's 1984 mark of 5.4 million. Her margin was second only to LBJ's 2.6 million-vote margin over Goldwater in New York State in 1964. She won everywhere except Orange County and the rural "mountain" counties.

In one of the most interesting races in the country, New Politics Liberal Barbara Boxer defeated Reagan Republican Bruce Herschensohn by 48–43% for California's six-year seat. In a bitter match-up of Marin County versus Orange County, Herschensohn was probably sunk by the national GOP debacle here in a seat that has been a burial ground for right-wingers since Alan Cranston beat ultra-conservative Max Rafferty in 1968. He was also undermined by his campaign's misguided strategy of writing off the Bay Area and campaigning only south of Fresno. Boxer won L.A. County by 53–40% and 347,000. Herschensohn wiped out this margin with a 52–38% victory and 435,000 margin in Southern California and went further ahead by carrying Rural California and the Central Valley cities easily. But all of Boxer's 529,000 statewide margin was delivered in the Bay Area, which she carried by 61–31% and 757,000 votes. Boxer's total of over 5.1 million votes was second only to Feinstein in a Senate race. Herschensohn also set a new record; his 4.6 million votes were the most ever received by the loser of a statewide race.

Among the social groups, Boxer actually lost the white vote but was saved by the state's three minority groups: Boxer won Asians by 52–46%, blacks by 82–16%, and Hispanics by 64–30%. In the end, the GOP statewide debacle and the changing demographics of the GOP contributed mightily to Herschensohn's loss. In the spring, Boxer enticed 300,000 young Republican women, mainly in the big cities, to switch parties and support her in the Democratic primary and in the fall. This was equal to roughly 3% of the state electorate. Herschensohn did get the votes he needed from white male "Reagan Democrats," but this missing 3% of the GOP's normal vote made the difference for Boxer. Herschensohn won the right, but failed to win enough of the centrist vote.

The Republicans were also disappointed by the legislative results. The California Supreme Court, dominated by Republican appointees, drew new districts that were supposed to produce a split delegation. Black and Hispanic voters were packed into safe Democratic seats creating many GOP-leaning suburban seats. But the Democrats made a net gain of one congressional seat (California gained seven new seats in redistricting) and one seat in the State Assembly. It could have been worse. Republicans won five congressional races by the narrowest of margins.

The watershed election of 1992 began a new era: the Clinton–Feinstein–Boxer Years. From 1992 until 2008, Democrats presidential nominees have carried the state five consecutive times by million-vote-plus margins, while Feinstein and Boxer have remained undefeated in the Senate and exactly two Republicans have won top-of-the-ticket races — Governor Wilson was re-elected in the GOP landslide of 1994 and Schwarzenegger had won under very special circumstances. Since 1992 was the turning point, it bears comparison to the Nixon–Reagan Republican re-alignment. Table 4–4 below shows the Democrats' improvements from the 1966–91 phase to the 1992–2008 years by region. The Democrats have scored solid gains in the big metro areas, thus turning their Reagan-era minority into a slight majority — and a big average lead over the Republicans because minor parties have usually received about

5–10% of the vote. Republicans have gained some ground in the Central Valley and Rural Areas, but those places only cast 15% of the state's vote.[1]

TABLE 4–4. DEMOCRATIC GAINS AFTER 1990

Region	Average Dem %	Average Dem %	Change %
	1966–91	1992–2008	
Bay Area	54%	62%	+8%
North/Central Coast	47%	51%	+4%
Central Valley Cities	47%	44%	-3%
Los Angeles County	50%	58%	+8%
Southern California	39%	41%	+2%
Rural California	42%	37%	-5%
Statewide	47%	50%	+3%

The mid-1980s, when Reagan and Deukmejian were being re-elected with roughly 60% of the vote was clearly the high-water mark for Republicans. In many ways, the 1994 win by Wilson was the "last hurrah" for conservative politics in California. The end of the Cold War and the closing down of military bases, particularly in Southern California, marked the beginning of economic issues coming to the fore on the political agenda. Unemployed aerospace workers began to questions their allegiance to the Republican Party. At the same time, organized labor was making advances, particularly in Los Angeles County, which shifted from a swing county to a reliably Democratic one. In the 1990s, L.A. County averaged 55–38% Democratic compared to a one-point lead in the 1980s. At the same time, Latino and Asian voters, though lagging behind white voters in terms of voter turnout, were growing voting blocs. The 1994 election win for the Republicans turned out to be a pyrrhic victory, for while Proposition 187 won and helped get Republicans elected that year, it energized Latino and other foreign-born ethnic groups to shift their allegiance more fully to the Democratic Party and vote.[2] In 1996, Clinton defeated Bob Dole 51–39%, the first California majority for a Democratic presidential candidate since LBJ in 1964. By 1998, Democrats were solidly in control of state government, and California was a solidly blue state. Gray Davis led the Democrat to their first across-the-board sweep since 1958. In 2002, Democrats won all the statewide constitutional offices for the first time since 1882. Only the unique appeal of Arnold Schwarzenegger, and an issue such as gay marriage that cuts across ethnic lines, have been the exception. In the 2008 election, Barack Obama received 61% of the vote, the highest for a Democrat since 1936 and the second highest in the last century.

---

1 See Chapter 7 for changes in the ethnic vote.
2 See Chapter 7.

Registration numbers in May 2009 shows Democrats continuing to extend their registration lead over Republicans. The financial crisis of the past two years has changed attitudes toward government at the national level, with people wanting a more activist government to restrain the greed of the private sector, particularly in financial services. But the financial crisis has put an enormous strain on the finances of the government as well as private enterprise, and result of this is the on going turmoil with the California state budget, which resulted in a new set of initiatives in a special election in May 2009 as part of the budget deal where voters powerfully rejected a new set of tax increase and borrowing schemes. What future shifts in the political landscape at the state and federal level will result from the financial crisis is yet to be seen. But no doubt, the ghost of Hiram Johnson's progressive reforms will continue to cast a shadow over California politics.

However, Johnson's ideas of non-partisanship, which helped bring Arnold Schwarzenegger to the governor's mansion, and Barack Obama's attempt at non-partisanship in his initial months in the White House have not fared so well, as recent events surrounding the California state budget and the Obama Administration's stimulus package have shown. The highly gerrymandered state legislative districts and the infamous 1933 two-thirds vote budget rule have created a highly partisan legislature. On the Republican side, the moderate Republican is an almost non-existent species, easily hunted down in primary elections by activist conservative Republican voters. On the Democratic side, more conservative areas, such as the Central Valley, still bring moderate-to-conservative Democrats to the state legislature to somewhat balance the more liberal members of the Democratic caucus, but it is still a fairly liberal lot. With the Republican minority able to stymie the budget process to promote their political ideology using the two-thirds rule, the state budget is now an annual fiscal train wreck papered over each year with the latest accounting gimmicks because there is no common ground between the Democrats' desire to raise taxes and the Republican desire to cut services.

The result of the convolutions of the last one hundred years of California politics is that the state is on the verge of financial bankruptcy, and whoever becomes governor in 2010 will be taking on a daunting task. The task will be made more difficult by the initiatives, referendums, and a key piece of budget legislation from seventy-five years ago that controls California's finances. All of these items may mean that the next governor could face another key political process if things do not go well — the recall.

5. The Structure of California Politics — Political Structures Affecting California Politics

The previous chapter outlined the history of California politics. This chapter will focus on those government institutions that have affected those politics. It should be no surprise that Progressives under the leadership of Hiram Johnson gave California its unique brand of politics. Some institutions, such as the initiative did not originate in California. That honor goes to the state of South Dakota, who originated the initiative in 1898. In fact eight other states, Utah, Oregon, Montana, Oklahoma, Missouri, Michigan, Arkansas, and Colorado, adopted the initiative before California did in Johnson's revolutionary special election of October 10, 1911, which also adopted the recall and referendum.[1] The recall and the referendum were also not original, but the three ballot measures function along with Johnson's other innovations combined to make California politics a unique process. This chapter will discuss them (primarily the initiative) along with the Two-Thirds Budget rule of 1933, term limits, redistricting, and other items. All of these structures will have a direct bearing on the 2010 election, next governor's ability to function, and the public's response to his program.

The Initiative

Perhaps more often interesting than their leaders is Californians' nationally famous use of "direct democracy" to shape state policy. California initiatives, propositions and referendums have settled issues ranging from labor law to open housing to taxes and spending, gun control, environmental protection, the death penalty, marijuana, gay rights, water rights, insurance rates, education policy, gambling, health care rules, immigration, affirmative action, rules for political parties, redistricting, bi-lingual education, budget rules, stem cell research, infrastructure-building plans, animal rights, abortion and term limits for state legislators.

---

1 California Secretary of State, *A History of California Initiatives* (Sacramento, 2003), http://www.sos.ca.gov/elections/init_history.pdf, 3.

Between the time the first initiative went on the ballot in 1912 and December of 2003, a total of 1,187 initiatives were titled and summarized for circulation. Of that total, 824 failed to qualify for the ballot, 290 qualified for the ballot and 99 were approved by the voters. Of those 99, 32 were constitutional amendments and 57 were statute revisions.[1] An analysis of these initiatives breaks them down into categories of the early initiatives before World War II, the liberal post-war initiatives to the mid-1960s, the more conservative initiatives from the mid-1960s, and various groups of initiatives advocating certain issues.

The Early Initiatives

In the special election of October 10, 1911, the constitutional amendment enabling the initiative passed by a margin of 168,744 to 52,093. The first initiatives to reach the ballot in 1912 were unnumbered. The practice of numbering began with the 1914 election.[2] The first items to make the 1912 ballot were related to county and city issues along with a gambling measure.[3] The first initiative to have a significant impact on an election was Proposition 28, which was approved in 1926, and redistricted the legislature along a modified federal plan, in which the forty Senate seats were drawn by county lines. This gave the control over the Senate to the smaller northern counties at the expense of Los Angeles and the larger southern counties. The north–south split was for many decades the most important political force behind many decisions of California's government, particularly water, as the population base shifted from north to south, but the power did not.[4] In 1930, Proposition 14 impacted voter registration.[5]

The most important initiative of the early period was in fact one that failed. Proposition 25 in 1938 was the first of the truly bizarre initiatives that would have a direct impact on an election. It was an outgrowth of the welfare-based Depression era policies that flourished in the country. It was similar to the famous Townsend Plan, which pre-staged the advent of Social Security. More importantly in the case of California, it was a continuation of writer and 1934 Democratic gubernatorial candidate Upton Sinclair's EPIC (End Poverty In California) program reformulated in a new form. Commonly known as the "Ham and Eggs" initiative or proposal, it was designed to give every unemployed person over fifty years of age $30 every Thursday. It was a half-baked proposal with some dubious sponsors, but it energized lower income voters who were also voting for the new majority Democratic Party. In the end, Proposition 25 lost by about 250,000 out of roughly 3 million voters cast. But it helped propel Culbert Olson to be the first Democrat elected governor in forty years, and just as important elected Democrat Sheridan Downey to the U.S. Senate, a position he would hold until 1950. It is credited by some historians with reviving the Democratic Party in California, although plenty of evidence existed that showed that the Democrats were on an upward trajectory long before that due to FDR's popular-

1 Ibid., 9.
2 Ibid., 2–3.
3 Ibid., 16.
4 Ibid., 18.
5 Ibid., 19.

ity. What did happen in 1938 was the election of Democrats in key statewide races, which was a tremendous breakthrough. Proposition 25 in 1938 was first of a long line of propositions to directly impact an election.[1]

In the thirty-three years between 1912 and 1944, one hundred eighty-one initiative petitions were circulated, an average of about five and a half a year. In fact there was less than that on a yearly basis as a few years had clusters of petitions. Most notable of the large petition years was 1914, the first time there was a two-year cycle for petitions, when twenty-one circulated, 1920 (fourteen) and 1922 (ten), and the Depression-era years of 1934 (twenty-three petitions), 1936 (twelve) and 1938 (sixteen). In 1944, conservatives put a "right-to-work" proposition (Proposition 12) on the ballot. It failed, just as it later would in 1958. In general, initiatives in the early period were not seen in the volume that we know them today, and aside from 1938, they did not have the impact on elections that they have had recently.

Early Post-World War II Initiatives to 1963

As was the case with the early initiatives, the initiatives circulated from 1946 to 1963 were relatively small, totaling sixty-three in all, or three and a half a year. After 1946 (twelve) and 1948 (twelve), the numbers fell off dramatically. As a result, the number of key initiatives affecting California was also small as well.[2] In the early post-war era, the Democrats were continuing on the ascent, even though Republicans continued to hold most of the key offices, primarily due their advantage from cross-filing. Needless to say, one of the important issues for Democrats during this period was the ending of cross-filing, and the initiatives reflected that. Another issue in the state was the apportionment of the seats in the State Senate, which was a North–South issue rather than a Republican–Democrat issue. Senate reapportionment came up no less than four times during the period, first in 1946 and 1948, then in 1960 and 1962. The last three times, it qualified at the ballot, but failed in the election.[3] It would not be until the one man–one vote court cases of the mid-1960s that the senate finally changed. As for cross-filing, two attempts were made by the Democrats to end it in the early years. The first was a failed effort in 1946 that did not even qualify for the ballot.[4] The second, which qualified in 1950, but did not go the ballot until 1952, was far more significant. It was what was known as an indirect initiative, which meant that it could be presented directly to the legislature for their approval, and if they did not approve it, could then go to the ballot. It was a rarely used method that was eventually revoked in 1966.[5] The 1950 cross-filing abolition measure was rejected by the legislature in 1951 and was put on the ballot as Proposition 13, at the same time the legislature did put on the ballot a referendum, Proposition 7, which kept cross-filing, but required party affiliation to be by the candidates' names. Proposition 13 was financed by a wealthy Democratic activist and was one of the first attempts by an

---

1 Peter Schrag, *California: America's High-Stakes Experiment* (Berkeley and Los Angeles: University of California Press, 2006), 133.
2 Sec of State, *Initiative History*, 21–23.
3 Ibid.
4 Ibid., 21
5 Ibid., 3.

individual or a small group to do an end around for political strategy rather than pro-moting a basic issue. At the same time, Proposition 7 was a strategy used many times by the legislature to put a competing proposition on the ballot to neutralize a more offensive one put on the ballot by the voters. In regards to political strategy, Propo-sitions 7 and 13 in 1952 were very modern uses of the initiative and referendum. As stated in the previous chapter, Proposition 13 just failed at 49.96%, but Proposition 7 was approved 72.8%.[1] This, however, turned out to be a delaying tactic as cross-filing was abandoned seven years later.

The most important initiative during this period was Proposition 18 in the 1958 election. This initiative demonstrated another strategy used during campaigns — the strategy of opposing an initiative to boost a campaign. It also shows an equally impor-tant lesson about initiatives and campaigns — supporting a failing initiative and its adverse effects on a campaign. Proposition 18 was an anti-labor "right to work" initia-tive. In the 1958 governor's race U.S. Senator William Knowland running as the Re-publican candidate for governor, tied himself to Proposition 18. His opponent Demo-crat Attorney General Pat Brown, saw collective bargaining as a basic right and op-posed Proposition 18, calling it "class warfare." Proposition 18 failed by a large margin in the 1958 election. Its effect on the gubernatorial campaign was that it united labor against the initiative and got them out to vote against Proposition 18 and Knowland. By opposing Proposition 18 and running a more independent non-partisan campaign, Pat Brown was a huge beneficiary.

The Democrats generally benefitted from the initiative process in the early post-war years. That was to change starting with a famous initiative on the 1964 ballot.

The Conservative Initiative Era 1964–1994

Starting in 1964, the political pendulum shifted the other way and initiatives tended to benefit conservatives and Republicans. This occurred even as the Demo-crats had a landslide victory across the nation. In California, the tide began to turn with Proposition 14. Proposition 14, which had qualified in 1963, sought to overturn the Rumford Fair Housing Act, which said that the owner of a house could not refuse to sell it to a buyer because of race. This act was passed while civil rights legislation was being hotly contested in the U.S. Congress with the Civil Rights Act of 1964 and the Voting Rights Act of 1965, two of the products of that debate. As was the case in other parts of the country, there was a backlash against this kind of fair housing legislation and Proposition 14 was one of the results that began a new conservative era. From the defeat of Fair Housing in 1964 to the passage of the immigrant bashing Prop 187 in 1994, most of the victories in issue campaigns went the conservatives' way. Californians have voted against a proposal to allow the union organization of farm workers on private property in 1976, for Proposition 13 to roll back property taxes and for the death penalty in 1978, for tax and spending limits and against school bus-ing in 1979, for victim's rights and against gun control and the inheritance tax in 1982 and against reconfirmation of liberal Supreme Court Justice Rose Bird in 1986. Liber-

---

1   Bruce, E. Cain, Elizabeth R. Gerber, University of California Berkeley Institute of Gov-ernment Studies, *Voting at the Political Fault Line: California's Experiment with the Blanket Primary* (Berkeley and Los Angeles: University of California Press, 2002), 16–17.

als did win a few major victories with the "Clean Water" Act of 1986 (Proposition 65) and by passing insurance reform in 1988 (Proposition 103), and guaranteeing that 40% of the state budget would be reserved for education (Proposition 98), but that last one has produced huge unintended consequences. A gas tax was also passed in 1990 to build more roads, but even the Republican Establishment supported it. The trends from 1964 through 1994 were clearly to the Right.

Proposition 14 heavily impacted the U.S. Senate race, which has been previously discussed. The key issue from the initiative's perspective is that Democrat Pierre Salinger's opposition to Proposition 14 galvanized its supporters without energizing its opponents. As a result, Proposition 14 and the Republican U.S. Senate candidate won easily.

The success of Proposition 14 in 1964 and the underlying conservative political reaction that it engendered set the stage for the conservative issues that were advanced by the use of the initiative. The most important of those issues was taxes. Although it really did not deliver a breakthrough until the now legendary Proposition 13 in June 1978, taxes or tax limitation became a frequent issue for initiatives. Howard Jarvis made numerous attempts at limiting taxes through the initiative process before his ultimate success in 1978. Tax limitation related initiatives were circulated just about every year from 1966 to 1978,[1] with the success of Proposition 13 generating subsequent initiative, such as Proposition 4 in 1979.[2]

Complementing taxes for conservatives was the issue of crime. Crime had been an important issue for conservatives since Barry Goldwater's 1964 presidential campaign, and it was a key issue for Ronald Reagan in the 1966 California governor's race. It first made its presence known with Proposition 17, the death penalty initiative that passed in 1972. Another version passed in 1978. 1982 saw two key crime and gun related initiatives on the ballot. Proposition 8, the victims rights initiative, passed while the gun control initiative, Proposition 15 failed.[3] Proposition 15 also played an important role in the 1982 governor's race between Democrat Tom Bradley and Republican George Deukmejian. Many believe that Proposition 15 brought out a larger pro-gun vote than normal for the Republicans and this helped decide a very close governor's race, although the Republican's pioneering strategic use of absentee ballots has been considered the most significant factor in that election, besides the added factor of race.[4] Crime has continued to be an important issue for conservatives when it comes to initiatives. While Hollywood may sometimes glamorize gangsters in films like *Scarface*, the California public has almost zero patience for such people; anti-crime initiatives like the death penalty and strict sentencing rules routinely pass with over 70% of the vote. For example, 71% of California voters supported re-instituting the death penalty in 1978 with 66% of Hispanics and even a majority of blacks voting yes. Sixteen years later, fully 88% of Californians voted to extend the death penalty to those who did "drive-by" shootings and opposition to the death penalty was a major reason for the ouster of Supreme Court Chief Justice Rose Bird in 1986. The most fa-

---

1 Sec of State, *Initiative History*, 108
2 Ibid., 29.
3 Ibid., 32.
4 See Chapter 4

mous crime initiative in recent years was Proposition 184, the three strikes initiative for repeat offenders, which passed in 1994.[1]

The 1994 election was the high water mark for conservative initiatives and their impact on a governor's race. Proposition 184 and Proposition 187 — which passed in 1994 and made illegal aliens ineligible for public services[2] — were an integral part of Republican Governor Pete Wilson's victory over Democrat Kathleen Brown. Since the 1994 election, race and social-cultural issues have been important for conservatives. Starting with Proposition 187, a series on race related, social and cultural initiatives have made the ballot. They include ending affirmative action (Proposition 209) in 1996,[3] ending bilingual education (Proposition 227) in 1998,[4] anti-gay initiatives (Proposition 22 in 2000[5] and Proposition 8 in 2008[6]), and parental consent for abortions (Proposition 73 in 2005, Proposition 85 in 2006 and Proposition 4 in 2008). In general, these initiatives have not had the same statewide impact after 1994 that those of the prior thirty years had for conservatives. The 1994 election was the last one where they had a major impact, and in fact, it is believed that the passage of Proposition 187 created a backlash among immigrants, particularly Latinos and Asians, which has decisively moved California into the Democratic column. While recent initiatives have not swung the initiative process completely to the left, it is clear that the advancement of conservative issues through the initiative process has been neutralized.

To be sure, voters have repeatedly rejected new taxes over the past 15 years, most notably in May of 2009, staunchly refused to repeal the two-thirds requirement for passing the state budget in 2004 (Proposition 56) and they also cancelled the John Burton health care mandate on business in 2004 (Proposition 72), but California voters have clearly come back to the center after their long run on the right from Proposition 13 in 1978 to Proposition 187 in 1994.

Other Issues

While the issues of crime and taxes have been key issues to advance conservative causes, other issues have been advanced through the initiative process, many of them more favorable to Democrats and liberals.

One of the key issues has been the environment. The first major initiative involving the environment was Proposition 20, the Coastal Zone Conservation Act, which passed in 1972. This act set up the Coastal Commission and has had a major impact on development on the coast. It has been a major force for the environmental movement. In 1986, Proposition 65 passed, which placed restriction on toxic discharges into drinking water and provide notices of exposure to toxics. Two years later, Proposition 70, the Wildlife, Coastal and Park Land Conservation Bond Act passed.[7] Then

---

1 Sec of State, *Initiative History*, 43.

2 Ibid., 44.

3 Ibid., 46.

4 Ibid., 49.

5 Ibid., 52.

6 For the election results of ballot measures after 2002, see the California Secretary of States web site http://www.sos.ca.gov/elections/elections_electiions.htm.

7 Secretary of State, *Initiative History*, 35.

in 1990, Proposition 117 on wildlife protection (including a ban on hunting mountain lions) and Proposition 132 on marine resources passed.[1] In the last ten years came passage of Proposition 4 (1998), banning the use of certain traps and animal poisons,[2] Proposition 50 (2002), which authorized the sale of bonds for coastal wetlands and water quality projects,[3] and most recently, Proposition 2 in 2008 for the protection of poultry. The environment has obviously been an important factor in initiative campaigns over the last twenty years.

Health care and health issues have been increasingly important, as the cost of health care has skyrocketed. Two failed ballot initiatives started the current wave in the 1992 election: Proposition 161 on terminal illness and assistance in dying, and Proposition 166, the basic health care initiative.[4] An initiative on the controversial subject of medical marijuana, Proposition 215, passed in 1996.[5] This initiative conflicted with federal law, so the George W. Bush Administration actively tried to suppress it while enforcing federal law in the states that had passed medical marijuana statutes. The Obama Administration has backed off enforcement in the medical marijuana states. In 2000, Proposition 36, an initiative involving drug treatment diversion programs, passed.[6] Health care issues continue to be a high priority with the public. The Obama administration is now attempting to put together a universal health care program as part of its initial budget. Due to the complexity of the issue, it will be some time before it is resolved, and there will no doubt be future initiatives circulated on the subject.

Election reform in its various forms has been a theme of the initiatives process right from the very beginning. Initiatives, referendums, and recalls were election reforms when they were first enacted in 1911. Many attempts have been made over the years through the initiative process as well as through the legislature. In addition to the 1911 actions, the ballot measures of 1926 and 1952 and the repeal of cross-filing in 1959 have already been noted. The law allowing for party endorsements in 1986 was another factor. However, in recent years there have been many initiatives involving election reform. The groundbreaking initiative on campaign disclosure was the passage of the celebrated Proposition 9, the Political Reform Act of 1974.[7] Promoted by then Secretary of State Jerry Brown, who was running for governor at the time, it created the Fair Political Practices Commission and created the structure for campaign disclosure, which has been used ever since with numerous modifications. In addition to boosting Brown's candidacy in 1974, it turned the Secretary of State office from a backwater operation into one of the most influential in the state. Campaign and spending contribution limits became another issue, and the first initiative passed on that subject was Proposition 68 in 1988.[8] The most recent law on the subject was the legislature created Proposition 34 in 2000, which is now the primary law covering

---

1 Ibid., 38–39.
2 Ibid., 50.
3 Ibid., 57.
4 Ibid., 40–41.
5 Ibid. 46.
6 Ibid. 54.
7 Ibid., 25.
8 Ibid., 35.

campaign contributions in state elections (federal elections fall under a different set of laws). The issue of clean money, or taxpayer-financed campaigns became an important issue in the current decade. Proposition 89, the clean money initiative sponsored by the California Nurses Association, failed at the ballot box in 2006. Clean money and campaign finance will continue to be an important issue in election reform and probably spur future initiatives.

Other aspects of election reform have been term limits, redistricting and the open primary. Term limits were adopted for state elections with the passage of Proposition 140 in 1990.[1] This statute allowed for members of the assembly to be limited to three two-year terms, and all other offices limited to two–four year terms. Many people thought that the law was too restrictive and there have been attempts on several occasions to extend terms. The most recent was the legislature enacted Proposition 93 in 2008, which failed at the ballot box. Attempts were made to extend term limits to federal offices with the passage of Proposition 164 in 1992,[2] but this act is pre-empted by the U.S. Constitution. Redistricting reform by taking the process out of the legislature's hands and placing it in a commission had been tried several times, and was part of Governor Arnold Schwarzenegger's reforms in the 2005 special election (Proposition 77). Lastly, Proposition 11, which covered only state legislative and board districts and excluded the House of Representatives, passed in November 2008. The full effect of this initiative will not be known until 2011. Finally, there have been attempts to re-institute another version of the open primary system in recent years. Along with the redistricting commission, it is felt that the open primary would allow for more moderate candidates being elected and create less partisanship in state government, a revised attempt to install Hiram Johnson's non-partisan Progressive ideas. An open primary initiative, Proposition 198, passed in 1996, but was thrown out by the courts.[3] The recent budget impasse was broken when both parties agreed to support Senator Abel Maldonado's proposal for putting an open primary measure on the ballot in June 2010. This ballot measure may influence the gubernatorial primary happening at the same time. Again, reform is in the California mainstream, which is partly why Schwarzenegger has repeatedly reached for it.

The final set of issues that have popped up in initiative proposals have been about labor. The most famous of them was the right to work initiative Proposition 18 in 1958, which galvanized labor and helped elect Pat Brown.[4] In fact, the key labor initiatives have failed because labor organized and successfully opposed them. This was true with the two "paycheck protection" initiatives, Proposition 226 in 1998,[5] and Proposition 75 in the 2005 special election. Labor has been a consistent winner over the past 60 years, especially when their ideas do not conflict with other popular themes like reform or low taxes. Californians realize that theirs is a high-cost state and simply do not want to see wages lowered.

---

1 Ibid., 39.
2 Ibid., 42.
3 Ibid., 44.
4 Ibid., 23.
5 Ibid., 49.

Initiative Activity

The final discussion about initiatives concerns the use of the initiative process as a political action tool, and the frequency of its use. As pointed out earlier, in the early days of the initiative, it was used far less that it is now, with 5.5 initiatives per year in circulation from 1912 to 1945, and 3.0 initiatives in circulation from 1945 to 1963, for a total of 234 petitions for the entire period of fifty-two years. In the thirty-nine years from 1964 to 2002, there were 953, or an average of 25.4.[1] The number of petitions that circulated continued to be modest from 1964 to 1971 with less than ten a year. In 1972 there were fifteen, and then in 1974 there were thirty-two. After a fall back to nine in 1975, the annual number of petitions circulated have been at least fifteen every year and as high as fifty-four in 1997.[2] The explosion in the 1970s coincided with advent of large statewide media campaigns and development of paid consultants and professional signature gatherers. Thus, the initiative has been transformed from Hiram Johnson's tool for the people to check their legislature to a professional political tool. It has also become for many the preferred way of enacting legislation by bypassing the legislature and engaging in direct democracy with all its attributes and pitfalls. As the recent passage of the redistricting commission initiative and the proposed primary initiative indicates, initiatives will continue to be an ongoing factor in the 2010 election and beyond.

STRUCTURAL ITEMS INVOLVING THE STATE BUDGET

Much of the drama currently involving the state government and the governor's race in 2010 involves the state budget. The state is currently trying to close a budget deficit in excess of $40 billion and the political dynamics in the legislature is such that there does not seem to be a solution because the votes are not there to pass a budget. It has to do with differing priorities and political ideology, but like political party organization in this state, it mostly has to do with ancient statutes, in this case, the Two-Thirds Budget rule of 1933. This and some additional legislative tweaking over the years has brought the present budgetary impasse.

The 1933 Two-Thirds Budget Rule

California is only one of three states that require a two-thirds majority of the legislature to pass a budget, and it is the only one that requires votes from both Republicans and Democrats to pass such a budget. As the partisan differences in the legislature, particularly regarding taxes, makes compromise nearly impossible, the current fiscal crisis and the inability to resolve it has put California on the brink of bankruptcy. Therefore, it is useful to discuss how the two-thirds rule came about in the first place.

Like the current impasse, the Two-Thirds Budget rule came about during another financial crisis — that brought on by the Great Depression. In the early 1930s, property tax revenue, the major source of government funding, was declining. In 1932, Proposition 9 was put on the ballot in order to authorize a sales and income tax. The

---

1 Ibid., 9.
2 Ibid., 23–58.

sales tax would have been dedicated to schools, leaving the property tax for the counties. But Proposition 9 was crushed at the ballot box, leaving the state in a deeper crisis. In response to this defeat, a proposal was made by State Controller Ray Riley and Senator Frank Stewart. This plan would authorize the legislator to raise taxes with a spending cap that would trigger a vote requirement; if the budget grew by more than 5%, a two-thirds vote would be required to approve it. This became Proposition 1, which was passed in a special election in 1933. Thus, California attempted to limit spending by increasing the voting requirement threshold to two thirds. Ironically, the spending limit was removed along with a lot of obsolete language in the California Constitution in a 1962 legislature sponsored initiative because the cap was not realistic. The two-thirds requirement did not become an issue until the mid-1960s, when the Republicans used the threat of a budget stalemate to get more money for education. Since that time, it has been increasingly used by partisan and bipartisan minority voting blocs to get certain pieces of legislation approved.[1]

The interesting aspect about the Two-Thirds Budget rule was that it was in fact a spending cap gimmick in order to raise taxes because a direct approach to addressing state state's financial problems would not have been accepted by the voters. Many of the same characteristics can be seen in Proposition 1A, which proposed a spending cap and a temporary increase in taxes, and which was voted down by voters in the May 2009 special election, just as Proposition 1 was voted on in a special election in 1933. The issues surrounding Proposition 1A were: (1) was it a gimmick to raise taxes, currently temporary in the proposition, but possibly permanent later on; (2) would the spending cap work, as recent analysis indicates that even if Proposition 1A passes, there will still be at least an $8 billion shortfall; and (3) would the spending cap create additional formulas that will complicate future budgets. Proposition 1 and 1A were the product of crisis finance seventy-five years apart. Proposition 1 left baggage that Proposition 1A tried to deal with, with the notion that it too may very well create problems for a future state government. Ultimately, the voters did not want any more baggage.

Other Items Affecting the Budget

Beyond the Two-Thirds Budget rule, other pieces of legislation have complicated the budget process by carving out parts of the general fund for special uses. The most important of these is Proposition 98, which under various formulas allocates 40% of the general fund to K–12 education. This initiative was passed in 1988.[2] Another attempt to solve the budget problems was the passage of Proposition 37 in 1984, which approved the state lottery. The money was supposed to go to education, but what it ended up doing was redirect non-lottery funds to other uses, thus proving the impetus for Proposition 98 four years later.[3]

---

1   Fred Silva, "California's Two-Thirds Legislative Vote Requirement and its Role in the State Budget Process," *Western City Magazine*, November 2008, http://www.cacities.org/index.jsp?zone=wcm&previewStory=27483
2   Sec of State, *Initiative History*, 37.
3   Ibid., 33.

General Budget Issues

All of the above items affecting the budget are the result of a state that currently relies too much on the income tax, whose sales tax is limited because the fastest grow-ing part of the economy, services, is not subject to the sales tax, and whose property tax is capped by Proposition 13 and subsequent pieces of legislation. This compounds the simple fact that California has been a state that historically has provided a high level of services which the public wants, but doesn't want to pay for. Most budget analysts agree that California needs to radically overhaul its budget process so that it is not held hostage by voting minorities, eliminate tax loopholes, and reduce some of the higher tax rates. It also needs to be more focused on what its spending priorities should be, particularly in economic downturns. The other question is whether the increasingly partisan nature of the legislature will allow it to conduct business and whether the initiative process that bypasses the legislature has made the politicians in Sacramento irrelevant when it comes to many key issues. Many polls have shown that the voters have more confidence in the initiative process than the legislature. In-deed, many analysts believe that the massive state budget and the budget stalemate in the legislature encouraged the voters to pass the redistricting initiative Proposition 11 in November 2008 in the hopes that commission-drawn legislative lines will bring more moderates into the legislature, reduce partisanship, and get things done. These budget issues will be some of the key questions that both the voters and politicians will have to face in the 2010 election.

The Recall

While referendums have not and will not have impact on government and the 2010 election that initiatives and the budget have already had, the recall process will, whether it is enacted in the near future for statewide races or not. The recall process of 2003 certainly has had an impact in the current situation. First, Arnold Schwarzenegger ran in 2006 as an incumbent, rather than the governor's race being for an open seat. The open seat occurs this time. Second, the 2003 recall was the only way a moderate Republican like Schwarzenegger could have become governor, as he never could have won a Republican primary, given his relationship with the party has clearly shown. The recall also operates under a looser election structure whereby more candidates can get involved in the election. For a modest fee, just about every-one could run for governor, and they did — 135 people were on the recall ballot, from crackpots and attention-seekers to legitimate candidates. Indeed, the circus atmo-sphere of the recall was ideally suited to someone from the entertainment industry like Schwarzenegger. The recall also had characteristics of cross-filing and the open primary, as party affiliations were optional.

Unless the conservatives currently attacking Schwarzenegger can come up with 1.5 million signatures by October, the recall process will not occur before or during the 2010 election. But after the election, the possibility increases as the events of 2003 showed. In the history of the recall, there have been only three serious attempts against a sitting governor: James Rolph in 1933, Culbert Olson in 1940, and the Gray Davis recall in 2003. Only the 2003 recall was successful or even went to the ballot, but all three had characteristics that the newly elected governor in 2011 should be worried about.

First and foremost, all three occurred in tough economic times. In the case of Rolph and Olson, it occurred during the Great Depression. The Great Depression was not a good time to be governor and the three governors of that time — Rolph (1931–1934), Frank Merriam (1934–1939), and Olson (1939–1943) — were ineffective. Rolph and Merriam were Republican hacks, not up to the job. In addition, Rolph was a very sick man and died in office as his health deteriorated due to the stress of the office. Olson was an extreme left liberal from the Upton Sinclair–EPIC mode and was too radical and partisan for the legislature and other government officials he had to work with; consequently, he got little done. The characteristics of Rolph and Olson, plus the serious economic crisis that they were dealing with made them both vulnerable to voter backlash.

In Rolph's case he became governor in the bottom of the Depression. In 1932, he supported the ill-fated Proposition 9 and the successful Proposition 1 in 1933. Then and now, supporting raising taxes in bad economic times is not the way to be popular, and Rolph was not popular. The possibility that property taxes would be raised after the failure of Proposition 9 got Rolph in trouble with the agricultural community, and the State Grange started a serious effort to recall Rolph in early in 1933. But there was not any real support for it, and so the recall movement ended almost as soon as it began.[1]

As for Olson, he ended up fighting with everybody. His appointments and his positions on legislation were opposed by the legislature, his labor platform was opposed big agriculture and his left wing leanings were always opposed by big business. By late 1939, he had offended so many people that some of them started organizing a recall, which failed after more than one attempt.

Gray Davis showed some of the same characteristics as Rolph and Olson. Having run some nasty campaigns during his career, he was not the most likeable politician, either with other politicians or with the public. When the natural gas/electricity crisis occurred followed by the massive budget deficits due to the bursting of the dot. com bubble, he had very little political capital to work with. He faced a Democratic legislature, then as now, trying to solve the budget crisis more through raising taxes than cutting unsustainable spending. With little or no support from his own party, he was vulnerable to a recall campaign orchestrated by conservative Republicans. Faced with a movie star in the recall, the rest was history. However, in the current budget crisis, Schwarzenegger faces approval ratings that rival the Davis lows of 2002–03. Being a top box office star does not protect you from the voters' wrath, as Schwarzenegger found out in the 2005 special election.

So, what does all this have to with the next governor in 2011? The next governor will be inheriting a financial nightmare and probably without the support engendered by President Obama. Unlike the president, the governor cannot print money. The next governor will in all probably be dealing with a deeply divided legislature, which has a Democratic majority steadfastly trying to protect existing programs

---

1 James Worthen, *Governor James Rolph and the Great Depression in California* (Jefferson, North Carolina: McFarland & Company, 2006), 155–156.

though taxes increases if necessary, and a Republican minority, fervently backed by their party's rank and file, opposing tax increases at any cost and noting that government spending was outstripping government revenue even during the boom years — all of this complicated by the two-third vote budget rule. The next governor not only risks trying to deal with the existing problem, but facing the real possibility that the economy and revenues will continue to sink, and that there will be no realistic option but slashing spending on a scale that not even Republicans can contemplate — or declaring bankruptcy. The situation reminds one of the story of the Detroit Zoo in 1932.[1] Staggered by the Great Depression and watching its city budget melt away with no way of taking care of the animals, the city took the drastic step of closing its zoo and slaughtering its animals for food. (In an eerie parallel, in April of 2009, the Bronx Zoo, the largest metropolitan zoo in the country, announced that, due to budget cuts, it would be shutting down four exhibits and shipping hundreds of animals to other zoos and aquariums around the country.[2] A similar situation is happening in Massachusetts, where a 61% cut in state contribution to two Boston-area zoos may result in the zoo having to euthanize as many as 200 animals.[3]) There will no doubt be the program equivalent on the 1932 Detroit Zoo either in Schwarzenegger's next budget after the failed 2009 Special Election or in the next governor's budget. It will not be pretty and the voters will not be amused. The need for unpopular decisions and the potential conflict with angry voters and divided politicians could leave the next governor as vulnerable to a recall as Rolph, Olson, and Davis were. Baring a miracle turnaround of the economy, it will be very difficult for the next governor to win re-election even if he or she does not face a recall.

The next governor will face these legal, political, and budgetary structural impediments. It will not be a job for weak stomachs.

---

1 Paul Farhi, "Lessons from 1929," *Washington Post National Weekly*, November 3–9, 2008, 23.
2 Sally Goldenberg, "Wild-Fired by the Zoo," *New York Post*, April 24, 2009, http://www.nypost.com/php/pfriendly/print.php?url=http%3A%2F%2Fwww.nypost.com%2Fseven%2F04242009%2Fnews%2Fregionalnews%2Fwild_fired_by_the_zoo_165956.htm.
3 The Buzz, "IOUs Seem Tame Compared to Massachusetts' Solution," *sacbee.com*, July 14, 2009, http://www.sacbee.com/capitolandcalifornia/story/2023570.html.

6. California in the 2010 Election And Beyond

The next governor will be facing a number of hurdles, some of which have been discussed in passing. The challenges are twofold. First, what will the candidates be facing during the election? What issues will they be facing, both inside and outside the state, which will impact the election? To what degree will those issues be advanced by initiatives and other ballot measures? What potential surprises, both issues and events, could change the political landscape? How will they affect the June primary and then the November general election? Second, what will the person who is elected governor be facing when that person is sworn in. What issues and fallout from the election will have an impact? What longer-term forces not focused on during the election will have a bearing on the next administration? These are the issues that will have to be addressed.

Administrative Issues for the 2010 Election

The Economic Crisis

The eight-hundred pound gorilla in the room for the 2010 election must inevitably be the economy and the global economic crisis affecting everyone. It is always difficult to make snap judgments in a California election because of the possibility of an issue-driven initiative, which moves the election in another unexpected direction. But the scale of the economic disaster is such that it is difficult to see how any issue could supersede it. Simply put, the current economic crisis is the biggest since the Great Depression and there does not appear to be any issue out there that will replace it. Virtually every issue that will come out of the 2010 election will in one form or another, emerge from or be reflected by the economy, the current crisis and its massive impact on the budget.

The core of California's economic problems is centered in real estate. Real estate has always been driving force in the California economy because of the explosive population growth the state has enjoyed through most of its history, particularly since 1880s.[1] California, along with Nevada, Arizona and Florida were "the Big Four" states at the heart of the sub-prime (aka "junk") real estate loan collapse, in part because they were fast growing states with exploding real estate markets — the most vulnerable to a big real estate bubble and the most likely where it was going to burst. In California, the areas where real estate has been most savaged has been in fast growing areas, such as in Stockton and Modesto, just south of Sacramento, which vied with Detroit for the highest foreclosure rate in the county, and Moreno Valley in Riverside County east of Los Angeles, the fastest growing large county in the state. But as it was in the rest of the country when the sub-prime crisis migrated out the Big Four states, the real estate crisis has migrated to all parts of the state and no area has been immune. As a result home prices have fallen by 58.3% from their peak in May 2007 of $594,530 to $247,590 in February 2009.[2] A large percentage of homes in the state have negative equity, homes worth less than the mortgages on them. As teaser rates on adjustable mortgages were re-priced to much higher rates and borrowers were unable to make the payments, foreclosures have exploded to the point where in many places of the state, a third or more of the house sales are homes that have been in foreclosure. Even where mortgage payments are being made, the loss of home equity is such that people feel less wealthy and are spending less, leading to a drop in consumer demand. That loss of demand, plus the loss of consumer demand from people in real financial distress has meant that overall consumer spending is down. That has led to a drop in sales and business activity, and a general economic retrenchment. In the past, California has often led the nation out of recessions due to its booming real estate market and defense spending. Neither of those factors may apply now.

The bursting of the real estate bubble not only affected real estate, but also the entire financial industry as securities based on real estate collateral collapsed. As a number of large commercial and investment banks ran into trouble, the stock and bond markets took a dive that saw the Dow Jones Industrial Average fall from 14,118 in October 2007 to less than 7,000 in March 2009 before the current modest rebound. A number of exotic real estate-based bonds and securities became financial toxic waste and became essentially worthless. This led to large losses in the financial industry, government bailouts, and a hemorrhaging of jobs on the financial industry to go along with the loss of jobs in the real estate and retail industries.

The result of the above has been skyrocketing unemployment. California's unemployment rate in May 2009 was 11.5%, the highest in modern records and the third highest in the country behind Michigan and Oregon.[3] And some analysts believe the state unemployment rate may reach 15% before it tops out. More importantly for the

---

1 See Appendix 1C

2 California Association of Realtors, "May 2008 Sales and Price Report (June 25, 2008 press release)," *California Association of Realtors (CAR.org)* http://www.car.org/newsstand/newsreleases/2008newsreleases/0508salesandpricereport/;Daniel Taub, "California Home Prices Decline 41% on Foreclosures (Update 1)," *Bloomberg.com*, March 25, 2009, http://www.boolmberg.com/apps/news?pid=20601087&sid=aRhTT4MNBjM&refer=home.

3 Dale Kasler, "State, Local Jobless Rates Tops 11 Percent," *Sacbee.com*, April 17, 2009, http://www.sacbee.com /1089/story/1788481.html; Shobhana Chandra, "Joblessness Reaches 10% in Indiana; Jumps in Oregon (Update 3)," *Bloomberg.com*, April 17, 2009, http://www.bloomberg.com/apps/news?pid=20601087&sid=aAF9sIUABJQ7c.

state government, the loss of real estate wealth, jobs, and business activity has meant a huge loss in revenue. California state government is particularly vulnerable to loss of revenue streams in economic downturns because so much of its income comes from the income tax, which can fall sharply during recessions, and capital gains, which can turn into capital losses during economic downturns.

The net result of California's revenue structure is that it is highly unstable during the course of the business cycle, with massive increases of revenue on the upswing and massive losses on the downswing. Legislators being who they are, tend to make tax cuts and fund programs in good times that are unsustainable when the economy takes a dive. Such a scenario occurred in the late 1990s when the dot.com bubble made legislators feel that they could afford a raft of tax cuts and new programs. The result was that when that bubble burst, the state was left with a deficit in excess of $20 million which ultimately got Governor Gray Davis recalled.

The bursting of the current financial bubble, which by all accounts exceeded anything that was seen in the twentieth century, including 1929 and the dot.com bubble,[1] created a budget shortfall in excess of $42 billion. To close the shortfall, the legislature passed a series measures including spending caps, tax increases and other budgetary devices designated Proposition 1A through 1F for the May 19, 2009 special election. The Democratic leaders in the legislature tried desperately to get the members of the Democratic State Central Committee to support the initiatives at the party's state convention in Sacramento on April 26, 2009, but the deeply divided party ultimately did not endorse 1A.[2] The Republican Party leadership opposed the initiatives, even though their legislators were part of the compromise. Some of the legislators could face recall.[3] Complicating the issue and driving part of the opposition to the initiatives is that even the supporters of the initiative admit that the budget gap is still expanding and that an $8 billion hole beyond the $42 billion has already opened up with no end in sight.[4] A gap of $60 billion is a possibility,[5] and continued decline in revenues could make it higher. All of this made the propositions on the May 19 ballot very dubious items and voters roundly rejected them

Regardless of the failures of Propositions 1A through 1E at the ballot box, it is clear that some very unpleasant choices are going to have to occur, from hatcheting prized programs to higher taxes, all guaranteed to enrage one constituency or another. The candidates from governor on down are going to have to run the gauntlet of these issues in both the 2010 primary and the general election.

---

1 "In Comes the Wave," *The Economist*, June 18, 2005, 66–68; cited in Stephen D. Cummings, *Red States, Blue States, and the Coming Sharecropper Society* (New York: Algora Publishing, 2008), 21.

2 California Speaker of the Assembly Karen Bass and Senate President pro Tempore Darrell Steinberg, letter sent to California State Central Committee members on the eve of the members' vote on a resolution supporting Propositions 1A through 1F on the May 19 special election at the State Democratic Convention, April 10, 2009.

3 Kevin Yamamura, "California GOP Leaders Reject All 6 Ballot Measures," *Sacbee.com*, April 19, 2008, http://www.sacbee.com/capitolandcalifornia/story/1791244.html

4 Jordan Rau and Evan Halper, "California Budget Faces New $8 Billion Shortfall," *Los Angeles Times*, March 14, 2009, http://www.latimes.com/news/local/la-me-budget14-2009mar14,0,3882637.story.

5 Patrick Reddy, Conversation with California State Senate staff indicated a projected gap of $40 to 60 billion, February, 2009.

Beyond the budget issues and the elections, there is still the fiscal reality that the state officers, particularly State Treasurer Bill Lockyer and State Controller John Chiang have to deal with. Chiang continues to see actual revenues falling behind projections.[1] Lockyer has to find a way to finance the state even with the current budget, as revenues normally trail expenses in the first half of the fiscal year even in good times. In the current situation, Lockyer has to fund at least $13 billion in revenue anticipation notes (RANs), and is asking the federal government to back the RANs in order to do it. Whether such large demands on the credit market coming from California and other government entities are doable is still open to question.[2] Then there is the shear scale of the crisis, the largest of its kind since the Great Depression. Since the Great Depression was some eighty years ago, there is no one active in government today with the experience to deal with such a crisis. It is not just a question of being able to control the economic chaos; it is a question of being able to comprehend it. There are no realistic benchmarks from which to construct or execute policy. The next governor will be flying blind into an economic nightmare he or she will be neither able to comprehend or control, with a fractious legislature from which will probably be more opposition than support, and from an increasingly restive public whose patience is wearing thin and who is ready to blame the most visible politician in sight, as they did to Gray Davis. It will not be pretty.

It is possible that a recovery could take hold in time for their re-election run in 2014. But if not, the chances are over 50% that the next governor could be only be given one term. After Hiram Johnson left for the Senate until Earl Warren's domination of the state, California governors often served only one term. That history could be about to repeat itself with another round of one-termers.

Infrastructure

While the economy will be the most pressing issue, there will be others. The state's sorry infrastructure will certainly be one of them. In 2005, the nonpartisan Government Performance Project gave the California a C minus rating which tied it with Alabama as the worst performing state in the country with regard to government functions such as public management and infrastructure. By that time, California had slipped below the national average in almost every measure of governance and public services, including the quality of its roads, highways, and other infrastructure such as public buildings.[3] Travel any distance on California highways and the deterioration is apparent. In 2004, highway expert David Hartgen ranked California last among the states in urban interstate congestion, forty-eighth in urban interstate road quality, and forty-third in rural interstate road quality. The industry-supported Road Information Program issued a study which that the four worst urban area roads in the country were all in California — Los Angeles, San Jose, San Francisco–Oakland

---

1 Capitol Alert, "Controller: State Cash Outlook 'Hammered' by Weak Retail Sales," *Sacbee.com*, April 10, 2009, http://www.sacbee.com/static/weblogs/capitolalertlatest/021447.html.

2 Steve Wiegand, "California Asks Feds to Back its IOUs," *Sacbee.com*, April 15, 2009, http://www.sacbee.com/topstories/story/1781008.html.

3 Peter Schrag, *California: America's High-Stakes Experiment* (Berkeley and Los Angeles: University of California Press), 94–95.

and San Diego. Two thirds of Los Angeles road miles were rated poor.[1] Much of his infrastructure was built in the glory days of Earl Warren, Goodwin Knight, and Pat Brown in the 1950s and 60s, when California led the way in government services. At that time, its per capita investment in infrastructure was among the highest in the nation.[2] In effect, California has been living off this investment and done an inadequate job to maintain it. Many older Californians have taken it for granted.

Compounding the infrastructure problem has been the financial crisis that has been previously discussed. Rebuilding the state's infrastructure will take a huge financial commitment, and in the current financial environment, that will be a very daunting task. The state has enough trouble funding its current budget deficit; funding long-term capital projects in a state that has the lowest state bond ratings in the union will be even more difficult.[3] There is a backlog of bonds to be funded now. The people of the state did make an attempt in November 2006 by approving Propositions 1A through 1E, a multi-billion dollar series of infrastructure bonds promoted by the Schwarzenegger Administration, the first major attempt to address the problem in many years.[4] But in a state where people want the services, but do not wish to authorize the taxes to pay for them, — "Build now, pay later" was the slogan for Arnold's bond campaign in 2006 — the real solution for funding the states infrastructure is up in the air.

Education

Education is one of the most important services in any state and California is no exception. As in the case of the state's infrastructure, California was one of the leaders in the 1950s and 1960s. Its University of California system and its Master Plan for Higher Education was the model that other states hoped to attain. It ranked in the top ten in the nation in per capita spent per school on public education.[5] By 2003–04, California was spending $7,772 per pupil versus the national average of $8,156 and well below comparable large industrial states. In percentage of personal income for K–12 schools, it ranked fortieth. California was last in the number of students per guidance councilor and librarians, and second to last in class size.[6] Test scores were among the lowest in the country.[7] Part of this may be attributed to the large number

1   David T. Hartgen, "The Looming Highway Condition Crisis: Performance of State Highway Systems, 1984–2002," manuscript, February 10, 2004, http://www.johnlock.org/policy_reports/2004020943.html; The Road Information Program, *Bumpy Roads Ahead: Cities with the Roughest Rides, and Strategies to Make Our Roads Smoother* (Washington DC: The Road Information Program, April 2004); cited in Schrag, *California*, 108–109.
2   Ibid., 93.
3   Stan Rosenberg, "Moody's Downgrades California GO Debt To 'A2' Stable," *The Wall Street Journal (WSJ.com)*, March 19, 2009, http://online.wsj.com/BT-CO-20090319-714047.html.; Kevin Yamamura, "Fitch Cuts California's Bond Rating, Now Worst in Nation," *Sacbee.com*, March 20, 2009, http://www.sacbee.com/politics/story/1714893.html.
4   California Secretary of State, *Statement of Vote 2006 General Election*, http://www.sos.ca.gov/elections/sov/2006_general/measures.pdf.
5   Schrag, *California*, 93.
6   National Education Association, *Rankings and Estimates, 2003–04* (Washington D.C.; National Education Association, 2004) Table 2: Summary of Selected Estimates Data, 2003–04; cited in Schrag, *California*, 102–03
7   Schrag, *California*, 95.

foreign and minority students in the state, but deterioration had been going on long before these new students were a factor. As for graduation rates, the National Center for Public Policy and Higher Education states in 2004 that after being a leader in higher education thirty years before, California ranked twenty-fifth in the percentage of its ninth-graders who got a bachelor's degree in six years or an associates degree in three years. Just 70% of ninth-graders finished high school and 19% got some sort of college diploma.[1]

As is the case with other infrastructure issues, educational infrastructure is falling seriously behind in the state. Despite the recent success of some bond issues, California is at least a decade behind in school construction. As of 1998 over a third of California's students were in portable classrooms, a total of some 2 million students. In 2002–03, Los Angeles had not opened a new general high school in over thirty years and few schools of any kind despite the fact that the city's population had increased by 30%. Nearly half the city's enrollment was on multi-track schedules.[2] No better example of the collapse of educational infrastructure spending can be found than the University of California. In the ten years from 1955 to 1965, the University of California system built campuses in Santa Cruz (1964) and Irvine (1965) from scratch and upgraded Santa Barbara, San Diego, Davis, and Riverside to general campuses. After the opening of UC Irvine in 1965, the UC system went some forty years before it opened a new campus at UC Merced (although new buildings have been built on the existing campuses). Similar drop-offs in building have also been seen in the California State University system, although not as extreme as the CSU system has recently opened campuses at San Marcos, Monterey Bay, and Channel Islands.

The thirty-year slide in education spending and infrastructure has not occurred without a fight. Led by the powerful California Teachers Association (CTA), there have been attempts to combat the decline, most notably in Proposition 98, passed in 1988, which requires the state to spend at least 40% of the state general funds on K–12 education.[3] Similarly, the successful passage of the state lottery initiative in 1984 (Proposition 37)[4], was also designed to boost education funding. However, politics being what they are, such funding plans have there own way of bringing nasty surprises. Proposition 98's formula's for future increases were such that only twice in the last twenty years has a governor voluntarily increased K–12 funding (Gray Davis in 2000–01) for fear of exploding funding of mandatory increases based on those formulas.[5] As for the lottery, while money from the lottery does go to K–12 education, it was used to replace other school funding so that there was no real increase, a result of both Proposition 98 formulas and the machinations of legislators who wanted the funds for their own pet projects. Still, the CTA and other teachers unions continue to be a powerful force in the negotiations for education funding, particularly in recent years with Governor Schwarzenegger. As discussed at length in Chapter 1, the gov-

1 *Policy Alert: The Educational Pipeline: Big Investment, Big Returns* (San Jose, CA: National Center for Public Policy and Higher Education, 2004); cited in Schrag, *California*, 116.

2 *Portable School Buildings: Scourge, Saving Grace, or Just Part of the Solution?* (Palo Alto, CA: Ed Source, April 1998); cited in Schrag, *California*, 110.

3 Schrag, *California*, 130.

4 Secretary of State, *Initiative History*, 33.

5 Schrag, *California*, 130.

ernor's breaking a 2004 funding pledge to restore $2 billion education funding cut in 2005 and subsequent proposal of an initiative to impose merit pay on teachers and revise tenure met with the wrath of the CTA when his initiative went down in flames in the 2005 special election. [1] More recently, he negotiated a deal with the teachers unions involving future restoration of education funding cuts in the current financial crisis through Proposition 1B in the May 19, 2009, special election that voters ended up rejecting.

Thus, the rebuilding of the educational system's funding and infrastructure, and the powerful impact education has on the political dynamics of the state will be an important factor that the next governor will have to deal with. Proposition 98, the CTA and the other unions, the political clout of the University of California alumni, and most importantly, the financial fallout from the current financial crisis, will all play a role as to how the governor proceeds with education.

Prisons and the Correctional System

One of the most controversial and fastest growing items in the state budget has been the growth of the correctional system and the building of the prison system. As the conservative political wave washed over the state starting in the mid-1960s, more and more attention was directed toward Barry Goldwater's 1964 presidential issue of "crime in the streets." More and more anti-crime laws were passed, and ultimately in 1994, Proposition 184 was passed. This was the famous (or infamous) "three-strikes law," which required judges to double the sentence on an offender's second felony conviction and to impose a sentence of twenty-five years to life for a third felony whether it was violent or nonviolent. Proposition 184 was the poster child for all the tough-on-crime legislation that had been passed over the decades. As a result of all this legislation, California's prison population exploded from under 25,000 at the beginning of the conservative era in the later 1960s to 135,000 by the end of the century. In conjunction with the growth in the prison population was a growth in prisons, with twenty of them built in the 1980s, and 90s. These actions caused the doubling the corrections budget and making it along with health and education, one of the biggest discretionary items (the third-largest item in the current budget if K–12 and higher education spending are counted together) in the state's general fund.[2] It also boosted the power of the influential California Correctional Peace Officers Association.

The problem with the correctional system is not only with its budget-busting capability, but also with the current scandal swirling around the whole system. Despite the heavily investment in prisons, the system has become overcrowded, much of it housing double the inmates it was supposed to. It was also being severely mismanaged; so mismanaged that in June 2005 federal Judge Thelton Henderson of San Francisco seized the entire prison health system saying that it was run so negligently

---

1   Ibid., 194, 210–11.
2   State of California, "Governor's Budget Summary, 2004–05," California Department of Finance, http://www.dof.ca.gov/HTML/BUD_DOCS/Bud_link.htm; cited in Schrag, *California*, 131.

that it was causing more than one unnecessary death a week.[1] Today, the system is still under federal receivership and the state has been unable to fund the reforms necessary. In refusing to terminate the receivership in March 2009, Henderson said "based on the entire record in this case, the court is far from confident that (state officials) have the will, capacity, or leadership to provide constitutionally adequate medical care in absence of a receivership, and (they) have presented no evidence to the contrary."[2]

The political and financial aspects of the corrections system have the potential of being a unique headache for the next governor. Crime is still a hot-button issue with many voters, but the combination of the financial crisis involving the budget and the huge potential liability emanating from prison health system from both the federal courts and individuals filing civil suits could pose an emerging problem for politicians. Moreover, unlike most budget issues that undermine key programs supported by the Democrats, this issue could give problems for Republicans, and especially a Republican governor. The prospect of having to empty the prisons *en masse* in order to save the finances of the state is one that most conservatives, in their zealous efforts to lock everyone up and throw away the key, would not want to contemplate.

Environment

Since the passage of Proposition 20, the coastal initiative in 1972, and the advent of the Jerry Brown Administration in 1975, the environment has been an important issue in California politics. Particularly in the coastal areas, no ambitious politician can make headway without a credible environmental policy, and if they do not have one, they make it up. Even in a statewide race, environmental issues can be an important factor. As noted earlier, a slew of environmental initiatives have been passed in recent years. California voters seem to be particularly fond of animals. The voters are also fond of parklands, clean air and clean water. A proposal from Governor Schwarzenegger to balance the state budget in 2008 by closing and even selling off some of the state parks met with a firestorm of protest. A pioneer in the regulation and control of air pollution and fuel-efficient cars, California's large market means that out of state and even foreign manufacturers have to consider California's environmental laws when developing their products.

Environmental issues are increasingly coming under attack from business groups in the current financial crisis because of their supposed "job killer" nature. This is heard during every California recession, and is being heard again. The data has shown that in most economic downturns California employment figures hold up better than most states. However, with the third highest unemployment rate among the states, such is not the case this time. Voters may be more susceptible to the business community's arguments in this election. In his previous runs for office, Arnold Schwarzenegger has run in both the business and environmental camps.

---

1 James Sterngold, "Judge Orders Takeover of the State's Prison Health Care System," *San Francisco Chronicle*, June 30, 2005; cited in Schrag, *California*, 201.

2 Denny Walsh, "U.S. Judge Won't Oust California Prison Medical Czar," *Sacbee.com*, March 25, 2009, http://www.sacbee.com/capitolandcalifornia/story/1726379.html.

If there are any key environmental issues that could have an impact on the 2010 governor's race, those issues would be energy and water. Energy was a key issue that first damaged the then highly popular Gray Davis when the natural gas crisis occurred in 2000–2001. It was the issue that began sending Davis on his way to the recall as it combined later with the deficit problems triggered by the bursting of the dot.com bubble. The spiking of gasoline prices in the $4.50 a gallon range last year led to a spike in disapproval ratings for politicians of all stripes. The financial crisis has led to the drop of consumption in gasoline, and the resultant price drop in gas prices. But this in turn could encourage more driving, which would force prices back up again; and demand around the world, especially in India and China, still outstrips supply. Renewable energy sources are always a sexy issue with the voters and are featured in most campaign materials. This topic certainly has been grabbed by the Obama Administration and is part of their strategy. Lower gas prices tend to discourage alternative energy development. On the other hand, developing alternative and renewable energy is an important long-term strategy to avoid future energy crises. Whether the economic situation advances or hinders the development of renewable energy remains to be seen.

Water has always been a major environmental issue by virtue of the fact that the bulk of the population of California lives in the semi-arid south and relies on water from up north. Also, the major farmlands in the San Joaquin Valley and further south rely on northern water as well. The great water projects of the state such as the Los Angeles, San Francisco, Colorado and California Aqueducts are anywhere from forty to nearly one hundred years old and are in need of repair. The crumbling levees in the San Joaquin–Sacramento Delta risk flooding the delta and polluting the water heading for use in the south. It is one of the oddities of politics that crisis of the levees in the delta have gotten former adversaries to seriously discuss the project that had divided them so much — the Peripheral Canal, which was designed to send water around the delta to the water projects and which voters rejected in 1982 by a 37–63% vote with over 85% of voters north of Santa Barbara voting no. Current thoughts on the Canal recognize that it could have a positive aspect on the environmental situation in addition to protecting the supply of water to the projects. The upshot of all this discussion is that there is growing support for issuing water bonds to create new water supplies and protect existing ones. But the cost of such bonds has got hung up with the economic and budget crises. Water is an issue that could be very crucial to agriculture and other communities in the coming election.

Healthcare

Healthcare continues to be a major issue at all levels of government as it becomes increasingly unaffordable for individuals and a budget buster for government. Under the Davis Administration, increased caseloads and inflation in healthcare was a major contributor to the growth in the state budget.[1] Healthcare issues continue to show up at the ballot box. In 2004, there were five health-care related initiatives alone; the most significant one was the stem cell research institute bonds that were passed.[2] In

---

1 Schrag, *California*, 119.
2 Ibid., 191.

the legislature, there have been numerous attempts to either expand health care or go to a full-blown single-payer system with the government doing the bookkeeping. A law to expand health care coverage in the waning days of the Davis Administration by requiring large businesses to provide health care or pay into an insurance fund was reversed in a rare referendum measure (Proposition 72), sponsored by the California Chamber of Commerce, which barely passed. This was one of the 2004 ballot measures.[1] The most radical effort in the legislature was the series of single-payer bills sponsored by State Senator Sheila Kuehl. In 2006, she was able to get the administrative bill without funding passed through the Legislature only to have it vetoed by Schwarzenegger. In response to the uproar from the veto and the growing pressure "to do something about healthcare," Schwarzenegger proposed his own insurance-friendly program, which was so inadequate that it failed to get out of the State Senate, even with the support of the legislative leadership. Kuehl has been termed out of the Senate, but others are now carrying her bill.

Healthcare will continue to be a major ongoing issue at all levels of government until a satisfactory means of controlling spiraling costs is implemented. All authoritative studies on the subject show that the U.S. citizens pay roughly double the cost as a percentage of Gross Domestic Product that citizens in other industrialized countries pay, with nowhere near the coverage. This should be a major issue in the 2010 gubernatorial campaign. However, in 2006 when Governor Schwarzenegger vetoed the single-payer administration bill, Democratic challenger Phil Angelides chose to sidestep the issue. Healthcare costs continue to skyrocket and erode the average voter's pocketbooks in tough economic times. It will be interesting to see if any gubernatorial candidate, Republican or Democrat, will try to elevate the healthcare issue as a means to attain the governor's mansion.

In addition to the issues involving domestic healthcare, the state is embroiled in a battle with the federal courts over its prison healthcare system, which has been previously discussed. The debate on how best to remedy the situation continues on between the state and the court-appointed receiver, as the state obviously does not have the funds to make the corrections to the system. This compounds the financial burden on the state's citizens that they already endure with the domestic health system. This in turn exacerbates the state's budget and financial problems, which are already acute.

Summary

The next Governor of California will have to curb a deficit ranging from $30 to even $60 billion, will have to face unfunded liabilities for pensions & health care in the range of $80 billion in the next generation and also began to pay back the bonds of Governor Schwarzenegger to the eventual tune of over $100 billion. There are certainly other issues that could be added to the above list of finance, infrastructure, education, the prisons, the environment, and healthcare. But these issues, all with major impacts on the state finances and the state budget, are a sufficient list to keep any governor or future governor, up late at night. They are certainly the major administra-

---

1 Ibid.

tive challenges that any incoming governor would have to face. But in addition to the administrative challenges, there are the political ones, which are in the next section.

POLITICAL ISSUES FOR THE 2010 ELECTION

In addition to the administrative problems that are discussed in the 2010 election and will have to be dealt with in the new state administration, the roadblocks put up by the political structure will also have to be addressed. These include a partisan and seemingly dysfunctional legislature, a flawed economic structure, and outside institutional forces that undermine the governmental apparatus.

Partisan and Dysfunctional Legislature

In just about every approval rating poll issues anywhere, the legislature tends to get a lower approval rating than the executive. Part of this is understandable, since a legislature is the collection of various political, social, and economic interests that have to be resolved before the sufficient consensus can be reached to enact legislation. The process in the United States was deliberately designed to be adversarial with its checks and balances so that legislation would be difficult to enact and only those issues with the broadest support would be enacted, as opposed to the parliamentary system where the majority government can enact legislation or programs fairly easily. The executive branch in the United States is a unitary branch, which can act unilaterally within its scope of jurisdiction, thus giving the impression that it more efficient in making decisions, however good or bad those decisions may be. Therefore, the executive branch usually has higher approval ratings than the legislative because it appears to be more decisive. This is even truer in California, where the legislature has had terrible approval ratings for years, as shown in Table 6–1 below. Even in the current economic crisis, Governor Schwarzenegger, whose approval ratings are terrible, has better ratings than the legislature.

The issue that encapsulated the current legislature's problem was the passage of Proposition 11, the redistricting initiative that passed in the November 2008 general election. The initiative replaces the current redistricting process for state constitutional and legislative offices, now drawn up by the legislature, with a process drawn up by an independent commission. One of the arguments that the proponents used is that the legislature is so ineffective (as shown by their inability to pass a budget) that they cannot be trusted with redrawing legislative lines. The ongoing wrangle over the budget with government jurisdictions all over the state thrown into chaos, certainly reinforced that image and helped pass the initiative. It was symbolic of how the public views the legislature, and why in poll after poll, the public trusts the initiative process more than they trust the legislature.[1]

At the core of the legislature's problems is the highly partisan nature of the institution as it currently stands. That was not always the case. Indeed, in the Progressive Era of Hiram Johnson and his associates, government was anything but partisan because Johnson and the Progressives structured it to be that way.

---

1 Field Poll, http://www.field.com/fieldpollonline/subscribers/COI-99-Nov-Legislation.pdf.

TABLE 6–1. FIELD POLL JOB RATINGS FOR THE LEGISLATURE

Date	Approve	Disapprove	No Opinion
April 2009	14%	74%	12%
Sept. 2008	15%	73%	12%
December 2007	39%	42%	19%
Sept 2006	34%	46%	20%
October 2005	26%	58%	16%
Sept 2004	33%	46%	21%
July 2003	19%	67%	14%
Sept 2002	35%	46%	19%
May 2001	39%	42%	19%
Feb 2000	49%	22%	29%
March, 1999	49%	23%	28%
August, 1998	44%	30%	26%
November, 1997	40%	40%	20%
1996 Average	41%	49%	10%
1995 Average	34%	59%	7%
1993 Average	28%	64%	8%
July 1992	23%	73%	4%

TABLE 6–2. JOB APPROVAL RATINGS FOR GOVERNOR SCHWARZENEGGER

Poll	Date	% Approve	% Disapprove
Field	April 2009	33%	55%
Field	September 2008	38%	52%
Field	May 2008	41%	48%
Field	December 2007	60%	31%
Field	March 2007	60%	29%
Field	September 2006	48%	37%

The parties were fragmented, cross-filing and the lack of party affiliation on the ballot tended to blur partisan lines, as did the ban on political parties making endorsements. This was all in addition to the initiative, referendum, and recall, which attacked the partisan structure from outside. The result was that Johnson and his cohorts were able to ram through radical legislation in the 1911 and subsequent legislatures. Nonpartisanship strongly influenced the state government for decades. However, it was a bogus nonpartisanship in many ways because in the early twentieth century, the Republican Party dominated the state and did not have to worry about nonpartisanship. Still, the more effective governors tended to be nonpartisan in their approach to running the state.

The nonpartisan focus in state government began to change in the 1930s, when the Democratic Party came back from the dead. By 1934, the Democrats led in registration and have led ever since. The long-term effects of cross-filing and some astute planning by Republicans through the California Republican Assembly (CRA) and other activities allowed the Republicans to control most statewide offices and the legislature through the incumbency and name recognition advantage that cross-filing gave them in the Democratic primary and the general elections. Nevertheless, the shift in registration forced the Republicans to be more moderate in order to get Democrat votes and that in turn kept the nonpartisan spirit. The advent of party affiliation on the ballot, the birth and development of the California Democratic Council (CDC), and the end of cross-filing, changed the whole Republican–Democratic relationship with the Democrats firmly in control the legislature and most of the statewide offices. At the same time, the arbitrary power of strong Democratic Speakers of the Assembly, such as Jesse Unruh and Willie Brown reduced the options for nonpartisanship.

In response to the ascendancy of Democratic power, the Republicans began to respond with conservatives taking over the party apparatus, creating a much more partisan tone on the Republican side. The conservative victories from the 1960s to the 1990s solidified the partisan nature of their activity. Increasingly, the Republicans became more doctrinaire in their approach to issues, particularly taxes. Opposing tax increases became a litmus test for political survival in the Republican Party. Republican office holders have been periodically threatened with challengers in their next primary campaign if they voted for a tax increase, a tactic dating back to the conservative takeover of the party forty years ago. The most recent version of this strategy is to run a recall process against a Republican office holder who voted for a tax increase as occurred in April 2009 when a recall petition was filed against Assemblyman Anthony Adams of Claremont (R-59thAD). Adams, one of six Republicans to vote with the Democrats to pass a budget out of the Assembly which included tax increases and whose district covers eastern Los Angeles County and western San Bernardino County, was served recall papers initiated by an organization called Atlas PAC, a political action committee based in Newport Beach, in Orange County.[1] That an out-of-area Republican operation could feel brazen enough to attempt such an action and in the midst of a financial crisis shows the level of partisan ideological commitment occurring in the Republican Party in 2009.

The Democrats have been less ideological for the simple reason that as the majority party, they have pitched a wider tent to include a more diverse set of values. As such, they have legislators, particularly from the more conservative Central Valley where they hold several seats in both houses, which are on the moderate to conservative spectrum of the party. They have also elected a number of moderate to con-

---

1 Brian Day, "Assemblyman Adams Served with Recall Papers," *pasadenastarnews.com*, April 8, 2009, http://www.pasadenastarnews.com/ci_12104064.

servative Democrats for the U.S. House of Representatives that would fit into the "Blue Dog Democrat" mold on budget issues in the House. Despite these moderate Democrats, there is a very strong liberal base in the Democrat Party, and as Assembly Speaker Karen Bass has found out, her Democratic legislators could also face recall battles if they agreed to items against the wishes of their various constituencies, as labor showed in the recent budget battle.[1] In turn, Bass has been tough on her own caucus, removing committee chairmanships from members who voted against the spending cap and other trailer bills after the budget was passed.[2] Therefore, the Democrats have their own share of ideologues' conformity, though not to the Republican extreme.

This partisan structure is compounded by two other problems — the 2001 redistricting and term limits. Redistricting is always a contentious issue because of its highly political and partisan nature — the 1991 redistricting was eventually done by the courts — but the 2001 redistricting brought the partisan issues to a head. A co-author of this book, Patrick Reddy worked for Speaker Robert Hertzberg's Task Force on Redistricting from 2000 to 2002. To prepare Speaker Hertzberg for negotiations with the Republicans, his consultants drafted what was gleefully called the "Republican Rest-in-Peace (RIP) Plan." Essentially, the Democratic districts were started in the center of every California big city and drawn out to the suburbs in a "spokes in a wheel" format. The net result was a map that handed Democrats 75% of all the legislative districts in California. Recognizing reality, Republican Leader Bill Leonard quickly accepted the Speaker's offer of a bi-partisan compromise plan where almost all incumbents of both parties were protected. The new maps basically froze the party balance for most of this decade. The only Congressional incumbents who lost in this decade were two men who had scandal problems, Gary Condit and Richard Pombo. Essentially, the Republicans agreed to give the Democrats a safe majority in both the Assembly and State Senate in return for protecting their existing seats in the legislature and the Congress. The Democrats got the new Congressional seat added in the Congressional reapportionment. What this did was create an incumbent protection plan with safe seats for everyone in both the legislature and the Congress. Moreover, it played into the hands of the ideologues of both parties, because the major battles were fought in the primaries, not the general election. Since only the activists vote in primaries and since they tend to be more extreme than the centrists who vote in the general election, the winners in the general election tend to be more liberal Democrats or conservative Republicans than the voters who elect them in November. This widens the partisanship gap even further. In the case of putting together a budget, requiring a vote of both parties with incompatible agendas, it is virtually impossible. The April Field Poll on the 2009 Special Election was a classic illustration of this. By a 67–23% margin, voters favored resolving the budget crisis more with budget cuts than with tax increases (a sentiment born out in the May 19 vote when all tax increases lost badly). But when asked which programs they favored

---

1 Steven Harmon, "Heat Coming from All Sides as Leaders Work on Budget," *Contracostatimes.com*, February 5, 2009, http://www.contracostatimes.com/localnews/ci_11631255?nclick_chck=1.

2 Capitol Alert, "Bass Doles Out Committee Perks, Penalties," *sacbee.com*, March 3, 2009, http://www.sacbee.com/static/weblogs/capitolalertlatest/020304.html.

cutting, 2–1 majorities opposed spending cuts in the big-ticket items like education, health care and law enforcement.[1] Democratic primary voters oppose cutting programs, while Republican primary voters utterly detest taxes. By representing the will of their voters, leaders of both parties maintain gridlock in the name of democracy. This is also true with any vote that requires a supermajority, such as raising taxes.

The other problem is term limits. Since there is such turnover in the legislature (at least one third of the Assembly members and one quarter of the Senate members leave each term), there is very little opportunity to develop relationships to offset the structural partisanship. It is also hard to put together long-term deals on certain issues because the people will not be around. Sheila Kuehl literally had to hand off her single payer project to Fran Pavley and others. It is the only major project continuing in that fashion because healthcare is such a commanding issue. In addition, others have attributed political reform legislation banning certain political-social activities with helping to create an impersonal wall between legislators that exacerbates the problem.[2]

The net result of the above is that it is very difficult to bridge the partisanship gap and get things done. However, the problem goes beyond partisanship and the dysfunction that it creates. Other structural forces at work complicate the problem.

Besides the institutional or structural problems noted, the Legislature has used bad political judgment. For example, in 2009 some of the wiser members of the State Assembly recognized the dreadful PR of having expensive independent commissions — like the Waste Management Board — whose members are paid over $100,000 per year for part-time work at a time of massive budget deficits. A bill was written to curb these Boards' funds. Those same Board members, many of whom are former Legislators, hired expensive private lobbyists at taxpayer expense to defeat such legislation.[3] So California citizens were essentially paying lobbyists to work against the public interest. The great reform governors like Hiram Johnson and Earl Warren would be horrified at such a turn of events.

Institutions That Create a Dysfunctional System

Hiram Johnson's progressive policies by their very nature created institutional roadblocks that encourage dysfunction in government. The initiative process has been discussed in detail, particularly with regard to the issues that influenced various elections. But initiatives also impact how government functions or dysfunctions. Most importantly, initiatives create ballot box democracy, in effect bypassing the channels that government normally uses — the legislature. Polls indicate the voters are very happy with this system, more so than they are with the legislature. However, the net result is that it makes the legislature even more irrelevant and dysfunctional, allowing the whole system to atrophy. It also helps the high level of partisanship to

---

1 Mark DiCamillo and Mervin Field, "While California Voters Prefer Spending Cuts to Tax Increases to Resolve the State Budget, Majorities Oppose Cutbacks in Ten of Twelve Spending Categories," *The Field Poll*, Release #2306, April 30, 2009, http://media.sacbee.com/smedia/2009/04/29/15/0429rls.source.prod_affiliate.4.pdf.

2 Schrag, *California*, 153.

3 Patrick Reddy, discussion with legislative staff, spring 2009.

continue because there are other avenues for party ideologues and special interest groups to get things done, and so there is no need to compromise.

The recall is increasingly adding to the problem. A little used process that primarily worked at the local level, the successful recall of Governor Gray Davis has showed that it can be a new weapon in trying to remove politicians between elections as well as during them. The attempted recall of Senator Jeff Denham of Merced (R-12thSD) in 2008 by then Senate President Pro Tem Don Perata, and the current effort against Assemblyman Anthony Adams shows that it is on the political radar at a much higher level than it has been before. The Denham recall attempt was a cross-party action because of a budget issue dispute. The Adams recall effort is an in-party dispute on a key Republican Party issue — taxes. Previously, such attacks would have waited for the primary or general election, or the terming out of the official. Not so anymore. This adds another dose of organizational uncertainness and dysfunction that previously wasn't there.

The other institutional problem for the legislature and the government as a whole is term limits, Proposition 140, which was passed in 1990. First, term limits reduces the experience level of the legislature. Like any other job, it takes quite a while to learn how things work, and the legislature is no exception. In addition to a loss of experience by the elected officials, the same has occurred with the legislative staff, which was cut by 40 percent in Proposition 140. Because of the loss of experienced personnel, the legislature was weakened in relation to both lobbyists and the executive branch. Without people knowledgeable about state government, the legislature is hindered in conducting oversight of the executive branch because it does not have the experienced legislators or staff to research and conduct that oversight. At the same time, without experienced personnel, legislators and their staff members have to rely on biased information from lobbyists advancing their own special interests.[1]

These institutional problems compound the partisan political problems and allow them to feed on each other. Until this cycle is broken, it will be difficult to get state government of track to make the next governor's job any easier.

SOLUTIONS

The May 19, 2009 Special Election

The continued dysfunction of state government has spawned a great deal of discussion and attempts at solutions. As has been the case in recent years, these solutions have come in the form of initiatives. The latest solution was in the form of Propositions 1A through 1F in the May 19 special election. This was a compromise between Governor Schwarzenegger and the legislature. As has been true of budgetary compromises in recent years, it was full of gimmicks that do not address some of the basic budgetary problems, such as the overreliance on the income tax and capital gains that makes revenues more volatile and encourages excessive spending in good times that is difficult to reduce in bad times. Proposition 1A attempted to put in a spending cap which requires money in good times to be put in a "rainy day" fund for future economic downturns. But it was a band-aid that did not solve the underlying

---

1 Schrag, *California*, 150–153.

structural budget deficit problem. Nor did it solve the inclination to use debt to cover those deficits rather than deal with them directly. The May 19 ballot measures faced a gauntlet of political problems on their own. They attracted a unique alliance of people that wanted to stop them, from anti-tax conservatives or labor and progressives who oppose the spending cap. These propositions clearly showed that from a political point of view they were a very limited solution. They were the best deal and the governor and the legislature could come up with, but there was no love or consensus regarding them that allowed them to be part of a long-term solution. Not surprisingly, they failed on May 19.

Redistricting — Proposition 11

The support and passage of Proposition 11 in November 2008 was based on the idea that if redistricting of the state legislature was taken out of the legislatures hands and placed in the hands of a redistricting commission, more competitive districts could be created that would allow for more moderates of both parties to get elected and make it easier for compromise on items such as the budget. While this is great in theory, it may not be so in practice. A commission may reduce some of the more egregious situations, but it probably would not reduce that many safe districts, due to the simple fact that in much of California, housing is still very segregated. Second, one cannot assume that such new map would elect more moderates from the party primaries. As conservatives in the Republican Party showed as far back as the early 1960s, an organized group of activists can take over a political party and get their people elected in an election with a legislative drawn map. The takeover of the Assembly by the Republicans in 1969 was based on maps drawn by Democrat Jesse Unruh in 1961. It is highly questionable whether redistricting reform will make for a better functioning legislature.

The Open Primary

The latest solution to make the legislature function better is a very old one — the open primary. The current version is one proposed by Senator Abel Maldonado of Santa Maria (R-15th SD) and adopted by the legislature *in toto* for the June 2010 primary, as a deal to get his vote to pass the state budget. It was another case of the Two-Thirds Budget rules being used to pressure (i.e., blackmail) the majority into accepting a questionable action. The 2010 version would have all the candidates of all parties on the primary ballot and the two highest vote getters in the primary run in the general election, even if they were from the same party. The idea here would be that with the Decline to State voters voting in the primary, centrist Republicans and Democrats would more likely come out of the primary for the general election. This theory is just as dubious as the ones in redistricting. As conservative Republicans have showed on many occasions, a well-organized minority (conservatives) can be very effective against a less well-organized majority (moderates). The least organized and the least predictable voters are Decline to States, who have known to disappear in primary elections, while the activists of both major parties are out getting the vote.

More important, California had a quasi-open primary system in the form of cross-filing for forty-four years, from 1914 to 1958. The result for most of that period was

Republican dominance in state government. As previously noted, cross-filing was advantageous to candidates with name recognition, since for most of the period, party identification was not on the ballot. Candidates with high name recognition tended to be incumbents, who had gotten it from previous campaigns, or the wealthy, who could buy it. In the first half of the twentieth century, it tended to benefit the Republicans, who had an advantage in both categories.

The current version of the open primary would list the party affiliation, although that may be voluntary (the details of this proposed initiative have not been seen in their final form). The incumbent advantage would be limited by term limits, but name recognition would still be a serious problem, and there would be the possibility in some districts that two Democrats or two Republicans would square off against each other, meaning that the party could not support a candidate, and it would come down to the individual resources of those candidates. The major parties would find themselves spending money in an internal party battle in those districts, when they should be competing against the other party in November. The minor parties would fare even worse, being wiped off the November ballot entirely. This is why all parties oppose the open primary, because they want to keep control of the nominating process of their own party.

Open primaries primary benefit wealthy moderate politicians like Maldonado, and former Controller Steve Westly and former Los Angeles Mayor Richard Riordan, who backed a previous open primary initiative. Aside from making it easier for the above people to get elected, how it makes the legislature more effective is open to question.

The Complete Overhaul

For many people the system is so broken that band-aid fixes like Propositions 1A, 11, and the open primary are too little, too late. The system needs a complete overhaul of how revenues are raised and expenditures are allocated. It requires that all the past initiative patches such as Proposition 13, Proposition 98, the Two-Thirds Budget rule, and all the others, including all the tax loopholes be put on the table. The idea would be to create a broader based set of taxes with lower rates. This would lower the burden for the highest incomes and straighten out the cash flow. It would probably be advisable to prohibit initiatives that tinker with the budget. The Two-Thirds Budget rule would be eliminated making it easier for the state to conduct business and allow the legislature to gain control of the process. This would make the governor's and the legislature's life a lot easier.

If none of the above work, we should expect to see some radical revisions of the State Constitution being discussed. Given the consistently dreadful job rating for the State Legislature, it is only a matter of time before some citizen group puts on the ballot a proposal for a "part-time" Legislature. Although the last Field Poll on this subject showed voters opposed by 52–33%, if the people continue to seethe in anger, anything is possible. We could even see the ultimate institutional "Big Bang": a constitutional convention. The State Constitution explicitly grants the people the right to modify their state government as they see fit, although the California Supreme Court has said in the past that while initiatives seeking constitutional amendments like Proposition 13 are perfectly valid, *revisions* to the State Constitution can only be put on the ballot via the Legislature. We may soon find out if the state Courts would be willing to block voters' desire for a new Convention. If the Court allows the process to go forward, all it would take is a few thousand determined volunteers with clipboards and 12% of the voters willing to sign petitions to put it on the ballot. Ask Gray Davis about what happens when voters' emotions get out of hand.

In fact, two groups are currently preparing major governmental reform efforts in California. The Bay Area Council, a collection of Northern California business executives openly favors calling a new "Constitutional Convention" as soon as possible to completely revamp state government. They have just begun to collect signatures for a 2010 ballot measure. The second civic organization is California Forward, led by former Assembly Speaker Bob Hertzberg who favors an official state commission appointed by the Legislature to recommend incremental changes such as reforming term limits and the two-thirds requirement to pass a budget. In a *Sacramento Bee* article, Hertzberg and his colleague Thomas McKernan advocated downsizing the state government's responsibilities by transferring many functions to county and city governments. With voter confidence in Sacramento collapsing by the week, either moderate or extreme constitutional surgery appears inevitable. George Skelton noted during the 2003 recall that every few years California goes through an upheaval driven by the Populist Right. These occurrences include the election of Ronald Reagan in 1966, Proposition 13 in 1978, term limits in 1990, and the 2003 recall. Based on those time frames, the next governor could be the victim of another one.

THE WAY FORWARD FROM 2010 — RED STATE VERSUS BLUE STATE CULTURE

Ultimately, for any future governor or legislature, the question of what they are faced with is entwined with what kind of state the voters want California to be. In the 1950s and early 1960s, Californians wanted the state to be the best it could be, and were willing to pay for it. In recent times, the voters wanted the high level of services, but did not want to pay for it. The current financial crisis has put paid to the idea that there is such a thing as a free lunch. California, currently the eighth largest economy in the world, was not built on the cheap. The highways, the water projects, the University of California system do not come cheap. So how will California operate in the future?

In his book *Red States, Blue States, and the Coming Sharecropper Society*, a co-author of this book, Stephen Cummings, postulated that the United States was developed on two competing economic models, a red state model, and a blue state model. The red state model was based on small government, low taxes, and the primacy of business over labor. This model originally was centered in the states of the Confederacy and spread out to those states that voted for George W. Bush in 2004. The blue state model was based on active government (particularly government infrastructure projects), high taxes, and a more balanced relationship between business and labor. This model was originally centered in the Northeastern states and spread out to those states that voted for John Kerry in 2004. Over time, the states that adopted a blue state culture have become wealthier than states with red state culture.[1] However, while a blue state culture or model is more successful, it is very expensive to maintain and takes a lot of commitment to maintain it. What kind of a state do Californians want to be?

For some forty years, Californians have wanted a blue state culture financed on a red state budget. That is no longer possible; they are going to have to choose one or the other. The current financial crisis leaves no alternative. Which culture they choose will be determined by whom they elect for governor and the ultimate solutions they make on the state finances.

It is difficult to see California abandoning its blue state culture when push comes to shove. After all, California has always been an entrepreneurial state. Its very remote location dictated that the immigrants that came here had to be quick on their feet to survive. The three Republican candidates for governor reside in or near Silicon Valley, two of them executives from Silicon Valley firms who made fortunes from the technological revolution. Those firms were made possible by the research infrastructure built up around the area, a lot of it supplied through the University of California, other public educational institutions, and other government support. It is impossible to see these candidates or their Democratic counterparts supporting a red state cultural model that would starve the very industries of the government support that made them successful. The people of this state want to see the California of Earl Warren and Pat Brown, not an oversized reproduction of Mississippi.

However even if the blue state model continues in California, there are changes that need to be made. The tax structure needs to be overhauled, not only changing the rates, but also broadening the base by closing loopholes and instituting taxes commonly levied in other states, such as the oil severance tax. At the same time, California is going to have to make some hard choices on how it spends its government revenues and how it can conserve cash. The blue state cultural model by its very nature emphasizes government expenditures in infrastructure, not social services. That is because infrastructure generates the wealth that funds the social services. The projects of the kind that occurred under Pat Brown and those necessary to a high tech economy that developed since Brown would be emphasized in a blue state cultural budget. There would still be substantial social services, but the needs of blue state economics and the unsustainable level of expenses in the present unbalanced budget and financial downturn make the current level of services not viable in the long run. It is highly debatable whether any state can survive financially when there are so many pressure groups chronically demanding more funds for an increasingly impoverished state. In addition, prison and health costs would have to be put into the mix, which might conserve cash for some social programs. It is difficult to see how California can surmount its current financial difficulties without moving to single-payer health care in order to conserve cash for budgets at all levels of government.

The other factor that has been and will continue to be brought to bear on a blue state cultural model that was not there in Pat Brown' time, but was initiated by his

---

1   For a more detailed discussion of red state and blue state culture, see Stephen D. Cummings, *Red States, Blue States, and the Coming Sharecropper Society* (New York: Algora Publishing, 2008), Part I.

son Jerry Brown, is the environment and environmental issues. California has been a leader in these issues, and as much as any state, attempted to develop new industries based on them. But the forces imposed by the environment on a state of nearly 40 million people will require changes as painful as those imposed by the budget.

The decisions made on budget and environmental issues are the very essence of the differences in blue state and red state culture. In red state culture, the attempt is to (1) keep taxes and services low, (2) reduce, finesse, evade or eliminate regulations, particularly environmental regulations, to benefit business, and (3) keep wages low, which along with low taxes, services and regulation would create a "business friendly" economic environment. In such an economic environment, the net result has been to attract and support economically declining, second-rate businesses with little real economic potential, staffed by management incapable of adapting to economic and environmental forces. In many cases, red state culture emphasizes minor short-term gains at the expense on long tern high economic growth. In the 2009 budget fight in the California legislature, the Republican Party clearly stood by the red state model.

In blue state culture, the attempt is to (1) maintain high taxes to sustain government infrastructure and the services needed for that infrastructure, (2) sustain regulations to maintain order in the community and the economy, (3) adapt to the environment and surmount its limitations to create genuine economic opportunity and not bleed old industries and workforces dry, and (4) create an environment for smarter businesses, not just be "business friendly" to obsolete ones. In many cases, blue state culture imposes short-term costs in the form of taxes, regulations and the like in order to generate long-term wealth. In the 2009 budget fight, the Democrats stood close to, but not quite at, the blue state model.

As stated earlier, it is difficult to see California abandoning the blue state model in the end, but the challenges to sustain a blue state model will be very difficult. It is hard to see the Republicans in the legislature working with any governor, Republican or Democrat, to sustain such a model, and with the Two-Thirds Budget rule, they can scuttle any blue state model plans. It ultimately comes down to the voters who will decide whether a red or blue state economic model predominates. The voters will take their cue from the candidates for governor and the next governor. Whom they select will determine which economic model is selected. The polling and the results of the May 19, 2009 special election indicates that the voters are tired of gimmicks, wants the governor and the legislature do their job, and are not interested in seeing taxes increased.[1] That is the only lead we have as to where the voters are heading, and it appears that they are looking at economic basics and not pie-in-the-sky programs. Based on the polling of the May 19 election, the current economic and political environment would indicate that the Republicans and the red state model are currently favored, at least in the short run, as that is what the voters are telling the pollsters. Even the Democrats have admitted that the current budget crisis can not be solved alone through tax increases, regardless of the results of the May 19 election

---

1   Peter Hecht, "Field Poll: California Voters Oppose Five of Six May 19 Ballot Measures," *sacbee.com*, April 29, 2009, http://www.sacbee.com/politics/v-print/story/1818253.html; Kevin Yamamura, "Voters Takes Dim View of Governor, Legislature," *sacbee.com*, May 1, 2009, http://www.sacbee.com/politics/v-print/story/1825240.html.

and whether there is a Two–Thirds Budget rule or not.[1] In the long run, however, the Democrats and blue state model still will probably prevail because it is difficult to see voters dismantling the state as the Republican ideologues would like, considering the dim view that the public has of Republicans and the business community after eight years of the George W. Bush Administration. However, where the voters will be in November 2010, which model of the state they will support, and which candidate will be able to communicate to the voters the right message, remains to be seen.

---

1   Steve Wiegand, "Looming State Cash Crisis Seen by California Analyst," *sacbee.com*, May 8, 2009, http://www.sacbee.com/capitolandcalifornia/v-print/story/184200.html.

PART III. CALIFORNIA IN 2010

7. CALIFORNIA STATISTICAL TRENDS — THE SIX REGIONS OF CALIFORNIA

REGIONAL CHANGES FROM 1958 TO 2010

For the purposes of this book, California is divided into 6 distinct regions, based on demographics, culture, history and voting patterns. Those regions are: 1) the San Francisco Bay Area; 2) the North & Central Coastal Counties; 3) the Central Valley; 4) Los Angeles County; 5) the remaining large suburban counties of Southern California (Orange, Riverside, San Bernardino, San Diego, and Ventura Counties) and 6) Rural California.[1]

Each one of these regions is similar to states and voting patterns elsewhere. The Bay Area as a giant Massachusetts or Minnesota, it is liberal on both social and economic issues. L.A. County was once dominated by middle class white voters and therefore, a reasonably accurate predictor of state and local returns. Now, it is a Third World metropolis that is less than one third white. The state's new black–Hispanic–Asian majority has conquered even the suburbs within L.A. County. Due to its changing demographics, Los Angeles County has now equaled New York City as the nation's premier source of Democratic presidential votes and a steady base for economic liberalism (unions) — though these minority voters sometimes still have a touch of social conservatism, as witness their vote against gay marriage in 2008. The Southern California suburbs are a bigger version of Phoenix; they tend to be both socially and especially, fiscally conservative. The Central Valley fifty years ago had a "populist" tradition on economics — as did their cousins in Oklahoma and Arkansas. That tradition has largely faded, being replaced by social conservatism. For example, the right-to-work Proposition was demolished in the Central Valley in 1958 and Proposition 13 did the worst here among the six regions. However, the bans on affirmative action and gay marriage passed by the biggest margins in the Valley. The North & Central Coast are a bigger and more ethnically diverse version of the Oregon Coast. If the Central Valley has moved to the right since the 1960s, the coastal counties have moved to the left, especially on social issues like women's rights — just like Washington and Oregon have done. The counties of Rural California are mostly

---

1 All Table sources in this chapter are from the Patrick Reddy database and the Appendix.

mountain areas, larger versions of Wyoming or Montana. Just as in those Mountain states, voters are both fiscally and especially, socially conservative.

TABLE 7–1. CALIFORNIA REGIONAL, ETHNIC AND CLASS VOTING BLOCS BY DECADE:

	1960s		1970s		1980s		1990s		2000–08	
	D	R	D	R	D	R	D	R	D	R
Statewide Wins	5	5	4	4	2	7	7	2	7	2
Regional:										
Bay Area	55%	44%	55%	41%	52%	43%	61%	31%	63%	29%
Nor/Cen. Coast	48%	51%	49%	47%	46%	50%	50%	41%	51%	40%
C. Valley Cities	54%	44%	51%	45%	43%	53%	44%	49%	43%	50%
L.A. County	51%	48%	52%	46%	49%	48%	55%	38%	59%	34%
Southern Cal.	44%	55%	43%	54%	36%	60%	39%	51%	41%	52%
Rural Cal.	52%	47%	48%	48%	38%	58%	38%	53%	37%	57%
Social Groups:										
Whites	46%	53%	45%	51%	39%	57%	44%	48%	44%	49%
Blacks	90%	10%	91%	8%	90%	9%	84%	12%	82%	14%
Latinos	83%	17%	81%	17%	67%	30%	69%	24%	68%	26%
Asians	62%	37%	53%	44%	46%	51%	54%	41%	58%	37%
White Voters:										
White Liberals	60%	40%	61%	36%	58%	37%	65%	28%	66%	27%
Conservatives	38%	61%	39%	58%	31%	66%	35%	56%	36%	58%
Bay Area Subs.	53%	46%	51%	45%	47%	48%	57%	36%	59%	34%
SoCal Whites	41%	58%	40%	57%	32%	65%	32%	59%	32%	62%
White Workers:										
Bay Area	59%	40%	58%	39%	51%	44%	59%	32%	64%	30%
L.A. County	52%	47%	53%	44%	46%	51%	45%	46%	54%	40%
Statewide	51%	48%	50%	46%	45%	51%	49%	43%	51%	42%

Sources: **America Votes**, Network and *L.A. Times* exit polls. Note: "Statewide" refers to races for president, governor, and U.S. Senator only. The "1960s" also includes the 1958 results for governor and U.S. Senator. See Appendix 2 for category descriptions.

Table 7-1 shows the average partisan vote by regions and social groups for the last five decades. California Democrats, just like their national counterparts declined in 3 phases: the 1950s, the 1960s, and the 1980s. In the 1950s, California voted for Eisenhower, as did most states outside the Deep South in broad middle class gains for Republicans. In the 1960s, racial issues like the Watts Riot and social issues like anti-war protests drove a wedge between the Democrats and white labor voters in the big metro areas and the Central Valley. Then in 1978, the tax-cutting Proposition 13 represented the final collapse of the New Deal Coalition over economic issues, which Reagan capitalized on in 1980 to win a decisive victory.

California Democrats revived themselves in three waves. First, Dianne Feinstein in her 1990 gubernatorial run brought in Bay Area women and as befitting the former Mayor of California's most heavily Asian city, she also carried Asian voters. In 1992, the loss of defense jobs in Southern California drove the white middle class Reagan Democrats and independents back toward Bill Clinton. While Kathleen Brown's 1994 defeat was a huge Democratic disappointment, her staunch opposition to the immigrant-bashing Proposition 187 paid huge dividends to Democrats with over a million Hispanics registering as Democrats by 2000. By 1996 and 1998, all these elements — Bay Area women, immigrants and their children, white workers in L.A. County — came together and Bill Clinton in 1996 and Gray Davis in 1998 dominated the California GOP. Despite Schwarzenegger's individual success, California Republicans have still not revived.

There are three regions of California where the Democrats have averaged over 50% of the vote for the last two decades: the Bay Area, Los Angeles County and the North & Central Coastal counties. Those three areas cast a slight majority of the California vote in any given election. And in recent decades, Democrats have become stronger in their base areas than the Republicans have in their best areas: the Southern California suburbs, the Central Valley and Rural California. Thus, the California Democrats have had a structural edge since 1992.

In terms of ethnic, class, and ideological voting trends, California's ethnic diversity is unique. While New York, Texas and Florida have ample black and Hispanic populations and Hawaii has the nation's largest Asian population, only California has sizable concentrations of all three minority groups. California also has almost as many Jews as New York, about as many white Catholics as Pennsylvania and as many "Okies" and "Arkies" as Tulsa, Oklahoma and Little Rock, Arkansas do today.

Since 1958, California has changed probably more than any other state due to both massive domestic migration and foreign immigration. At the end of the 1940s, California passed Pennsylvania to become the nation's second most populous state after New York. In 1960, California was more middle class and suburban than the nation. California's population was also better-educated as 10% of Californians had college degrees compared to 8% nationally; and wealthier with median family incomes 118% of the US average, while only 12% of California families were below the federal poverty line compared to 19% nationally. And this better-educated, more upwardly mobile society was largely based in California suburbia. For example, the national population was 35% city, 33% suburban, and 32% rural in 1960. By contrast, the Golden State was then 33% city, a solid 54% majority suburban and only 13% rural. The defense boom of the World War II era had attracted millions of Americans who quickly built homes in the suburbs around Los Angeles. L.A. County's population jumped from 2.8 million in 1940 to just over 6 million in 1960, with roughly two thirds of the growth outside the city of Los Angeles. Therefore, California suburbanized sooner than the rest of the nation and this showed in the 1960 election results; Kennedy carried New York, Illinois and Pennsylvania where central city voters were more dominant while losing suburban-majority California narrowly to California native Richard Nixon. Since 90% of suburban voters in California were white, these same white suburbanites were a majority of statewide voters, a first among the 10 biggest states. California was the first big state outside the South to elect a Goldwater-style conservative as governor in Reagan (1966), while the big eastern states were still electing Republican moderates like Nelson Rockefeller in New York, Bill Scranton in Pennsylvania and George Romney in Michigan.

For the next 30 years after the 1960 election, the largely white suburban middle class dominated California politics. White suburbanites were in the forefront of the racial backlash, the tax revolt, the environmental movement, and the sexual revolution. Their consistent votes for local Republicans like Nixon and Reagan were the reason California went Republican seven of eight times from 1960 to 1988 with Lyndon Johnson in 1964 the sole Democratic exception. For the past 50 years, nearly 90% of "white non-Hispanic" Californians have been living above the poverty line. From the 1960s until the mid-1990s, the political portrait of the typical California voter was a middle-aged middle class white suburbanite. Until about 1990, white suburbanites were a majority of voters and they retain a small plurality even today.

While California has remained more suburban than the nation as a whole (See Appendix 1A), the ethnic make-up of the Golden State has shifted tremendously over the past five decades. And these ethnic changes have crossed city, suburban and even rural lines. These ethnic changes affected California society first, the economy second and the politics last.

In the 1960 Census, California had a slightly lower percentage of blacks than the nation and a significantly higher Hispanic population. Overall, both California and America were over 80% "non-Hispanic white." Over the next four Censuses, the nation would grow more diverse and California led the way. These changes were largely caused by immigration as California's Hispanic share soared from 9% in 1960 to 19% in 1980 and 32% in 2000 (the comparable figures for the nation were 3% in 1960 and 13% in 2000 (See Appendix 1A). The Asian population grew even faster, going from 2% in California and 1% nationally in 1960 to 11% in California and 4% nationally 40 years later. As Appendix 1 shows, all six of California's regions were 80% white or more in 1960. By 2007, four regions — the Bay Area, the Central Valley, L.A. County and somewhat surprisingly, the suburbs of Southern California — had non-white majorities. As might be expected, L.A. County changed the most, going from 80% white in 1960 to just 30% in 2007. However, the white percentages of the Bay Area, the Central Valley, and Southern California declined to 52–53% in 2000 and slid below 50% in this decade. Only the North & Central Coast (59%) and Rural California (71%) still have white majorities.

Rural Californians (i.e., farmers and those living in towns smaller than 50,000 people) have declined to just 5% of the state population, compared to 20% nationally. Not only have the cities and suburbs grown faster relative to the rural areas, they have also swallowed up some land that was once considered "rural" in 1960. For example, Riverside and San Bernardino Counties were considered part of their own small town areas out in the desert. Ventura County was labeled a farming area. Now all three are called suburbs by the Census and are included in the Consolidated Los Angeles Metropolitan Area.

Which California region has voted most often for the statewide winner and which social group is the best predictor of state elections? The answers are that the North & Central Coast Region has gone with the state winner the most times since 1958, and the social groups with the best track record of predicting California elections are the so-called "Reagan Democrats" in Los Angeles County and Asian Americans.

TABLE 7–2. CALIFORNIA STATISTICAL SUMMARY

Population 1960: 15,717,204	Population 2009: 38,293,000	Growth 1960–2009: +144%
Ethnic Breakdown		
1960:	2007:	
83% white	45% white	
6% black	6% black	
2% Asian/Pacific Islander	12% Asian/Pacific Islander	
9% Hispanic	36% Hispanic	
	1% Other	
	5% Mixed Race	
Voter Registration		
1958:	2009:	
58% Democrat	45% Democrat	
39% Republican	31% Republican	
3% Decline-to-State	20% Decline-to-State	
	4% Other	
Best Performance		**Worst Performance**
Democratic:	Barack Obama (2008) Alan Cranston (1974 Senate) 61%	Jimmy Carter (1980) 36% Cruz Bustamante (2003 recall) 31%
Republican:	George Deukmejian (1986 Governor) 61%	George Bush (1992) 33%
Voter Breakouts		
	2007:	
	Poor: 13%	College Degrees: 26%

The Bay Area: Republicans Need Not Apply

In his 1969 classic *The Emerging Republican Majority*, author Kevin Phillips noted that San Francisco is the Pacific outpost of the Northeast liberal Establishment.[1]

---

1 Kevin Phillips, *The Emerging Republican Majority*, (New Rochelle, New York: Arlington House, 1969), 415.

Key Proposition/Special Election votes:	Statewide
1958 Right-to-work	40%
1964 Repeal Fair Housing	65%
1972 Establish Coastal Commission	55%
1978 Proposition 13	65%
1978 Restore Death Penalty	71%
1982 Gun Control	37%
1988 40% Education budget set-aside	51%
1988 Insurance reform	51%
1990 Term Limits:	52%
1992 Right-to-Die	46%
1994 Proposition 187 — Illegal Immigration	59%
1996 Proposition 209 — Ban Affirmative Action	55%
2003 Recall Gray Davis	55%
2004 Stem Cell research	59%
2006 Road Bonds	61%
2008 Ban Gay Marriage	52%
2008 Abortion — Parental Consent Law	48%

Since the 1980s, the San Francisco Bay Area has emerged as one of the top five Democratic bastions in the country, matching the metro areas of New York, Boston and Washington, DC as sources of Democratic votes and money. Ronald Reagan in 1980 is the last Republican presidential nominee to carry the San Francisco Bay Area and that was in a 3-way race. President Nixon in 1972 was the last Republican nominee to win here in a two-way race. Governor Deukmejian won 55% in the Bay Area in his successful 1986 re-election, making him the last GOP candidate for major office in California to win the Bay Area. Even Walter Mondale won 51% in the Bay Area in 1984 despite losing 49 states nationally. With 2% of the nation's population — and 4% of the nation's wealth — the Bay Area is now a national powerhouse and easily the equal of the Republican stronghold of Dallas–Fort Worth. Even on the world stage, from the 49ers in their Super Bowl years to Silicon Valley, "San Francisco" has become a brand name that is stylish, expensive, progressive, technologically advanced, environmentally sensitive and intellectual. Thirty-seven percent of Bay Area residents have a college degree, the highest region in California.

After Walter Mondale was nominated in San Francisco, Jeanne Kirkpatrick, the Democrat-turned-Republican, who was President Reagan's Ambassador to the United Nations, famously excoriated what she called "the San Francisco Democrats" who "always blame America first." It is no surprise Republicans do not think much of the Bay Area because it is filled with groups the modern conservative movement loves to hate — liberals, sometimes radical intellectuals, politically-correct feminists, "good-government" reformers, moderate-to-liberal Republicans, slick city powerbrokers, union bosses, gays and immigrants.

TABLE 7–3. BAY AREA SUMMARY

Counties: Alameda (Oakland), Contra Costa, Marin, Napa, San Francisco, San Mateo, Santa Clara (San Jose), Solano, Sonoma.		
Population 1960: 3,636,400	Population 2009: 7,375,678	Growth 1960–2009: +103%
Percent of State		
1960:	2009:	
23%	20%	
Ethnic Breakdown		
1960:	2007:	
82% white	49% white	
7% black	7% black	
4% Asian/Pacific Islander	21% Asian/Pacific Islander	
7% Hispanic	23% Hispanic	
	1% Other	
	5% Mixed Race	
Voter Registration		
1958:	2009:	
58% Democrat	52% Democrat	
39% Republican	20% Republican	
3% Decline-to-State	23% Decline-to-State	
	4% Other	
Best Performance		**Worst Performance**
Democratic:	Barack Obama (2008) 74%	Jimmy Carter (1980) 41%
Republican:	Thomas Kuchel (1962 Senate) 57%	Dick Mountjoy (2006 Senate) 21%
Democratic % and Ranking		
1960s:	2000-2008:	
55%, 1st of 6	63%, 1st of 6	
Voted for State Winner		
1958-2008:	2007:	
69% (4th of 6)	Poor: 9%	College Degrees: 37%

Key Proposition/Special Election votes:	Percent Yes	Statewide
1958 Right-to-work	36%	40%
1964 Repeal Fair Housing	58%	65%
1972 Establish Coastal Commission	60%	55%
1978 Proposition 13	62%	65%
1978 Restore Death Penalty	62%	71%
1982 Gun Control	46%	37%
1988 40% Education budget set-aside	56%	51%
1988 Insurance reform	54%	51%
1990 Term Limits:	50%	52%
1992 Right-to-Die	51%	46%
1994 Proposition 187 — Illegal Immigration	45%	59%
1996 Proposition 209 — Ban Affirmative Action	46%	55%
2003 Recall Gray Davis	36%	55%
2004 Stem Cell research	67%	59%
2006 Road Bonds	64%	61%
2008 Ban Gay Marriage	39%	52%
2008 Abortion — Parental Consent Law	37%	48%

Conservatives have long seen San Francisco as a prime example of immoral behavior and corruption. Even today, many massage parlors in San Francisco are fronts for the sex trade, a practice apparently tolerated by city leaders.

As Republican analyst Tony Quinn has pointed out, the Bay Area is home to all the various species of California Democrat. There are the "Wine-and-Cheese" liberals of San Francisco and Marin Counties, the hippies and gays in the city, the Berkeley radicals, the high-tech youngsters in San Jose's Silicon Valley, the Hispanic immigrants struggling for a foothold in the United States, the white union members living just south of Oakland (who still go to Raiders games), and the new Asian population that is soaring both demographically and economically. Somehow, all these disparate groups have united to form a coalition that has delivered literally millions of votes to Bill Clinton, Dianne Feinstein, Barbara Boxer, and Barack Obama. The Bay Area is one of the few places in America that would vote for keeping affirmative action, legalizing gay marriage, tolerating even illegal immigrants and preserving union power.

Unlike Los Angeles, which is economically liberal but with a touch of social conservatism, the Bay Area is liberal on both economic and social issues. The Bay Area did go through a brief phase of fiscal conservatism in the late 1970s, voting for Proposition 13 and the Gann Spending Limit. But that quickly passed and the region often votes for higher taxes, especially for "sin taxes" like on tobacco.

San Francisco was the dominant city in California at the turn of the last century and the ninth largest city in America with roughly 20% of the state's population. The whole Bay Area contained nearly 50% of California voters, while all of Los Angeles County was less than half the size of San Francisco. Accordingly, many California governors came from the Bay Area, including Hiram Johnson, Earl Warren, Pat Brown and James Rolph, who was also the longest-serving Mayor of San Francisco. Much has changed since then as the Los Angeles and San Diego metro areas became a majority of California's population during the boom caused by the Second World War in the 1940s. But the Bay Area still exercises much statewide influence due to its high turnout rates and Democratic solidarity as evidenced by the fact that two Bay Area women have won seven straight races for the US Senate.

Back in the 1950s, the Bay Area was a stronghold for liberal Republicans like Warren and Thomas Kuchel, just as New York was for Nelson Rockefeller, John Lindsay and Jacob Javits. As late as 1960, Nixon earned 48% in the Bay Area, including a highly respectable 42% in San Francisco, thus contributing greatly to his 50.1% California victory. Two years later, Senator Kuchel scored the best Republican performance in the Bay Area over the last five decades with 57%. But the nomination of Barry Goldwater in 1964, who defeated the Republican Establishment's favorite Rockefeller, began a process where moderate-liberal Republicans and independents grew alienated from the GOP. That fall, Lyndon Johnson scored his biggest California gains in the Bay Area and North–Central Coast, just as he did with Rockefeller's base in the New York suburbs. It was no accident that the Republican who ran best in the Bay Area and North Coast was Kuchel, a Senator with a solidly liberal voting record on social issues. When conservatives dumped Kuchel for right-winger Max Rafferty in the 1968 GOP primary, Republicans lost some votes in the Bay Area forever (Democrats Alan Cranston and Barbara Boxer have held Kuchel's seat since 1968). Republicans have fallen down to just 20% of the registered voters in the Bay Area, a record low for the GOP and in 2002, Republican gubernatorial nominee Bill Simon finished behind the Green Party in San Francisco. No Republican candidate for president, governor, or senator has carried the Bay Area in over 20 years — even Pete Wilson lost it in the Republican landslide of 1994.

So why is the Bay Area so liberal and Democratic? It starts with the people who settled the Bay Area after the Gold Rush and continuing into the twentieth century. Coming from the northern states and Asia, these people tended to be very tolerant on social issues. Adding to the Democratic base were Irish, Italian and Hispanic immigrants who were often union members — the Bay Area, particularly San Francisco and Oakland, has above-average union membership. As a result, Franklin Roosevelt ran a few points better in the Bay Area than he did nationally in all four of his elections.

Pat Brown's election in 1958 was the ultimate flowering of the New Deal Coalition in California. Since Pat Brown's 1958 landslide of 65% in the Bay Area, only four Republicans have carried the Bay Area: Kuchel, Reagan, Nixon in 1972, and Deukmejian in 1986. It has been nearly a quarter-century since a Republican candidate for major office won the Bay Area and GOP prospects do not look good in 2010.

That explains the past. The two forces currently driving Bay Area liberalism are Third World immigration and the alienation of white suburbanites from the New

Right. The tide of immigration from Asia and Latin America reshaped the face of the Bay Area. In 1960, the ethnic breakdown was 82% white, 7% black, 4% Asian/Pacific Islander and 7% Hispanic. By 2007, the Census Bureau estimated the Bay Area to be still 7% black, while Asians had surged to 21%, Hispanics to 23% with whites dropping to minority status at 49%. Five percent of Bay Area residents are mixed-race children, twice the national average. These immigrants began to mobilize after the Proposition 187 campaign, helping to fuel the increase in the average Democratic vote from 55% in the 1960s to 63% this decade. (To put this Democratic strength in perspective, John F. Kennedy won only 60.2% in his native Massachusetts in 1960). Data from the California Secretary of State's Office show voters in Alameda and San Francisco Counties have higher turnout rates than L.A. County and most of Southern California.

While Proposition 187 will be discussed at length later for its impact in Greater Los Angeles, 187 also had a significant impact in the Bay Area. Asian Americans never had the overwhelming loyalty to the Democrats that blacks and some Hispanics had. For example, Chinatown in San Francisco voted for Eisenhower twice in the 1950s. They were much more of a swing group, generally voting for whoever was popular and strong at that time, whether that was Reagan or Pat Brown. However, the intensity of the Proposition 187 campaign when Wilson ran ads with the tagline "They just keep coming" revived memories of the Chinese and Japanese Exclusion Acts. Roughly, half of Asian Americans voted for Kathleen Brown, the first time they had swung toward a landslide loser. Shortly after the 1994 election, a co-author of this book, Patrick Reddy appeared on the radio show "Which Way L.A." and told the audience that the statistic that should scare Republicans was that Asians who went nearly two-to-one for Reagan in 1984 turned against Republicans in their biggest across-the-board win since the 1950s. Combined with Dianne Feinstein's personal following among Asians, Proposition 187 caused yet another group in the Bay Area to begin drifting toward the Democrats. Since 1994, Matt Fong (who is of Chinese descent) and Arnold Schwarzenegger are the only two Republicans to do well with Asians.

The white middle class voters (including gays) who have migrated to the Bay Area since the 1960s disdain the hard-edged social conservatism that has defined the Republican Party in recent years. The well-educated, successful white-collar workers who often have Asian or Hispanic spouses simply have little use for the "fire-and-brimstone" preachers of the Deep South or the race baiting of a Jesse Helms. Accordingly, the Republican vote in the Bay Area suburbs has declined sharply since the 1980s from a 48–47% GOP lead during the Reagan Era to a dismal 34% in the first decade of the twenty-first century. Moreover, along with Asian voters, those suburbs are the swing groups in the Bay Area. Excluding ultra-liberal Marin County, the all-suburban counties of the Bay Area (Contra Costa, Napa, Solano and Sonoma) have voted for the eventual statewide winner in 36 of the last 45 elections — an 80% accuracy rate.

The trends that made the Bay Area a true Democratic bastion ironically evolved during the 1980s when the Republicans under Reagan were dominating California politics, winning seven of nine major statewide races. In 1980, the Bay Area shared the national disappointment with the Carter Administration as he hit rock bottom in the Bay Area with just 41%, the worst performance for any Democrat in the past 50 years. Democrats then began a revival with the Bay Area seemingly becoming more

Democratic almost every election cycle. In 1982, Tom Bradley received 54% in the Bay Area, slightly better than he did in his native L.A. County. Two years later, Walter Mondale won 51% in the Bay Area, one of his best performances in the country for any large combined metro area. In 1986, Bay Area voters saved Alan Cranston's career for one more term with a 300,000-vote plurality (58–40%), nearly three times his state margin. In 1988, Michael Dukakis carried the Bay Area by a surprising 58% and nearly 400,000 votes, although the first George Bush overcame this deficit with big win in the Southern California suburbs. In 1990, former San Francisco Mayor Dianne Feinstein carried the Bay Area by an overwhelming 20 points, but once again, Republican Pete Wilson triumphed based on a bigger vote in Southern California.

The surge continued after 1990. Bay Area voters always regretted that Feinstein was not elected governor. Her percentages during her Senate career in the region — 67% in 1992, 63% in 1994, 64% in 2000, 73% in 2006 — make her the most popular Democrat in these parts since FDR. In this decade, the only Democratic candidates to poll significantly less than 60% in the Bay Area were Cruz Bustamante and Phil Angelides, both of whom lost badly to Schwarzenegger.

To summarize, economic liberalism and labor unions keep the blacks, Hispanics, and white union members in the Democratic fold and social liberalism attracts the Asians and white yuppies. The key issues in the Bay Area are the environment and high-tech industry. Only Republicans with extraordinary personal popularity like Schwarzenegger who won 45% here in 2006 can hope to compete in the Bay Area. Getting a near-bloc vote from the roughly 25% of California voters who live in the Bay Area will continue to give California Democrats a big advantage in state elections. To regain their overall political health, California Republicans will need to recover in the Bay Area suburbs. All three Republican candidates for governor 2010 have Silicon Valley roots. It remains to be seen if their local ties can loosen the Democratic grip on the Bay Area.

The North and Central Coast Goes Left

Kevin Phillips in *The Emerging Republican Majority* said that the "social currents that wash Northern Pacific shores are more cosmopolitan than the factors at work in the Sun Belt" and that the North Pacific Coast is much more liberal.[1] Much the same could be said of the North & Central Coast of California. As noted in the Bay Area section, the same voting trends impacting the Bay Area are visible in the nearby North & Central Coast counties. One key difference is the North & Central coast has much smaller concentrations of black, white labor and Asian voters, while its Hispanic population is bigger than the Bay Area due to the prevalence of agriculture. Since a fair part of the Coast's Hispanic population is guest farm workers, the net result is that white voters are much more dominant here than in the Bay Area or L.A. County. Nevertheless, social liberalism has allowed Democrats to post impressive gains on the Coast since the 1980s, much like the story in Oregon and Washington. For example, Coast voters went heavily against bans on gay marriage and abortion in recent years, while supporting medical marijuana, stem cell research and drug treatment as a sentencing alternative for non-violent drug users. There is still a touch of fiscal conservatism here as a small majority voted against the Burton health care mandate

---

1 Philips, *The Emerging Republican Majority*, 424.

(Proposition 72 in 2004) and a big majority voted against the 2009 tax increases (see Appendix 3). Overall, the focus on social concerns has moved the North & Central Coast much closer to San Francisco than to Orange County.

TABLE 7–4. NORTH & CENTRAL COAST SUMMARY

Counties: Del Norte, Humboldt, Mendocino, Monterey, San Luis Obispo, Santa Barbara, Santa Cruz		
Population 1960: 706,298	Population 2009: 1,654,778	Growth 1960–2009: +134%
Percent of State		
1960	2009	
4%	4%	
Ethnic Breakdown		
1960:	2007:	
87% white	59% white	
2% black	2% black	
3% Asian/Pacific Islander	5% Asian/Pacific Islander	
8% Hispanic	33% Hispanic	
	1% Other	
	4% Mixed Race	
Voter Registration		
1958:	2009:	
54% Democrat	46% Democrat	
43% Republican	29% Republican	
3% Decline-to-State	20% Decline-to-State	
	6% Other	
Best Performance		**Worst Performance**
Democratic:	Barack Obama (2008) 64%	Jimmy Carter (1980) 34%
Republican:	Thomas Kuchel (1962 Senate), Ronald Reagan (1966 Governor) 61%	Dick Mountjoy (2006 Senate) 30%
Democratic % and ranking		
1960s:	2000–2008:	
48%, 5th of 6	51%, 3rd of 6	
Voted for State Winner		
1958–2008:	2007:	
89% (1st of 6)	Poor: 13%	College Degrees: 27%

Both Republican registration (from 43% in 1960 to 29% in 2009) and perfor-mance (from an average of a 51–48% GOP lead in the 1960s and 50–46% GOP lead in the 1980s to a 40–51% Republican deficit in this decade peaking with Obama's record 64% in 2008) have collapsed in the last generation on the North & Central Coast. Considering that Jimmy Carter and Walter Mondale averaged less than 40% of the white vote in the 1980s, things have really changed.

Key Proposition/Special Election votes:	Percent Yes	Statewide
1958 Right-to-work	45%	40%
1964 Repeal Fair Housing	60%	65%
1972 Establish Coastal Commission	54%	55%
1978 Proposition 13	66%	65%
1978 Restore Death Penalty	67%	71%
1982 Gun Control	36%	37%
1988 40% Education budget set-aside	50%	51%
1988 Insurance reform	44%	51%
1990 Term Limits:	51%	52%
1992 Right-to-Die	50%	46%
1994 Proposition 187 — Illegal Immigration	57%	59%
1996 Proposition 209 — Ban Affirmative Action	56%	55%
2003 Recall Gray Davis	51%	55%
2004 Stem Cell research	61%	59%
2006 Road Bonds	58%	61%
2008 Ban Gay Marriage	43%	52%
2008 Abortion — Parental Consent Law	39%	48%

Who lives here? Mostly white voters in smaller cities like Santa Barbara, Monterey, Salinas, Santa Cruz, San Luis Obispo, and Mendocino who have populated the North and Central Coast of California. There are also a good number of small towns like Crescent City, Eureka, and Pismo Beach. There were not many urban New Deal vot-ers (union members) on the Coast and there was a tradition of moderate Republi-cans doing well here like former Assemblyman Brooks Firestone of Santa Barbara. For example, Nixon carried this area against Kennedy in 1960 and Pat Brown in 1962. Thomas Kuchel was even more popular here than in the Bay Area. From the late 1950s to the late 1980s, Republicans usually ran slightly ahead in this region. But begin-ning in the late 1980s and early 1990s as Republicans under the two President Bushes began to pitch their appeals more to the fundamentalists in the South, they began to lose support on the North & Central Coast (just as they did in Northern tier states like Oregon, Michigan, Maine and Iowa). The national Republican Party essentially traded Santa Barbara for Beaumont, Texas and Mobile, Alabama. Ronald Reagan was the exception — a conservative who consistently ran better on the North and Central Coast than his state average, partly because he owned a ranch in Santa Barbara. Reagan tied Kuchel for the best GOP showing in this region with 61%. In the last two decades, Republicans have only carried the North & Central Coast in national landslide years like 1994 or when they have an exceptional individual like Schwarzenegger, whose support for environmental laws like AB32 locked up the Coast's vote.

Since 1958, the North & Central Coast region has the best track record of any California region in picking statewide winner, getting it right almost 90% of the time. (Pete Wilson in 1990 was the last winner to lose the Coast). Voters here have a 19-win election streak, the longest in California. Is it because of all that medical marijuana grown in Humboldt County? The best guess is that the percentage of white voters, the percentage of adults with college degrees and the percentage of poor families here is virtually identical to the statewide share. Twenty-seven percent of residents over age 25 on the North & Central Coast have college degrees, as do 27% of Californians. Thirteen percent of families live below the poverty line just like in California as a whole. White voters are about 65% in both California and on the North & Central Coast. On the North & Central Coast, there is a majority of white voters combined with a large Hispanic minority (about 20%) and much smaller concentrations of Asian and black voters — the same as the statewide electorate.

The key issue on the North & Central Coast is the environment and other social issues. To return to competitiveness on the North & Central Coast, Republicans will have to develop a more pro-environment stance and candidates. They will have to think more like Schwarzenegger and Earl Warren and less like Dick Cheney.

The Central Valley Cities: Tom Joad Becomes a Republican?

The cities of California's Great Central Valley Sacramento, Stockton, Modesto, Fresno and Bakersfield, which John Gunther called "the heart of California," have repeatedly entered American popular culture and folklore. First, the discovery of gold near Sacramento in 1848 made California a household name all over the world associated with "striking it rich" and populated the state almost instantly, with the state's non-Indian population more than tripling in 1849 alone. Then, in the Depression, the John Steinbeck novel *The Grapes of Wrath* detailed the struggles of fruit-pickers through the fictional Joad family migrating from the drought-ridden "Dust Bowl" in Oklahoma for the Promised Land of California. Around the same time, a picture of an exhausted, poverty-stricken woman and her children by Dorothea Lange, dubbed "Migrant Mother," achieved worldwide fame. In the 1960s, the seemingly eternal struggles of farm workers had a sequel with the poor whites of the Depression now in the upper class and Mexican immigrants playing the roles of the Joads. The late United Farm Workers Union leader Cesar Chavez became a national figure in the 1960s and 1970s. In 1973, the film *America Graffiti*, set in Modesto and featuring classic themes of young love, cars and coming of age, was massively popular and helped spark a re-examination of, and nostalgia for, the 1950s and early 1960s. Also in the 1970s, the University of California at Davis near Sacramento drew national attention for a Supreme Court case involving affirmative action. Though the Central Valley has been quiet lately, it has seen plenty of drama and history.

TABLE 7–5. CENTRAL VALLEY CITIES SUMMARY

Counties: Fresno, Kern (Bakersfield), Kings, Merced, Sacramento, San Joaquin (Stockton),Stanislaus (Modesto),Tulare (Visalia),Yolo (Davis)		
Population 1960: 1,942,520	Population 2009: 5,471,904	Growth 1960–2009: +182%
Percent of State		
1960	2009	
12%	14%	
Ethnic Breakdown		
1960:	2007:	
82% white	46% white	
4% black	6% black	
3% Asian/Pacific Islander	9% Asian/Pacific Islander	
11% Hispanic	37% Hispanic	
	1% Other	
	5% Mixed Race	
Voter Registration		
1958:	2009:	
64% Democrat	42% Democrat	
34% Republican	38% Republican	
2% Decline-to-State	16% Decline-to-State	
	4% Other	
Best Performance		**Worst Performance**
Democratic:	Pat Brown, Claire Engle (1958 Governor, Senate) 66%	Tom Bradley (1986 Gov.) 30%, Cruz Bustamante (2003 recall) 26%
Republican:	George Deukmejian (1986 Governor) 68%	William Knowland, Goodwin Knight (1958 Governor, Senate) 34%
Democratic % and ranking		
1960s:	2000–2008:	
54%, 2nd of 6	43%, 4th of 6	
Voted for State Winner		
1958–2008:	2007:	
76% (3rd of 6)	Poor: 17%	College Degrees: 18%

The Central Valley was predominantly rural but is now a mixture of agriculture and growing cities and even suburbia. Fresno County, in the heart of the Valley, has got to be the only county in America that has a central city of over a half million people and also produces nearly $5 billion worth of agricultural commodities, including grapes, almonds, tomatoes, poultry and beef.

Key Proposition/Special Election votes:	Percent Yes	Statewide
1958 Right-to-work	39%	40%
1964 Repeal Fair Housing	64%	65%
1972 Establish Coastal Commission	53%	55%
1978 Proposition 13	57%	65%
1978 Restore Death Penalty	76%	71%
1982 Gun Control	28%	37%
1988 40% Education budget set-aside	48%	51%
1988 Insurance reform	38%	51%
1990 Term Limits:	52%	52%
1992 Right-to-Die	41%	46%
1994 Proposition 187 — Illegal Immigration	65%	59%
1996 Proposition 209 — Ban Affirmative Action	61%	55%
2003 Recall Gray Davis	64%	55%
2004 Stem Cell research	49%	59%
2006 Road Bonds	60%	61%
2008 Ban Gay Marriage	64%	52%
2008 Abortion — Parental Consent Law	55%	48%

The Central Valley cities have also attracted many commuters. Today, thousands of Valley residents are making commutes of over 75 miles to the Bay Area. From 2000 to 2009, the California Department of Finance estimates that the Central Valley gained nearly one million residents, for a growth rate of roughly 20%, compared to 13% for the state. The Central Valley is now a combination of California's breadbasket and booming "Sun Belt" cities and suburban sprawl. This combination has pushed the Valley closer to the Republicans.

California agriculture is mostly divided between the Central Valley counties and the rest of what we call "Rural California." The state's "Mediterranean" climate plus the rich soil of the Central Valley have combined to make California America's leading agricultural producer. With cash revenues of over $31 billion in 2006, the state's farm revenue was more than the combined total of Texas (second) and Iowa (third). Roughly one third of California products were exported in 2006 to over 150 countries. California produces over $1 billion each of the following commodities: milk and cream, grapes, nursery products, almonds, cattle, lettuce, strawberries, tomatoes, flowers and hay. California also leads the nation in the production of milk and nearly 80 categories of crops, including apricots, broccoli, flowers, lemons, lettuce, onions, peaches, strawberries and tomatoes, while growing virtually 100% of the nation's almonds, artichokes, figs, grapes, raisins, olives, peaches, plums, pomegranates, rice and walnuts.[1] And all of this bounty is produced by less than 10% of California's population. California is famous for its large-scale farms. While some Valley residents have expressed concern over population growth and farms being paved over, the fact is the Valley has plenty of room for both farms and suburbia. While the population of both Fresno and Bakersfield has doubled in the last 30 years, they are a long, long way from being overrun by urban sprawl. Fresno County has roughly 150 persons per acre and Kern less than 100. By contrast, L.A. County has 2500 persons per acre. Anyone who drives along Interstate 5 will see nothing but miles of fields and pastures from Bakersfield to Stockton. In addition, the Williamson Act, which was passed in the 1960s, offers farmers financial incentives through lower property taxes in exchange for continuing to farm, also helps prevent over-development. Given the amount of food and money produced by Central Valley farms, it is very difficult to imagine this way of life disappearing anytime soon.

Due to its large farm labor population, the Valley and Rural California have the highest poverty rates of any California region with twice as many Valley residents on welfare as the state average and individual poverty rates 30% higher than the state as a whole. However, as the *Los Angeles Times* pointed out, that has not stopped the Republicans who represent the Valley from voting for massive cuts in social services. The *Fresno Bee* quoted the economic research firm IHS Global Insight as predicting the lower Central Valley will not recover the jobs lost in the 2007–2009 recession until at least 2012. One result of California's latest budget crunch will be much social and economic pain in the Valley. It will be interesting to see if there is any political fallout in the Valley in the 2010 campaign.

The Central Valley had a tradition of populist whites voting Democratic until the 1960s. During the farm Depression of the 1920s and 1930s, hundreds of thousands of poor Democrats from the Southern (Texas, Arkansas) and Border states (Oklahoma, Missouri) moved out west and worked in the fields. These Southern/Border transplants retained their Democratic loyalties all through the 1930s and 1940s — FDR ran better in the Valley than he did statewide all four times and the Valley delivered Harry Truman's 1-point margin of victory in 1948 after he and Thomas Dewey ran essentially even in California's big metro areas. Dwight Eisenhower was personally popular for a while in the Valley, but Democrats at the local level remained strong. In 1958 and 1962, the Valley was Pat Brown's best region along with the Bay Area (see Appendix 2).

Like so much else in America, the Valley's politics began to change in the 1960s. As Democrats came to be seen as more into in urban programs than Valley agriculture, the Valley began to drift away. Following up on the Valley's 64–36% vote to repeal the Fair Housing Act in 1964, Ronald Reagan easily defeated Pat Brown in the Valley by 11 points. There was still some residual loyalty to the Democratic Party when Hu-

---

1 California Department of Agriculture, *2006 Annual Report.*

bert Humphrey carried the Valley with just 47% in 1968 as Nixon and Wallace split the conservative vote. However, the easy Democratic victories in the days of FDR, Truman and Pat Brown were over. The Valley was a swing area in the 1970s: when Democrats like Alan Cranston, John Tunney, and Jerry Brown carried the Valley, they won statewide. (Proposition 13 was relatively unpopular here, losing in Kern County and running 8 points behind its state total).

In retrospect, the flashpoint for the Valley's permanent defection from the Democratic Party came in 1982 when a gun control measure, Proposition 15, drove a massive wedge between California Democrats and the conservative "Valleycrats." Although the handgun control proposal lost badly statewide by 37–63%, it was annihilated in the Central Valley (28–72%) and especially Rural California (19–81%). The wipeout of Proposition 15 played a big role in Tom Bradley's upset loss. Bradley lost the Central Valley by 100,493 votes compared to his statewide deficit of 93,345. If the L.A. Mayor had just broken even in the Valley (as Jerry Brown had essentially done so in the last close gubernatorial contest in 1974), he would have won statewide by a few thousand votes. This was the only time in the last 50 years that the Valley provided any candidate of either party with their margin of victory because there have not been that many close elections in California, and the Bay Area and the suburbs of Southern California have historically had more clout than the Valley.

A turning point in the Valley's political evolution came in 1982. In the 1960s and 1970s, Democrats generally ran even or slightly ahead of their statewide percentages in the Central Valley, even with losing candidates like Salinger and McGovern. But since that big gun control vote, virtually every Democratic candidate for president, governor or senator has run behind their statewide showing in the Valley, even winners like Clinton, Feinstein and Obama. Democrats now only carry the Valley in landslide years like 1998 or 2008. In his 60% landslide in 1958, Pat Brown received 66% in the Central Valley. By contrast, 50 years later in his 61% landslide, Obama carried the Valley with only 52%. Since the Valley's black and Hispanic populations were still voting heavily Democratic, that must mean there has been a massive shift away from the Democrats among white voters. Democratic registration has dropped from 64% in 1960 to just 42% in 2009 with most of the losses concentrated among formerly white Democrats. The children and grandchildren of Tom Joad have largely left the Democrats. The key issues in the Central Valley are agriculture, jobs, crime and guns, and while the North & Central Coast had moved leftward, the Valley has moved to the right.

Los Angeles County: From Iowa by the Sea to Baywatch to a Hispanic City

The great chronicler of California Carey McWilliams spoke of Los Angeles as "the great city of the Pacific, the most fantastic city in the world."[1] Los Angeles County passed Chicago's Cook County in the 1960 Census to become the nation's most populous county and topped the population of New York City in the mid-1970s, an apt symbol of the growth of the West. In 2009, the California Department of Finance estimated Los Angeles County to have 10,293,000 people — roughly the population of Michigan. Its five County Supervisors represent districts with over 2 million people

---

1 Carey McWilliams, *Southern California: An Island on the Land* (1946; reprint Salt Lake City: Peregrine Smith Books, 1988), 377.

each, more than the combined populations of Philadelphia and Boston. While the growth rate in L.A. County has slowed down to single-digits over the last two decades, it will probably have over 12 million people by 2020 — more than Ohio and catching up to Pennsylvania.

TABLE 7–6. LOS ANGELES COUNTY SUMMARY

Counties: Los Angeles		
Population 1960: 6,038,771	Population 2009: 10,393,185	Growth 1960–2009: +72%
Percent of State		
1960	2009	
38%	27%	
Ethnic Breakdown		
1960:	2007:	
80% white	30% white	
8% black	9% black	
2% Asian/Pacific Islander	13% Asian/Pacific Islander	
10% Hispanic	47% Hispanic	
	1% Other	
	5% Mixed Race	
Voter Registration		
1958:	2009:	
58% Democrat	52% Democrat	
39% Republican	24% Republican	
3% Decline-to-State	20% Decline-to-State	
1% Other	4% Other	
Best Performance		**Worst Performance**
Democratic:	Barack Obama (2008) 69%	Jimmy Carter (1980) 40%, Cruz Bustamante (2003 recall) 37%
Republican:	Ronald Reagan (1966 Governor) 57%	Bill Jones, Dick Mountjoy (2004 & 2006 Senate) 28%
Democratic % and Ranking		
1960s:	2000-2008:	
51%, 4th of 6	59%, 2nd of 6	
Voted for State Winner		
1958–2008:	2007:	
82% (2nd of 6)	Poor: 15%	College Degrees: 25%

Key Proposition/Special Election votes:	Percent Yes	Statewide
1958 Right-to-work	40%	40%
1964 Repeal Fair Housing	67%	65%
1972 Establish Coastal Commission	55%	55%
1978 Proposition 13	67%	65%
1978 Restore Death Penalty	71%	71%
1982 Gun Control	42%	37%
1988 40% Education budget set-aside	55%	51%
1988 Insurance reform	63%	51%
1990 Term Limits:	47%	52%
1992 Right-to-Die	45%	46%
1994 Proposition 187 — Illegal Immigration	56%	59%
1996 Proposition 209 — Ban Affirmative Action	46%	55%
2003 Recall Gray Davis	49%	55%
2004 Stem Cell research	65%	59%
2006 Road Bonds	65%	61%
2008 Ban Gay Marriage	50%	52%
2008 Abortion — Parental Consent Law	46%	48%

For many years, L.A. County usually picked the winners of California elections. In the 1960s for example, L.A. went for the winner nine of ten times, missing only in 1960. In the 1970s, L.A. County picked six out of eight winners, missing only in the 1976 presidential and senate contests. Back then, Los Angeles County was majority white suburban, as was the rest of California. But as the County's population became more minority-influenced, Democrats grew stronger in L.A. during the 1980s even as the Republicans were winning most state elections. Now L.A. County is solidly Democratic, in line with California, but not necessarily with the rest of the country.

Spanish settlers coming north from Mexico in 1781 founded the Pueblo of Los Angeles. After California achieved independence and then statehood in the 1840s and 1850s, American migrants from the Midwest, Northeast, and South moved here to enjoy the weather and seek a fresh start. These transplants remade Los Angeles into a distinctly mainstream American city, solidly middle class with very few of the ethnic enclaves that used to characterize cities like New York or Chicago — or San Francisco, for that matter. From 1920 to 1984, Los Angeles voted for the winner of every presidential election. Beginning in the late 1960s, due mainly to the Immigration Reform Act of 1965, L.A. changed as much as any city in America, going from a largely white middle class area to a Third World metropolis. President Reagan's 55% in 1984 was the last time a GOP presidential nominee carried L.A. County and Cruz Bustamante in 2003 is the only Democrat to lose L.A. in the last 15 years.

Since the L.A. of today represents such a sharp break from the past, it makes political sense to analyze the "Old" L.A. of the 1950s, 1960s and 1970s and the "New" Los
Angeles County that began to emerge in the 1980s.

In the first 30 years of the twentieth century, Los Angeles County grew more
than ten-fold, from 170,000 in 1900 to 2.2 million in 1930. Spurred by the real estate
boom, enticed by the beautiful climate, empowered by the automobile, and inspired
by Hollywood newsreels, millions of American came to L.A. to chase the dream of
new wealth and enjoy the weather. The Depression of the 1930s caused a slowdown
in L.A.'s growth, but that was temporary. Modern California as a national powerhouse based in Los Angeles County was essentially created in two related decades
— the 1940s, which saw a massive mobilization for the Second World War, and the
1950s, which continued the defense build-up for the Cold War and the growth of new
industries to supply the booming Southwest market. From 1940 to 1960, the population of L.A. County more than doubled.

Because so much of the World War II mobilization was focused on the Pacific
Theater, California became both a hub of military production and training ground
for American soldiers. Millions of Americans (including African-Americans whose
numbers in L.A. rose from 170,000 in 1940 to 462,000 in 1960) came to work in the
wartime factories and millions passed through on the way to Asia. Many service-
men liked what they saw and stayed after the war. After a brief recession in 1945–46
caused by re-converting defense industry to civilian purposes, which resulted in the
election of Richard Nixon to a Republican-majority Congress, the great post-war
boom in L.A. was on. After the war, a modern, middle class society based on the automobile was created in L.A. Because of its usually booming real estate market and
the stimulus provided by continued high defense spending, L.A. County usually was
much better off than the rest of the country (see Appendix 1).

In addition, the old L.A. County was part of California's mainstream; in the
1960 Census, 83% of Californians were white, as were 80% of L.A. County residents.
Roughly, 12% of Californians were poor; the figures were virtually identical for L.A.
County. A majority of California's population was in the suburbs and L.A. County
had a suburban majority in 1960. From the death of FDR in 1945 to the re-election
of Eisenhower in 1956, Republicans of all stripes from liberals Warren, Knight and
Kuchel to conservatives Nixon and Knowland, did well in California, and they all carried L.A. County as well. When Pat Brown finally ended the GOP winning streak in
1958, he actually ran a few points behind his statewide total in L.A. County. Until the
1980s, the typical voter in L.A. County was white and middle class.

The middle class dominance of Los Angeles County, which helped Republicans
win statewide, continued in the 1960s and 1970s. JFK barely carried L.A. County with
50%, but Nixon easily overcame that margin in the Southern California suburbs. In
1964, 67% of voters in L.A. County voted to repeal the Fair Housing law, helping spur
George Murphy's upset of Pierre Salinger. Two years later, when Reagan helped re-
align California politics by demolishing Pat Brown's bid for a third term, he won 57%
in both L.A. County and the entire state. Beyond partisan campaigns, the middle class
orientation of L.A. County was proven when Proposition 13 scored 67% in L.A., compared to 65% statewide. From Reagan's election in 1966 to the first election of Pete

Wilson in 1990, the relatively small Democratic margins in L.A. County were usually overmatched by Republican votes in the Southern California suburbs and Rural California. Nixon carried L.A. in both 1968 and 1972 and Reagan won L.A. County (his hometown) in all four of his campaigns for governor and president.

The population of L.A. County began to change with immigration reform in the 1960s and by 1980, white non-Hispanics were down to just 52% of L.A. County with Asians and Hispanics tripling their share compared to 1960 with 6 and 28% respectively. It took a few years for the voting population to catch up to these changes, but by 1988, Michael Dukakis carried L.A. County by 52–47% despite a lackluster campaign. A new Democratic coalition was emerging in L.A., based on liberals and minorities as many Reagan Democrats and their children had moved out of the County. The 1990 Census showed that whites had officially slipped to minority status at 41% with Hispanics almost even at 38% and almost as many Asians as blacks (see Appendix 1).

The new demographics were about to join with a new politics in L.A. County. Pete Wilson's 47% and 867,000 votes in L.A. helped him narrowly defeat Dianne Feinstein in the 1990 gubernatorial race that would turn out to be nearly the last hurrah for the Reagan Coalition (Wilson would be re-elected in 1994, but that was largely due to the national GOP tide and the backlash against immigration.)

However, trouble was already brewing in paradise. In 1990, California had slipped into the national recession. In 1991, however, the quick end of the first Persian Gulf War combined with the winding down of the Cold War led to steep cuts in defense spending, which had become the base of L.A. heavy industry. The economic result was the deepest recession since 1945 for Los Angeles County (over 70% of California's job losses in that recession occurred in L.A. County). The political result was the end of the Reagan Coalition in L.A. and the rest of Southern California.

The events of 1992 seem as extraordinary as the recall election. The first President Bush had soared to over 80% in the polls in 1991 after the defeat of Iraq. However, in the winter of 1992, the L.A. economy had crashed due to defense cuts. Unemployment and underemployment (wage cuts and lost hours) approached 20%. After the post-Rodney King trial riots had caused over $1 billion in damages, the president was briefly running third behind Clinton and Perot in the spring. The recession caused by defense cuts had impacted white swing voters the most, causing devastating defections up and down the GOP ticket. Taking advantage of the Bush–Perot split, Clinton carried L.A. County by the astonishing margin of 650,000 votes, while Bush dropped to just 29%, thus re-aligning L.A. County for the next two decades. The New L.A. was born in 1992.

As noted above, Wilson carried L.A. County in 1994 with a bare majority of 50.4% — the last time a Republican would win the County in a non-special election. Since then, L.A. County has turned in huge Democratic percentages — 59% for President Clinton in 1996, 66% for Davis in 1998, 63% for Gore in 2000, 67% for both Feinstein and Boxer in their Senate re-elections, 69% for Obama in 2008. Even Schwarzenegger could only gather 46% here in his 2006 landslide. Most Democratic candidates receive a 500,000 margin in L.A. County, usually overpowering the Republican vote in the Southern California suburbs.

The demographic shifts revealed by the 1990 Census continued all through the next two decades. The 1970 Census showed that L.A.'s once white-majority population with small groups of blacks and Mexicans (10-15%) had by 2000 given way to a dazzling array of minority sub-groups: of 50,000 residents each of Armenians, Chinese, Filipinos, Guatemalans, Iranians, Japanese, Indians, Israelis, Koreans, Russians, Salvadorans, various South Americans, Sub-Sahara Africans, Vietnamese, etc. Working and middle class whites in the southern and eastern part of L.A. County had moved out and were largely replaced by Hispanic and Asian immigrants. These dramatic ethnic changes also transformed some of the L.A. County suburbs. In terms of population density, poverty and population mix, Compton, Inglewood, Pomona, Pasadena, plus East Los Angeles and the heavily black and Hispanic unincorporated areas south and east of Los Angeles should now be considered central cities. Adding them to Los Angeles and Long Beach gives the County an urban majority for the first time since 1945.

The 2000 Census had L.A. County's white population down to 33% and the 2007 estimate was 30%. Meanwhile the Hispanic population was officially 45% in 2000 and probably a majority in 2009. Antonio Villaraigosa's election in 2005 as the first Hispanic Mayor of Los Angeles in over a century symbolized this tremendous ethnic shift. Due to the immigrant bashing of Proposition 187, the Hispanic mobilization sought as long ago by the "Viva Kennedy" effort of 1960 finally occurred. In the 1990 Governor's race, an East Los Angeles Assembly District cast approximately 21,500 votes. A decade later, that figure rose to nearly 56,000, an increase of over 250% with Al Gore defeating Bush 83-15% in East L.A. Unless Republicans can start attracting middle class Hispanics and win back the Asians who used to vote for Reagan, they will be looking at huge losses in Los Angeles County. Los Angeles was founded by Spanish-speaking immigrants from Mexico. With the city of Los Angeles now over 50% Hispanic and the County soon to follow, perhaps Los Angeles is going back to the future.

The key issues in contemporary L.A. County vary by sections. On the West Side, the environment (no offshore oil drilling) and social issues dominate, much as they do on the North Coast. In South Central, on the East Side and in the San Fernando Valley north of downtown, the keys are jobs, poverty, schools, and crime. Further out into the suburbs of the eastern part of the County, traffic and schools are most important. Since the County voted against gay marriage and almost voted for curbing abortion rights, one would have to say that economics has been driving the Democratic Party's gains in Los Angeles in the last fifteen years. Social issues keep the Westside of L.A. Democratic and broader economic issues do the same for the Central, Eastern, and Southern sections of L.A. County.

Of L.A.'s white population, probably 10% are Jewish and another 5% are gays. Both of those groups are liberal on social issues. Therefore, L.A. County is now almost certainly out of reach for a socially conservative Republican presidential nominee from the South. As Schwarzenegger proved, a charismatic mainstream Republican can be very competitive within L.A. County. In order to do well here, Republican candidates in 2010 and beyond would be well advised to mimic the Governator's pro-green, pro-choice, pro-gay rights message.

Southern California: The Good Life Endangered — or Enlarged?

James Q. Wilson said in 1967 that "the important thing to know about Southern California is that the people who live there, who grew up there love it...the way people love the realization that they have found the right place."[1] "Southern California" is defined in this book as the five mostly suburban counties south of the Tehachapi Mountains: Orange, Riverside, San Bernardino, San Diego, and Ventura Counties. (San Diego County is 40% city, 60% suburban). For many years, Southern California was *the* source of Republican victories in the Golden State. The votes of Southern California made Richard Nixon president and help keep Reagan in office as Governor. Now the ethnic shifts overwhelming Los Angeles have reached the Southern California suburbs with blacks, Hispanics and Asians an estimated 52% of the people in 2007. Orange County, nationally famous for launching the Goldwater–Reagan movement in the 1960s has not been immune to these winds of change as it became a "majority of minorities" shortly after 2001. One of the oldest political/demographic rules is that the bigger a constituency gets, the more likely it is to divide. The once white suburban monolith that backed the campaigns of Nixon, Reagan, Deukmejian, and Wilson has now been eroded by massive migrations of minorities to the suburbs who are chasing their own version of the California Dream. San Bernardino and Riverside Counties will soon follow Los Angeles into Hispanic-majority status. Combined with the economic collapse of 1992, the Southern California Republicans have never been the same.

Kevin Phillips once dubbed Florida and the Southwest the "Sun Belt." The Sun Belt was the essence of modern conservatism, and Southern California, especially San Diego and Orange Counties, was the essence of the Sun Belt. Who are these people? Just as important, who were they? Right around the time Phillips wrote about the Sun Belt, the 1970 Census showed Southern California to be 82% white, 2% black, 3% Asian and 13% Hispanic. Since the immigrants were then voting only about a third of their potential strengths, the electorate of Southern California was roughly 90% white in 1968 and 1972 when Southern California native Richard Nixon won the presidency. Southern California is the region that has grown the fastest in the last 50 years, more than tripling its population and raising its share of California's electorate from 15% in 1958 to 28% in 2008. In the last presidential election, Southern California cast nearly four million votes, more than New York City and Philadelphia together.

The "Sun Belt" conservative Republican phenomenon described by Phillips was very real. For an entire generation, from 1960 to 1990, Southern California turned in a string of spectacular performances for GOP candidates that literally changed California and even American history. Southern California and the rest of the Sun Belt (Texas, Florida, and Arizona) were the muscle behind the elections of Nixon, Reagan, and both Bushes.

---

1 James Q Wilson, "A Tour of Reagan Country," *Commentary*, June, 1967.

TABLE 7-7. SUBURBAN SOUTHERN CALIFORNIA SUMMARY

Counties: Orange, Riverside, San Bernardino, San Diego, Ventura		
Population 1960: 2,745,856	Population 2009: 11,317,107	Growth 1960–2009: +312%
Percent of state		
1960	2009	
17%	30%	
Ethnic Breakdown		
1960:	2007:	
87% white	48% white	
3% black	5% black	
1% Asian/Pacific Islander	10% Asian/Pacific Islander	
9% Hispanic	36% Hispanic	
	1% Other	
	4% Mixed Race	
Voter registration		
1958:	2009:	
53% Democrat	36% Democrat	
44% Republican	40% Republican	
3% Decline-to-State	20% Decline-to-State	
1% Other	4% Other	
Best Performance		**Worst Performance**
Democratic:	Alan Cranston (1974 Senate), Jerry Brown (1978 Governor) 53%	Walter Mondale (1984), Tom Bradley & Phil Angelides (1986 & 2006 Gov.), 30%. Cruz Bustamante (2003 recall) 21%
Republican:	Ronald Reagan (1984) 69%	George Bush (1992) 39%
Democratic % and Ranking		
1960s:	2000–2008:	
44%, 6th of 6	41%, 5th of 6	
Voted for State Winner		
1958–2008:	2007:	
69% (4th of 6)	Poor: 11%	College Degrees: 25%

Key Proposition/Special Election votes:	Percent Yes	Statewide
1958 Right-to-work	47%	40%
1964 Repeal Fair Housing	72%	65%
1972 Establish Coastal Commission	52%	55%
1978 Proposition 13	66%	65%
1978 Restore Death Penalty	78%	71%
1982 Gun Control	33%	37%
1988 40% Education budget set-aside	46%	51%
1988 Insurance reform	48%	51%
1990 Term Limits:	58%	52%
1992 Right-to-Die	44%	46%
1994 Proposition 187 — Illegal Immigration	68%	59%
1996 Proposition 209 — Ban Affirmative Action	63%	55%
2003 Recall Gray Davis	69%	55%
2004 Stem Cell research	55%	59%
2006 Road Bonds	59%	61%
2008 Ban Gay Marriage	59%	52%
2008 Abortion — Parental Consent Law	55%	48%

During the Republican post-war 1946–56 period of dominance, Southern California was strongly Republican, even more so than the state as a whole, giving Warren, Knight, Nixon, Knowland and Kuchel all 60% of their votes. In 1958, Pat Brown won Southern California by 52–47%, but well below his state percentage of 60%, making it his worst region. Then in 1960, Southern California conservatives began a run that was doubly impressive because it gave Republicans control of what soon to be the nation's most powerful state.

In 1948, the five counties of Southern California cast just 12% of California's votes compared with 43% for L.A. County as Truman carried the state by one point. By 1960, Southern California's population was growing twice as fast as the state. In the 1960 election, Nixon beat Kennedy by 56–43% in Southern California, providing him with his entire statewide margin of victory. When Ronald Reagan buried Pat Brown in 1966, he carried all six California regions, but Southern California was his best at 66%. By 1968, Southern California's share of the state vote had grown again to nearly 20% and this time it again helped deliver California to Nixon, giving him his margin of victory in the Electoral College. Regardless of what one thinks of the Nixon Presidency, there can be no doubt that history would have been quite different had Humphrey shifted California by two points.

In 1976, a huge margin for Gerald Ford in Southern California (56% and twice his state margin) carried the Golden State for the GOP again and denied Jimmy Carter a national mandate. In 1982, Los Angeles Mayor Tom Bradley was seeking to become the nation's first black governor since Reconstruction. Bradley won narrowly all over the state, not counting Southern California, where a 42%–56% loss sealed his state-wide defeat by one point.

Eight years later, voters in Southern California, especially Orange County and Pete Wilson's hometown of San Diego combined to defeat former San Francisco Mayor Dianne Feinstein in her bid to become California's first woman governor. White sub-urbanites in Southern California were the GOP's base and Orange County was the banner GOP territory. Orange County and the rest of Southern California was the California Republicans' impregnable fortress and secret weapon in a close race as Republican presidential candidates won the state six straight times from 1968–88.

The Republican winning streak came to a screeching halt in 1992, when Bill Clinton carried California by more than 1 million votes. As noted in the L.A. County section above, economics drove the political change of the early 1990s. The end of the Cold War devastated the aerospace industry, as more than 500,000 jobs were lost in Los Angeles County alone. However, some of those L.A. jobs were also lost by commuters from Orange County and the Southern California suburbs.

The first beneficiary of this shift was Ross Perot. Clinton won the same 36% in Southern California as 1988 Democratic candidate Michael Dukakis. However, Perot's split of the conservative vote pretty much wiped out the GOP majority. George Bush the elder carried Southern California by a massive 717,000 vote in 1988, more than twice his state margin. Four years later, President Bush's margin had dropped to only 86,000 as he lost the state badly.

In 1994, Gov. Pete Wilson bounced back, using Proposition 187 to divide white voters from immigrants and carry Southern California by 65–31% and win a 40-point victory in Orange County, but the gain was short-lived. In 1996, President Clinton held Bob Dole to just 47% here with 8% for Perot. Hispanics, mobilized by Proposition 187, turned out in droves, and keyed Loretta Sanchez's upset of right wing Republican Congressman Bob Dornan in the Anaheim area.

By the late-1990s, the ethnic changes that were making Southern California almost half non-white were beginning to trickle down to the voters. Minorities were now casting about 25% of the region's vote compared to a 90% white electorate a generation earlier. Santa Ana in central Orange County was 75% Hispanic in the 2000 Census and nextdoor neighbor Anaheim is also majority-Hispanic. Both Riverside and San Bernardino are now also "majority–minority" with San Bernardino almost as heavily black and Hispanic as Los Angeles County. Only Ventura and San Diego still have white majorities, but they are slowly changing too. The movement of blacks and Hispanics to the Southern California suburbs has given Democrats a small toehold here, which the Democrats have been building on for the past 20 years.

In 1998, Gray Davis actually carried Southern California, the first Democrat to do so since Alan Cranston in 1980, while Barbara Boxer received 44%, an impressive improvement over her 38% six years earlier. The 2000 results proved that 1998 was no fluke. Al Gore held George W. Bush to just 52% in Southern California and his margin in L.A. County was three times the size of the GOP margin in the Southern California suburbs. And Dianne Feinstein won Southern California for the first time in her career. Not surprisingly, both Democrats won the home state of Nixon and Reagan by over a million votes. Schwarzenegger, of course, was strongly popular here in his two elections with 60% in 2003 and 66% in 2006. But he is the only Republican in the last 15 years to rally a huge vote in Southern California. Obama even won Southern California by a few points (51–47%) in 2008, winning all but Orange County.

There is also a subtle coastal/inland split within these largely suburban counties. According to the latest Census data, the Inland Empire counties of Riverside and San Bernardino are more blue-collar, with lower incomes than the coastal counties of Orange, San Diego and Ventura. Bill Leonard, the former Republican Assembly-man of San Bernardino County, says the Inland Empire is more like Fresno than Los Angeles. Most of the growth in Southern California since 1990 has been in the Inland Empire. In the 1960 Census, the Inland Empire counties had 800,000 people and 5% of the state. Today, they have nearly 4.2 million and 11% of the population. Since the coastal areas of Southern California are so built up, most of the future growth will likely come in the Inland Empire. However, will the growing minority base make it more like L.A.?

Minorities, like everyone else want to move to Southern California because they see an improved quality of life — more affordable housing, less crime, better schools, and a quieter lifestyle. The suburban good life that so many white Southern Californians enjoyed after the Second World War is now being enjoyed by millions of non-white immigrants and their children.

Why does the fate of a few suburban counties far away from the nation's capital matter? As real estate agents would say, for three reasons — location, location and location. Southern California's bloc conservative Republican vote could once swing the nation's largest state. The best way of explaining it would be to say that in the 1980s, white Southern California suburbanites cast as many votes as all of New Jersey and were about as conservative as Barry Goldwater's home state of Arizona. With the once-Democratic South moving more Republican every decade, Democrats had to win the West Coast to have any chance of winning an electoral majority. As long as Southern California kept the Golden State in the GOP column, Democratic presidential candidates faced a severe uphill battle, one that Humphrey, McGovern, Carter, Mondale, and Dukakis all lost.

From the Watts riot in 1965 to the end of the Cold War in 1991, the only Democratic president elected was Jimmy Carter, who won almost every Southern state in a Watergate-induced fluke. Now that the "Orange Curtain" has fallen, however, Southern California is no longer turning over massive decisive GOP margins and California is back in the Democratic coalition, Democrats are competitive again nationally.

During the heyday of Republican power in Southern California, Tom Fuentes, the county GOP chairman, told an enthusiastic pre-election rally that Orange County would "anchor the ship of state strongly to the right." That was true two decades ago, but history's wheel has turned. Working-class Asian and Hispanic immigrants have brought down the Orange Curtain and spread though the Southern California suburbs as Republican registration in this region has fallen to just 40% in 2009. Republicans still do well with white suburbanites in Southern California; the first George Bush won 65% from this group in 1988 when he beat Dukakis as did his son sixteen years later when he beat Kerry. But there are just fewer of them compared to twenty years ago and there will be even fewer twenty years from now given the high minority birthrates and continuing immigration.

Orange County and the rest of Southern California will simply no longer turn over the massive conservative majorities Republicans need to overcome Democratic strength in Los Angeles and San Francisco. The right-wing tail will no longer wag the moderate–liberal dog.

The fundamental problem for Republicans is that older Anglos who used to go two-to-one Republican have now been replaced by immigrants who will, at best, someday be swing voters, but are now strong Democrats. California Republicans will have to get away from their diet of strident anti-government conservatism to deal with this new reality.

With a new generation of immigrants tilting both Southern California and the Golden State to the Democrats, the Republican Party will have to change. California Republicans face the same evolutionary challenge that Democrats in the South face — adapt or die. Their task now is to either find a conservative with massive ethnic appeal (no one comes to mind in the current generation of California Republicans) or an outspoken "reform" candidate like Schwarzenegger or Earl Warren.

The Southern California of Ronald Reagan, the Beach Boys, John Wayne, and Howard Jarvis has been replaced by that of Barack Obama, Fernando Valenzuela, Oscar De La Hoya, Los Angeles Mayor Antonio Villaraigosa, Salma Hayek and Los Lobos. It is quite possible that the succeeding generations of the current immigrants will be middle class and conservative. That, however, is a while off. Suburban conservatives are no longer a majority in California, or for that matter, even in the Southern California region.

The key issues in the Southern California suburbs are taxes, real estate, traffic, crime, and immigration. Southern California voted for most of the "social conservative" Propositions like 209, 187, and bans on gay marriage and abortion. Therefore, one would have to say that recent Democratic gains here are due to ethnic shifts and economic concerns.

Rural California: Red Country in a Sea of Blue

Rural California is every county outside the metro areas of Los Angeles, San Diego, the Central Valley cities, the North and Central Coast and the San Francisco Bay Area. They are often referred to as "Mountain Counties." Every county in the Rural category is in Northern California except Imperial County, a farming area on the Mexican Border. Rural California represents the last vestiges of frontier California. It is the part of the state that shown the least growth in raw numbers and demographically, the least change over the last five decades. Of course, it has also shown the most partisan change, moving from being dominated by conservative rural Democrats to Republicans.

Who lives in Rural California? In 1960, Rural California was the most heavily white part of the Golden State at 87%. It still is today at 71% white. (Imperial County, which was 75% Hispanic in 2007, is the exception). While the black and Asian percentages in Rural California have hardly grown, Hispanics have slowly climbed from 9% in 1960 to 22% in 2007. While the Bay Area and all of California south of the

Tehachapi were transformed due to immigration, Rural California is still dominated by the "good old boys."

TABLE 7–8. RURAL CALIFORNIA SUMMARY

Counties: Alpine, Amador, Butte, Calaveras, Colusa, El Dorado, Glenn, Humboldt, Imperial, Inyo, Lake, Lassen, Madera, Mariposa, Modoc, Mono, Nevada, Placer, Plumas, San Benito, Shasta, Sierra, Siskiyou, Sutter, Tehama, Trinity, Tuolomne, Yuba.

Population 1960: 647,359	Population 2009: 1,780,348	Growth 1960–2009: +175%
Percent of state		
1960	2009	
4%	5%	
Ethnic Breakdown		
1960:	2007:	
85% white	71% white	
2% black	2% black	
2% Asian/Pacific Islander	3% Asian/Pacific Islander	
9% Hispanic	22% Hispanic	
	2% Other	
	4% Mixed Race	
Voter registration		
1958:	2009:	
61% Democrat	34% Democrat	
37% Republican	43% Republican	
2% Decline-to-State	18% Decline-to-State	
	5% Other	
Best performance		**Worst performance:**
Democratic:	Claire Engle (1958 Senate) 72%	Phil Angelides (2006 Governor) 25% , Cruz Bustamante (2003 recall) 20%
Republican:	George Deukmejian (1986 Governor) 71%	Goodwin Knight (1958 Senate) 28%
Democratic % and ranking		
1960s:	2000–2008:	
53%, 3rd of 6	37%, 6th of 6	
Voted for State Winner		
1958–2008:	2007:	
62% (6th of 6)	Poor: 18%	College Degrees: 19%

Like the Central Valley, the economy of Rural California is based on extractive industries — once mining and logging, now more agriculture. And like the Central Valley, this area had a tradition of voting for moderate "populist" Democrats such as 1958
Senate candidate Clair Engle (who holds the Democratic record in Rural California
with 72%). Franklin Roosevelt and Harry Truman ran better than their state totals in
Rural California as did Pat Brown in 1958 and 1962. However, the social turmoil of the
1960s hurt Democrats in Rural California just as it did in the Central Valley.

Key Proposition/Special Election votes:	Percent Yes	Statewide
1958 Right-to-work	38%	40%
1964 Repeal Fair Housing	64%	65%
1972 Establish Coastal Commission	48%	55%
1978 Proposition 13	72%	65%
1978 Restore Death Penalty	77%	71%
1982 Gun Control	19%	37%
1988 40% Education budget set-aside	40%	51%
1988 Insurance reform	38%	51%
1990 Term Limits:	59%	52%
1992 Right-to-Die	45%	46%
1994 Proposition 187 — Illegal Immigration	71%	59%
1996 Proposition 209 — Ban Affirmative Action	71%	55%
2003 Recall Gray Davis	69%	55%
2004 Stem Cell research	48%	59%
2006 Road Bonds	52%	61%
2008 Ban Gay Marriage	62%	52%
2008 Abortion — Parental Consent Law	55%	48%

Pat Brown ran three points worse among rural voters than his state percentage in
his 1966 loss to Reagan and a broad change in Rural California voting trends was soon
under way. After the Reagan landslide, Democrats became much more of an urban
party and even successful Democrats like Alan Cranston and Jerry Brown in the 1970s
generally ran worse in Rural California than they did statewide.

The streaming away from the Democrats in Rural California during the 1970s
became a flood in the 1980s when the Democratic nominee for Governor was the
black Mayor of Los Angeles. Tom Bradley received only 39% from Rural California in
1982 and 26% in 1986. While Rural California did not deliver Deukmejian's margin
of victory, as did the Central Valley and Southern California, it did give Deukmejian
his highest percentage in both years. (Deukmejian won statewide by 93,000 in 1982
and carried Rural California by 81,000 votes). The issue that damaged Democrats in

Rural California was guns as much race; the handgun control Proposition 15 lost by 19–81% in the rural areas and Jerry Brown ran 4 points worse than Bradley. The 1980s continued, and capped, the Democrats' decline in Rural California, from an average of 52% in the 1960s, to 48% in the 1970s and collapsing to just 38% in the 1980s. Even though the California Democrats re-emerged as the majority party in the last two decades, they are not doing much better in Rural California. The good news for California Republicans is they have averaged a 55–37% lead in Rural California over the last decade. The bad news for Republicans is Rural California casts less than 10% of the total vote and the GOP is being swamped in the big urban areas of Los Angeles and San Francisco.

Is it possible that Rural California could become the next boom area like the Central Valley or the Inland Empire? Certainly yes, because the big coastal urban areas like San Francisco and L.A. are so crowded. However, the guess here is that the North & Central Coast will become the next destination for retiring Baby Boomers in the coming decade. Rural California will likely be the last region to go through a massive boom.

Since the 1960s, Rural California has generally voted conservative on both social (Fair Housing, guns, gays, abortion) and economic (Proposition 13, insurance reform) initiatives. Whatever economic populism existed in Rural California has been overridden by the social issues. The key issues in Rural California are agriculture, economic development, and guns. It is not likely that Democrats can reclaim their competitiveness here due to their social liberalism and stance on gun control.

ETHNIC AND SOCIAL GROUPS IN CALIFORNIA

One side effect of California's diversity is ethnic friction. Unlike a mostly white state, like Vermont, there has been plenty of ethnic conflict in the last 150 years, from the Chinese Exclusion Act to the Internment of the Japanese during World War II, to the Zoot Suits riots of the 1940s, to the L.A. riots of 1965 and 1992, to the loud arguments over immigration and affirmative action.

For roughly a quarter century, from the election of Ronald Reagan in 1966 to Pete Wilson in 1990, California Republicans benefited from ethnic friction. Republican victories came from attracting the votes of angry white Democrats. Republicans like Nixon, Reagan, Murphy, Deukmejian, and Wilson were quite ruthless in exploiting these ethnic divisions to win elections. Besides division, some of these Republicans victories also relied on a low turnout of minorities. As Kevin Phillips wrote, "given the ethnocentricity of white Southern California, the Negro-Mexican population is large enough to provoke white anger and counter-solidarity but seemingly not large enough to achieve a balance of power."[1]

The Republican "backlash" era ended in 1992, when the recession, exacerbated by cuts in defense spending, pummeled the Los Angeles area. Bill Clinton convinced the Reagan Democrats to come home. Republicans, led by Pete Wilson, panicked and reached back to racial divisiveness for one last big victory. Then the black and Mexican population of Greater L.A. got strong enough to do more than "achieve a balance of power." They almost completely wiped out California Republicans. By the end of

---

1 Phillips, *The Emerging Republican Majority*, 446.

the 1990s, Clinton and Company had re-united white and minority Democrats, plus added independents and a few Republicans. The California GOP was left with just a shrinking core of suburban conservatives and the rural voters who are less than 5% of the state. The "anti-intellectual and ethnocentric" politics of California Republicans led them to a dead end. The Democrats now have a broad multi-ethnic coalition that fits the New California and has proved formidable since 1992.

A Note on White Voters

Unlike white voters in Texas (74% for Bush in 2004) or Mississippi (88% for Mc-Cain in 2008), white voters in California are not a solid racial bloc. In fact, they are all over the map, generally voting in patterns that can be linked more to sex, class, ideology, geography, and religion than to race. Bay Area residents, women, lower-income and urban whites, liberals and Jewish voters usually go Democratic, while wealthy non-Jews, men, rural voters, conservatives, Southern California suburbanites and born-again Christians vote Republican. To write that a certain candidate got x percent of the white vote in California would be to miss several key nuances. Perhaps the better way to look at the Golden State white electorate is to see which sets of white voters are voting for whom. Back in their 1966–90 winning days, California Republicans usually received the 55–60% of the white vote they needed to win statewide, most often from white voters in the Southern California suburbs, Central Valley and Rural California. Since white voters were over 80% of the electorate, a 60% showing was enough to guarantee a GOP victory (60% of 84% equals 50%, any Republican votes from minorities were pure bonus). But it was rare for Republicans to exceed 60% among white voters as Republicans now consistently do in the South. Only Reagan in 1966 and 1984 and Deukmejian in 1986 were able to achieve that goal. There were simply too many moderate and liberals whites in California, especially in the big cities, for Democrats to write the state off, unlike Wyoming or Nebraska, for example.

California Republicans have had an across-the-board decline among white votes since the 1980s with the biggest losses coming in white liberal areas (-10), among the L.A. County white working class (-11), in the Bay Area suburbs (-14) and among Bay Area white workers (-15). Overall, the Republicans' average lead among white voters dropped from 57–39% in the 1980s to just 49–44% in the last decade. That is a fatal decline for a party that consistently loses among minorities and is dependent on white voters.

Asian-Americans: Affluent, Educated, Assimilated

Demographic Background

Although some Asian activists are mildly embarrassed by the "Model Minority" label, the fact is that this stereotype is mostly accurate. The latest Census data from 2007 show that nearly half (47%) of Asians in California over age 25 have at least a college degree, compared to 37% of whites, 21% of blacks and 10% of Hispanics. Since in California's technically advanced society, income often rises with education levels, it's not surprising that Asians have emerged as the wealthiest racial group in the Golden State. Such success should have made them prime targets for Republicans, but the GOP squandered this opportunity with reckless immigrant bashing in the 1990s and Schwarzenegger is the only Republican to have carried this constituency in the last decade.

Asians have had a presence in California since the Gold Rush in 1849. However, the latest wave of immigration from Asia was jump-started by the Immigration Reform Act of 1965, which abolished the "national quota" system that had maintained numerical dominance for mostly European immigrants. The first wave of Asian immigrants came mainly from Japan and China after the Civil War and worked as farmers or on the new Western railroads.

A look at recent Census data indicates that immigrants from South and East Asia are succeeding so rapidly that they may earn the title of the next "super-Americans." On average, Asian-Americans in California are better educated, more prosperous and less afflicted with social problems like crime and divorce than the national average. Once the victims of ferocious discrimination, Japanese, Korean and Chinese-Americans are now solidly in the professional/ownership ranks.

The Census Bureau defines Asian-Americans as "those having origins in any of the original peoples of the Far East, Southeast Asia or the Indian subcontinent, including, for example: Cambodia, China, India, Japan, Korea, Laos, Malaysia, Pakistan, the Philippines, Thailand and Vietnam." In the 1960 Census, Asians and Pacific Islanders made up 2% of California's population or slightly more than 300,000. Japanese-Americans were the largest Asian sub-group at 157,000, followed by the Chinese at 96,000, Filipinos at 65,000, those from India (39,000) and all other Asians, including Koreans, at 21,000.

By 2000, the Asian population was up to 11% — and with a growth rate that averaged 500% over the past generation. And given the vast numbers of undocumented immigrants, the true number of Americans with at least one Asian parent is more than 12% and heading toward 16 to 20% by 2020. While there are greater raw numbers of Hispanic immigrants, the Asian share of the population is growing faster in terms of percentages — multiplying by a factor of six since 1960. With China and India both having more than a billion people, these trends will likely continue.

Besides mushrooming in size, the Asian-American community also went through extensive internal change. Prior to the 1965 law, Japanese-Americans accounted for more than half of all Asian-Americans. Forty years later, the Chinese are the largest Asian sub-group (23%), followed by Filipinos (20%), Asian Indians (16%), Koreans (10%), Vietnamese (10%), and the Japanese (9%). There are currently over 1 million Chinese and Filipinos living in California with over 500,000 Vietnamese, Koreans and Asian Indians.

Where have the 4 million post-1965 immigrants and their children settled? According to the 2007 Census estimates, one third of all Asian-Americans live in the Bay Area, particularly San Francisco (over 30% Asian), San Mateo, and Santa Clara Counties (where many work in the computer software industry). Another 30% live in Los Angeles County, especially in San Gabriel Valley suburbs like Monterey Park (64%), Walnut (59%), Rosemead (57%), Arcadia (56%), and Alhambra (52%). In addition, roughly 11% of California Asians live in Orange County. The Central Valley (9%), the

North & Central Coast (5%), and Rural California (3%) have below-average Asian populations.

Asian Politics

Of non-white minorities, Asians are the most bipartisan. Hawaii is unique for its Asian majority and has been a Democratic stronghold since just after it became a state in 1959. Beginning in 1962, when Japanese-American politicians led by Daniel Inouye built a powerful political machine, the Aloha State voted Republican only in landslide years like 1972 or 1984, when Presidents Nixon and Reagan each carried 49 states.

On the West Coast, Asians tend to assimilate quickly into the local political mainstream. In liberal areas like San Francisco or L.A., they tend to be Democrats. On the other hand, they vote Republican in the more conservative Southern California suburbs. Orange County in 2004 elected the first Vietnamese-American to any state legislature when Republican Assemblyman Van Tran won in the Little Saigon area. Observers note that most Asian-American legislators tend to be practical problem-solvers rather than partisan ideologues.

Statewide Asian Voting Trends, 1958–2008

Since Asians were only 2% of California's population in the 1960s and less than 2% of the actual voters, polling data is hard to come by. So this book uses precinct data from San Francisco's Chinatown neighborhood for the elections of 1958 through 1968. The 1960 Census showed that the only overwhelmingly Asian enclave (i.e., over 80% Asian) in California was Chinatown. By the 1970s, when the Asian population topped 1 million people, Asians began to be sampled by the Field Poll and exit polls. Therefore, in the 1970 elections, this book switches to using statewide polls to measure Asian voting trends.

Like many big-city voters, the residents of Chinatown were Democrats in the 1960s. Pat Brown received 75% in Chinatown in 1958, substantially more than his rural running mate Clair Engle's 62%. All through the 1960s, Chinatown turned over impressive Democratic majorities; 58% for JFK, 75% for LBJ in 1964, 61% for Pat Brown in 1966, 62% for Humphrey and 70% for Alan Cranston in 1968. Democrats averaged 62% in Chinatown for the decade 1958–68. The only Republican to carry Chinatown in the 1960s was the liberal Thomas Kuchel in 1962, although Nixon with his fierce anti-Communist reputation did get 48% there when he ran against Pat Brown in 1962.

In partisan elections during the 1970s, the Field Poll, *Los Angeles Times* and network exit polls showed that Asians went a perfect eight for eight in picking winners of statewide elections. But what about their ideology? Using voting patterns on the various Propositions, one can make an educated guess on what Asians believe. The Field Poll showed that Asians favored Proposition 13 at a margin very close to the statewide yes vote. They also voted heavily for the death penalty in 1978, against firing gay teachers and to ban busing — just like the rest of the state. During the 1980s, the Asian community's votes on gun control, Proposition 65 (water pollution regulations), ousting Rose Bird, and insurance reform were very similar to the state average. On most issues, Asian voters were in the California mainstream. Two interesting patterns stand out among Asian voters. First, they are very tough on crime, supporting the death penalty and the "3-strikes" law solidly, and second, they are also consistent votes for reform measures like term limits, open primaries and redistricting reform. But perhaps one should not be surprised that a largely middle and upper class group would strongly support "law-and-order" and "good government" principles.

During the conservative 1980s, Asian-Americans drifted toward the Republican Party as much of the nation did. President Reagan particularly had a close relationship with the Asian community, dating back to the 1940s when he publicly opposed the internment of Japanese-Americans. He was the first conservative Republican to carry the Asian vote in his 1970 gubernatorial campaign and was rewarded with more than 60% of the Asian vote in 1984. (President Reagan also signed a bill granting reparations to the World War II internees). Thanks to Reagan's popularity, Republicans had an average lead of 51–47% among Asians in the 1980s. Bill Schneider once described the phenomenon of "anti-communist refugees" voting for conservatives with the classic example being the anti-Castro Cubans in Florida. The Vietnamese voters of Orange County also fit that description — as did some Chinese-American voters during the Reagan years.

However, Republicans lost much of this support when they supported Proposition 187 to deny illegal immigrants public services. Dianne Feinstein had carried the Asian vote narrowly in her gubernatorial loss in 1990 and easily in her 1992 win. In 1994, Asians supported Feinstein again and Democratic gubernatorial candidate Kathleen Brown due to the Proposition 187 issue (the *L.A. Times* exit poll had Asians voting 47–53% against Proposition 187. Since then, majorities of Asians have voted to keep affirmative action and against banning collection of racial data. They split evenly on gay marriage in 2008). According to Assemblyman Warren Furutani (who is Japanese-American), Pete Wilson's vehement immigrant-bashing scared Asian voters by reviving memory of past discrimination, whether it was the Japanese internment camps or the "No Asians Need Apply" signs of the 1930s. Republicans then compounded this damage when they put anti-immigrant language in their 1996 platform, dropping Bob Dole to 40% with Asians against Clinton. According to Assemblyman Furutani, Republicans further offended the Asian Community when they were targeted for investigations of the Clinton fundraising operations shortly after the election. In 1998, Gray Davis won 67% in the Asian community, the best showing for a Democrat since Jerry Brown in 1978. George W. Bush attempted to repair the damage in the last two elections and posted modest gains with Asian-Americans compared to Dole and Lundgren. Moreover, Schwarzenegger, as a pro-business, socially tolerant moderate Republican, certainly has proved popular with Asians, doing the best in this community since Reagan. However, his was personal popularity. Feinstein and Boxer continued to win easily among Asians and the 2008 economic crisis allowed Obama to poll 64% from California Asians. (President Obama was also helped by the fact that he grew up in Hawaii and Indonesia and has Asian in-laws).

In general, Indian, Japanese, and Filipinos are the most Democratic Asian voters with Korean and Vietnamese the least and Chinese being a swing vote unless Dianne Feinstein is running. Reagan was the most popular Republican in the Asian community, while Pat Brown and Feinstein have been the most popular Democrats.

Since they comprise a smaller portion of the population than Hispanics, Asians are more likely to have an impact on the economy and the academic/scientific world than the political scene. However, as 2000 and 2004 reminded us all, in close elections, every vote counts. Moreover, with a growth rate more than three times the national average, their political influence can only grow.

Many Asian-American activists still feel that the community does not get the political attention it deserves. However, this problem is slowly being solved by the weight of numbers (their share of the electorate has risen from 3% in 1992 to 6% in 2008) and Asian skill at fundraising and coalition-building. The State Legislature now has a record 11 Asian members or 9% of all legislators, slightly more than the Asian share of the voters, if not the population. On the State Board of Equalization, which oversees taxes, three of the four members were Asian before Judy Chu's election to Congress.. In addition, State Controller John Chiang has gotten much publicity during the state budget crisis. He will be a candidate for Governor or Senator sometime in the next decade.

If present trends continue and the Asian and Hispanic populations increase at more than twice the national average, by 2040 we could see a competition for national influence among Hispanics (roughly 20%), Asians (15%) and African-Americans (15%), with (ironically) the white minority holding the balance of power. Such a process is already under way in cities like San Jose and San Francisco and in some suburbs of Los Angeles.

California Blacks: Struggle and Triumph

Demographic Background

As the land of fresh starts and bold dreams, it was also thought that California might be the Promised Land for African Americans. Although many of their material dreams came true, increasing social problems after 1965 helped derail the goal of economic equality and many of their political hopes until the 2006 and 2008 political cycles when much was accomplished. Prior to that, there seemed to be a "glass ceiling" for African American candidates. Legislative offices were certainly attainable, big-city mayors were elected, minor statewide posts such as Lt. Governor and Schools Superintendent had been won, but the big prizes of Governor and US Senator looked to be out of reach. Now with blacks winning state legislative races in the Southern California suburbs and with Obama carrying California with 8.2 million votes and by a 3.2 million-vote margin, one must conclude that race will no longer be an insurmountable barrier to a good candidate.

Since California achieved statehood in 1850, its African American population has always been less than the national average. Slavery was banned under Mexican laws through the 1840s, so there was no existing base of former slaves, as in the South. There were less than 1,000 blacks in the 1850 Census. After the First World War, the first "Great Migration" of African-Americans from the South to the cities of the North and West began. In the 1920s, the African American population in California more than doubled, but still stood at only 1.4% of the state because numerous whites and Mexicans were also coming to California. During the World War II, a second great migration happened as African Americans, especially women, came to work in the wartime defense industries. In the 1940s, the African American population more than tripled to 462,000. Since the 1950 Census, the African American population has increased by nearly 2 million, giving California the second largest black population after New York. But at the same time, the white population increased by more than 10 million, Asians by more than 4 million and Hispanics by a stunning 11 million. In short, the African American population has failed to keep pace and never gotten above the 6–8% range.

However, politics in California has always been about more than raw numbers; personality and ideas count too. One very attractive quality of the West's growth and need for labor is that it encourages acceptance of other cultures. So for tasks large (building ships and planes during World War II, completing the Trans-continental railroad) or small (a family farm's grape harvest), the West's labor shortages make the region tolerant by necessity. And that has certainly been in true in California where literally millions of immigrants and migrants have found work.

Black Politics since 1932

Most California blacks, like most American blacks were Republicans due to the memory of Lincoln at the turn of the last century. Even a majority of African Americans stayed loyal to Herbert Hoover in the Depression year of 1932 when African American unemployment/poverty rates were approaching 50%. Led by Augustus Hawkins, who ousted California's first African American legislator, Republican Assemblyman Frederick Roberts, in 1934, California's black community largely became Democrats in the Roosevelt–Truman Era. With his New Deal relief programs, FDR became a hero to black America. "A lot of blacks are still voting for him (Roosevelt) and he's been dead for 40 years," commented Republican activist Gerti Thomas in 1987. Liberal Republicans like Warren, Knight and Kuchel occasionally would win 25–30% of the African American vote in the 1950s, but Pat Brown received 90% in urban black precincts in 1958. Under Governor Pat Brown and Speaker Jess Unruh, California became a pioneer in social legislation, with laws to ban discrimination in jobs and housing before the federal Civil Rights Acts were passed. After Pat Brown's extremely strong showing with African Americans in 1962 (93%), Lyndon Johnson pushed these levels even higher by passing the Civil Rights Act in 1964. Republican nominee Barry Goldwater pursued a "Southern Strategy" of appealing to white voters by opposing civil rights laws. Johnson carried black voters in California by 98–2%.

Watching the tense racial brawling in Birmingham, Alabama in 1963, Pat Brown predicted that such racial strife was highly unlikely in California due to his civil rights laws and anti-poverty programs. Unfortunately for Governor Pat Brown and for the state, this prediction was proved disastrously wrong in Watts two years later. The 1965 Watts Riots changed the political landscape.

Voters viewed Watts through a distinct racial prism. Whites saw a breakdown in order, while blacks cited poverty, discrimination, and police brutality. However, the white majority's view would rule and they were in an angry "backlash" mode.

As is well known, the resentments of the suburbs, especially the "Berkeley–Watts-crime-high taxes" social issue matrix, drove Ronald Reagan's campaign to an easy million-vote victory. In many ways, Reagan would use the African American community, especially the urban underclass, as his foil for the rest of his career. The result was that according to precinct studies done by NBC News and the Field Poll, Reagan never won more than 5% of the African American vote. Until George Deukmejian and Pete Wilson came along, Reagan was the most racially divisive governor in California history.

Reagan, Deukmejian, and Wilson were California Republican governors who seemed to go out of their way to antagonize African Americans. Reagan made opposition to black interests a conservative staple. Deukmejian used hardball negative (some say racist) tactics against the first serious black candidate for governor. Wilson had a moderate record as Mayor of San Diego on civil rights. In 1994, the L.A. Times exit poll showed that he scored gains with the African American middle class, nearly doubling his share of the black vote in that big Republican year. But he immediately frittered away these gains by endorsing Proposition 209 to ban affirmative action in order to cynically revive his failing presidential ambitions. Schwarzenegger is the only California Republican nominee for president, governor, or Senator to exceed 20% of the black vote since Warren and Knight in the 1950s. Future Republicans would be wise to follow his path rather than the Reaganites.

However, Reagan's reign as Governor had one surprising impact on the African American community; it motivated them to vote. From the 1960s on, black turnout has usually come close to white turnout and vastly exceeded Hispanic turnout. The late Sixties saw an energizing of the African American vote that eventually produced results. In 1969, Tom Bradley almost got elected Mayor of Los Angeles, then prepared for another run in 1973. From 1970 to 1981 was the heyday of emerging black political power in California. In 1970, Wilson Riles ousted the outspoken rightwing Max Rafferty as Superintendent of Public Instruction, becoming California first African American elected statewide official. A study of hiring in state government during the 1980s found that African Americans were over-represented in state and L.A. County jobs. In 1973, Bradley won his rematch with Mayor Sam Yorty, building a coalition of African Americans, Jews and Hispanics that would run the city for 20 years. Willie Brown was elected Speaker of the Assembly and promoted several black legislators like Maxine Waters to key committee chairs. Mervin Dymally was elected Lt. Governor in the Democratic landslide of 1974. Also in the 1970s, Berkeley, Oakland and Richmond elected their first black mayors. After being re-elected in 1981 with 63% and carrying every district in the city, Mayor Bradley became the frontrunner for Governor in 1982. It seemed that the West Coast offered a new paradigm of ethnic politics where race did not really matter.

However, the promise of overcoming race in politics was never quite fulfilled. In the Proposition 13 year of 1978, Lt. Governor Dymally was defeated, and Bradley lost the 1982 and 1986 gubernatorial campaigns. For the next 25 years after 1982, no African American candidate even came close to winning a statewide office; none were even nominated by California Democrats.

All through the 1990s and early part of the 2000s, African Americans seemed to be losing ground politically. Partly due to the cuts mandated by Proposition 13, the black big-city mayors failed to reverse inner city poverty. Willie Brown was forced to leave the State Assembly by term limits. The African American Democrats in the California Congressional delegation lost their committees after the Republican takeover of 1994. Richard Riordan, a white Republican businessman, succeeded Bradley in Los Angeles. African American candidates for the legislature were simply not winning seats outside of solidly black districts, unlike Asian and Hispanic who were beginning to pick up influence due to increased turnout and population growth. Elihu Harris, the former Mayor of Oakland, suffered the ultimate humiliation of losing to a Green Party candidate in a special Assembly election in 1999. After the Harris defeat, no African American represented a legislative seat in the Bay Area for the first time since Byron Rumford's election in 1948. In the 1999 Legislative Session, there were as many Latino Republicans in the State Assembly as African Americans — four members.

Many political analysts blamed the African American leadership for focusing solely on racial issues and failing to build coalitions with moderate whites and other minorities. Black activists countered that they faced worst prejudice than other groups. Both points were true. Encouraged by the New Right and talk radio, conservatives gleefully scored politically by portraying African American politicians as captives of a violent, drug-addicted, welfare-dependent urban underclass. On the other hand, after Mayor Bradley left the scene in L.A., no African American politician has remotely shown his ability to attract votes beyond the black community. In several Assembly districts in the Bay Area and Los Angeles County, seats formerly won by blacks had Asian or Hispanic replacements.

The conventional wisdom on African American voters is that they are liberals on both social and economic issues. That is still true on economic questions, but a majority of blacks (and Hispanics) voted to require "parental notice" before a minor could get an abortion and also against gay marriage. Whether this new trend of African American cultural conservatism on non-racial issues continues will be a fascinating question.

Blacks and Hispanics have voted the same in partisan elections since 1958 for all 45 Democratic nominees for president, governor, and senator. They are not swing voters at all. Before there were exit polls, Lyndon Johnson won an estimated 98% in predominantly black precincts due to his successful push for the 1964 Civil Rights Act and Goldwater's opposition. Not surprisingly, Bradley and Obama did the best among African Americans, with exit polls in the 95–97% range, while Angelides had the Democratic low of 70%. Schwarzenegger in his 2006 re-election campaign turned in the best GOP performance among blacks with 27% with Goldwater in 1964, Deukmejian in 1982 and McCain in 2008 bringing up the rear with less than 5%. Obviously, a non-celebrity Republican would have a tough time matching Schwarzenegger's showing in 2010 as polls show that African American voters are very much enthralled with President Obama.

Black political prospects did not measurably improve until 2006 when Ms. Amina Carter was elected to the State Assembly from San Bernardino County, the first time an African American candidate had won in the Inland Empire suburbs. The Black Legislative Caucus is now up to nine members, its high water mark. Ironically, for all the talk a decade ago of black influence fading, the percentage of African Americans in the Legislature (7.5%) now exceeds their share of the population (6%).

Obviously, the biggest (and best) news for the African American community was Obama's record-breaking 2008 landslide in California, winning more votes here in both raw numbers and percentages than Reagan ever did. The old truism that there was a hidden anti-black vote was overwhelmed by the desires of California for change. The "Bradley Effect" did not entirely disappear. A map on the cover of the *New York Times* showed a slice of territory in the South and Border states where Obama actually lost some Kerry voters from 2004. However, no California counties were in that category as the Golden State was hit hardest by the mortgage meltdown and swung toward Obama. Also, times have changed and the combination of older white voters being replaced by Hispanics and Asians and white voters also becoming more tolerant added up to a massive Obama victory. We can now truly say that any quality candidate can win in California regardless of race. However, despite this good news, there is currently no African American candidate who is favored to win statewide office in 2010. San Francisco District Attorney Kamala Harris is running for Attorney General, but the liberal baggage of her hometown (she opposes the death penalty and has talked of de-criminalizing prostitution) could sink her, just as it might hurt San Francisco Mayor Gavin Newsom. Perhaps the best bet for a African American governor or US Senator would be a black celebrity, either an entertainer or sports figure. Before he was stricken with AIDS, basketball star Magic Johnson talked of running for L.A. Mayor and then governor. Actors Will Smith and Denzel Washington have also been mentioned as possible candidates.

Whichever black candidates run in 2010 and beyond, if they avoid the "radical" label, they can win. Thanks to the Obama victory, things really have changed for black candidates.

Hispanics: The Sleeping Giant Awoken

Demographic Background

For years, even decades, Hispanics have been described as the "sleeping giant" of California politics. Their slumber lasted a whole generation and might have gone on for another had not California Republicans made a fatal error that shocked them awake. Studies done by the Census Bureau and exit polls repeatedly showed that all through the 1960s, '70 and '80s, Hispanics were only voting at one quarter to one third of their potential strength. The combination of low citizenship rates, poverty, and youth consistently led to low Hispanic turnouts. After her narrow 1990 loss for Governor, Dianne Feinstein spoke for many Establishment Democrats when she said that the Party could not count on the poor to vote and must woo the middle class. Then events came to the Democrats' rescue; the deepest recession since 1945 caused the election of Bill Clinton in 1992, the first Democratic nominee to carry California since 1964. In response to the Clinton victory, Governor Pete Wilson and the California Republican Party turned to immigrant bashing as a way to recover in 1994. It worked in the short run, but achieved what was previously believed to be impossible — Wilson shook the "Sleeping Giant" wide awake. Over the next dozen years, Hispanic turnout rose by over 300% in an unprecedented mobilization. Sometimes, having a good old-fashioned political villain works better than a hero and Wilson played the villain's role to the hilt, engaging in constant disputes with the Latino Community. Hispanics are now a solid presence in Sacramento with 23% of all legislators with the big upsurge coming in the 1990s as term limits forced the older generation of mostly white office-holders to retire. Cruz Bustamante was the first Hispanic elected to statewide office in a century, and in the next decade, Hispanics will be in strong contention for governor and the US Senate. This change has happened so quickly that it is forgotten how long it was in coming. Nevertheless, it is definitely here to stay and Hispanics will be major players in 2010 and beyond.

Spanish-speaking explorers discovered the American Southwest for Europeans and California, Texas, Arizona, Nevada, Colorado, New Mexico, Wyoming, and Utah were once part of Mexico. Therefore, Hispanics have always had a major impact on California culture. After the immigration laws were changed in the mid-1960s, Hispanics had a large impact on the economy. Finally, in the mid-1990s, they started to have a major political impact as well.

To give a very brief history, Spanish-speaking immigrants from Mexico were a majority of California's tiny population when gold was discovered in 1848. A year later, 100,000 persons from all over the world had come to California and Hispanics were below 10% of the population where their share stayed until the Second World War. In the 1940 Census, Hispanics were only 6% of Californians. In the 1940s, California agribusiness interests began to recruit farm workers from Mexico to meet wartime labor shortages and Congress later formalized the guest-worker ("Bracero") program. In the 1950 Census, the number of Hispanics had increased sharply and the population boom and poverty of Latin America guaranteed a steady source of immigration. By 1960, Hispanics were nearly 10% of the state, and probably higher due to undercounting.

Due to their relative poverty, labor ties and (sometimes) minority consciousness, Hispanics have always been registered Democrats. All of their political heroes in the old days — Al Smith, FDR, Pat Brown, JFK — were Democrats. According to studies of predominantly Hispanic precincts done by NBC News, no Republican candidate in the 1960s surpassed 25% of the Hispanic vote, not even Reagan. The Field Poll Archive backs up this conclusion. (As exit poll data was not available until the 1970s, we use barrio precincts in 90%-plus Hispanic East Los Angeles to estimate older Hispanic voting trends). Since the Democrats were the party of labor, Republicans had little to say to the working class Hispanic neighborhoods.

Then in 1965, the most significant event in the history of Hispanic America occurred. Congress passed the Immigration Reform Act, which abolished a notorious quota system that had been designed to maintain the nation's ethnic balance. For example, if 3% of the population was of Italian descent, then no more than 3% of the new immigrants could be from Italy. The new law abandoned national quotas in favor of a "demand" system (that almost, by definition, favored the most populous Third World nations), expressed a preference for "family unification" (so immigrants could then send for family members) and increased legal immigration limits. Although signed by President Johnson after JFK's death, the 1965 Immigration Reform Act promoted by President Kennedy, drafted by Attorney General Robert Kennedy and pushed through the Senate by Ted Kennedy resulted in a wave of immigration from the Third World and has been called "the Kennedy's family greatest gift to the Democratic Party."

The Immigration Reform Act had an immediate impact on the Southwest. Immigrants, legal and illegal, began pouring over the Mexican borders. Since then, their population has exploded. The number of California Hispanics rose by over 1.3 million "officially" in the 1970 Census, nearly doubling and there was probably a 10% undercount. By 1980, Hispanics (4.5 million) were up to 19% of Californians and jumped up to 26% (nearly 7.7 million residents) in 1990.

Hispanic Politics from 1960

For all of their population growth, Hispanics had little impact on the politics of the late 1960s as the Vietnam War and race riots were the leading issues. All this social turmoil led, of course, to the rise of the Reagan Coalition in 1966. Even though Pat Brown, Hubert Humphrey and Jess Unruh all received bloc votes in East L.A., they still could not beat Reagan and Nixon. The strength of this new conservative alignment was demonstrated when Presidents Nixon, Reagan and the first Bush combined most of the Wallace vote with traditional Republican business support to carry California 6 straight times from 1968 to1988. Back then, it seemed that California Democrats faced a chronic deficit of white votes and Hispanics were then too young a constituency to be mobilized.

As a social and economic symbol, Mexican farm workers came to the fore in the Central Valley when Cesar Chavez began to organize them and he made the cover of *Time*. Hispanics occasionally affected state politics, as in the close 1974 gubernatorial election when Jerry Brown lost the white vote, but his 3-point victory margin was provided by the black and Hispanic communities. Despite being almost 20% of California's people, Hispanics were only about 5–6% of the actual voters. For at least two decades after the Immigration Reform Act was passed, Hispanics were slow to register because some were only residents and not full citizens yet, or too young to vote, and many were more interested in working for economic advancement and even survival, than politics.

As it was, the Hispanic population kept growing, but not their share of voters. About once a decade, Democratic leaders and Hispanic activists were hopeful a new era of rising Hispanic turnout was imminent, but these were a series of false starts. After Chavez organized the Farm Workers in the late 1960s, it was widely assumed that Hispanics would follow blacks into heavy politics, but it did not occur. After Hispanics helped Jerry Brown become governor, some thought the Hispanic political moment had arrived, but it hadn't. In 1982, Tom Bradley's camp was stunned by the low Hispanic turnout and this helped cost him the election. While the percentage of California blacks voting has pretty much been equal to that of Anglos since the 1960s, Hispanic (and Asian) turnout has lagged badly. From about 1970 to 1990, Hispanics voted at only 25–30% of their potential strength.

Unlike the black vote, which Republicans had pretty much written off after 1964 with their (white) Southern strategy, GOP presidents Nixon and Reagan courted the Hispanic vote with "family values" speeches and some appointments. Reagan's efforts — along with a booming California economy that helped create an emerging

Hispanic middle class — were rewarded as the GOP made steady incremental gains among Hispanics in the 1980s. In 1974, Jerry Brown had swept 84% of the Hispanic vote in his successful gubernatorial bid. By 1984, at least a third of Hispanics were supporting President Reagan (as were over 60% of Asians). In the 1982 governor's race, George Deukmejian's 23% showing among Hispanics contributed to his narrow 1-point win and ironically, Wilson in 1990 got crucial votes from Hispanics and Asians in his narrow win. If either the Duke or Wilson had lost the Hispanics by four-to-one as Lundgren did in 1998, they would not have been governor. By 1990, the GOP had doubled its share of the Hispanic vote from the low-point of 1974 (see Appendix 2).

For much of this time, when the California economy was growing spectacularly, not too many people seemed to care about the state's changing demographics. However, that situation changed radically in the recession of the early 1990s. Pete Wilson was elected in 1990 as a moderate Republican. Upon taking office, Wilson had to sign a then record $8.6 billion tax increase to keep the state solvent and the schools open. Wilson was hit with so many disasters in his first term — recession, fires, floods, earthquakes, race riots, government shutdowns, etc. — that Joe Scott called "the perils of Pete" and Wilson himself later joked that they had every "Biblical plague but locusts." Sure enough, California agriculture was soon threatened by a bizarre insect called the glassy-winged sharpshooter.

By 1992, Clinton, Feinstein, and Boxer were riding a wave of popular demand for change and swept the state, including the Hispanic vote. Meanwhile, Wilson's job approval ratings were down in the 20% range and he was 23 points behind Kathleen Brown in the Field Poll. Republicans were in a full-scale panic. White "Reagan Democrats" appeared to be coming back home and they were about to lose the governor's office again to a third member of the hated Brown Dynasty.

Wilson then turned to what can sometime be the most devastating strategy — when all else fails, change the subject. Wilson hitched his re-election to an initiative known as Proposition 187 that sought to deny social services to illegal immigrants and their children, and required teachers to report any suspected illegal aliens to the government. He ran ads showing immigrants sneaking across the Mexican border with the tag line "they just keep coming" and attacking Brown for opposing Proposition 187. This strategy worked superbly in the short run. Both Proposition 187 and Wilson won by more than a million votes.

However, beneath the surface of the GOP victories were some interesting trends: Wilson made significant gains among white (+6%) and black (+9%) voters, but Brown carried the Asian vote narrowly and Hispanics by three to one. For the first time ever, the Asian and Hispanic vote moved in the opposite direction of white voters. Previously, the immigrants had swung along with the broad (mostly white) electorate.

The record Asian and Hispanic turnout was another sign of realignment. Proposition 187 was the proximate cause of these changes as the immigrants voted identically on the governor's race and the so-called "Save Our State" initiative. Proposition 187 shook the Hispanic giant out of its slumber because it threatened the one thing they consider most precious — their children.

Most immigrants express a libertarian desire to be left alone. They usually do not ask for anything special from the government. However, denying health care and education to immigrant children and turning teachers into INS agents went too far. Many Hispanics and a good number of Asians saw Wilson's ads as race baiting. In addition, Wilson's claim that immigrants were a burden to the state was a bad rap; Asians and Hispanics both have higher-than-state-average labor force-participation rates and lower divorce rates.

Hispanic activists wondered whether Proposition 187 and Wilson would finally be the cause of increasing Hispanics turnout. The 1994 election and thereafter provided the answer. After 1994, a big change went on in the Hispanic community. Politics became something more than just candidates attacking each other on TV; it was now the way to respect and to protect one's children. Hispanics who were eligible to become American citizens began to exercise their options. Voter registration workers funded by organized labor ventured forth in East L.A., the blue-collar suburbs of L.A., in the Mission District of San Francisco, on the Southside of San Jose, in Downtown San Diego, the farm worker precincts and barrios of the Central Valley, even in Santa Ana in Orange County. Unlike the 1970s and 1980s, they began to get results.

Even without Proposition 187, Hispanic influence probably would have slowly increased as they had more voters eligible every election. However, Wilson sped up the clock immeasurably. Statewide exit polls done by the *Los Angeles Times* and the networks show that the Hispanic share of California voters began increasing steadily since the low-turnout gubernatorial race of 1990, when they were only 6% of the voters despite being more than 20% of the adult population. In 1992, the Hispanic share edged up to 7% and went even higher in the immigration-crazed year of 1994. After that, as Table 7–9 shows, the floodgates opened; 1996 was the first election where over 1 million Hispanics voted. More than 75% voted against Proposition 209 and for Clinton, the Democrats' best performance among Hispanics since the 1970s. The Democratic margin in the Hispanic community jumped by over 500,000 votes. In the decade after 1996, Hispanic margins for Democratic candidates got even bigger, hitting an all-time high in 2008. A special Field survey done in 2000 confirms these data findings of an increase in Hispanic voters of 1 million from 1995 to 2000. These new voters were mostly poor, mostly young and mostly Democrats.[1]

After Proposition 187 passed, Hispanics legislators like Senator Richard Polanco and Assembly Speaker Antonio Villaraigosa made a concentrated effort to recruit and finance Hispanic candidates. Their efforts paid off as the number of Hispanic Democratic legislators doubled in the 1990s, from seven to 14, while the number of Republican Hispanics in the Assembly went from zero to four. In co-author Reddy's early days as a Democratic consultant to Speaker Villaraigosa, he attended a fundraiser where Senator Polanco proudly detailed how Hispanic turnout was about to soar. An older white lobbyist commented that he had been hearing that same speech from Polanco for 20 years. Reddy replied that this time it might be real — and it was.

---

1 Field Poll, http://www.field.com/fieldpollonline/subscribers/COI-00-May-Latinos.pdf.

TABLE 7–9. THE IMMIGRANTS BEGIN TO COME OF AGE

The votes below are for the "top of the ticket" races, i.e., governor and president (all votes are in thousands).

Year	Latino Votes	% of State	%Dem	Dem Votes	Dem Margin
1990	462,000	6%	62%	286,000	134,000
1992	779,000	7%	63%	491,000	327,000
1994	780,000	9%	73%	569,000	421,000
1996	1,106,000	11%	76%	841,000	664,000
1998	1,174,000	14%	75%	881,000	475,000
2000	1,755,000	16%	72%	1,263,000	842,000
2004	2,236,000	18%	65%	1,453,000	693,000
2008	2,438,000	18%	74%	1,804,000	1,243,000

Year	Asian Votes	% of State	%Dem	Dem Votes	Dem Margin
1990	154,000	2%	52%	80,000	12,000
1992	445,000	4%	45%	200,000	22,000
1994	433,000	5%	50%	217,000	18,000
1996	501,000	5%	53%	264,000	65,000
1998	503,000	6%	67%	337,000	191,000
2000	658,000	6%	58%	382,000	120,000
2004	870,000	7%	65%	565,000	278,000
2008	949,000	7%	64%	608,000	275,000

Table 7–9 shows distinct and pro-Democratic trends at work among Latinos and Asians since the early 1990s. Not only has turnout among these voters surged, but Democratic solidarity also increased significantly since 1990. The net result is that Republican leads among white voters are generally overcome by Democratic bloc votes from California minorities — who made up nearly 40% of the electorate in 2008. Minorities used to make up 15% of the California electorate in the 1980s. By 1996, that figure was up to nearly 25%. As of 1996, there had been such a large ethnic shift among California voters that if the 1982 and 1990 governors' races were re-run under the 1996 line-up with each candidate holding onto the same level of every ethnic group's support, the narrow defeats of Tom Bradley and Dianne Feinstein would have been reversed. After the even higher Hispanic turnout of 2000, Ronald Reagan's 500,000 margin over Jess Unruh in 1970 would also have been reversed. Moreover, with Obama's massive turnout in 2008, Pat Brown would have narrowly defeated Reagan in 1966.

Since the economic turmoil of the early Nineties hit the previously Republican middle class of Southern California so hard, Democrats have won every US Senate race and Democratic presidential nominees have carried California by over a million votes five times in a row. After the Republican collapse of 1992, the only Republican winners of a top-of-the-ticket race have been Wilson in the landslide Republican year of 1994 and Schwarzenegger — who happened to have been the world's most popular movie star.

Another way to view the changing California electorate is analyze each age cohort by ethnicity. Table 7-10 illustrates how the oldest group of voters, those over age 65 in 1998, represented the "Old California" of an overwhelming majority of white voters that existed in the Nixon–Reagan era. On the other hand, the 18–29 age group is the multi-ethnic "New California" where white voters will not be a majority. Nineteen ninety-eight was the beginning of the minority growth cycle.

Table 7-10. 1998 Exit Poll

Age Group (% of all)	White	Black	Asian/Pacific Islander	Hispanic
18–29 (14%)	56%	9%	10%	25%
30–49 (30%)	70%	9%	6%	15%
50–64 (29%)	78%	5%	5%	12%
Over 65 (27%)	87%	5%	3%	6%
State Totals	73%	7%	6%	14%

Source: CNN, November 3, 1998.

Table 7-11 shows the patterns of a growing minority a decade later in 2008. As can be seen, white voters are a minority in the youngest age cohort and Hispanics are almost equal to them. Older voters are still solidly white, but they are now only one of every six voters. Obama did best with the youngest voters, winning 76%. The only age group McCain won was over 65 and just by 50–48%. California's political future certainly looks ethnic and Democratic.

Table 7-11. 2008 Exit Poll

Age Group (% of all)	White	Black	Asian/ Pacific Islander	Hispanic
18–29 (20%)	44%	10%	6%	36%
30–49 (28%)	63%	10%	7%	17%
50–64 (36%)	65%	10%	4%	15%
Over 65 (16%)	77%	8%	3%	9%
State Totals	63%	10%	6%	18%

Source: CNN, November 4, 2008.

Summary

In all likelihood, the full story of Hispanics in California cannot be written until immigration slows down substantially. Even if Republicans start doing well with middle class Hispanics again, immigration will continue to replenish the inner city barrios with working class voters desiring all kinds of social spending and the "New Deal" political cycle will repeat itself. For the near future, Hispanics will be the base of California Democrats.

For many years, high levels of immigration gave California Republicans the best of both worlds. The growing Hispanic population caused California to gain House seats in re-apportionment and more influence in Electoral Votes (jumping from 32 in 1960 to 52 in 1990), while the fact that Hispanics were slow to register allow Republicans to carry the state based on the votes of white conservatives. That era came to a crashing end in the late 1990s and will not return. Given the state's rapidly growing minority vote, one should expect a major Republican bid for their support in the next generation by nominating black and Hispanic candidates for governor and US Senate. Competition between the two parties for the new ethnic voters should be healthy for everyone.

Summing Up: The Future of Ethnic Politics in California

In 2010, California is approaching two decades of Democratic dominance based on 1) the return of white voters due to economics, 2) the defection of some former moderate Republicans over social issues, and 3) the massive mobilization of the post-1960s immigrants. While the state was more ethnically polarized in the 1970s, white and Latino Democrats now find themselves agreeing more on issues like economics. (Asians and whites have often agreed in the past and still do). The 2009 special election where almost every ethnic group rejected spending and tax increases was a perfect example. One must hope that the days of racial brawling, as in Propositions 187 and 209, are over.

The two million Asian and Hispanics who have registered as Democrats and Decline to State (independents) since 1990 obviously give any Republican a huge hurdle to overcome. However, it occasionally can be overcome, as Schwarzenegger has proved. In most presidential elections, where the minority turnout is consistently higher, Democrats will rate a solid favorite to carry California. In off-year elections, however, where the turnout mix is less liberal and less Democratic, the Republicans will have a better chance.

The Voter Registration Paradox

Table 7-12 shows voter registration patterns in presidential years over the last generation. Democratic registration has declined steadily since the 1960s (except for two brief times after Watergate and in 2008). Republican registration had two upward blips after Reagan's election as governor in the mid-1960s and president in the 1980s, but has declined after Reagan left office. Since 1990, both major parties have lost strength while the number of independent voters has more than tripled since the 1970s. Since 1988, Republicans have lost nearly 20% of their faithful.

TABLE 7–12. VOTER REGISTRATION TRENDS

Year	Democrat	Republican	Other	% of Adults Registered	% of Eligible Who Voted	% Turnout of Registered Voters
1960	39%	3%	78%	69%	88%	58 %
1964	58 %	39%	3%	75%	66%	88%
1968	55%	40%	5%	73%	62%	86%
1972	56%	37%	7%	79%	65%	82%
1976	57%	35%	8%	70%	57%	82%
1980	53%	35%	12%	74%	57%	77%
1984	52%	36%	12%	79%	59%	75%
1988	50%	39%	11%	74%	54%	73%
1992	49%	37%	14%	72%	55%	75%
1996	47%	36%	17%	70%	53%	66%
2000	45%	35%	20%	73%	52%	71%
2004	43%	35%	23%	75%	57%	76%
2008	44%	31%	25%	75%	59%	79%

And herein lies the paradox. From 1960 to 1988, there were over one million more registered Democrats, but Republicans won most elections for president, governor, and senator during that time frame. Why? The answer lies in the fact that roughly 25% of all Democrats (mostly older, mostly male, mostly white, mostly suburban or rural) defected from Pat Brown in 1966, Hubert Humphrey in 1968, Jimmy Carter in 1980, Tom Bradley in 1982, Mike Dukakis in 1988, Dianne Feinstein in 1990 and Kathleen Brown in 1994. But in the 1990s, the smaller number of voters remaining as registered Democrats is much more loyal to the party. The main reason for this is that many former white Democrats have shifted to registered independents and the Democrats left are mostly women and minorities who are a lot more loyal to the party. For example, Barack Obama, Bill Clinton, Senators Dianne Feinstein and Barbara Boxer and Gray Davis have all won over 90% of the Democratic vote — plus about half of the independents. Suffice to say that the number of Democratic defections has declined by half since 1990. With only 31% of registered voters and many fewer Democratic defections, it is easy to see why California Republicans have truly become a minority party.

Going into the 1990s, Democrats had a decent, but small base in the Bay Area (about 25% of voters) and slight edges in the North–Central Coast and L.A. County (where the loss of the Reagan Democrats limited their strengths to the low-50 percentage range). Republicans could usually match the Democratic votes in the Bay Area and L.A. with an almost equal bloc of white suburbanites and then go over the top with solid support in the Central Valley and Rural California. After Wilson narrowly defeated Feinstein for Governor in 1990, it was assumed by some pundits that these patterns would go on for the near future

What happened next, however, was the defense bust in L.A. County made the "Reagan Democrat" white workers think like their counterparts in the Rust Belt and the Hispanic voter eruption energized L.A. County Democrats. Beginning in 1992, Democrats held their bases in the Bay Area and North & Central Coast, while winning back the white labor vote in L.A. and benefited from a massive Hispanic turnout, thus turning defeat in the Reaganite 1980s into victory.

One reprieve for the Republicans is that the governor's office in California has often been bi-partisan. Since Democrats obtained a majority of registered voters upon the upsurge in FDR's popularity in 1934, they have only won seven gubernatorial elections compared to the Republicans' 11 (counting Schwarzenegger in 2003 and not counting Earl Warren's landslide in 1946 when he won both nominations). Therefore, the very real Democratic edge in presidential elections of the past generation may not necessarily carry over to the 2010 Governor's race. Nevertheless, the huge demographic and ethnic advantage that the Democrats have will give them a strong edge in 2010 and beyond, even in the governor's races.

8. Gubernatorial Profile and the Candidates

As of the spring of 2009, there is a crowded field in the race for governor, much like there was for president at this time two years ago. As was the case with the presidential race, the incumbent Arnold Schwarzenegger is termed out, and so there will be a new person in the executive office in January 2011. We cannot say executive mansion, as the state does not have an active one, only the old 1877 governor's mansion which was used from 1903 to 1967 and is now a museum (including one of Jerry Brown's 1974 Plymouths). As for the candidates themselves, they come from a wide background and bring various assets to the job. This chapter is designed to illuminate those backgrounds.

Gubernatorial Profile

What does a successful gubernatorial profile look like? It is best to look at the people who have been governor. This list this chapter will look at is Hiram Johnson (1911–1917) and all the governors since Earl Warren (1943–1953), including Goodwin Knight (1953–1959), Pat Brown (1959–1967), Ronald Reagan (1967–1975), Jerry Brown (1975–1983), George Deukmejian (1983–1991), Pete Wilson (1991–1999), Gray Davis (1999–2003), and Arnold Schwarzenegger (2003–).

Backgrounds

Prior governors can be categorized into four backgrounds: Attorney General, Lieutenant Governor, politicians, and neophytes. Most political observers have felt that the most important office to hold as a stepping-stone to the governorship is Attorney General. Three of the ten governors in this chapter were Attorney General in their prior job, Warren, Pat Brown and Deukmejian. There are other AGs who ran for governor. If Jerry Brown became governor again, he would be the fourth, although his situation does not really count since he has already been governor. The other job that might appear to be a stepping-stone is Lieutenant Governor. Two of the ten stepped up to the governorship, Knight and Davis. But in fact, only Davis was a sitting Lieuten-ant Governor who was elected governor for an open seat. Knight succeeded to the gov-ernorship on Earl Warren's resignation to become Chief Justice of the U.S. Supreme Court and was elected as an incumbent. In that regard, the Lieutenant Governor isn't any different than other elected office holders that became governor. Two other elect-ed positions produced a governor: Jerry Brown, who was Secretary of State, and Pete Wilson, who was a U.S. Senator. What all these seven elected positions have in com-mon is that they were all elected statewide offices, like the governor. Three other gov-ernors came from the other end of the spectrum; they were neophytes who had never held elective office: Johnson, Reagan and Schwarzenegger. Reagan and Schwarzeneg-ger were actors with great name recognition. Johnson was at the head of a powerful political movement, the Progressives, that took over the state in 1911.

So how do these backgrounds apply to our candidates in 2010? As of the spring of 2009, there were seven acknowledged candidates on the Democratic side and three or four on the Republican side. According to the Capitol Weekly/Probolsky Research Poll taken in early February 2009, Senator Dianne Feinstein led the Democrats in the poll with 36%, followed by Attorney General Jerry Brown at 14%, San Francisco Mayor Gavin Newsom 9%, Los Angeles Mayor Antonio Villaraigosa 9%, Lieutenant Governor John Garamendi 4%, Superintendent of Public Instruction Jack O'Connell 3%,and former Controller Steve Westly 1% with 22% unsure. On the Republican side, former Congressman Tom Campbell narrowly leads with 15%, former eBay CEO Meg Whitman 14%, Insurance Commissioner Steve Poizner 4%, and Ventura County Su-pervisor Peter Foy 1% with 62% unsure.[1] It is believed in some circles that Foy is not a serious candidate for Governor but is using the race to gain visibility for another office. In any event, he polls as well as Westly, who was a serious candidate for gov-ernor in 2006.

The Mervin Field organization, the most famous name in California polling, did a poll in March 2009 with a different set of candidates. In that poll, Feinstein had 38%, Brown 16%, Villaraigosa 16%, Newsom 10%, Garamendi 4%, and Westly, O'Connell and Treasurer Bill Lockyer less than 2% on the Democratic side. Without Feinstein, who is undecided about leaving the Senate despite her commanding position in the governor's race, the poll shows Brown with 26%, Villaraigosa 22%, Newsom 16% and Garamendi 8%. The poll also shows Villaraigosa leading Brown 29% to 22% in Southern California. On the Republican side, Whitman had 21%, Campbell 18% and Poizner 7%, with 54% undecided.[2]

The job descriptions given in the polls provides the answers to backgrounds of the 2010 candidates. Brown holds the job with the most frequent paths to the gover-norship by being the only current or former Attorney General in the race. Feinstein and Garamendi hold jobs where office holders stepped directly into the governor's of-fice. Westly, Newsom and Campbell held jobs that other governors held on their way to being governor. O'Connell and Poizner hold statewide offices that have not led to

---

1 Capitol Alert, "Poll: Feinstein Tops Dems Field: GOP Race Tight in 2010," *sacbee.com*, Febru-ary 6, 2009, http://www.sacbee.com/static/weblogs/capitolalertlatest/019330.html.

2 Capitol Alert, "AM Alert: Feinstein, Whitman Atop Early 2010 Poll," *sacbee.com*, March 5, 2009, email from capitolalert@sacbee.com, Thu, 05 Mar 2009 08:00:51 -600 to sc@cumming-sresearch.com

the governorship, No one who has served as Mayor of Los Angeles has been governor, although mayors of other large cities have. Whitman is the neophyte in the election, but does not have the unique background that other neophytes like Johnson, Reagan and Schwarzenegger had.

Based on the past, it would appear that Brown, Feinstein and Garamendi have the best political offices from which to run for governor — highly visible statewide offices. Newsom and Villaraigosa also are in a decent position as leaders coming from large visible cities. On that basis, they have a leg up on everyone else, and it shows in the polls.

Successful Political Models

From a political approach to the election, which of the 2010 candidates are best positioned? From the list of earlier governors, it is clear that the non-partisan vision of Hiram Johnson from his 1910 campaign had a profound impact on political campaigns, which should not have been very surprising. Johnson and his Progressives structured their campaigns in that fashion and much of the political development of California politics flowed out in that fashion right until the 1960s. Therefore, it should be no surprise that governors like Hiram Johnson, Earl Warren, Goodwin Knight and Pat Brown should come out of that mold. In the case of Warren and Brown in their first campaigns in 1942 and 1958 respectively, this was particularly true as they ran non-partisan campaigns against the highly partisan campaigns of Culbert Olson and William Knowland. Added to these governors would have to be Gray Davis, who ran as a moderate Democrat and was often in battle with his more liberal Democratic legislature. Arnold Schwarzenegger also has the non-partisan (or post-partisan in modern political language) approach, first in the 2003 recall campaign and then after the disastrous 2005 special election. In general, Schwarzenegger has had a better relationship with the Democrats in Sacramento than the Republicans. Jerry Brown also has had a unique combination of liberal and conservative viewpoints that has been difficult to pin him in the partisan mold. The success of all these governors was in the fact they appealed across a broad range of constituencies, which has generally been the most successful road to the governorship.

A second smaller group of governors were those who identified with conservative policies, particularly law and order, in the period 1967 to 1999. This covers the governorships of Ronald Reagan, George Deukmejian and Pete Wilson. Jerry Brown was also part of that period, and to the extent that he advocated the limitations of government, he fits into this category. However, as he has shown throughout his career, Brown is a multifaceted politician and not a true conservative like the other three governors of the period. The period began with the most famous conservative Republican of his era in Reagan and Deukmejian and Wilson followed. However, as he showed throughout his career, Reagan could also reach out to voters beyond the hard core conservative camp. It first showed up in his 1966 win against Pat Brown, when he was able to win in labor-based Democratic strongholds. Later in his presidential runs, he was famous for wooing the celebrated "Reagan Democrats." So Reagan had his own non-partisan appeal, which often frustrated his staunch conservative supporters who always blamed Reagan's staff for not allowing "Reagan to be Reagan"; but there was never any doubt that Reagan was a conservative. Deukmejian and Wilson did not have Reagan's popularity and they ran at a time when the Republican Party was becoming increasingly more conservative. In Wilson's case, he was considered too moderate for the party stalwarts for many years until he won a highly contested U.S. Senate primary in 1982. These gubernatorial candidates were successful in a time when conservative political philosophy was the dominant philosophy in California and the nation. California's political blue shift, which started in the late 1980s and has resulted in five straight Democratic presidential wins since 1992, would appear to make another conservative era less likely in the near future. The current financial crisis could change that, however.

A third and equally important group of governors, which overlaps the other two groups, is the personality governors. As the home to the entertainment industry, personalities have always been a part of California culture, and politics has been a part of that. Hollywood celebrities have always been a part of political campaigns, and starting with Helen Gahagan Douglas's election to Congress in 1944, entertainers from California have been elected officials. Two people from the entertainment industry, actors Ronald Reagan and Arnold Schwarzenegger have been governors. To these two must be added Jerry Brown, certainly the most unique personality (entertainer or otherwise) to have been in the governor's office. Brown, of course, had his own connections to the entertainment industry with his relationship with singer Linda Ronstadt. But Brown has shown throughout his political career that he is his own man and cannot be categorized in any particular box. He remains the most interesting politician in the current gubernatorial candidate field and must rank with Ronald Reagan and Richard Nixon has the most intriguing politician California has ever produced.

So where does the current crop of candidates aside from Brown fit into these three categories? In looking at the field, very few of them do. Four candidates, Campbell, Feinstein, O'Connell and Westly tend to be centrists and would fit in the non-partisan role. Campbell, Feinstein and Westly have all at one time it another alienated the more extreme members their party. O'Connell represented a swing district for many years and had strong supporters in both parties. Garamendi could also be put in this category as he has been able to win statewide in down-ticket races, although he has been considered more of a liberal than a moderate Democrat.

In the conservative category, there are certainly no Democrats and Campbell is an anathema to the conservatives in the Republican Party. His support of Proposition 1A in the May 19, 2009 special election certainly confirms that in their eyes. That leaves Steve Poizner and Meg Whitman among the Republicans. They have certainly sounded like conservatives so far during the primary, but then one would expect them to move to the right during the Republican primary campaign. Where they are really remains to be seen. They could end up being as moderate as Campbell. It is difficult to believe that former business people from Silicon Valley hold extreme conservative views. Added to this is the fact that while both of them oppose Proposition 1A, neither one of them funded the "No on 1A" campaign although both are in a position to do so, as they have shown in their own campaigns. There is still the possibility that a candidate with true conservative credentials could enter the race, but aside from Tom

McClintock, who was just elected to Congress and has stated that he will not enter the governor's race[1], it is difficult to see who could challenge Whitman or Poizner if rank and file conservatives became disenchanted with them.

While there are legitimate conservatives in the race, there is certainly a flock of liberals. Extreme liberals have not done well in the governorship. Only one has been elected, Democrat Culbert Olson in 1938. His election was an outgrowth of the liberal surge during the Great Depression. Olson's term was not a successful one, and he was defeated for re-election by Earl Warren in 1942. Still, with the country in its biggest economic crisis since the Depression and the political landscape making its first leftward shift in years, liberals do have a chance. Gavin Newsom, Antonio Villaraigosa and John Garamendi fill that role.

Along with Jerry Brown, who positions himself as a nonpartisan as well as a personality, the candidates cover a wide range of political viewpoints, and given the uncertainty of state finances and the national economy, more roads to the governorship are available this time than has been the case in many previous elections.

Prior Occupations

Of the occupations that previous governors has before they went into politics, there is basically only one — attorney. Johnson, Warren, Knight, the Browns, Deukmejian, Wilson, and Davis were all attorneys. The only two exceptions were Reagan and Schwarzenegger, who were actors, something that could only happen in California. Surprisingly, none of the previous governors were in business outside of practicing the law. Therefore, in California it has been easier to become governor by being an actor than by being a successful businessman.

The current crop of candidates offers a mixed bag of occupations. In fact, only two, Brown and Campbell, are attorneys (none are actors). Four started out as business people — Newsom, Poizner, Westly and Whitman. Villaraigosa was a labor organizer; O'Connell was a teacher; Feinstein was a social worker, and Garamendi was in public service. If there is a chance to break out of the attorney mold, this is the election.

Regarding business people in the governor's race, particularly those with a lot of money, there has obviously been a notable failure for them to win the top jobs in California. As Jerry Roberts and Phil Trounstine noted in *Calbuzz*, rich candidates have been unsuccessful in California while such candidates have succeeded in states like Texas and New Jersey.[2] Campaign strategist Garry South points out that rich candidates from the business world have an inflated view of their accomplishments in that arena and fail to understand what it takes to succeed in the political field — their business wins do not translate to the political world. Many of them think that they can buy their way to an office, but they do not have a clear message that they can target to voters. In addition, there is a great deal of mistrust of wealthy candidates by

---

1 Capitol Alert, "McClintock Douses Conservative Fire Over Gubernatorial Bid," *sacbee.com*, May. 4, 2009, http://www.sacbee.com/static/weblogs/capitolalertlatest/022030.html.
2 Jerry Roberts and Phil Trounstine, "Why Rich Guys Don't Win Top Offices in California," *Calbuzz*, May 4, 2009, http://calbuzzer.blogspot.com/2009/05/why-rich-guys-don't-win-top-offices-in.html.

the average voter, particularly if that candidate is not a known quantity. Most U.S. senators are wealthy, but many of them have built political reputation over the years with their various constituencies. Wealthy California candidates with no record of political accomplishment run for governor or U.S. Senator with a handicap.[1]

How does the above affect the business candidates Newsom, Poizner, Westly and Whitman? Only Whitman has no political experience and is most at risk in falling in the footsteps of Al Checchi or Bill Simon who crashed and burned in the political campaign. But Westly was barely able to beat Tom McClintock for the state Controller job in 2002 despite heavily outspending him and failed in the gubernatorial primary against Phil Angelides in 2006. Poizner beat a politically badly damaged Cruz Bustamante for Insurance Commissioner in 2006 in the only race he has ever won after losing an Assembly race to Ira Ruskin in 2004, again heavily outspending Ruskin. Newson was first appointed to the San Francisco City and County Board of Supervisors and then won reelection in 1998, 2000, and 2002 before being elected Mayor in 2003 and reelected in 2007 with 72% of the vote.[2] Based on electoral victories in San Francisco, Newsom would appear to have broken out the potential trap that is in store for Poizner, Westly and Whitman. Unlike Poizner and Whitman, Newsom is running in a much more crowded field on the Democratic side with a lot of experienced politicians with a lot of varied political successes.

A final word on businessmen running for political office. The current economic crisis and resultant exposés on the activities of businessmen on Wall Street and the bonus culture surrounding them has given the average voter a bad taste in their mouths. The man in the street resents the bailout money thrown at the banks while average citizen is losing or afraid for their job and being thrown out of their foreclosed home. The approval ratings for the business community in general have plunged and being linked with the business community is no longer the asset it was prior to 2007. Candidates with a limited political resume to go with their business background may be fighting an uphill battle, even with the low approval ratings of California politicians. As long time pollster Mervin Field said rich candidates in the current economic environment, "the state is in one hell of a mess. I believe voters will be looking for someone with a different resume."[3]

Summary

So what does the above profile analysis tell us about what is going on the governor's race? It mirrors very closely what the polls are telling us. On the Democratic side, the most experienced candidates, Feinstein and Brown lead the way. On the Republican side, the most experienced candidate, Campbell leads one poll and is a strong second in the March Field poll, even though his moderate views and support of Measure 1A are a huge handicap with the kind of conservative Republican voters that will vote in the primary. Of course, it is still early in the campaign and many of

---

1 Ibid.; Garry South, "Meg Whitman: a Female Checci or Simon?," *Capitol Weekly*, May 7, 2009, http://capitolweekly.net/article.php?1&_c=xynb684e779dgp&xid=xyl4lnkv7fhkum&done=, xyn9ajv66gqu0j&_ce=1241720339.fc23d8db8503f2c45328fb2a5f9d68f8.

2 *Wikipedia*, s.v. "Gavin Newsom," http://en.wikipedia.org/wiki/Gavin_Newsom (accessed April 29, 2009).

3 Roberts and Trounstine, "Why Rich Guys Don't Win."

the poll responses is based on name recognition and there is plenty of time for political bombshells to upturn both primaries. Still the poll responses are holding true to form and provide a window as to what likely will happen next year.

CANDIDATE BIOGRAPHIES

The following is a brief rundown of the major Republican and Democratic candidates based on the polling done so far. The Democratic candidates will be listed in alphabetical order, followed by the Republicans in the same order.

Democrats

Edmund Gerald "Jerry" Brown, Jr.[1]
Born: April 7, 1938 San Francisco CA
Education: Studied at Santa Clara University. Entered Sacred Heart Novitiate, a Jesuit Seminary intending to become a priest. Left the seminary and entered U.C. Berkeley, graduating with a B.A. in Classics, 1961. J.D. Yale Law School 1964.
Religion: Catholic
Field Poll (March 2009): 16% (T-Second). Without Feinstein 26% (First)
Personal Background: Third of four siblings and only son of former Governor Edmund Gerald "Pat" Brown and Bernice Brown. After passing the bar, Brown practiced law in Los Angeles. In the late-1960s, he began his political career. After losing the U.S. Senate race to Pete Wilson leaving the governorship in 1983, Brown traveled to Asia studying Buddhism in Japan as well as working with Mother Teresa in Kolkata (Calcutta), India. Known for an austere life a governor and his friendship with singer Linda Ronstadt, Brown remained a bachelor until 2005, when he married his girlfriend of some 15 years, Anne Gust, former chief counsel for The Gap, a clothing company. Since the mid 1990s, Brown and Gust have lived in Oakland, where Brown was a radio talk show host before getting back into politics
Political Background: Got actively involved in politics by organizing migrant workers and anti-Vietnam war activities (he was part of CDC's anti-war slate in the 1968 Democratic presidential primary). Elected to the newly created Los Angeles Community College Board of Trustees, placing first in a field of one hundred twenty-four, 1969. Elected California Secretary of State 1970. Elected governor of California 1974 and re-elected 1978. Ran for president 1976, 1980 and 1992. Elected chair of the California Democratic Party against Steve Westly 1989. In 1998, announced that he was leaving the Democratic Party and changed his registration to "Decline to State." He reregistered as a Democrat in 1999. Elected Mayor of Oakland in 1998 and re-elected in 2002. Elected California Attorney General in 2006.
Comment: Jerry Brown continues to be the most unique politician in California today, and may very well be the most unique politician in California history. Probably the most intelligent person to ever be governor, he continues to confound friend and foe alike with the originality of his though processes and the way he continually re-invents himself. Brown was the first politician to understand how to wield power

---

1 *Wikipedia* s.v. "Jerry Brown," http://en.wikipedia.org/wiki/Jerry_Brown.(Accessed April 29, 2009).

in the less visible state constitutional offices when he used the Secretary of State's office to promote campaign finance disclosure. Jess Unruh subsequently took up this strategy in 1975, when he took the state Treasurer's position and made it an advocate for large shareholders in corporations and pension funds. Brown advocated highly progressive ideas in his tenure as governor in terms of farm worker rights and the environment. He also was the first governor to promote a large number of women and minorities to key government jobs. But he was also capable of taking what appeared to be conservative positions in contrast to his father, particularly on budget matters. He did the same as mayor of Oakland when he took many centrist positions on local issues. In both cases as governor and as mayor, he explained the apparent changes from his earlier liberal positions by saying that he was dealing with the realities of running a state in an era of limitations or being a big city mayor with big city problems. Much the same kind of philosophy appears to be operating in his discussions about the current financial problems of the state.

In his interview on *Calbuzz*, Brown compared the approach he would take today as governor as opposed to the one he took when he was in that office from 1975 to 1983: he said "then, I emphasized new ideas; now, I would emphasize management more. He went on to say "its was very exciting then, but without that sense of innovation, I'd be more practical-minded, very detailed, focus on follow through and consensus building...I'd be looking for people who are seasoned administrators." In discussing bridging the ideological divide in the legislature, he said "I'm going to be the apostle of common sense. I am going to disabuse them of their ill-conceived predilections...if eliminating the structural problems in the California budget were easy, Wilson, Davis and Schwarzenegger would have done it." Brown also pointed out his four key concerns as governor: renewable energy, prison reform, education reform, and water policy. Brown commented that California is a "very high tax" state and that regulation undermining California's competitiveness must be challenged.[1]

One asset he has against his rivals in the governor's race is his incomparable understanding of state government, having either observed or been involved in it since his father became Attorney General in 1951. He has said "I have a greater sense of how things get done...I have a much better, hands-on understanding of how (government functions...a sense of how things work...a much better sense of sizing people up and how you go about building an administration."[2] Brown was a reluctant supporter of Proposition 1A on the May 19, 2009 special election, saying that it had problems, but that it was the best that could be achieved at this point.[3]

As for Brown's opinion of what kind of a governor will succeed Arnold Schwarzenegger, Brown says, "I kind of think a guy who knows his way, is pretty down to earth, no bells and whistles, just meat and potatoes. That's kind of where I am....It's

---

1 Jerry Roberts and Phil Trounstine, "Jerry Brown: I'm Going to be an Apostle of Common Sense," *Calbuzz*, April 13, 2009, http://calbuzzer.blogspot.com/2009/04/jerry-brown-im-going-to-be-apostle-of.html.

2 Ibid.

3 Capitol Alert, "Brown Says Prop 1A Will Help 'Next Governor,'" *sacbee.com*, April 14, 2009, http://www.sacbee.com/static/weblobs/captolalertlatest/021519.html.

back to basics."[1] Jerry Brown turned 71 on April 7 and assuming Dianne Feinstein does not enter the race would be far and away the oldest candidate in the field. Already Gavin Newsom and Steve Poizner have tried to make Brown's age an issue. But Brown has shown time and again that he is an original thinker whose ability to remake himself into something entirely new almost makes the age issue irrelevant. Only three years ago he won the Attorney General's office at the age of 68 with the highest percentage vote on any statewide constitutional officer (Feinstein had the highest percentage overall in her Senate race). Whether his view of what kind of governor the voters want turns out to be accurate and whether he is that person remain to be seen. One thing is for sure; he is not to be underestimated.

Dianne Feinstein[2]
Born: June 22, 1933 San Francisco, CA
Education: B.A. Stanford 1955
Religion: Jewish
Field Poll (March 2009): 38% (First)
Personal Background: Born Dianne Goldman and raised in San Francisco. Family came to San Francisco in 1890. Studied criminology and did social work before being appointed to the Women's Parole Board 1960–66. Married Jack Berman in 1956 and had a daughter Katherine (now Judge Katherine Feinstein Mariano) in 1957. Divorced in 1959. Married Bertram Feinstein (died 1978) in 1962. Married Richard C. Blum January 20, 1980.

Political Background: Elected to the San Francisco Board of Supervisors 1970–1978; President of the Board of Supervisors 1970–71, 1974–75, 1978. As the presiding president of the Board, succeeded to the mayoralty of San Francisco on the murder of Mayor George Moscone on September, 1978. Elected as Mayor of San Francisco 1979 and 1983. Democratic nominee for Governor in 1990, losing to Republican Pete Wilson 49% to 46%. Elected to U.S. Senate 1992, 1994, 2000, and 2006, for the term ending in 2013.

Comment: Although she continually faces criticism from liberal Democrats for her moderate to conservative votes on security and foreign policy issues, particularly the Iraq War Resolution, Dianne Feinstein is considered by most political analysts as the most popular politician in California. Many politicians wanted Feinstein to run in the 2003 recall to keep the governorship in Democratic hands. It was telling that Arnold Schwarzenegger did not enter the recall race until Feinstein bowed out. Feinstein has said that the one political job that she covets the most is the governorship. Based on her commanding position in California politics, the job would no doubt be hers if she wanted it. But at this point in time there are key negatives to her getting in the race. First, as one of the senior members of the U.S. Senate now in the

1 George Skelton, "Jerry Brown Wants to be a Back-to-Basics Governor," *Los Angeles Times*, April 20, 2009, http://www.latimes.com/news/local/la-me-cap20-2009apr20,0,2315392.column.
2 U.S. Congress. Joint Committee on Printing. *Congressional Directory 2007-2008, 110ᵗʰ Congress* (Washington DC: Government Printing Office, 2007), 17; Michael Barone and Richard E. Cohen, eds. *The Almanac of American Politics 2006* (Washington D.,C.: The National Journal Group, 2005), 160-161; *Wikipedia* s.v. "Dianne Feinstein," http://en.wikipedia.org/wiki/Dianne_Feinstein. (Accessed May 11, 2009)

majority with the key committee chairmanship of the Senate Select Committee on Intelligence (prior to that, the chairwoman of the Senate committee on Rules and Administration), she would be giving up a lot if she left at this point. The second big negative would be her age. She would be 77 upon taking office. While she appears to be in good health, she would be taking on a thankless, brutal job at an advanced age. She would probably serve only one term, but oddly enough, her position in California without having to run for a second term might be that she is in the best position to accomplish something. Feinstein is not expected to make a decision on running for governor until later this year. It may be the single most important announcement in the 2010 election.

John Garamendi[1]
Born: January 24, 1945 Mokelumne Hill CA
Education: B.A., U.C. Berkeley 1966: M.B.A., Harvard 1974
Religion: Presbyterian
Field Poll (March 2009): 4% (Fifth). Without Feinstein 8% (Fourth)

Personal Background: Garamendi's family is of Basque origin. His father came from Utah and Nevada to run his in-laws cattle ranch in the gold country area around Mokelumne Hill. John Garamendi was one of seven children. Garamendi went to the University of California at Berkeley at was a second team All-American offensive guard in football and the 1964 West Coast heavyweight wrestling champion. He married his wife Patti in 1965 and they have six children. Garamendi and his wife served in the Peace Corps in Ethiopia from 1966 to 1968. He worked in private business and went to Harvard before entering politics in 1974.

Political Background: Elected to the California State Assembly in 1974. Elected to the State Senate 1976 and re-elected 1980, 1984 and 1988. Lost the Democratic Primary for governor in 1982 and 1994. Elected the State's first Insurance Commissioner in 1990. After losing the gubernatorial primary in 1994 was appointed Deputy Secretary of the Interior by President Bill Clinton and served until 1998. In private business until 2002, was elected to a second term as Insurance Commissioner. Elected Lieutenant Governor in 2006.

Comment: Although held in high regard by Democrats and elected to legislative and statewide office over the past thirty-five years, John Garamendi has never been able to generate the kind of name recognition that Dianne Feinstein or Jerry Brown has achieved statewide, nor does he come from the population base that launches urban candidacies like Antonio Villaraigosa and Gavin Newsom. Also, coming from a rural area, he has not generated the fundraising base necessary for a run for governor. As a result, he has trailed the other four major candidates in the early polls.

---

1 *Wikipedia* s.v. "John Garamendi," http://en.wikipedia.org/wiki/John_Garamendi; "About John," *Garamendi for Governor 2010*, http://www.garamendi.org/index-php?option=com_conrent&view=article&id=48&Itemid=58 (Accessed April 29, 2009); "Meet John," *Office of the Lieutenant Governor John Garamendi*, http://www.ltg.ca.gov/index.php?option=com_content&view=article&id=24&Itemid=42.; California Joint Committee on Legislative Organization, *California Blue Book, 1975* (Sacramento: California Office of State Printing, 1975), 145; Nancy Zubrini, *A Travel Guide to Basque America*, 2nd ed., (Reno, NV: University of Nevada Press), 221.

With this in mind, on April 22, 2009, Garamendi announced that he would run for the 10th Congressional District seat being vacated by Representative Ellen Tauscher, who had accepted the position of Undersecretary of State for Arms Control and International Security. A special election would be set pending Tauscher's confirmation.[1] Assuming the confirmation and the setting of the special election, Garamendi would be considered the favorite, given his years of service to the area and name recognition. However, the field would be a crowded one and there is no guarantee that Garamendi would be the winner. If Garamendi were not successful in obtaining the 10th District congressional seat, he could resume his campaign for governor. However, there is strong interest by certain people to have Garamendi to run for the 3rd District congressional seat. Garamendi's ranch is in the 10th district bordering of the 3rd, and so he has been active in both districts in various elected positions. While the 10th is a heavily Democratic district where winning the primary is tantamount to winning the general election. The 3rd district is a Republican district where Garamendi could easily win the nomination but would have to fight hard to win in November. But Garamendi's name recognition is such is that he would have reasonable chance to win such a seat.

Gavin Newsom[2]
Born: October 10, 1967 San Francisco CA
Education: B.A. Santa Clara University, 1989
Religion: Catholic
Field Poll (March 2009): 10% (Fourth). Without Feinstein 16% (Third)
Personal Background: A fourth-generation San Franciscan, Newsom's parents divorced in 1972 and Newson moved with his mother and sister to Marin County when Newsom was ten. Newsom's severe dyslexia made schooling difficult, but he was able to get through Santa Clara University and in 1991 created a company Plump-Jack Associates L.P., which opened the PlumpJack Wine Shop on Fillmore Street, San Francisco in 1992. The business became a multi-million dollar operation with several shops and restaurants. He sold his share of the business when he became mayor in 2004. Newsom married Kimberly Guilfoyle in 2001; the couple was divorced in 2005. In 2008, he married actress Jennifer Siebel; they are now expecting a child.

Political Background: Appointed to the San Francisco Board of Supervisors 1997 and re-elected 1998, 2000 and 2002. During his time on the board, Newsom was best known for the voter initiative "Care Not Cash," which offered supportive services for the homeless instead of direct cash aid. In 2003, he was elected mayor of San Francisco, and was considered a moderate in the Dianne Feinstein mold. He was re-elected in 2007. While Newsom has worked on a number of issues as mayor as homelessness, housing, health care and the environment, he garnered national attention when he allowed gay couples to marry in San Francisco, an action that was later quashed by the courts. Newsom's activity on behalf of gay rights and his opposition to the anti-gay

1 Capitol Alert, "AM Alert: Garamendi to Drop Gov bid and Run for Congress," *sacbee*.com, April 22, 2009, email from capitolaltert@sacbee.com, Wed, 22 Apr, 2009 08:01:36-0500 to sc@cummingsresearch.com.
2 *Wikiperia* s.v. "Gavin Newsom," http://en.wikipedia.org/wiki/Gavin_Newsom.(Accessed April 29, 2009)

marriage Proposition 8 on the November 2008 ballot made his activity a focal point for the Yes on 8 forces. He announced his candidacy for governor on April 21, 2009 on YouTube, Facebook, and Twitter.[1]

Comment: With his announcement on YouTube, Facebook, and Twitter, Gavin Newsom clearly showed where he was aiming his campaign — younger voters and a younger mindset. In his announcement statement, Newsom said that the state needed fresh blood and fresh ideas to tackle its problems; clearly an attack on the 71-year-old Jerry Brown. "We can't afford to keep returning to the same old tired ideas and expect a different result," he said. He also noted in an interview with the San Francisco Chronicle that his outlook toward technology as well as his entrepreneurial experience would allow him to draw clear distinctions between himself and other candidates.[2] This may be true on the Democratic side of the ballot; it would be much tougher to make that distinction against the Republican candidates, particularly Steve Poizner and Meg Whitman, who are far wealthier entrepreneurs. Newsom describes himself as a pro-business Democrat.[3] In this regard, Newsom may have the same problem that Poizner and Whitman have in being business candidates in an anti-business economic environment.

With regard to specific issues, the campaign web site, www.gavinnewsom.com has lots of them. The overriding theme in the issues tab is to compare the state's problems with what Newsom did in San Francisco, which may or may not be an adequate model. Under the page, "The San Francisco Story of Progress," Newsom points out that San Francisco is the "only city in America on its way to providing universal health care...has one of the best performing urban school districts in America...recycles 70% of its waste, the highest recycling rate of any American city...helped create thousands of new high-wage jobs by attracting economic engines like the California Center for Regenerative Medicine...implemented a local Earned Income Tax Credit that helps families earning less than $42,000 annually keep more of their hard earned money." The page ends with the sentence, "time after time, on issue after issue, San Francisco is leading the state with bold new solutions and proven policy ideas...Under Gavin Newsom, San Francisco has generated a wealth of new ideas that look beyond the tired slogans of yesterday's politics to forge new solutions for the California of tomorrow."[4] The web site and the campaign has clearly borrowed from two important other campaigns — the Obama campaign with its emphasis on technology and its message of hope, and the Schwarzenegger recall campaign with its message of a new kind of politics to fix things in Sacramento. The problem will be how those themes work in 2010. Schwarzenegger was unable to bring post-partisanship to California politics, and now his approval ratings are in the tank. The appeal of the Obama message may not be so attractive after eighteen months of political battles in Wash-

1 Capitol Alert, "Newsom: I'm a Candidate for Governor," *sacbee.com*, April 21, 2009, http://.www.sacbee.com/static/weblogs/capitolalertlatest/021685.html.

2 Carla Marinucci, "Newsom Declares for Governor in High-Tech Style," *San Francisco Chronicle*, April 22, 2009, http://www.sfgate.com/cgi-bin/article.cgi?f=/c/a/2009/04/21/MNJO176EKA.DTL.

3 Ibid.

4 "The San Francisco Story of Progress," *Gavin Newsom: For a Better California*, http://www.gavinnewsom.com/learn/the_san_francisco_story/. (Accessed May 13, 2009)

ington. Nevertheless, it is certainly a strategy worth following, and will no doubt give Newsom a sizable bloc of votes in the 2010 primary.

Antonio Villaraigosa[1]
Born: January 23, 1953 Los Angeles (Boyle Heights) CA
Education: East L.A. College, 1972. B.A. UCLA 1977.
Religion: Catholic
Field Poll (March 2009): 16% (T-Second). Without Feinstein 22% (Second)

Personal Background: Born Antonio Villar to a Mexican immigrant father and a California-born mother of Mexican descent, the oldest of four children. Father abandoned the family when Antonio was five years old. Mother raised four children in a two-bedroom apartment. Volunteered at 15 for Cesar Chavez's first grape boycott. Kicked out of a Catholic high school at 15 for fighting after a football game, he finished high school at night. Developed a benign tumor on his spine at 15 that required surgery and left him in constant pain; had a second surgery in 2001. From high school, he was a campus agitator for civil rights. At UCLA, he led protests against the Vietnam War, Chicano and farm worker rights. Fathered two daughters out of wedlock, charged with assault for hitting a man who smeared his mother. Married Corina Raigosa in 1987 and combined their two names; had two more children. In 2007, they divorced and it was announced that he was having a relationship with Mirthala Salinas, a Spanish-language reporter. The scandal cost him key political supporters. Became a labor organizer, rising to prominence with the United Teachers of Los Angeles.

Political Background: Appointed to Metropolitan Transportation Board 1990–1994. Elected to the California State Assembly 1994. Re-elected 1996 and 1998. Speaker of the Assembly 1997–2000. Lost race for Los Angeles Mayor to James Hahn in 2001. Elected to the 14th District of the Los Angeles City Council, 2003. Elected Mayor of Los Angeles 2005. Re-elected 2009.

Comment: Like Gavin Newsom, Antonio Villaraigosa grew up in a single mom household and had to overcome numerous handicaps to get where he is. Like Newsom, he has had to suffer from a divorce and a messy public affair. Unlike Newsom, who built his career in the private sector, Villaraigosa is an avowed liberal who grew up in the civil rights and labor movement. He has overcome his handicaps through tireless work, energy and campaigning. He also has a reputation for consensus and coalition building. In winning the 2005 mayoralty election, he was able to build from his solid Latino base by adding a large number of African-Americans to his coalition, including such key figures as Congressmember Maxine Waters and former L.A. Lakers star Magic Johnson. He is the first Latino mayor of Los Angeles since Cristóbal Aguilar left office in 1872, no mean achievement.

As for Villaraigosa's performance as mayor, the record has been mixed. The mayor has cited his accomplishments as fewer crimes and potholes and less graffiti, more homeless housing, police officers, recycled trash and planted. He has made progress,

---

1 *Wikipedia* s.v. "Antonio Villaraigosa," http://en.wikipedia.org/wiki/Antonio_Villariagosa (Accessed April 29, 2009); "Biography of Antonio Villaraigosa, Mayor of Los Angeles," *Los Angeles Almanac,* http://www.laalmanac.com/government/gl12.htm; Deborah White, "Antonio Villaraigosa, Mayor of Los Angeles: The Bumpy Road of a Rising Democratic Superstar," *About.com,* http://usliberals.about.com/od/peopleinthenews/a/Antonio.htm.

but not as much as he promised in the 2005 election. He promised an additional 1,000 police officers, but showed a net gain of 694. He planted about 200,000 of 1 million trees he planned. He pledged to take control of the Los Angeles Unified School District, but had to back off due to hostility of the teacher' unions, the L.A. Board of Education, and weak support of the idea from the community. He ended having to settle for getting allies elected to the board of education and install his deputy mayor for education as superintendent. The proposed "subway to the sea" has showed some progress, but has not moved as fast as the mayor hoped. However, he did have a resounding success with the building of the dedicated road express bus Orange Line through the San Fernando Valley, established the proposed Exposition Line to USC and Exposition Park, and is near the completion of the Gold Line expansion to East Los Angeles.[1] Expanding public transit, reducing crime, reforming education, greening Los Angeles, and promoting economic development have been Villaraigosa's top priorities. He has been criticized for spending too much time on promotion and too little time of the job. One of his harshest critics, the alternative paper L.A. Weekly has accused Villaraigosa for being an "all-about-me mayor" whose frenetic self-promotion leaves little time for his job." But Villaraigosa believes that politicians need to communicate with the public. As he says, "It's important to get public support for what you do....I believe that the success of what we've been able to do has everything to do with that." Villaraigosa's promotion of the downtown has helped turn it around, according to Samuel Garrison, vice president of public policy for the Greater Los Angeles Chamber of Commerce.[2]

Villaraigosa has not announced that he is running for governor at this time and did not attend the California Democratic Party state convention, officially saying that he needed to attend to city business. In fact, the decision had been made to lie low after his recent re-election so as to not appear that he was job-hopping at the convention. However, interested in the governor's job he most certainly is. He brings tremendous assets to the governor's campaign, starting with the fact that he is the leading Latino politician in the state and has a large built-in bloc of votes. He has shown an ability to put together coalitions of various blocs of voters as he did in his 2005 race. He also has tremendous support in Southern California. In the March Field Poll, Villaraigosa led Brown 29% to 22% in Southern California. Since Southern California constitutes two thirds of the vote, Villaraigosa's showing in the Southland is an important reason why Villaraigosa leads Newsom in the polls, even though Newsom has been out campaigning and Villaraigosa has not.

If Villaraigosa were to be elected governor, he would be the first Latino to hold the office since Romualdo Pacheco in 1875. He would also be the first born and raised in Southern California since the nineteenth century. He has overcome many obstacles, some of his own doing, to get this far. It is certainly within his capability to reach the governor's office.

---

1 Tom Tugend and Brad A. Greenberg, "Villaraigosa Runs Hard for Second Term on Record, Future," *Jewish Journal.com*, February 25, 2009, http://www.jewishjournal.com/community/article/villaraigosa_runs_hard_for_2nd_term_on_record_future_20090225/.

2 Peter Hecht, "L.A. Mayor's Star on the Rise Again as Higher Office Beckons," *Sacramento Bee*, February 2, 2009, http://www.sacbee.com/capitolandCalifornia/story/1590994-p2.html.

Republicans

Tom Campbell[1]
Born: August 14, 1952 Chicago IL
Education: B.A., M.A. University of Chicago, 1973. J.D. Harvard 1976. PhD. University of Chicago 1980.
Religion: Catholic
Field Poll (March 2009): 18% (Second)
Personal Background: Native of Chicago and one of eight children of a U.S. Federal Judge in a Democratic household, Campbell became a Republican at the University of Chicago, getting a Ph D in economics. His faculty advisor was Milton Friedman. Campbell states on his campaign web page that it was at that time that he developed his beliefs on the importance of fiscal responsibility and individual liberty. He married his wife Susanne in 1978. Since then, he has switched between government and academia. After serving in the Reagan Administration from 1981 to 1983, he came west to take a professorship at Stanford Law School until being elected to Congress in 1988. He left politics in 2000 to return to Stanford before being appointed Dean of the Hass School of Business at U.C. Berkeley in 2002. He took a leave in 2004–05 to serve the Schwarzenegger Administration. He left Haas in 2008 to join the Chapman School of Law in Orange County for a two-year visiting appointment starting in January 2009.

Political Background: Served as the Director of the Bureau of Competition, Federal Trade Commission 1981–1983. Elected to Congress from California's 12th Congressional District 1988. Re-elected 1990. Unsuccessful candidate for the Republican nomination for the U.S. Senate seat vacated by Alan Cranston and eventually won by Barbara Boxer. Elected to the California State Senate 11th District in a 1993 special election. Elected to Congress in California's 15th Congressional District 1994. Re-elected 1996 and 1998. Unsuccessful Republican nominee for the U.S. Senate against Dianne Feinstein 2000. Appointed to Governor Schwarzenegger's newly formed Council of Economic Advisors 2004. Director of California's Department of Finance, 2004–2005. In July 2008, Campbell set up his exploratory committee for the governor's race.

Comment: Tom Campbell's greatest asset in the Republican gubernatorial primary is his greatest liability — he is a moderate Republican, which means that he has been a fiscal conservative and a social liberal. During the May 2009 special election, he supported Proposition 1A while Whitman, Poizner and most rank and file Republicans oppose it. As such, he has been unable to win the Republican nomination for statewide office when there was an open seat, specifically the 1992 U.S. Senate race. He did obtain the Republican nomination for the U.S. Senate when no one wanted to run against Dianne Feinstein. At the same time, in a three way race where the conservatives may split between Steve Poizner and Meg Whitman, Campbell has a chance. In fact, Poizner, Whitman and Campbell are all moderate Republicans, which makes

---

1 *Wikipedia* s.v. "Tom Campbell (California politician), "(Accessed April 29, 2009) http://en.wikipedia.org/wiki/Tom_Campbell_(California_politician); "About Tom," *Tom Campbell:Join the Conversation on California's Future*, http://www.campbell.org/about/. (Accessed May 14, 2009)

the conservatives choices that more difficult unless a leading conservative politician gets in the race.[1] In addition, Campbell and Jerry Brown were the only candidates in this race with a real grasp of the current finance situation of the California government. As Director of California's Department of Finance in 2004–05, he has an understanding of the state budget that no other gubernatorial candidate can match. In a political environment where the state's finances become an important issue, Campbell's expertise could be highly valued by voters more set in economics than ideology. In addition, Campbell has lots of experience campaigning, and in a high-visibility primary like the governor's race, where more people vote than vote down ticket, that could also be an issue. Finally, more pragmatic Republicans wanting to keep the governorship in Republican hands, may prefer a candidate like Campbell who has demonstrated that he can win in Democratic districts. Like Poizner and Whitman, Campbell has worked most of his adult life in Silicon Valley, and could neutralize their advantage in terms of Silicon Valley money, although he has nowhere near Poizner or Whitman's wealth. All this stacks up as to why Campbell was a close second to Whitman in the Field Poll and well ahead of Poizner. Campbell's candidacy is viable on many fronts. The question is whether he can survive the ideology of the current Republican Party.

Steve Poizner[2]
Born: January 4, 1957 Houston TX
Education: B.A. Texas 1978. M.B.A. Stanford 1980.
Religion: Jewish
Field Poll (March 2009): 7% (Third)
Personal Background: Neither web sources such as Wikipedia nor his gubernatorial campaign give much information on his background prior to 1980, except that he is married to Carol Poizner and they have one daughter Rebecca. After graduating from Stanford Poizner pent several years as a management consultant at the Boston Consulting Group. In 1983 Poizner founded Strategic Mapping, Inc. a software mapping firm. He sold Strategic Mapping in 1995 and founded SnapTrack, Inc., a GPS tracking technology firm, which was sold to Qualcomm in 2000 for approximately $1 billion. He is believed to have a net worth of $1 billion. After SnapTrack, he went into politics.

Political Background: Served as White House Fellow where he worked in the National Security Council Office of Cyberspace Security 2001–02. Was the Republican nominee for the California State Assembly in the 21st Assembly District, but lost to Democrat Ira Ruskin after Poizner spent $5 million of his own money on the race. Elected California Insurance Commissioner in 2006. Set up an exploratory committee for governor in 2008.

---

1 Shane Goldmacher, "Republican Whitman Launches 2010 Bid for Governor," *Sacramento Bee*, February 10, 2009, http://www.sacbee.com/capitoland California/story/1612318.html.

2 *Wikipedia* s.v. "Steve Poizner," http://en.wikipedia.org/wiki/Steve_Poizner (Accessed April 29,2009); "Meet Steve," *Steve Poizner Governor 2010*, http://www.stevepoizner.com/meet/bio/?_c=xz98a49tu6xcc7(Accessed May 14, 2009).

Comment: The paucity of information regarding Steve Poizner and his campaign is reflected in an article on his campaign from the Los Angeles Times. The article entitled "Poizner Runs a Rocky Path to Governor's Race" noted that the campaign is on its third campaign manager and that several top advisors have also left and reduced their visibility. At the same time it was noted that the fund set up to pay for his 2007 inauguration spent more than $375,000 on celebrations in San Jose and Sacramento and had nearly $150,000 in bills unpaid. Poizner eventually wrote personal checks in April 2009 to cover the deficit. The difficulty of the inaugural fund undermines Poizner primary claim that he will solve the state's financial woes by running it more efficiently. It also indicates a lack of funding support beyond Poizner's personal fortune. In April 2009, Poizner issued a sharp attack on rival Med Whitman, accusing her of a "disastrous record on fiscal mismanagement." The basis for the attack was Whitman's former company eBay taking a loss of $1.4 billion on the sale of Skype, which was purchased for $2.5 billion when Whitman was CEO of the company.[1] It indicates what kind of a campaign the Republicans could be in for in their gubernatorial primary. Despite his fortune and his statewide election to a minor office, Poizner is already trailing badly in the Field Poll, which also shows the problems that his campaign is having. The campaign is showing some of the signs that relatively inexperienced business candidates run into.[2] His response to Sacramento Bee reporter Peter Hecht in February 2009 on the California budget did not show any great insight into the state's financial crisis beyond the usual pro-business boilerplate regarding businesses fleeing California because the anti-business environment in the state.[3] There is plenty of time to turn things around, but it is clear that Poizner's campaign has some work to do.

Meg Whitman[4]
Born: August 4, 1956 Cold Spring Harbor, Long Island, NY
Education: A.B. Princeton 1977, M.B.A. Harvard 1979
Religion: Presbyterian
Field Poll (March 2009): 21% (First)
Personal Background: Born Margaret Cushing Whitman in an affluent Long Island community, Meg Whitman was the youngest of three children. Went to Princeton to study pre-med but switched to economics. After leaving Harvard she worked for several businesses, starting with Proctor & Gamble in 1979. While at P&G she met and married her husband Griffith Rutherford Harsh IV, a neurosurgeon in 1981. They have two sons. In March 1998 she was approached by a corporate headhunter who was looking to find someone who could supervise day-to-day operations and establish the brand for an Internet company founded in 1995 that was initially named

1 Capitol Alert, "Poizner Campaign Mounts Attack Against Whitman," *sacbee.com*, April 16, 2009, http://www.sacbee.com/static/weblogs/capitolalertlatest/021597.html.

2 See text cited in notes 4 and 5.

3 Peter Hecht, "Q&A: Poizner Explains Views on California Budget," *Sacramento Bee*, February 18, 2009, http://www.sacbee.com/capitolandcalifornia/v-print/story/1632869.html.

4 *Wikipedia* s.v. "Meg Whitman," http://en.wikipedia.org/wiki/Meg_Whitman (Accessed April 29, 2009); "Meg Whitman 1956-," *Reference for Business-Business Biographies S-Z*, http://www.reference forbusiness.com/biography/S-Z/Whitman-Meg-1956.html; "Meg," *Meg Whitman for Governor*, http://www.megwhitman.com/aboutMeg.php (Accessed May 14, 2009).

Auction Web, but had changed its name to eBay, Whitman was at first not interested, but took the job. EBay at the time had about thirty employees. The company grew to be one of the most successful Internet companies online with some 15,000 employees and $8 billion in revenues. Whitman resigned as CEO of eBay in November of 2007, but remained on the board as an advisor. She served on the board of the eBay Foundation, Proctor and Gamble, and Dream Works SKG until early 2009. Her estimated net worth is $1.4 billion.

Political Background: Meg Whitman has never been elected to office. Until recently, her primary political activity was donating money to candidates of both parties, but primarily Republicans. She first got actively involved politically in Mitt Romney's abortive presidential campaign in 2008 and was on his finance committee. When Romney left the race, Whitman supported John McCain as a national co-chair. She announced on February 9, 2009 that she would run for governor.[1]

Comment: As the only women currently active in the governor's race and as an acknowledged successful businesswoman from a well-known company, Meg Whitman comes into the campaign with some important assets. No doubt, that has helped take the lead in the Field poll on the Republican side. However, her campaign poses problems itself as its gets underway. First, although she opposes Proposition 1A along with Steve Poizner and supported the anti-gay marriage initiative Proposition 8 on the November 2008 ballot, she supports abortion rights, same-sex civil unions, and adoption rights for same-sex couples — social positions that conservative Republicans are bound to gag on. In that regard, she is not that much different than the so-called moderate in this race Tom Campbell. In addition to philosophical conflicts with conservative Republicans, there is the problem that she has not been one for very long — she only registered as a Republican in 2007. Her claim is that she needed to stay politically neutral for the sake of eBay, and she changed her registration for the sake of her friend Mitt Romney.[2] Not only does Whitman have registration problems, but she didn't vote in four statewide elections since 2003, including the 2003 recall. To top it off, Whitman gave money to former eBay co-worker and Democrat Steve Westly in his 2006 governor's race and has also given money to none other than liberal Senator Barbara Boxer.[3] Such revelations, when they are widely known, are bound to give moderate, let alone conservative, Republicans second thoughts about such a candidate. Whitman also comes with all the problems associated with green candidates, and, unlike Arnold Schwarzenegger, a beneficiary of the 2003 recall's short campaign window, will have to campaign for a full year, which will allow more experienced candidates plenty of time to target the Whitman campaign.[4]

In discussing issues such as the budget deficit Whitman has yet to go beyond generalities, stating that spending, regulations and the bureaucracy need to be cut, but without citing specific solutions. She noted at a Silicon Valley leadership group

---

1 Goldmacher, "Republican Whitman Launches 2010 Bid for Governor,"

2 Michael Finnegan, "Whitman Unveils Conservative Positions," *Los Angeles Times*, February 11, 2009, http://articles.latimes.com/2009/feb/11/local/me-whitman11?page_type=article&exci=2009/02/11/local/me-whitman11&pg=1

3 South, "Meg Whitman: a Female Checci or Simon?"

4 Ibid.

meeting the standard Republican line that "California does not have a revenue problem, it has a spending problem."[1] Michael Finnegan of the *Los Angeles Times* stated that she sounded like "an ill-at-ease novice who has studied stacks of policy binders, but has yet to master the art of political maneuvering."[2] Like Poizner, Whitman has the resources to run a campaign; she also has the unique asset of being the only woman in the field — but like Poizner's, her campaign has a lot to learn.

1 Stu Woo, "Whitman Lays Out Plans to Solve California's Fiscal Woes," *The Wall Street Journal*, April 27, 2009, http://blogs.wsj.com/washwire/2009/04/27/Whitman-lays-out-plan-to-solve-californias-fiscal-woes/.
2 Finnegan, "Whitman Unveils Conservative Positions."

9. HANDICAPPING THE HORSE RACE

As of this writing, the primary election for governor is just under a year away, and the general election is some seventeen months way with the next governor taking office in nineteen months. The country is in the grips of its worst financial downturn since the Great Depression. While some government officials are trying to promote the idea that the economy is bottoming out every time a favorable piece of news or a less awful piece of news is made public, it is clear that the economic problems of the country will be with us for some time, and will be around during next year's election. The results of the Obama Administration's recovery package have yet to be seen.

California in the meantime continues to be one of the hardest hit states in the nation. In May 2009, California's unemployment rate climbed to 11.5 %, the highest in modern record keeping (although it dropped from the fourth worst to the fifth worst rate in the country, behind Michigan, Oregon, Rhode Island and South Carolina).[1] Its housing situation, while showing increased sales through foreclosures and auctions, continues to be bad, with delinquencies rising and prices falling. The weak housing market continues to depress the economy, although state GDP surprisingly rose 0.4% in 2008, while other parts of the nation fell.[2] At this stage, there is no recovery in sight for the state. This is the overall picture as the 2010 California governor's election comes into focus.

---

1 Associated Press Writer, "Calif. Unemployment Climbs to Record 11.5 Percent." *Sacramento Bee*, June 19, 2009, http://www.sacbee.com/state_wire/v-print/story/1960877.html
2 The Buzz, "The Buzz: California's GDP Grew in 2008, Analyst Find," *sacbee.com*, June 9, 2009, http://www.sacbee.com/capitolandcalifornia/v-print/story/1930331.html.

Issues Impacting the 2010 Election

The Economy and the State Budget

The current polls on the subject on the economy and the budget offer some interesting background information. In a Probolsky Research (a Republican campaign consultancy)/Capitol Weekly Poll conducted between May 25 and May 29, 2009, voters cited the economy (31.2 %) as their top concern; more than double any other category, including public safety (15.3 %), government (12.5%), and education (12.0%).[1] The commanding position of the economy in this poll shows that it is the driving force behind current electoral politics in the state. It also shows that it is the economy itself, not its fallout on government, which is the primary issue. This could because voters are looking at more than California government at this point, and are giving the new Obama Administration a pass at this time.

They certainly did not give the California government a pass in the May 19, 2009 special election. Two key pollsters, Mark DiCamillo of the Field Poll and Mark Baldassare of the Public Policy Institute of California believe that the May 19 vote was a message to the state government to fix the state budget mess and do it quickly.[2]

How to fix it is another matter. While Governor Schwarzenegger and Republicans have stated that May 19 was a referendum against further taxes, Baldassare and DiCamillo indicated that the public might go for certain taxes as long as, in Dan Walter's words, they didn't tax themselves. That is why there is some interest in taxes on cigarettes and liquor, and very-high income people.[3] Although being rebuffed on May 19, the Democrats are still trying to approve taxes on cigarette, and an oil severance tax[4] and pass a budget sparing cuts in some of the social service safety net programs.[5] The impasse over taxes and the budget continues.

While the budget maneuvering continues between the two parties, the budget continues to sink. State Controller John Chiang released his May 2009 report showing that the revenue projections for May alone, which had been made earlier in the month as part of the governor's revised budget, were off $827 million.[6] As for State Treasurer Bill Lockyer, the legislature needs to balance the books now, even if future budget holes open up. "People somehow think they can have all the services and not pay the taxes," said Lockyer. "They're going to have to experience the cuts. Do an honest budget. Then possibly you can go to the voters and say, 'If you want some of this

---

1 John Howard, "Economy Trumps Education, Public Safety in New Poll," *Capitol Weekly*, June 4, 2009, http://www.capitolweekly.net/article-php?l&_c=y2gz9h3kg5titn&xid=y0zd934yqrl 1up&done=.y2gzfu5pu7ij7h#.

2 Peter Hecht, "Pollsters Evaluate California Special Election Results," *Sacramento Bee*, June 17, 2009, http://www.sacbee.com/capitolandcalifornia/v-print/story/1952810.html

3 Dan Walters, "Dan Walters: California Ballot Message Was 'Don't Tax Me,'" *Sacramento Bee*, June 17, 2009, http://www.sacbee.com/politics/v -print/story/1953095.html.

4 Shane Goldmacher and Eric Bailey, "Legislative Panel Approves Oil and Tobacco Taxes," *Los Angeles Times*, June 17, 2009, http://www.latimes.com/news/local/la-me-budget17-2009jun17,0,1715367.story.

5 Steve Wiegand, "Dems Vow to Pass 'Share-the-Pain' Budget," *Sacramento Bee*, June 17, 2009, http://www.sacbee.com/topstories/v-print/story/1955307.html.

6 Capitol Alert, "State Cash Hole Deepens," *sacbee.com*, http://www.sacbee.com/weblogs/capitolalertlatest/023001.html.

stuff back, you'll have to pay for it.'"[1] As Lockyer points out, the voters could very well change their minds on budget priorities when they are confronted with the realities of a slash-and-burn budget.

With the economic horror show continuing to unfold, the question in the 2010 governor's race is which candidate is best positioned to withstand the economic issue? The voters are obviously angry. Will they want to throw all the rascals out, regardless of party and search for new blood? They did that in the case of Barack Obama. But the voters are also nervous. Having one amateur in the White House groping his way, they may not want to have another one in the governor's executive office. Would they rather have someone more experienced in state government? Are they fed up with politicians, old and new, and prefer someone from the outside in the business community? Or having been burned by the bankers on Wall Street and the oil men from the Bush Administration, are they turned off to the idea of businessmen as politicians? The answer to these questions would obviously favor one gubernatorial candidate over another.

If the answer to the above question is an Obama clone, then someone like Gavin Newsom clearly has an advantage. As Jerry Roberts and Phil Trounstine noted in *Callbuzz*, Newsom "is positioning himself to run an Obama Lite campaign of generational change, promising new ideas, new approaches, and new outcomes to old and intractable California problems."[2] The question is how much staying power this approach will have if there is no substance behind the flash.

If the answer to the above question is an experienced politician, then a Jerry Brown, Tom Campbell or Antonio Villaraigosa would have an advantage. Brown's "back to basics" approach to the budget, Campbell's budget experience and Villaraigosa's ability to generate consensus in the legislature when he was Speaker of the Assembly would more likely appeal to a populace that wants an experienced hand at the helm. Brown's recent email fundraiser alludes to his long years of being closely involved in state government starting" — in the fifties — when my father ran for attorney general and then for governor, and again when I was governor."[3] Similarly, Campbell has shown his vast knowledge of the state budget. A nervous voter might be comfortable with such people regardless of the political baggage they bring.

If the answer to the above question is someone who has successfully run a business and could transfer those business skills to government, then Meg Whitman and Steve Poizner become the logical candidates. As is always the case with candidates from the business community is how well those business skills transfer. As Roberts and Trounstine noted about Whitman, her "biggest strength is her potential to ana-

1 George Skelton, "Note to Budget Doctors: Don't Spare the Knife; Treasurer Bill Lockyer Tells Democratic Lawmakers That Voters Are Angry and Want Them to Solve the Fiscal Problems Now," *Los Angeles Times*, June 11, 2009, http://www.latimes.com/news/local/la-me-cap11-2009jun11,0,4963544,print.column.

2 Jerry Roberts and Phil Trounstine, "The Calbuzz Primary Starts Today," *Calbuzz*, June 8, 2009, http://calbuzzer.blogspot.com/2009/06/calbuzz-primary-starts-today.html.

3 Jerry Brown, "Help Me Fight the Corrosive Politics of California," June 16, 2009 15:12:00 -0400(EDT) email from Jerry Brown 2010 ‹jerry@jerrybrown.org› to sc@cummingsresearch.com.

lyze and articulate fresh approaches to chronic economic and political problems; her greatest weakness is her failure to come close to doing so"[1] (in the campaign).

Finally, given voter proclivities, the answer to the above question could be "none of the above," in which case the voters would be searching for some other kind of candidate. Odds are, however, that economic reality will focus the voters' attention on the above categories.

While other issues might not have the impact of the economy on the election, they will still be important. The key ones will be Education, Public Safety, and Health. All three have been long time high priorities with the voters.

Education

The big issue regarding education is the severe cuts that education, both K through 12 and higher education, will suffer in the state budget, as education, prisons, and health-welfare are by far the largest budget items in the general fund. Some of this will be covered by the federal government, but not all. Education cuts impact a wide section of the voting public, including the middle class which is not as exposed in some of the other categories. Education cutbacks are also an issue of concern to Republicans, unlike welfare issues. The candidate who can craft a persuasive message on this issue will have a powerful asset among a wide range of people in the campaign. At this time, no candidate stands out on the subject.

Public Safety

Public safety was a distant second, but still second in the Probolsky Research/ Capitol Weekly poll.[2] Public safety is always a top priority among voters, particularly in the Republican Party. It has been the foundation of conservative and Republican Party message for decades. Yet to some degree, the voters only give lip service to public safety. The stories of the disregard and abandonment of U.S. service members returning from overseas or in peacetime is legion. Some of those attitudes have shown up in the recent financial crisis in California regarding law enforcement and correctional officers. The April 2009 Field Poll that showed voters rejecting nearly all the May 19 special election propositions and opposition to higher taxes, also showed that when asked to cut state services, the top target was the prisons and correctional officers. In fact, only two services of the long list given to voters, prisons and state parks, had majority support for cutting. The Schwarzenegger plan for balancing the state budget includes laying off 5,000 state employees, the majority of which are in the corrections department[3] In addition, hostility to government workers, including public safety personnel, has been palpable in the discussion of public worker salaries and pensions. As in the case of U.S. service members, support for public safety people

---

1 Roberts and Trounstine, "The Calbuzz Primary Starts Today."

2 Howard, "Economy Trumps Education"

3 Peter Hecht, "Field Poll: California Voters Oppose Five of Six May 19 Ballot Measures," *sacbee.com*, April 29, 2009, http://www.sacbee.com/politics/v-print/story/1818253.html; Kevin Yamamura, "Voters Takes Dim View of Governor, Legislature," *sacbee.com*, May 1, 2009, http://www.sacbee.com/politics/v-print/story/1825240.html.; Associated Press Writer, "AP News-Break: Proposed Deal for Calif. Inmate Care," *Sacramento Bee*, May 28, 2009, http://www.sacbee.com/state_wire/v-print/story/1900432.html.

ends when it affects the voter's pocket books. Still, the cuts in these programs at the state and local level represent a cut in services generally supported by middle-class, working-class and Republican voters that undermine the Republican position on safety issues, as under the Two-Thirds Budget requirement, Republican legislators are required to vote on and Republican Arnold Schwarzenegger is required to sign the budget. In addition, since the majority of the public safety personnel are in Republican-dominated unions, there will be increased interest from those union members to join forces with the traditional Democrat-dominated unions in the organized labor movement.

Health

Healthcare continues to be a major issue that cuts across party lines. A Field Poll survey of health care conducted between May 5 and May 24, 2009 "showed that 88% of Democrats, 73% of nonpartisans, and 55% of Republicans agree that the health care system either needs significant restructuring or should be completely rebuilt." In addition, 85% of those polled "said they support the general concept of allowing people a choice between privately run and government-run health plans." Sixty-nine percent support requiring employers to offer heath care and 74% support expanding Medicare to cover people between 55 and 64. There is a sharp split between Republicans and Democrats over whether to pay for health care with higher taxes[1], but what is evident is that the vast majority are open to fundamental changes in health care, and a new system funded by higher taxes may not be that far off in California. This could be especially true if the advocates for single-payer can convince California voters that a government-funded system would be substantially cheaper than a privately run system. Healthcare is an issue in which a gubernatorial candidate can make headway in the 2010 primary and general election if he or she can craft the right message.

THE CANDIDATES

Recent Polling

The most recent poll on the gubernatorial candidates was the Probolsky Research/Capitol Weekly poll taken between May 25 and 29, 2009 which showed Jerry Brown leading the Democrats at 21.3%, followed by Gavin Newsom at 16.4% and Antonio Villaraigosa at 14.3%. John Garamendi, who dropped out of the race to run for Congress polled 6.2%. On the Republican side, the polling was close with Tom Campbell at 11.6%, Meg Whitman at 8.2% and Steve Poizner at 7.8%.[2] In the prior Capitol Weekly poll in February with Dianne Feinstein in the polling, Brown was 14% and Newsom and Villaraigosa both at 9%. Therefore, there has been relatively little change between the Democratic remaining candidates. In the case of the Republicans, the prior poll was Campbell 15%, Whitman 14% and Poizner 4% — so

---

1 Peter Hecht, "Poll: Californians Want Health Care Overhaul, but They're Divided On Taxes," *Sacramento Bee*, June 18, 2009, http://www.sacbee.com/capitolandcalifornia/v-primary/story/1956233.html.
2 Howard, "Economy Trumps Education"

Campbell has widened his lead against Whitman, but both have dropped back while Poizner increased.[1]

The last Field Poll was in March and showed Brown at 26%, Villaraigosa at 22%, and Newsom at 16% with Garamendi at 8%. The Republicans showed Whitman with 21%, Campbell 18%, and Poizner 7%.[2]

The Democrats

On Monday, June 22, 2009, Los Angeles Mayor Antonio formally took himself out of the race for governor and instead plans to focus on managing the city's financial problems brought on by the recession.[3] With this news, it is increasingly looking like a Democratic primary between Jerry Brown and Gavin Newsom. If that is the contest, the primary will revolve around the issue of whether Democrats want an old face (Brown) or a new face (Newsom) as their nominee. In such a contest, Brown would have to be the favorite because a financially shell-shocked electorate would probably want to have a known quantity as their nominee and as their governor. Brown also benefits from Villaraigosa leaving the race. Among Los Angeles Democrats in a recent L.A. Times poll, Villaraigosa barely beat Attorney General Jerry Brown 36% to 32%, so Brown would be the strongest candidate in Los Angeles without the mayor.[4] As pointed out by *Sacramento Bee* columnist Dan Walters, Brown has long-standing ties to L.A. politics, having lived in the city for many years and having worked closely with the political organizations of Congressmen Howard Berman and Henry Waxman. Brown has equally long ties with the state's Latino leadership, dating back to when he was governor and helped promote the cause of farm workers by getting the farm labor relations law passed. He also appointed Latinos to key positions in his administration and to the state Supreme Court.[5] All of this puts Newsom in a difficult position.

However, with Villaraigosa and Garamendi out of the race, it opens up the field for someone like state Superintendent of Public Instruction Jack O'Connell to jump in. O'Connell would provide Sacramento experience without Brown's political baggage. O'Connell's problem would be that he would have little name recognition and no money to fight a primary, and he would have to have many voters feel that Brown and Newsom pose too big a political liability. With Brown having carried the 2006 Attorney General's election by the biggest margin for a state constitutional officer that year, it is difficult to see how O'Connell could get any traction on the liability issue against Brown. In the end, Brown would probably be the Democratic nominee.

---

1 Capitol Alert, "Poll: Feinstein Tops Dems Field: GOP Race Tight in 2010," *sacbee.com*, February 6, 2009, http://www.sacbee.com/static/weblogs/capitolalertlatest/019330.html.

2 Capitol Alert, "AM Alert: Feinstein, Whitman Atop Early 2010 Poll," *sacbee.com*, March 5, 2009, email from capitolalert@sacbee.com, Thu, 05 Mar 2009 08:00:51 -600 to sc@cummingsresearch.com

3 Dan Walters, "Villaraigosa Says He Won't Run for Governor," *Sacramento Bee*, June 22, 2009, http://www.sacbee.com/1095/v-print/story/1967562.html.

4 Phil Willon, "Villaraigosa's Future, Once Bright, Looks Dimmer Now," *Los Angeles Times*, June 20, 2009, http://www.latimes.com/news/local/la-me-poll21-2009jun21,0,3001867.story.

5 Dan Walters, "Villaraigosa's Departure Boosts Brown," *Sacramento Bee*, June 23, 2009, http://www.sacbee.com/capitolandcalifornia/v-print/story/1968293.html.

The Republicans

The polls show the Republican race as essentially as toss-up and with a huge block of undecided voters. Right now, the race features three moderate Republicans from Silicon Valley, two from the business community and another with ties to the business and legal schools in the Bay Area. The two business people, Steve Poizner and Meg Whitman, have very little experience in politics let alone political campaigns. Tom Campbell does have that experience but has been too politically moderate for activist Republicans to support, save for an unwinnable race against Dianne Feinstein.

A recent article in the San Jose Mercury News on Campbell pointed out his situation. It noted that he had been relatively strong against Whitman and Poizner, and that in the three-way race where Whitman and Poizner would split the conservative vote that they are targeting, Campbell might win a primary by seizing the smaller moderate Republican vote along with the Decline-To-State voters that vote in the Republican Primary.[1] But the article also pointed out what many others have said: that the reason Campbell is competing in this race is that none of the three announced candidates is of any real interest to die-hard conservative Republicans, particularly those in Southern California, which would dominate any primary. Many believe that the primary is wide open for a conservative from Southern California. However, the only candidate to step forward is Ventura County Supervisor Peter Foy, hardly a commanding figure in his own party let alone statewide. Nevertheless, the names of more familiar GOP leaders in Southern California have not been heard, and the most important conservative name in the party, Congressmember Tom McClintock, ruled out a run earlier. In part, Republicans have been hurt more than Democrats by term limits because Republicans don't enough long-term incumbents that can run in increasingly Democratic districts and can be effective gubernatorial candidates. They have been unable to crack into the statewide four-year constitutional officer jobs that are a stepping stone to the governorship, except by the recall and against the occasional weak Democratic candidate. At this point, the Republican nomination would be a complete crap-shoot with Campbell or a Southern California conservative having a slight edge.

The November Election

If the general election is between Brown and a conservative Brown will win. The Republicans have simply no one to match up with him. Brown's political baggage (and for anyone under the age of 35, no one would know or care) would be offset by the conservative Republican's ideological baggage, particularly that from the George W. Bush Administration. A Brown–Campbell race would be more intriguing because Campbell has a shot at getting the Decline To State vote from Brown. The question then would be where would the conservatives go? Would they vote for Campbell or stay home? In such a campaign, Brown's experience would be the decisive factor, and Brown would win a closer race.

---

1 Ken McLaughlin, "Can Tom Campbell Upset Billionaires Running for California Governor?" *San Jose Mercury News*, June 20, 2009, http://www.mercurynews.com/fdcp?1245689984089.

One final point. Because the new governor would be inheriting the greatest financial crisis since the Great Depression, that person, in all likelihood, would be unelectable in 2014. Many believe that Villaraigosa and some leading Republicans are keeping out of this election for that reason. At age 72, Jerry Brown is probably running his last statewide race, unless he chooses to run for U.S. Senate in 2012 or 2016, assuming those seats open up. By the end of his term, he would have passed Earl Warren as the longest serving governor, and would have no other attainable political mountains to climb. For younger candidates, assuming the governor's office in 2011 could easily be the last step in a short political career, ending by 2015, with no other opportunities on the horizon. Ultimately, that consideration may well determine who runs and finally wins.

APPENDIX 1. CALIFORNIA CENSUS DATA, 1960 TO 2010

All Census percentages are rounded off to whole numbers. Numbers may not add up to 100% due to rounding. *2008 figures are estimates. X = less than 1%. The "Asian" category includes Pacific Islanders also. N/A means not available. Source for Appendixes 1, 1A & 1B: Census Bureau.

CENSUS

	1960	1970	1980	1990	2000
Total Population	15,717,204	19,953,134	23,667,902	29,760,021	33,871,648

ETHNICITY: POPULATION (IN THOUSANDS)

Asian/Pacific Islander	318,376	552,364	1,253,818	2,845,659	3,814,474
Non-Hispanic Blacks	883,861	1,400,143	1,784,281	2,092,801	2,263,882
Non-Hispanic Whites	13,028,692	15,022,519	15,884,103	16,891,459	16,493,390
Non-Hispanic Other Race	59,737	239,595	201,369	242,164	333,346
Hispanics (all races)	1,426,538	2,738,513	4,544,331	7,687,938	10,966,556

PERCENT OF STATE

Census	1960	1970	1980	1990	2000	2008
Asian/Pacific Islander	2%	3%	5%	10%	11%	13%
Non-Hispanic Blacks	6%	7%	8%	7%	7%	6%
Non-Hispanic Whites	83%	75%	67%	57%	49%	44%
Non-Hispanic Other Race	X	1%	1%	1%	1%	1%
Hispanics (all races)	9%	14%	19%	26%	32%	36%
Two or More Races					(5%)	

RESIDENCY

Census	1960	1970	1980	1990	2000
Cities	33%	36%	37%	38%	39%
Suburbs	54%	55%	58%	58%	58%
Rural	13%	9%	5%	4%	3%
Homeowners	58%	55%	56%	52%	57%
Median Age (years)	30	28	32	31	33

EDUCATION

5 or More Years College	4%	7%	11%	8%	10%
College Graduates	6%	7%	20%	28%	27%
High School Grads	52%	63%	74%	76%	77%
No High School Diploma	48%	37%	26%	24%	23%

ECONOMICS

Median family income as % of US average	118%	112%	108%	115%	108%
Per capita income as % of US average	123%	114%	115%	114%	107%
Families below poverty line	12%	8%	9%	9%	11%
National Rank by Median Family Income	4th	9th	12th	8th	17th
Born in State	40%	43%	53%	46%	50%
Foreign-Born	9%	9%	15%	22%	26%
Married Couples	68%	65%	56%	53%	51%

TOTAL POPULATION BY REGION (IN THOUSANDS) (% OF STATE)

Census	1960	1970	1980	1990	2000	2009
Bay Area	3,626 (23%)	4,628 (23%)	5,180 (22%)	6,024 (20%)	6,784 (20%)	7,376 (20%)
North/Central Coast	706 (4%)	909 (4%)	1,126 (5%)	1,395 (5%)	1,544 (5%)	1,655 (4%)
Central Valley Cities	1,943 (12%)	2,308 (12%)	2,882 (12%)	3,836 (13%)	4,572 (13%)	5,472 (14%)
Los Angeles County	6,039 (38%)	7,032 (35%)	7,478 (32%)	8,863 (30%)	9,519 (28%)	10,393 (27%)
Southern California	2,746 (17%)	4,294 (22%)	5,882 (25%)	8,166 (27%)	9,668 (29%)	11,317 (30%)
Rural California	647 (4%)	778 (4%)	1,121 (5%)	1,476 (5%)	1,785 (5%)	1,780 (5%)
State Total	15,717	19,953	23,668	29,760	33,872	38,293

POPULATION OF REGIONS BY ETHNICITY

Note: the 1960 and 1970 Censuses combined Native Americans with Asians and Pacific-Islanders. After 1970, the category "Others" include only Native Americans, Eskimos and Aleutians.

1960 Census	Whites	Blacks	Asians	Hispanics	Others
Bay Area	82%	7%	4%	7%	N/A
North/Central Coast	87%	2%	3%	8%	N/A

Central Valley Cities	82%	4%	3%	11%	N/A
Los Angeles County	80%	8%	2%	10%	N/A
Southern California	87%	3%	1%	9%	N/A
Rural California	87%	2%	2%	9%	N/A
State Total	83%	6%	2%	9%	N/A

1970 Census	Whites	Blacks	Asians	Hispanics	Others
Bay Area	77%	8%	6%	10%	N/A
North/Central Coast	81%	2%	4%	12%	
Central Valley Cities	76%	5%	4%	15%	
Los Angeles County	68%	11%	4%	17%	
Southern California	82%	3%	2%	13%	
Rural California	85%	2%	3%	10%	
State Total	73%	7%	4%	16%	N/A

1980 Census	Whites	Blacks	Asians	Hispanics	Others
Bay Area	70%	9%	8%	12%	1%
North/Central Coast	76%	3%	3%	16%	2%
Central Valley Cities	71%	5%	3%	20%	1%
Los Angeles County	52%	13%	6%	28%	1%
Southern California	75%	4%	4%	16%	1%
Rural California	83%	1%	1%	12%	2%
State Total	67%	8%	5%	19%	1%

1990 Census	Whites	Blacks	Asians	Hispanics	Others
Bay Area	61%	9%	15%	15%	1%
North/Central Coast	70%	3%	4%	22%	1%
Central Valley Cities	62%	5%	7%	25%	1%
Los Angeles County	41%	11%	10%	38%	X
Southern California	64%	5%	7%	24%	1%
Rural California	80%	1%	2%	15%	2%
State Total	57%	7%	9%	26%	1%

2000 Census	Whites	Blacks	Asians	Hispanics	Others	Mixed
Bay Area	53%	8%	20%	19%	1%	5%
North/Central Coast	62%	2%	4%	30%	1%	4%
Central Valley Cities	52%	6%	8%	33%	1%	5%
Los Angeles County	33%	10%	12%	45%	1%	5%

Southern California	53%	5%	9%	32%	1%	4%
Rural California	74%	2%	3%	19%	2%	4%
State Total	49%	7%	11%	32%	1%	5%

"Mixed" means "two or more races."

2007 Census estimates	Whites	Blacks	Asians	Hispanics	Others
Bay Area	49%	7%	21%	23%	X
North/Central Coast	59%	2%	5%	33%	1%
Central Valley Cities	46%	6%	9%	37%	1%
Los Angeles County	30%	9%	13%	47%	1%
Southern California	48%	5%	10%	36%	1%
Rural California	71%	2%	3%	22%	2%
State Total	45%	6%	12%	36%	1%

INCOME LEVELS AND POVERTY RATES BY RACE/ETHNICITY:
MEDIAN FAMILY INCOMES BY ETHNICITY AS PERCENTAGE OF STATE AVERAGE:

Census	1960	1970	1980	1990	2000
Asian/Pacific Islander	83%	N/A	108%	107%	116%
Non-Hispanic Blacks	73%	69%	69%	73%	74%
Non-Hispanic Whites	105%	101%	105%	115%	108%
Non-Hispanic Other Race	56%	N/A	77%	76%	77%
Hispanics (all races)	60%	81%	70%	69%	77%
State Total	100	100	100	100	100

INDIVIDUAL POVERTY RATES BY ETHNICITY:

Census	1960	1970	1980	1990	2000
Asian/Pacific Islander	19.6%	N/A	13.6%	14.3%	12.9%
Non-Hispanic Blacks	22.8%	24.6%	26.4%	21.1%	22.4%
Non-Hispanic Whites	10.1%	9.9%	7.9%	7.3%	10.5%
Non-Hispanic Other Race	N/A	N/A	20.4%	18.6%	22.0%
Hispanics (all races)	16.1%	16.3%	23.7%	21.6%	22.1%
State Total	11.6%	11.1%	12.2%	11.1%	14.2%

| LA County Poverty Rates | 12.1% | 10.9%% | 13.4% | 15.1% | 17.9% |

(INDIVIDUALS, ALL ETHNIC BACKGROUNDS)
CALIFORNIA SUBURBIA BY RACE/ETHNICITY:

Census	1960	1970	1980	1990	2000
Asian/Pacific Islander	2%	3%	5%	9%	12%
Non-Hispanic Blacks	3%	4%	5%	6%	6%
Non-Hispanic Whites	87%	77%	70%	60%	50%
Non-Hispanic Other Race	X	X	1%	1%	1%
Hispanics (all races)	9%	16%	19%	24%	31%

APPENDIX 1A. CALIFORNIA/USA CENSUS DATA, 1960, 1980 AND 2000

(All Census percentages are rounded off to whole numbers. Numbers may not add up to 100% due to rounding. X = less than 1%).

Census	1960		1980		2000 (Y)	
	Calif.	USA	Calif.	USA	Calif.	USA
% of Total Population	8.7%	100%	10.4%	100%	12.0%	100%
Ethnicity:						
Asian/Pacific Islander	2%	1%	5%	2%	11%	4%
Non-Hispanic Blacks	6%	10%	8%	12%	7%	12%
Non-Hispanic Whites	83%	86%	66%	79%	49%	70%
Non-Hispanic Other Race	X	X	1%	1%	1%	1%
Hispanics (all races)	9%	3%	19%	6%	32%	13%
Percent in 2000 Census that were "two or more races"					4.7%	2.4%
Residency:						
Cities	33%	35%	37%	30%	39%	30%
Suburbs	54%	33%	58%	44%	58%	50%
Rural	13%	32%	5%	26%	3%	20%
Homeowners	58%	62%	56%	64%	57%	66%
Gender and Age:						
Men	50%	49%	49%	49%	50%	49%
Women	50%	51%	51%	51%	50%	51%
Median Age (years)	30	30	32	30	33	35
Married Couples	68%	68%	56%	60%	51%	52%

Census	1960		1980		2000 (Y)	
	Calif.	USA	Calif.	USA	Calif.	USA
Education:						
Median Age (years)	30	30	32	30	33	35
Married Couples	68%	68%	56%	60%	51%	52%
Advanced Degrees	N/A	N/A	N/A	N/A	10%	9%
College Graduates	10%	8%	20%	16%	27%	24%
High School Graduates	52%	41%	74%	66%	77%	80%
Foreign-born	9%	5%	15%	6%	26%	11%
Economics:						
Cost of Living Index	N/A	N/A	N/A	N/A	135%	100%
Median Family Income as % of US Average	118%	100%	109%	100%	108%	100%
Families below poverty line	12%	19%	9%	10%	11%	9%

(Y) In 2007, the Census Bureau estimated that California had 12.5% of the national population or one-eighth of all Americans.

Appendix 1B. Los Angeles City & County by Ethnicity, 1960 to 2008

Census	1960	1970	1980	1990	2000	2008*
Total Population	6,038,771	7,032,075	7,477,503	8,863,164	9,519,338	9,883,649
Ethnicity: Population						
Asian/Pacific Islander	123,359	262,732	434,850	907,810	1,306,108	
Non-Hispanic Blacks	461,546	762,844	943,968	934,776	883,911	
Non-Hispanic Whites	4,877,156	4,812,362	3,984,462	3,618,850	2,988,576	
Non-Hispanic Other	N/A	N/A	48,120	50,486	48,176	
Hispanics (all races)	576,710	1,194,137	2,066,103	3,351,242	4,656,878	
Percent of LA County						
Asian/Pacific Islander	2%	4%	6%	10%	12%	13%
Non-Hispanic Blacks	8%	11%	13%	11%	10%	9%

Non-Hispanic Whites	80%	68%	53%	41%	33%	30%
Non-Hispanic Other	N/A	N/A	1%	1%	1%	1%
Hispanics (all races)	10%	17%	28%	38%	45%	47%

City of Los Angeles						
Census	1960	1970	1980	1990	2000	2008
Ethnicity:						
Asian/Pacific Islander	82,291	101,615	198,436	341,398	375,169	
Non-Hispanic Blacks	334,916	503,606	495,292	485,949	415,195	
Non-Hispanic Whites	1,801,419	1,715,740	1,444,764	1,257,737	964,683	
Non-Hispanic Other	N/A	N/A	14,731	29,838	29,412	
Hispanics (all races)	260,389	481,668	815,305	1,370,476	1,719,073	
Percent of LA City						
Asian/Pacific Islander	3%	4%	7%	10%	10%	11%
Non-Hispanic Blacks	14%	18%	17%	14%	11%	10%
Non-Hispanic Whites	73%	61%	49%	36%	26%	29%
Non-Hispanic Other Race	N/A	N/A	X	1%	1%	1%
Hispanics (all races)	11%	17%	27%	39%	47%	49%

Note: In 2000, 5.2% of Los Angeles residents were "two or more races."

Census	1960	1970	1980	1990	2000	2008
Rest of Los Angeles County (Suburbs)						
Total Population	3,559,756	4,220,274	4,508,975	5,377,766	5,824,518	
Ethnicity: Population						
Asian/Pacific Islander	41,068	161,117	236,414	566,412	789,384	

Non-Hispanic Blacks	126,630	259,238	448,676	448,827	515,762	
Non-Hispanic Whites	3,075,737	3,096,622	2,539,698	2,361,113	2,139,944	
Non-Hispanic Other Race	N/A	N/A	33,389	20,648	47,576	
Hispanics (all races)	316,321	712,469	1,250,798	1,980,766	2,523,140	
Percent of LA County						
Asian/Pacific Islander	1%	4%	6%	11%	14%	15%
Non-Hispanic Blacks	4%	6%	10%	8%	9%	8%
Non-Hispanic Whites	86%	73%	56%	44%	37%	30%
Non-Hispanic Other Race	N/A	N/A	1%	X	1%	1%
Hispanics (all races)	9%	17%	28%	37%	43%	46%

APPENDIX 1C. CALIFORNIA'S GROWTH, 1850–2000

Year	Population	Growth	% Increase	% of USA	National Rank
1850	92,597	N/A	N/A	0.4%	29
1860	379,994	287,397	310%	1.2%	26
1870	560,247	180,253	47%	1.4%	24
1880	864,694	304,447	54%	1.7%	24
1890	1,208,398	343,704	40%	1.9%	22
1900	1,485,053	276,655	23%	1.9%	21
1910	2,377,549	892,496	60%	2.6%	12
1920	3,426,861	1,049,312	44%	3.2%	8
1930	5,677,251	2,250,390	66%	4.6%	6
1940	6,907,387	1,230,136	22%	5.2%	5
1950	10,586,223	3,678,836	53%	7.0%	2
1960	15,717,204	5,130,981	48%	8.8%	2
1970	19,953,134	4,235,930	27%	9.8%	1
1980	23,667,902	3,714,768	19%	10.4%	1
1990	29,760,021	6,092,119	26%	12.0%	1
2000	33,871,648	4,111,627	14%	12.0%	1
2009@	38,293,000	4,421,352	13%	12.5%	1

*2009 estimate courtesy of California Department of Finance; others are official Census totals.

Appendix 1D. Assembly & Senate Trends, 1950–2008

	ASSEMBLY		STATE SENATE	
ELECTION YEAR	DEM.	REP.	DEM.	REP.
1952	26	54	11	29
1954	32	44	16	23
1956	38	42	20	20
1958	48	32	27	13
1960	47	33	30	10
1962	52	28	27	13
1964	49	31	27	13
1966*	42	38	21	19
1968	39	41	20	20
1970	43	37	21	19
1972	49	31	22	18
1974	55	25	25	15
1976	57	23	26	14
1978	50	30	25	15
1980	47	33	23	17
1982	48	32	25	15
1984	47	33	25	15
1986	44	36	24	15
1988	47	33	24	15
1990	48	32	26	13
1992	47	33	24	15
1994	39	41	22	16
1996	43	37	23	16
1998	48	32	25	15
2000	50	30	26	14
2002	48	32	25	15
2004	48	32	25	15
2006	48	32	25	15
2008	50	30	25	15

Source: California State Blue Book

*Special redistricting ordered by the Supreme Court in 1966.

Note: seats won in special elections are counted in the next year's line-up. Assembly seats may not add up to 80 or Senate seats to 40 due to the presence of independent members.

APPENDIX 2. SUMMARIES OF CALIFORNIA PARTISAN VOTING FOR PRESIDENT, GOVERNOR AND US SENATE, 1958–2008

Definitions of regional categories: The "Bay Area" includes San Francisco, Alameda (Oakland), Santa Clara (San Jose), Contra Costa, Napa, San Mateo, Solano, and Sonoma Counties. The North and Central Coast Counties are Del Norte, Humboldt, Mendocino, Monterey, San Luis Obispo, Santa Barbara, & Santa Cruz. The Central Valley Cities include Fresno, Kern, Kings, Merced, Sacramento, San Joaquin, Stanislaus, Tulare, & Yolo Counties. Los Angeles County also includes the City of Los Angeles. Southern California includes Orange, Riverside, San Bernardino, San Diego and Ventura Counties. "Rural California" is every other county in the state. In the technically non-partisan recall/replacement 2003 race, Cruz Bustamante is counted as the Democratic candidate and Arnold Schwarzenegger as the Republican. All state and county election returns were obtained from the America Votes series. The Regional categories provided by Tony Quinn. These categories apply to every election analyzed below.

Definitions of Social Groups: Racial and ethnic voting data comes from Network and LA Times exit polls after 1979.From 1970 to 1978, Field Poll data are used along with the LA Times exit polls, plus precinct studies done by NBC News and CBS News. Prior to 1970, precinct, city and district data are used from the California State Archives. "Asian" voters in the 1958-68 period are represented by San Francisco's Chinatown. Hispanics trends from the early period were taken from pre-dominantly Hispanic (89% in the 1960 Census) East Los Angeles, plus also urban Hispanics precincts in San Francisco and San Jose. Blacks were sampled in the overwhelmingly African-American precincts of South-Central Los Angeles, Inglewood and Compton plus the black neighborhoods of Oakland & San Francisco. For some elections in the 1960-72 period, the data for blacks and Hispanics comes from precinct studies done for NBC News and reported in The Ethnic Factor by Michael Kramer and Mark Levy. White Liberals are represented by Marin County, the city of Berkeley and the West Los Angeles assembly districts. Wealthy Conservatives are portrayed by Orange County and Placer County (after 1995).The Bay Area all-suburban Counties are Contra Costa, Marin, Napa, San Mateo, Solano and Sonoma. The category "Southern California Whites" means (mostly suburban) white voters in Orange, Riverside, San Bernardino, San Diego and Ventura Counties. White workers are from the blue collar neighborhoods of southeastern Los Angeles County and San Francisco's "Sunset" neighborhood plus the cities of South San Francisco and the "I-880 Corridor" (San Leandro, Fremont, Hayward, Milpitas, Newark, Union City) in the Bay Area. The social categories were provided by Bill Schneider, Bill Cavala and Patrick Reddy. The "Ethnic Vote" category may not add up to 100% because of mixed-race or "Other Race" voters. All state, Assembly District and county election returns were obtained from the America Votes series. All precinct and city returns were obtained from the California Secretary of State Archives.

Note: N/A means "not available." (All turnout figures and election statistics are rounded off to whole numbers). "Turnout" means the percentage of registered voters who participated in a given election.

Year: 1958   Democrat: Pat Brown
Election: Governor   Republican: William Knowland
Turnout: 79%

Geographic Breakdown:

Region	% of State	Dem (%)	Rep (%)	Total Votes	Margin
Bay Area	25%	850,763 (65%)	465,907 (35%)	1,317,603	D 384,256
Nor/Central Coast	4%	118,106 (56%)	93,851 (44%)	212,063	D 24,255
Cent. Valley Cities	11%	376,565 (66%)	194,429 (34%)	571,382	D 182,443
LA County	41%	1,254,226 (58%)	909,429 (42%)	2,165,771	D 344,797
South. Cal.	15%	402,571 (52%)	363,546 (47%)	766,899	D 39,025
Rural Cal.	4%	137,845 (62%)	84,056 (38%)	222,059	D 53,789
State	100%	3,140,076 (60%)	2,110,911 (40%)	5,255,777	D 1,029,165

Ethnic Breakdown /Social Group Voting

Group	D%	R%	% of State Voters
Asians	75%	25%	1%
Blacks	90%	10%	5%
Hispanics	85%	15%	4%
Whites	57%	43%	90%

White Sub-Groups:

White Liberals	63%	37%
Conservatives	46%	54%
Bay Area Suburbs	63%	37%
South Cal. Whites	50%	49%
Bay Area White Workers	70%	30%
LA County White Workers	66%	34%

Sources: Asians – Chinatown; Blacks – South Central Los Angeles; Hispanics – East Los Angeles.

Year: 1958   Democrat: Clair Engle
Election: US Senate   Republican: Goodwin Knight

Geographic Breakdown:

Region	% of State	Dem (%)	Rep (%)	Total Votes	Margin
Bay Area	25%	759,805 (59%)	518,740 (41%)	1,279,223	D 241,065
Nor/Central Coast	4%	112,268 (54%)	95,679 (46%)	208,070	D 16,589
Cent. Valley Cities	11%	370,305 (66%)	191,641 (34%)	562,234	D 178,664
LA County	41%	1,135,669 (54%)	974,618 (46%)	2,111,556	D 161,051
South. Cal.	15%	391,767 (52%)	362,054 (48%)	754,549	D 29,713
Rural Cal.	4%	157,879 (72%)	61,605 (28%)	219,589	D 96,274
State	100%	2,927,693 (57%)	2,204,337 (43%)	5,135,221	D 723,356

Ethnic Breakdown /Social Group Voting

Group	D%	R%	% of State Voters
Asians	62%	38%	1%
Blacks	74%	26%	5%
Hispanics	79%	21%	4%
Whites	54%	46%	90%

White Sub-Groups:

White Liberals	57%	43%
Conservatives	48%	52%
Bay Area Suburbs	59%	41%
South Cal. Whites	50%	50%
Bay Area White Workers	61%	39%
LA County White Workers	60%	40%

Sources: Asians – Chinatown; Blacks – South Central Los Angeles; Hispanics – East Los Angeles.

Year: 1960   Democrat: John F. Kennedy
Election: President   Republican: Richard Nixon
Turnout: 88%

Geographic Breakdown:

Region	% of State	Dem (%)	Rep (%)	Total Votes	Margin
Bay Area	24%	821,350 (52%)	751,719 (48%)	1,578,030	D 69,641
Nor/Central Coast	4%	119,940 (45%)	145,352 (55%)	266,430	R 25,412
Cent. Valley Cities	11%	368,722 (52%)	332,177 (47%)	704,049	D 36,545
LA County	41%	1,323,818 (50%)	1,302,661 (49%)	2,634,499	D 21,157
South. Cal.	16%	460,365 (43%)	598,357 (56%)	1,062,332	R 137,492
Rural Cal.	4%	129,894 (49%)	129,456 (49%)	263,238	D 438
State	100%	3,224,099 (50%)	3,259,722 (50%)	6,506,578	R 35,623

Ethnic Breakdown /Social Group Voting

Group	D%	R%	% of State Voters
Asians	58%	42%	1%
Blacks	86%	14%	5%
Hispanics	83%	17%	4%
Whites	45%	54%	90%

White Sub-Groups:

White Liberals	56%	44%
Conservatives	39%	61%
Bay Area Suburbs	50%	50%
South Cal. Whites	41%	59%
Bay Area White Workers	56%	44%
LA County White Workers	55%	45%

Sources: Asians – Chinatown; Blacks and Hispanics – NBC News.

Year: 1962   Democrat: Pat Brown
Election: Governor Republican: Richard Nixon
Turnout: 79%

Geographic Breakdown:

Region	% of State	Dem (%)	Rep (%)	Total Votes	Margin
Bay Area	24%	787,694 (56%)	607,604 (43%)	1,410,606	D 180,090
Nor/Central Coast	4%	117,873 (49%)	121,288 (50%)	242,629	R 3,415

Cent. Valley Cities	11%	367,271 (56%)	281,314 (43%)	658,198	D 85,957
LA County	39%	1,171,724 (52%)	1,080,113 (47%)	2,219,282	D 111,611
South. Cal.	17%	442,012 (44%)	539,810 (54%)	997,783	R 97,798
Rural Cal.	4%	130,535 (53%)	110,222 (45%)	244,772	D 20,313
State	100%	3,037,109 (52%)	2,740,351 (47%)	5,853,270	D 296,758

Ethnic Breakdown /Social Group Voting

Group	D%	R%	% of State Voters
Asians	52%	48%	1%
Blacks	93%	7%	6%
Hispanics	81%	18%	5%
Whites	48%	51%	88%

White Sub-Groups:

White Liberals	61%	38%
Conservatives	39%	59%
Bay Area Suburbs	54%	45%
South Cal. Whites	41%	56%
Bay Area White Workers	62%	37%
LA County White Workers	54%	45%

Sources: Asians – Chinatown; Blacks – South Central Los Angeles; Hispanics – East Los Angeles.

Year: 1962   Democrat: Richard Richards
Election: US Senate   Republican: Thomas Kuchel

Geographic Breakdown:

Region	% of State	Dem (%)	Rep (%)	Total Votes	Margin
Bay Area	24%	580,566 (43%)	766,492 (57%)	1,349,150	R 185,926
Nor/Central Coast	4%	89,701 (39%)	142,087 (61%)	232,235	R 52,386
Cent. Valley Cities	11%	258,514 (41%)	376,075 (59%)	635,228	R 117,561
LA County	39%	1,045,121 (47%)	1,171,678 (53%)	2,223,335	R 126,557
South. Cal.	17%	385,060 (40%)	568,487 (60%)	973,207	R 198,427
Rural Cal.	4%	93,877 (40%)	140,664 (60%)	234,797	R 46,787
State	100%	2,452,839 (43%)	3,180,483 (56%)	5,647,952	R 727,644

Ethnic Breakdown /Social Group Voting

Group	D%	R%	% of State Voters
Asians	42%	58%	1%
Blacks	83%	17%	6%
Hispanics	78%	22%	5%
Whites	38%	61%	88%

White Sub-Groups:

White Liberals	49%	51%
Conservatives	36%	63%
Bay Area Suburbs	41%	58%
South Cal. Whites	38%	62%
Bay Area White Workers	49%	51%
LA County White Workers	50%	50%

Sources: Asians – Chinatown; Blacks – South Central Los Angeles; Hispanics – East Los Angeles.

Year: 1964
Election: President
Turnout: 88%

Democrat: Lyndon Johnson
Republican: Barry Goldwater

Geographic Breakdown:

Region	% of State	Dem (%)	Rep (%)	Total Votes	Margin
Bay Area	24%	1,116,215 (66%)	579,528 (34%)	1,698,161	D 536,687
Nor/Central Coast	4%	178,476 (60%)	117,647 (40%)	296,613	D 60,829
Cent. Valley Cities	11%	490,249 (64%)	273,266 (36%)	764,389	D 216,983
LA County	39%	1,568,300 (57%)	1,161,067 (43%)	2,730,918	D 407,233
South. Cal.	18%	649,692 (51%)	632,215 (49%)	1,282,877	D 17,477
Rural Cal.	4%	168,945 (59%)	115,385 (41%)	284,628	D 53,560
State	100%	4,171,877 (59%)	2,877,108 (41%)	7,057,586	D 1,292,769

Ethnic Breakdown /Social Group Voting

Group	D%	R%	% of State Voters
Asians	76%	24%	1%
Blacks	98%	2%	7%
Hispanics	90%	10%	5%
Whites	54%	46%	87%

White Sub-Groups:

White Liberals	69%	31%
Conservatives	44%	56%
Bay Area Suburbs	64%	36%
South Cal. Whites	48%	52%
Bay Area White Workers	67%	33%
LA County White Workers	58%	42%

Sources: Asians – Chinatown; Blacks and Hispanics – NBC News.

Year: 1964   Democrat: Pierre Salinger
Election: US Senate   Republican: George Murphy

Geographic Breakdown:

Region	% of State	Dem (%)	Rep (%)	Total Votes	Margin
Bay Area	24%	898,545 (53%)	793,393 (47%)	1,692.374	D 105,212
Nor/Central Coast	4%	145,735 (49%)	149,134 (51%)	294,920	R 3,399
Cent. Valley Cities	11%	400,784 (53%)	358,860 (47%)	759,772	D 41,924
LA County	39%	1,285,738 (47%)	1,435,745 (52%)	2,722,923	R 151,007
South. Cal.	18%	540,669 (42%)	746,994 (58%)	1,287,854	R 206,325
Rural Cal.	4%	140,441 (49%)	143,489 (51%)	283,978	R 3,048
State	100%	3,411,912 (48%)	3,628,555 (52%)	7,041,821	R 216,643

Ethnic Breakdown /Social Group Voting

Group	D%	R%	% of State Voters
Asians	60%	40%	1%
Blacks	96%	4%	7%
Hispanics	75%	25%	5%
Whites	42%	58%	87%

White Sub-Groups:

White Liberals	59%	41%
Conservatives	35%	65%
Bay Area Suburbs	50%	48%
South Cal. Whites	39%	61%
Bay Area White Workers	55%	45%
LA County White Workers	45%	55%

Sources: Asians – Chinatown; Blacks – South Central Los Angeles; Hispanics – East Los Angeles.

Year: 1966
Election: Governor
Turnout: 79%

Democrat: Pat Brown
Republican: Ronald Reagan

Geographic Breakdown:

Region	% of State	Dem (%)	Rep (%)	Total Votes	Margin
Bay Area	24%	760,610 (48%)	806,716 (51%)	1,571,609	R 46,106
Nor/Central Coast	4%	104,699 (38%)	167,524 (61%)	272,829	R 62,825
Cent. Valley Cities	11%	321,502 (44%)	401,047 (55%)	723,256	R 79,545
LA County	37%	1,037,663 (43%)	1,389,995 (57%)	2,431,093	R 352,332
South. Cal.	19%	417,621 (34%)	809,968 (66%)	1,229,728	R 392,347
Rural Cal.	4%	107,079 (39%)	167,663 (61%)	274,930	R 60,584
State	100%	2,749,174 (42%)	3,742,913 (57%)	6,503,445	R 993,739

Ethnic Breakdown /Social Group Voting

Group	D%	R%	% of State Voters
Asians	61%	39%	1%
Blacks	96%	4%	7%
Hispanics	80%	20%	5%
Whites	35%	64%	87%

White Sub-Groups:

White Liberals	59%	41%
Conservatives	28%	72%
Bay Area Suburbs	45%	55%
South Cal. Whites	30%	69%
Bay Area White Workers	50%	50%
LA County White Workers	39%	61%

Sources: Asians – Chinatown; Blacks and Hispanics – NBC News.

Year: 1968
Election: President

Democrat: Hubert Humphrey
Republican: Richard Nixon
Independent: George Wallace

Turnout: 86%

Geographic Breakdown:

Region	% of State	Dem (%)	Rep (%)	Ind (%)	Total Votes	Margin

Bay Area	24%	890,650 (51%)	725,304 (41%)	116,516 (7%)	1,755,226	D 165,346
Nor/Cen Coast	4%	128,793 (42%)	155,934 (51%)	20,572 (7%)	307,655	R 27,141
C. Val Cities	11%	367,704 (47%)	347,762 (44%)	62,976 (8%)	781,725	D 19,942
LA County	37%	1,223,251 (46%)	1,266,480 (48%)	151,050 (6%)	2,657,982	R 43,229
South. Cal.	20%	514,896 (35%)	831,533 (57%)	108,227 (7%)	1,461,117	R 316,642
Rural Cal.	4%	119,024 (41%)	140,646 (49%)	27,929 (10%)	287,882	R 21,622
State	100%	3,244,318 (45%)	3,467,664 (48%)	487,270 (7%)	7,251,587	R 223,346

Ethnic Breakdown /Social Group Voting

Group	D%	R%	I%	% of State Voters
Asians	62%	29%	8%	1%
Blacks	91%	8%	1%	7%
Hispanics	87%	12%	1%	5%
Whites	39%	54%	7%	87%

White Sub-Groups:

White Liberals	60%	36%	4%
Conservatives	30%	63%	7%
Bay Area Suburbs	47%	44%	8%
South Cal. Whites	30%	61%	8%
Bay Area White Workers	54%	37%	8%
LA County White Workers	44%	48%	8%

Sources: Asians – Chinatown; Blacks and Hispanics – NBC News.

Year: 1968   Democrat: Alan Cranston
Election: US Senate   Republican: Max Rafferty

Geographic Breakdown:

Region	% of State	Dem (%)	Rep (%)	Total Votes	Margin
Bay Area	24%	1,020,529 (60%)	662,508 (39%)	1,708,5111	D 358,021
Nor/Central Coast	4%	147,659 (49%)	148,847 (50%)	300,434	R 1.188
Cent. Valley Cities	11%	403,795 (54%)	337,815 (45%)	750,666	D 65,980
LA County	37%	1,344,953 (52%)	1,232,231 (47%)	2,613,002	D 112,722
South. Cal.	20%	613,832 (43%)	811,620 (56%)	1,440,905	R 197,788
Rural Cal.	4%	149,584 (52%)	136,127 (47%)	288,947	D 13,457
State	100%	3,680,352 (52%)	3,329,148 (47%)	7,102,465	D 351,204

Ethnic Breakdown /Social Group Voting

Group	D%	R%	% of State Voters
Asians	70%	28%	1%
Blacks	91%	6%	7%
Hispanics	87%	12%	5%
Whites	47%	52%	87%

White Sub-Groups:

White Liberals	65%	33%
Conservatives	38%	61%
Bay Area Suburbs	56%	43%
South Cal. Whites	38%	61%
Bay Area White Workers	61%	38%
LA County White Workers	51%	48%

Sources: Asians – Chinatown; Blacks and Hispanics – NBC News.

Year: 1970   Democrat:Jess Unruh
Election: Governor   Republican: Ronald Reagan
Turnout: 76%

Geographic Breakdown:

Region	% of State	Dem (%)	Rep (%)	Total Votes	Margin
Bay Area	25%	777,396 (49%)	784,914 (49%)	1,598,346	R 11,518
Nor/Central Coast	4%	113,477 (41%)	158,861 (57%)	278,709	R 45,384
Cent. Valley Cities	11%	354,375 (49%)	360,264 (50%)	726,902	R 5,889
LA County	36%	1,095,899 (47%)	1,173,161 (51%)	2,312,263	R 77,262
South. Cal.	20%	482,362 (36%)	815,137 (61%)	1,326,248	R 332,775
Rural Cal.	4%	115,098 (43%)	147,327 (55%)	267,604	R 32,229
State	100%	2,938,607 (45%)	3,439,664 (53%)	6,510,072	R 501,057

Ethnic Breakdown /Social Group Voting

Group	D%	R%	% of State Voters
Asians	44%	52%	1%
Blacks	95%	3%	7%
Hispanics	82%	16%	5%
Whites	39%	59%	87%

White Sub-Groups:

White Liberals	59%	38%
Conservatives	31%	67%
Bay Area Suburbs	44%	54%
South Cal. Whites	33%	65%
Bay Area White Workers	50%	48%
LA County White Workers	46%	52%

Sources: Asians – Field Poll; Blacks and Hispanics – NBC News.

Year: 1970   Democrat: John Tunney
Election: US Senate   Republican: George Murphy

Geographic Breakdown:

Region	% of State	Dem (%)	Rep (%)	Total Votes	Margin
Bay Area	24%	932,218 (59%)	619,019 (39%)	1,587,214	D 313,199
Nor/Central Coast	4%	144,083 (52%)	125,204 (45%)	276,106	D 18,879
Cent. Valley Cities	11%	415,254 (57%)	298,494 (41%)	725,738	D 116,760
LA County	36%	1,257,262 (54%)	1,022,408 (44%)	2,315,967	D 234,854
South. Cal.	20%	609,027 (46%)	691,859 (52%)	1,322,555	R 82,332
Rural Cal.	4%	138,714 (52%)	120,633 (46%)	264,577	D 18,081
State	100%	3,496,558 (54%)	2,877,617 (44%)	6,492,157	D 618,941

Ethnic Breakdown /Social Group Voting

Group	D%	R%	% of State Voters
Asians	68%	28%	1%
Blacks	94%	3%	7%
Hispanics	86%	13%	5%
Whites	49%	49%	87%

White Sub-Groups:

White Liberals	64%	33%
Conservatives	41%	58%
Bay Area Suburbs	56%	43%
South Cal. Whites	43%	55%
Bay Area White Workers	61%	37%
LA County White Workers	54%	44%

Sources: Asians – Field Poll; Blacks and Hispanics – NBC News.

Year: 1972   Democrat: George McGovern
Election: President Republican: Richard Nixon
Turnout: 82%

Geographic Breakdown:

Region	% of State	Dem (%)	Rep (%)	Total Votes	Margin
Bay Area	25%	990,560 (48%)	1,007,615 (49%)	2,052,982	R 17,055
Nor/Central Coast	5%	168,992 (42%)	213,844 (54%)	397,966	R 44,852
Cent. Valley Cities	11%	397,630 (44%)	475,385 (52%)	906,600	R 77,755
LA County	34%	1,189,977 (42%)	1,549,717 (55%)	2,830,370	R 359,740
South. Cal.	22%	590,186 (32%)	1,168,037 (64%)	1,837,255	R 577,851
Rural Cal.	4%	138,502 (40%)	187,498 (55%)	342,689	R 48,996
State	100%	3,475,847 (42%)	4,602,096 (55%)	8,367,863	R 1,126,249

Ethnic Breakdown /Social Group Voting

Group	D%	R%	% of State Voters
Asians	46%	54%	1%
Blacks	90%	9%	7%
Hispanics	74%	23%	5%
Whites	37%	60%	87%

White Sub-Groups:

White Liberals	57%	41%
Conservatives	29%	68%
Bay Area Suburbs	43%	51%
South Cal. Whites	28%	68%
Bay Area White Workers	48%	50%
LA County White Workers	38%	58%

Sources: Asians – Field Poll; Blacks and Hispanics – NBC News.

Year: 1974   Democrat: Jerry Brown
Election: Governor   Republican: Houston Flournoy
Turnout: 64%

Geographic Breakdown:

Region	% of State	Dem (%)	Rep (%)	Total Votes	Margin
Bay Area	24%	809,962 (54%)	660,411 (44%)	1,510,775	D 149,551
Nor/Central Coast	5%	153,194 (49%)	151,783 (49%)	315,005	D 411
Cent. Valley Cities	11%	349,556 (50%)	333,324 (48%)	699,256	D 16,232
LA County	32%	1,059,533 (53%)	898,808 (45%)	2,005,165	D 160,725
South. Cal.	23%	623,405 (44%)	763,149 (54%)	1,424,607	R 139,744
Rural Cal.	5%	135,998 (46%)	144,479 (49%)	293,262	R 8,481
State	100%	3,131,648 (50%)	2,952,954 (47%)	6,248,070	D 178,694

Ethnic Breakdown /Social Group Voting

Group	D%	R%	% of State Voters
Asians	53%	42%	1%
Blacks	89%	10%	7%
Hispanics	84%	15%	5%
Whites	44%	52%	87%

White Sub-Groups:

White Liberals	58%	39%
Conservatives	41%	57%
Bay Area Suburbs	49%	48%
South Cal. Whites	39%	59%
Bay Area White Workers	59%	39%
LA County White Workers	57%	40%

Sources: Asians & Hispanics – Field Poll, Blacks – CBS News.

Year: 1974   Democrat: Alan Cranston
Election: US Senate   Republican: H.L. Richardson

Geographic Breakdown:

Region	% of State	Dem (%)	Rep (%)	Total Votes	Margin
Bay Area	24%	1,007,136 (69%)	409,543 (28%)	1,465,597	D 597,593
Nor/Central Coast	5%	184,757 (60%)	111,325 (36%)	308,666	D 73,432
Cent. Valley Cities	11%	425,834 (61%)	233,507 (34%)	692,926	D 192,327

LA County	32%	1,175,843 (60%)	736,423 (38%)	1,961,418	D 423,420
South. Cal.	23%	740,136 (53%)	612,283 (44%)	1,402,705	D 127,853
Rural Cal.	4%	159,454 (59%)	107,186 (40%)	271,120	D 52,268
State	100%	3,693,160 (61%)	2,210,267 (36%)	6,102,432	D 1,482,893

Ethnic Breakdown /Social Group Voting

Group	D%	R%	% of State Voters
Asians	63%	34%	1%
Blacks	92%	6%	7%
Hispanics	83%	14%	5%
Whites	57%	40%	87%

White Sub-Groups:

White Liberals	69%	28%
Conservatives	49%	47%
Bay Area Suburbs	66%	31%
South Cal. Whites	49%	48%
Bay Area White Workers	72%	25%
LA County White Workers	64%	33%

Sources: Asians & Hispanics – Field Poll, Blacks – CBS News.

Year: 1976   Democrat: Jimmy Carter
Election: President   Republican: Gerald Ford
Turnout: 81%

Geographic Breakdown:

Region	% of State	Dem (%)	Rep (%)	Total Votes	Margin
Bay Area	24%	950,055 (50%)	872,920 (46%)	1,905,498	D 77,135
Nor/Central Coast	5%	191,507 (48%)	191,774 (48%)	398,623	R 267
Cent. Valley Cities	11%	430,691 (50%)	410,225 (48%)	863,076	D 20,466
LA County	31%	1,221,893 (50%)	1,174,926 (48%)	2,459,077	D 46,967
South. Cal.	24%	770,293 (41%)	1,055,643 (56%)	1,874,072	R 285,350
Rural Cal.	5%	177,845 (48%)	176,756 (48%)	366,771	D 1,089
State	100%	3,742,284 (48%)	3,882,244 (49%)	7,867,117	R 139,960

Ethnic Breakdown /Social Group Voting

Group	D %	R%	% of State Voters
Asians	45%	52%	1%
Blacks	87%	13%	7%
Hispanics	83%	15%	5%
Whites	42%	55%	87%

White Sub-Groups:

White Liberals	55%	42%
Conservatives	35%	62%
Bay Area Suburbs	47%	49%
South Cal. Whites	37%	60%
Bay Area White Workers	54%	42%
LA County White Workers	54%	44%

Sources: Asians & Hispanics – Field Poll, Blacks – CBS News.

Year: 1976   Democrat: John Tunney
Election: US Senate   Republican: S.I. Hayakawa

Geographic Breakdown:

Region	% of State	Dem (%)	Rep (%)	Total Votes	Margin
Bay Area	25%	943,032 (50%)	869,507 (46%)	1,872,280	D 73,525
Nor/Central Coast	5%	182,885 (47%)	195,055 (50%)	393,102	R 12,170
Cent. Valley Cities	11%	382,793 (46%)	432,255 (51%)	840,945	R 49,462
LA County	28%	1,061,839 (50%)	992,752 (47%)	2,108,061	D 69,087
South. Cal.	25%	776,431 (41%)	1,066,921 (56%)	1,895,404	R 290,490
Rural Cal.	5%	155,882 (43%)	192,483 (53%)	362,476	R 36,601
State	100%	3,502,862 (47%)	3,748,973 (50%)	7,442,268	R 246,111

Ethnic Breakdown /Social Group Voting

Group	D%	R%	% of State Voters
Asians	34%	64%	1%
Blacks	87%	11%	7%
Hispanics	73%	25%	5%
Whites	42%	55%	87%

White Sub-Groups:

White Liberals	58%	39%
Conservatives	37%	61%
Bay Area Suburbs	47%	50%
South Cal. Whites	37%	59%
Bay Area White Workers	55%	43%
LA County White Workers	52%	45%

Sources: Asians & Hispanics – Field Poll, Blacks – CBS News.

Year: 1978   Democrat: Jerry Brown
Election: Governor   Republican: Evelle Younger
Turnout: 70%

Geographic Breakdown:

Region	% of State	Dem (%)	Rep (%)	Total Votes	Margin
Bay Area	24%	998,201 (60%)	503,713 (30%)	1,654,700	D 494,488
Nor/Central Coast	5%	196,338 (55%)	135,730 (38%)	358,633	D 60,608
Cent. Valley Cities	11%	421,432 (54%)	303,542 (39%)	787,507	D 117,890
LA County	30%	1,178,368 (57%)	744,491 (36%)	2,055,012	D 433,877
South. Cal.	25%	907,432 (53%)	700,296 (41%)	1,707,832	D 207,136
Rural Cal.	5%	177,041 (49%)	138,762 (39%)	358,694	D 38,279
State	100%	3,878,812 (56%)	2,526,534 (36%)	6,922,378	D 1,532,278

Ethnic Breakdown /Social Group Voting

Group	D%	R%	% of State Voters
Asians	67%	29%	1%
Blacks	91%	6%	7%
Hispanics	82%	12%	5%
Whites	52%	40%	87%

White Sub-Groups:

White Liberals	64%	27%
Conservatives	49%	44%
Bay Area Suburbs	55%	36%
South Cal. Whites	50%	44%

Bay Area White Workers	60%	29%
LA County White Workers	62%	34%

Sources: The ethnic vote breakdowns came from averaging the exit polls of the Los Angeles Times and CBS News.

Year: 1980
Election: President

Democrat: Jimmy Carter
Republican: Ronald Reagan
Independent: John Anderson

Turnout: 77%

Geographic Breakdown:

Region	% of State	Dem (%)	Rep (%)	Ind (%)	Total Votes	Margin
Bay Area	24%	827,309 (41%)	904,100 (44%)	230,678 (11%)	2,034,033	R 76,791
Nor/Cen Coast	5%	152,845 (34%)	233,554 (51%)	50,464 (11%)	455,043	R 80,709
C. Val Cities	11%	381,483 (39%)	504,885 (51%)	74,861 (8%)	83,229	R 123,402
LA County	28%	971,830 (40%)	1,224,533 (50%)	175,882 (7%)	440,185	R 244,703
South. Cal.	26%	596,865 (27%)	1,399,236 (63%)	156,783 (7%)	220,185	R 802,371
Rural Cal.	5%	145,329 (32%)	258,550 (60%)	51,165 (11%)	453,755	R 113,221
State	100%	3,083,661 (36%)	4,524,858 (53%)	739,833 (9%)	8,587,063	R 1,441,197

Ethnic Breakdown /Social Group Voting

Group	D%	R%	I%	% of State Voters
Asians	33%	60%	5%	2%
Blacks	87%	11%	2%	7%
Hispanics	59%	33%	8%	6%
Whites	29%	60%	10%	85%

White Sub-Groups:

White Liberals	46%	38%	11%
Conservatives	23%	68%	7%
Bay Area Suburbs	37%	50%	10%
South Cal. Whites	22%	67%	7%
Bay Area White Workers	43%	45%	9%
LA County White Workers	39%	53%	6%

Sources: Asians & Hispanics – NBC News; Blacks & Whites are an average of NBC and CBS News exit polls.

Year: 1980   Democrat: Alan Cranston
Election: US Senate   Republican: Paul Gann

Geographic Breakdown:

Region	% of State	Dem (%)	Rep (%)	Total Votes	Margin
Bay Area	24%	1,271,312 (64%)	575,540 (29%)	1,980,805	D 695,772
Nor/Central Coast	5%	265,121 (60%)	146,204 (33%)	443,124	D 118,917
Cent. Valley Cities	11%	544,090 (57%)	339,805 (36%)	952,162	D 204,285
LA County	28%	1,348,919 (57%)	898,712 (38%)	2,367,188	D 454,207
South. Cal.	26%	1,053,965 (49%)	958,625 (45%)	2,145,984	D 95,340
Rural Cal.	5%	221,992 (50%)	174,540 (40%)	438,218	D 47,452
State	100%	4,705,399 (57%)	3,093,426 (37%)	8,327,481	D 1,611,973

Ethnic Breakdown /Social Group Voting

Group	D%	R%	% of State Voters
Asians	63%	31%	2%
Blacks	91%	7%	7%
Hispanics	75%	22%	6%
Whites	53%	41%	85%

White Sub-Groups:

White Liberals	68%	25%
Conservatives	44%	50%
Bay Area Suburbs	61%	32%
South Cal. Whites	46%	48%
Bay Area White Workers	66%	28%
LA County White Workers	58%	36%

Sources: Asians & Hispanics– Field Poll; Blacks & Whites – CBS News exit polls.

Year: 1982   Democrat: Tom Bradley
Election: Governor   Republican: George Deukmejian
Turnout: 70%

Geographic Breakdown:

Region	% of State	Dem (%)	Rep (%)	Total Votes	Margin
Bay Area	23%	992,329 (54%)	778,669 (43%)	1,831,339	D 213,660
Nor/Central Coast	5%	207,875 (50%)	193,539 (47%)	415,083	D 14,336
Cent. Valley Cities	12%	415,714 (43%)	516,207 (54%)	958,132	R 100,493
LA County	28%	1,173,149 (52%)	1,024,946 (46%)	2,244,236	D 148,203
South. Cal.	25%	827,334 (42%)	1,115,821 (56%)	1,988,383	R 288,487
Rural Cal.	6%	171,268 (39%)	251,832 (57%)	439,525	R 80,564
State	100%	3,787,669 (48%)	3,881,014 (49%)	7,876,698	R 93,345

Ethnic Breakdown /Social Group Voting

Group	D%	R%	% of State Voters
Asians	53%	45%	2%
Blacks	97%	2%	8%
Hispanics	72%	24%	6%
Whites	41%	55%	84%

White Sub-Groups:

White Liberals	60%	37%
Conservatives	37%	61%
Bay Area Suburbs	49%	48%
South Cal. Whites	37%	60%
Bay Area White Workers	50%	46%
LA County White Workers	46%	51%

Sources: Asians & Hispanics are an average of the Field & LA Times exit polls; Blacks & whites are an average of the Field, NBC, CBS & LA Times exit polls.

Year: 1982   Democrat: Jerry Brown
Election: US Senate   Republican: Pete Wilson

Geographic Breakdown:

Region	% of State	Dem (%)	Rep (%)	Total Votes	Margin
Bay Area	23%	922,153 (51%)	821,833 (45%)	1,817,036	D 100,320
Nor/Central Coast	5%	172,004 (42%)	220,035 (53%)	411,883	R 48,031
Cent. Valley Cities	12%	402,374 (42%)	508,641 (54%)	949,533	R 106,267

LA County	29%	1,130,954 (51%)	1,037,174 (47%)	2,228,000	D 93,780
South. Cal.	25%	714,864 (36%)	1,177,521 (60%)	1,965,618	R 462,657
Rural Cal.	6%	152,619 (35%)	257,361 (59%)	433,468	R 104,742
State	100%	3,494,968 (45%)	4,022,565 (52%)	7,805,538	R 527,597

Ethnic Breakdown /Social Group Voting

Group	D%	R%	% of State Voters
Asians	48%	50%	2%
Blacks	87%	9%	8%
Hispanics	72%	24%	6%
Whites	38%	59%	84%

White Sub-Groups:

White Liberals	57%	40%
Conservatives	31%	66%
Bay Area Suburbs	44%	51%
South Cal. Whites	33%	65%
Bay Area White Workers	50%	45%
LA County White Workers	48%	49%

Sources: Asians & Hispanics are an average of the Field & LA Times exit polls; Blacks & whites are an average of the Field, NBC, CBS & LA Times exit polls.

Year: 1984   Democrat: Walter Mondale
Election: President Republican: Ronald Reagan
Turnout: 75%

Geographic Breakdown:

Region	% of State	Dem (%)	Rep (%)	Total Votes	Margin
Bay Area	24%	1,157,855 (51%)	1,090,115 (48%)	2,277,500	D 67,740
Nor/Central Coast	5%	210,333 (42%)	283,908 (57%)	501,041	R 73,575
Cent. Valley Cities	12%	464,595 (41%)	655,651 (58%)	1,132,840	R 191,076
LA County	27%	1,158,912 (44%)	1,424,113 (55%)	2,612,914	R 265,201
South. Cal.	26%	748,348 (30%)	1,693,135 (69%)	2,469,713	R 944,787
Rural Cal.	5%	182,476 (36%)	320,067 (63%)	511,415	R 137,591
State	100%	3,922,519 (41%)	5,467,009 (58%)	9,505,423	R 1,544,490

Ethnic Breakdown /Social Group Voting

Group	D%	R%	% of State Voters
Asians	34%	65%	2%
Blacks	90%	10%	8%
Hispanics	63%	36%	6%
Whites	35%	64%	84%

White Sub-Groups:

White Liberals	57%	41%
Conservatives	24%	75%
Bay Area Suburbs	46%	53%
South Cal. Whites	26%	73%
Bay Area White Workers	47%	53%
LA County White Workers	39%	60%

Sources: The ethnic vote breakdowns came from averaging the exit polls of CBS News, ABC, NBC and the Los Angeles Times.

Year: 1986
Election: Governor
Turnout: 59%

Democrat: Tom Bradley
Republican: George Deukmejian

Geographic Breakdown:

Region	% of State	Dem (%)	Rep (%)	Total Votes	Margin
Bay Area	23%	740,369 (42%)	967,133 (55%)	1,748,323	R 226,764
Nor/Central Coast	6%	147,254 (38%)	233,922 (60%)	389,817	R 86,568
Cent. Valley Cities	12%	272,505 (30%)	624,565 (68%)	913,461	R 352,060
LA County	28%	930,576 (45%)	1,090,138 (53%)	2,058,248	R 159,562
South. Cal.	26%	580,545 (30%)	1,289,627 (67%)	1,912,124	R 709,082
Rural Cal.	6%	110,465 (26%)	301,216 (71%)	421,578	R 190,751
State	100%	2,781,714 (37%)	4,506,601 (61%)	7,443,551	R 1,724,887

Ethnic Breakdown /Social Group Voting

Group	D%	R%	% of State Voters
Asians	45%	54%	2%
Blacks	96%	3%	8%

Hispanics	61%	38%	6%
Whites	32%	66%	84%

White Sub-Groups:

White Liberals	51%	47%
Conservatives	27%	72%
Bay Area Suburbs	35%	62%
South Cal. Whites	22%	74%
Bay Area White Workers	37%	61%
LA County White Workers	38%	60%

Sources: The ethnic vote breakdowns came from averaging the exit polls of ABC, NBC and the Los Angeles Times.

Year: 1986   Democrat: Alan Cranston
Election: US Senate   Republican: Ed Zschau

Geographic Breakdown:

Region	% of State	Dem (%)	Rep (%)	Total Votes	Margin
Bay Area	24%	1,055,808 (58%)	701,395 (40%)	1,745,362	D 304,413
Nor/Central Coast	5%	191,854 (49%)	184,894 (48%)	387,864	D 6,960
Cent. Valley Cities	12%	414,897 (46%)	466,170 (51%)	908,550	R 51,273
LA County	28%	1,110,614 (54%)	876,250 (43%)	2,039,232	D 234,364
South. Cal.	26%	749,960 (39%)	1,084,633 (57%)	1,900,251	R 334,673
Rural Cal.	6%	173,539 (42%)	228,462 (55%)	417,290	R 54,923
State	100%	3,646,672 (49%)	3,541,804 (48%)	7,398,549	D 104,868

Ethnic Breakdown /Social Group Voting

Group	D%	R%	% of State Voters
Asians	55%	43%	2%
Blacks	93%	6%	8%
Hispanics	71%	24%	6%
Whites	44%	53%	84%

White Sub-Groups:

White Liberals	66%	32%

Conservatives	35%	62%
Bay Area Suburbs	52%	46%
South Cal. Whites	36%	62%
Bay Area White Workers	55%	42%
LA County White Workers	51%	46%

Sources: The ethnic vote breakdowns came from averaging the exit polls of CBS News, ABC, NBC and the Los Angeles Times.

Year: 1988   Democrat: Mike Dukakis
Election: President   Republican: George Bush
Turnout:

Percent of Registered Voters Turning Out: 73%
Geographic Breakdown:

Region	% of State	Dem (%)	Rep (%)	Total Votes	Margin
Bay Area	23%	1,338,533 (58%)	945,802 (41%)	2,315,792	D 392,731
Nor/Central Coast	5%	261,904 (50%)	250,040 (48%)	519,960	D 11,864
Cent. Valley Cities	12%	533,046 (46%)	617,258 (53%)	1,164,558	R 84,212
LA County	27%	1,372,352 (52%)	1,239,716 (47%)	2,644,671	D 132,636
South. Cal.	27%	975,582 (36%)	1,692,123 (63%)	2,702,331	R 716,541
Rural Cal.	5%	220,816 (41%)	309,978 (57%)	539,753	R 89,162
State	100%	4,702,233 (48%)	5,054,917 (51%)	9,887,065	R 352,684

Ethnic Breakdown /Social Group Voting

Group	D%	R%	% of State Voters
Asians	43%	56%	2%
Blacks	86%	13%	8%
Hispanics	67%	32%	6%
Whites	41%	58%	84%

White Sub-Groups:

White Liberals	63%	36%
Conservatives	31%	68%
Bay Area Suburbs	53%	45%
South Cal. Whites	34%	65%

Bay Area White Workers	56%	43%
LA County White Workers	48%	52%

Sources: The ethnic vote breakdowns came from averaging the exit polls of CBS News, ABC, NBC, and the Field Poll.

Year: 1988   Democrat: Leo McCarthy
Election: US Senate   Republican: Pete Wilson

Geographic Breakdown:

Region	% of State	Dem (%)	Rep (%)	Total Votes	Margin
Bay Area	23%	1,199,961 (53%)	970,303 (43%)	2,243,232	D 229,658
Nor/Central Coast	5%	244,654 (47%)	256,206 (49%)	520,631	R 11,552
Cent. Valley Cities	12%	487,278 (42%)	622,789 (54%)	1,150,714	R 135,511
LA County	27%	1,261,449 (48%)	1,265,582 (49%)	2,603,311	R 4,133
South. Cal.	28%	888,536 (33%)	1,719,667 (64%)	2,689,951	R 831,131
Rural Cal.	5%	205,375 (38%)	308,862 (58%)	535,759	R 103,487
State	100%	4,287,253 (44%)	5,145,409 (53%)	9,743,598	R 856,156

Ethnic Breakdown /Social Group Voting

Group	D%	R%	% of State Voters
Asians	43%	54%	2%
Blacks	82%	16%	8%
Hispanics	64%	33%	6%
Whites	40%	57%	84%

White Sub-Groups:

White Liberals	58%	39%
Conservatives	29%	68%
Bay Area Suburbs	49%	48%
South Cal. Whites	28%	69%
Bay Area White Workers	52%	44%
LA County White Workers	46%	51%

Sources: The ethnic vote breakdowns came from averaging the exit polls of CBS News, ABC, NBC, and the Field Poll.

Year: 1990   Democrat: Dianne Feinstein
Election: Governor   Republican: Pete Wilson
Turnout: 59%

Geographic Breakdown:

Bay Area	24%	1,072,379 (58%)	698,178 (38%)	1,851,976	D 374,201
Nor/Central Coast	6%	208,073 (48%)	197,606 (46%)	430,471	D 10,467
Cent. Valley Cities	13%	404,631 (42%)	515,591 (53%)	965,968	R 110,960
LA County	24%	911,413 (49%)	867,781 (47%)	1,861,893	D 43,632
South. Cal.	27%	739,395 (35%)	1,241,460 (59%)	2,100,500	R 502,065
Rural Cal.	6%	189,306 (39%)	271,288 (56%)	488,659	R 81,982
State	100%	3,525,197 (46%)	3,791,904 (49%)	7,699,467	R 266,707

Ethnic Breakdown /Social Group Voting

Group	D%	R%	% of State Voters
Asians	52%	44%	2%
Blacks	87%	11%	8%
Hispanics	61%	33%	6%
Whites	41%	54%	84%

White Sub-Groups:

White Liberals	62%	34%
Conservatives	32%	63%
Bay Area Suburbs	54%	42%
South Cal. Whites	32%	64%
Bay Area White Workers	58%	37%
LA County White Workers	44%	51%

Sources: The ethnic vote breakdown comes from the LA Times exit poll.

Year: 1992   Democrat: Bill Clinton
Election: President   Republican: George Bush
                         Independent: Ross Perot
Turnout: 75%

Geographic Breakdown:

Region	% of State	Dem (%)	Rep (%)	Ind (%)	Total Votes	Margin
Bay Area	24%	1,476,971 (56%)	658,202 (25%)	470,385 (18%)	2,627,702	D 818,769

Nor/Cen Coast	5%	281,232 (47%)	184,476 (31%)	133,174 (22%)	603,968	D 96,756
C. Val Cities	12%	561,138 (41%)	522,605 (38%)	266,774 (20%)	1,360,075	D 38,533
LA County	25%	1,446,529 (53%)	799,607 (29%)	488,624 (18%)	2,753,403	D 646,922
South. Cal.	28%	1,122,213 (36%)	1,209,669 (39%)	774,903 (25%)	3,131,187	R 86,456
Rural Cal.	6%	232,242 (35%)	256,015 (39%)	162,146 (25%)	655,386	R 23,773
State	100%	5,121,325 (46%)	3,630,574 (33%)	2,296,006 (21%)	11,131,721	D 1,490,751

Ethnic Breakdown /Social Group Voting

Group	D%	R%	I%	% of State Voters
Asians	45%	40%	15%	4%
Blacks	83%	9%	8%	7%
Hispanics	64%	23%	13%	9%
Whites	42%	35%	21%	79%

White Sub-Groups:

White Liberals	63%	20%	15%
Conservatives	32%	44%	24%
Bay Area Suburbs	51%	28%	20%
South Cal. Whites	29%	43%	27%
Bay Area White Workers	54%	25%	20%
LA County White Workers	41%	37%	22%

Sources: The ethnic vote breakdowns come from averaging the LA Times and networks' consortium exit polls.

Year: 1992   Democrat: Dianne Feinstein
Election: US Senate (Short Term)*   Republican: John Seymour
(*Special election to replace Pete Wilson when he became Governor.)

Geographic Breakdown:

Region	% of State	Dem (%)	Rep (%)	Total Votes	Margin
Bay Area	24%	1,723,912 (67%)	684,371 (27%)	2,555,613	D 1,039,541
Nor/Central Coast	5%	330,894 (56%)	213,726 (36%)	588,440	D 117,168

Cent. Valley Cities	12%	634,908 (48%)	585,098 (44%)	1,326,384	D 49,810
LA County	25%	1,552,223 (59%)	899,656 (34%)	2,643,495	D 652,567
South. Cal.	28%	1,327,918 (44%)	1,413,463 (47%)	3,026,519	R 85,545
Rural Cal.	6%	283,796 (44%)	297,187 (46%)	642,292	R 13,391
State	100%	5,853,651 (54%)	4,093,501 (38%)	10,782,743	D 1,760,150

Ethnic Breakdown /Social Group Voting

Group	D%	R%	% of State Voters
Asians	62%	36%	4%
Blacks	88%	7%	7%
Hispanics	70%	25%	9%
Whites	50%	41%	79%

White Sub-Groups:

White Liberals	71%	24%
Conservatives	40%	51%
Bay Area Suburbs	63%	31%
South Cal. Whites	37%	54%
Bay Area White Workers	66%	27%
LA County White Workers	47%	44%

Sources: The ethnic vote breakdowns come from averaging the LA Times and networks' consortium exit polls.

Year: 1992   Democrat: Barbara Boxer
Election: US Senate   Republican: Bruce Herschensohn

Geographic Breakdown:

Region	% of State	Dem (%)	Rep (%)	Total Votes	Margin
Bay Area	23%	1,535,671 (61%)	779,155 (31%)	2,535,136	D 756,516
Nor/Central Coast	5%	286,774 (49%)	241,887 (41%)	583,597	D 44,887
Cent. Valley Cities	12%	555,803 (42%)	645,753 (49%)	1,325,392	R 89,950
LA County	25%	1,410,423 (53%)	1,062,974 (40%)	2,684,066	D 347,449
South. Cal.	28%	1,146,412 (38%)	1,581,878 (52%)	3,028,963	R 435,466
Rural Cal.	6%	238,384 (37%)	332,535 (52%)	642,549	R 94,151

State	100%	5,173,467 (48%)	4,644,182 (43%)	10,799,703	D 529,285

Ethnic Breakdown /Social Group Voting

Group	D%	R%	% of State Voters
Asians	52%	46%	4%
Blacks	82%	16%	7%
Hispanics	64%	30%	9%
Whites	43%	52%	79%

White Sub-Groups:

White Liberals	65%	29%
Conservatives	33%	58%
Bay Area Suburbs	56%	35%
South Cal. Whites	32%	58%
Bay Area White Workers	58%	32%
LA County White Workers	41%	51%

Sources: The ethnic vote breakdowns come from averaging the LA Times and networks' consortium exit polls.

Year: 1994　　　　　Democrat: Kathleen Brown
Election: Governor　　Republican: Pete Wilson
Turnout: 60%

Geographic Breakdown:

Region	% of State	Dem (%)	Rep (%)	Total Votes	Margin
Bay Area	23%	1,056,206 (52%)	877,189 (44%)	2,012,223	D 179,017
Nor/Central Coast	6%	208,225 (43%)	257,670 (53%)	489,262	R 49,445
Cent. Valley Cities	13%	392,670 (35%)	671,396 (61%)	1,108,966	R 278,726
LA County	24%	953,301 (46%)	1,043,835 (50%)	2,069,889	R 90,534
South. Cal.	28%	745,075 (31%)	1,568,779 (65%)	2,428,460	R 823,704
Rural Cal.	6%	164,322 (30%)	362,897 (65%)	556,575	R 198,575
State	100%	3,519,799 (41%)	4,781,766 (55%)	8,665,375	R 1,261,967

Ethnic Breakdown /Social Group Voting

Group	D%	R%	% of State Voters
Asians	50%	46%	5%
Blacks	77%	20%	7%

Hispanics	72%	24%	9%
Whites	36%	60%	77%

White Sub-Groups:

White Liberals	55%	42%
Conservatives	28%	68%
Bay Area Suburbs	47%	49%
South Cal. Whites	21%	75%
Bay Area White Workers	49%	45%
LA County White Workers	36%	60%

Sources: The ethnic vote breakdown comes from the LA Times exit poll.

Year: 1994   Democrat: Dianne Feinstein
Election: US Senate   Republican: Michael Huffington

Geographic Breakdown:

Region	% of State	Dem (%)	Rep (%)	Total Votes	Margin
Bay Area	23%	1,246,261 (63%)	600,898 (30%)	1,981,600	D 845,363
Nor/Central Coast	6%	227,268 (47%)	206,289 (43%)	481,046	D 20,979
Cent. Valley Cities	13%	440,305 (40%)	556,162 (51%)	1,088,916	R 115,857
LA County	24%	1,046,026 (52%)	819,594 (40%)	2,029,897	D 226,432
South. Cal.	28%	830,091 (35%)	1,324,878 (56%)	2,383,577	R 494,787
Rural Cal.	6%	189,201 (34%)	309,204 (56%)	549,053	R 120,003
State	100%	3,979,152 (47%)	3,817,025 (45%)	8,514,089	D 162,127

Ethnic Breakdown /Social Group Voting

Group	D%	R%	% of State Voters
Asians	52%	40%	5%
Blacks	80%	14%	7%
Hispanics	67%	22%	9%
Whites	43%	49%	77%

White Sub-Groups:

White Liberals	69%	27%
Conservatives	32%	59%

By Area Suburbs	58%	35%
South Cal. Whites	26%	65%
Bay Area White Workers	57%	35%
LA County White Workers	39%	52%

Sources: The ethnic vote breakdown comes from the LA Times exit poll.

Year: 1996   Democrat: Bill Clinton
Election: President   Republican: Bob Dole
                       Independent: Ross Perot

Turnout: 66%
Geographic Breakdown:

Region	% of State	Dem (%)	Rep (%)	Ind (%)	Total Votes	Margin
Bay Area	23%	1,417,511 (61%)	588,755 (25%)	137,657 (6%)	2,342,889	D 828,756
Nor/Cen Coast	6%	270,227 (48%)	211,446 (38%)	42,177 (8%)	560,203	D 58,781
C. Val Cities	13%	579,858 (46%)	572,841 (45%)	79,750 (6%)	1,266,023	D 7,017
LA County	24%	1,430,629 (59%)	746,544 (31%)	157,752 (7%)	2,411,014	D 684,085
South. Cal.	28%	1,180,172 (42%)	1,317,541 (47%)	227,097 (8%)	2,804,889	R 137,369
Rural Cal.	6%	241,438 (38%)	391,253 (62%)	53,414 (8%)	634,466	R 149,815
State	100%	5,119,835 (51%)	3,828,380 (39%)	697,847 (7%)	10,019,484	D 1,291,455

Ethnic Breakdown /Social Group Voting

Group	D%	R%	I%	% of State Voters
Asians	53%	40%	4%	5%
Blacks	87%	6%	5%	7%
Hispanics	75%	18%	6%	11%
Whites	42%	46%	8%	76%

White Sub-Groups:

White Liberals	63%	26%	5%
Conservatives	37%	52%	7%
Bay Area Suburbs	57%	33%	7%
South Cal. Whites	32%	54%	11%
Bay Area White Workers	62%	28%	7%

LA County White Workers	51%	38%	9%

Sources: The ethnic vote breakdown comes from the LA Times exit poll.

Year: 1998   Democrat: Gray Davis
Election: Governor   Republican: Dan Lundgren

Turnout: 58%
Geographic Breakdown:

Region	% of State	Dem (%)	Rep (%)	Total Votes	Margin
Bay Area	23%	1,340,185 (68%)	542,648 (28%)	1,962,347	D 797,537
Nor/Central Coast	6%	263,172 (56%)	179,392 (38%)	469,704	D 83,780
Cent. Valley Cities	13%	560,160 (52%)	494,188 (46%)	1,080,638	D 65,972
LA County	24%	1,297,896 (66%)	615,642 (31%)	1,975,672	D 682,254
South. Cal.	28%	1,140,789 (49%)	1,101,894 (47%)	2,328,026	D 38,895
Rural Cal.	7%	258,500 (45%)	294,266 (50%)	568,809	R 25,766
State	100%	4,860,702 (58%)	3,218,030 (38%)	8,385,196	D 1,642,672

Ethnic Breakdown /Social Group Voting

Group	D%	R%	% of State Voters
Asians	67%	29%	6%
Blacks	83%	11%	7%
Hispanics	78%	17%	14%
Whites	50%	46%	71%

White Sub-Groups:

White Liberals	71%	25%
Conservatives	44%	53%
Bay Area Suburbs	64%	32%
South Cal. Whites	41%	55%
Bay Area White Workers	69%	28%
LA County White Workers	57%	40%

Sources: The ethnic vote breakdown comes from the networks' consortium exit poll.

Year: 1998   Democrat: Barbara Boxer
Election: US Senate   Republican: Matt Fong

Geographic Breakdown:

Region	% of State	Dem (%)	Rep (%)	Total Votes	Margin
Bay Area	23%	1,223,233 (63%)	648,106 (33%)	1,948,220	D 575,127
Nor/Central Coast	6%	240,783 (52%)	200,224 (43%)	461,553	D 40,559
Cent. Valley Cities	13%	499,106 (46%)	533.786 (50%)	1,074,472	R 34,680
LA County	24%	1,198,403 (61%)	704,782 (36%)	1,969,788	D 493,621
South. Cal.	28%	1,019,839 (44%)	1,183,822 (51%)	2,307,871	R 163,983
Rural Cal.	7%	230,341 (42%)	305,631 (55%)	553,049	R 75,290
State	100%	4,411,705 (53%)	3,576,351 (43%)	8,314,953	D 835,354

Ethnic Breakdown /Social Group Voting

Group	D%	R%	% of State Voters
Asians	54%	44%	6%
Blacks	85%	13%	7%
Hispanics	72%	23%	14%
Whites	46%	50%	71%

White Sub-Groups:

White Liberals	68%	29%
Conservatives	39%	57%
Bay Area Suburbs	60%	37%
South Cal. Whites	34%	61%
Bay Area White Workers	62%	34%
LA County White Workers	53%	44%

Sources: The ethnic vote breakdown comes from the networks' consortium exit poll.

Year: 2000   Democrat: Al Gore
Election: President Republican: George W. Bush
                     Independent: Ralph Nader

Turnout: 71%
Geographic Breakdown:

Region	% of State	Dem (%)	Rep (%)	I (%)	Total Votes	Margin
Bay Area	23%	1,741,931 (64%)	825,220 (30%)	139,755 (5%)	2,732,632	D 916,711
Nor/Cen Coast	5%	296,775 (50%)	241,757 (41%)	43,726 (7%)	588,420	D 55,018
C. Val Cities	12%	610,598 (45%)	692,191 (51%)	42,941 (3%)	1,360,206	R 81,593

LA County	25%	1,710,505 (63%)	871,930 (32%)	83,731 (3%)	2,695,154	D 838,575
South. Cal.	28%	1,380,068 (44%)	1,606,920 (52%)	94,500 (3%)	3,118,251	R 226,852
Rural Cal.	6%	255,762 (37%)	402,799 (58%)	29,957 (4%)	697,077	R 147,037
State	100%	5,861,203 (53%)	4,567,429 (42%)	418,707 (4%)	10,965,856	D 1,293,774

Ethnic Breakdown /Social Group Voting

Group	D%	R%	I%	% of State Voters
Asians	63%	33%	4%	6%
Blacks	85%	14%	1%	6%
Hispanics	75%	23%	2%	16%
Whites	47%	49%	4%	70%

White Sub-Groups:

White Liberals	68%	25%	6%
Conservatives	38%	58%	3%
Bay Area Suburbs	60%	35%	4%
South Cal. Whites	33%	62%	4%
Bay Area White Workers	65%	31%	3%
LA County White Workers	56%	40%	3%

Sources: The ethnic vote breakdown comes from the LA Times exit poll.

Year: 2000   Democrat: Dianne Feinstein
Election: US Senate   Republican: Tom Campbell

Geographic Breakdown:

Region	% of State	Dem (%)	Rep (%)	Total Votes	Margin
Bay Area	23%	1,570,041 (64%)	695,215 (28%)	2,453,725	D 874,826
Nor/Central Coast	5%	298,026 (52%)	217,179 (38%)	577,012	D 80,847
Cent. Valley Cities	13%	681,375 (51%)	557,208 (42%)	1,331,270	D 124,167
LA County	25%	1,677,668 (64%)	743,872 (29%)	2,605,254	D 933,796
South. Cal.	28%	1,419,213 (48%)	1,332,403 (45%)	2,972,375	D 86,810
Rural Cal.	6%	286,199 (42%)	340,976 (50%)	683,978	R 54,777
State	100%	5,932,522 (56%)	3,886,853 (37%)	10,623,614	D 2,045,669

Ethnic Breakdown /Social Group Voting

Group	D%	R%	% of State Voters
Asians	64%	33%	6%
Blacks	86%	9%	6%
Hispanics	74%	19%	17%
Whites	48%	45%	70%

White Sub-Groups:

White Liberals	67%	24%
Conservatives	42%	55%
Bay Area Suburbs	62%	32%
South Cal. Whites	38%	53%
Bay Area White Workers	66%	28%
LA County White Workers	59%	35%

Sources: The ethnic vote breakdown comes from the LA Times exit poll.

Year: 2002   Democrat: Gray Davis
Election: Governor   Republican: Bill Simon
Turnout: 51%

Geographic Breakdown:

Bay Area	23%	985,829 (57%)	487,394 (28%)	1,715,810	D 498,435
Nor/Central Coast	6%	204,247 (47%)	176,056 (40%)	435,300	D 28,191
Cent. Valley Cities	13%	399,191 (40%)	487,224 (49%)	999,417	R 88,033
LA County	23%	975,162 (56%)	594,748 (35%)	1,706,059	D 358,414
South. Cal.	28%	812,586 (39%)	1,103,393 (53%)	2,081,567	R 290,807
Rural Cal.	7%	178,475 (33%)	320,986 (60%)	538,158	R 142,511
State	100%	3,533,490 (47%)	3,169,801 (42%)	7,476,311	D 363,689

Ethnic Breakdown /Social Group Voting

Group	D%	R%	% of State Voters
Asians	54%	37%	5%
Blacks	82%	10%	5%
Hispanics	65%	24%	13%
Whites	40%	47%	75%

White Sub-Groups:

White Liberals	61%	24%
Conservatives	32%	59%
Bay Area Suburbs	53%	33%
South Cal. Whites	31%	61%
Bay Area	62%	28%
LA County	53%	39%

Sources: The ethnic vote breakfdown comes from the LA Times exit poll

Year: 2003   No on Recall of Gray Davis
Election: Recall Governor Davis?   Yes on Recall of Gray Davis
Turnout: 61%

Note: The 2003 special election had two parts; the first to recall Governor Gray Davis and the second to choose a replacement.

Geographic Breakdown:

Region	% of State	No (%)	Yes (%)	Total Votes	Margin
Bay Area	23%	1,322,443 (64%)	751,994 (36%)	2,074,437	N 570,449
Nor/Central Coast	5%	242,412 (49%)	247,463 (51%)	489,875	Y 5,051
Cent. Valley Cities	13%	416,960 (36%)	746,397 (64%)	1,163,357	Y 329,437
LA County	22%	1,024,341 (51%)	984,222 (49%)	2,008,563	N 40,119
South. Cal.	29%	805,852 (31%)	1,812,149 (69%)	2,618,001	Y 1,006,297
Rural Cal.	7%	195,775 (31%)	434,049 (69%)	629,824	Y 238,274
State	100%	4,007,783 (45%)	4,976,274 (55%)	8,984,057	Y 968,491

Ethnic Breakdown /Social Group Voting

Group	No %	Yes %	% of State Voters
Asians	53%	47%	6%
Blacks	79%	21%	6%
Hispanics	55%	45%	15%
Whites	40%	60%	73%

White Sub-Groups:

White Liberals	65%	35%
Conservatives	27%	73%
Bay Area Suburbs	58%	42%

South Cal. Whites	22%	78%
Bay Area White Workers	61%	39%
LA County White Workers	44%	56%

Sources: The ethnic vote breakdown comes from the LA Times exit poll.

Year: 2003   Democrat: Cruz Bustamante
Election: Replacement of Gray Davis   Republican: Arnold Schwarzenegger
                                             Other: Tom McClintock

Although this "replacement" special election was technically non-partisan, Arnold Schwarzenegger was endorsed by the California Republican Party and Cruz Bustamante was endorsed by the California Democrats. Over 100 candidates of all parties ran. For the purposes of our study, Arnold is the Republican candidate and Cruz is the Democrat. Republican State Senator Tom McClintock finished third and his votes are in the "O" column in the above chart.

Geographic Breakdown:

Region	% of State	Dem (%)	Rep (%)	O (%)	Total Votes	Margin
Bay Area	22%	875,254 (46%)	631,502 (33%)	223,917 (12%)	1,910,050	D 243,752
Nor/Cen Coast	5%	159,547 (34%)	198,844 (43%)	62,053 (13%)	465,771	R 39,297
C. Val Cities	13%	292,923 (26%)	592,350 (52%)	186,154 (16%)	1,131,798	R 299,427
LA County	23%	735,066 (37%)	78,747 (45%)	217,404 (11%)	1,960,605	R 143,681
South. Cal.	30%	540,519 (21%)	1,554,708 (60%)	367,744 (14%)	2,578,491	R 1,014,189
Rural Cal.	7%	121,565 (20%)	350,133 (57%)	104,015 (17%)	611,200	R 228,568
State	100%	2,724,874 (31%)	4,206,284 (49%)	1,161,287 (13%)	8,657,915	R 1,481,410

Ethnic Breakdown /Social Group Voting

Group	D%	R%	I%	% of State Voters
Asians	34%	46%	15%	6%
Blacks	67%	18%	8%	6%
Hispanics	56%	32%	9%	15%
Whites	25%	54%	14%	73%

White Sub-Groups:

White Liberals	47%	36%	9%
Conservatives	17%	63%	16%

Bay Area Suburbs	40%	38%	14%
South Cal. Whites	10%	71%	15%
Bay Area White Workers	46%	34%	14%
LA County White Workers	35%	45%	14%

Source: Los Angeles Times exit poll.

Year: 2004
Election: President
Turnout: 76%

Democrat: John Kerry
Republican: George W. Bush

Geographic Breakdown:

Region	% of State	Dem (%)	Rep (%)	Total Votes	Margin
Bay Area	22%	1,926,726 (69%)	815,225 (29%)	2,782,707	D 1,111,501
Nor/Central Coast	5%	379,664 (58%)	267,018 (40%)	659,384	D 112,646
Cent. Valley Cities	12%	664,958 (43%)	851,509 (56%)	1,533,190	R 186,551
LA County	24%	1,907,736 (63%)	1,075,225 (36%)	3,023,280	D 831,511
South. Cal.	29%	1,551,130 (43%)	2,009,958 (56%)	3,605,791	R 458,828
Rural Cal.	7%	315,271 (39%)	489,891 (60%)	817,500	R 174,620
State	100%	6,745,485 (54%)	5,509,826 (44%)	12,421,852	D 1,235,659

Ethnic Breakdown /Social Group Voting

Group	D%	R%	% of State Voters
Asians	65%	34%	7%
Blacks	83%	16%	6%
Hispanics	66%	32%	18%
Whites	47%	51%	67%

White Sub-Groups:

White Liberals	72%	27%
Conservatives	38%	61%
Bay Area Suburbs	64%	34%
South Cal. Whites	34%	65%
Bay Area White Workers	69%	30%
LA County White Workers	58%	41%

Sources: The ethnic vote breakdowns come from averaging the LA Times and networks' consortium exit polls.

Year: 2004   Democrat: Barbara Boxer
Election: US Senate   Republican: Bill Jones

Geographic Breakdown:

Region	% of State	Dem (%)	Rep (%)	Total Votes	Margin
Bay Area	22%	1,877,470 (70%)	701,624 (26%)	2,684,720	D 1,175,846
Nor/Central Coast	5%	376,449 (58%)	233,678 (36%)	645,514	D 142,771
Cent. Valley Cities	12%	729,973 (49%)	718,078 (48%)	1,504,128	D 11,895
LA County	24%	1,940,493 (67%)	822,351 (28%)	2,907,036	D 1,118,142
South. Cal.	29%	1,694,926 (48%)	1,647,995 (47%)	3.507,414	D 46,931
Rural Cal.	7%	336,417 (42%)	432,196 (54%)	804,483	R 95,779
State	100%	6,995,728 (58%)	4,555,922 (38%)	12,053,295	D 2,399,806

Ethnic Breakdown /Social Group Voting

Group	D%	R%	% of State Voters
Asians	66%	30%	7%
Blacks	85%	13%	6%
Hispanics	72%	23%	18%
Whites	51%	46%	67%

White Sub-Groups:

White Liberals	73%	23%
Conservatives	42%	54%
Bay Area Suburbs	65%	31%
South Cal. Whites	40%	55%
Bay Area White Workers	73%	25%
LA County White Workers	63%	32%

Sources: The ethnic vote breakdowns come from averaging the LA Times and networks' consortium exit polls.

Year: 2006   Democrat: Phil Angelides
Election: Governor   Republican: Arnold Schwarzenegger
Turnout: 56%

Geographic Breakdown:

Region	% of State	Dem (%)	Rep (%)	Total Votes	Margin

Bay Area	23%	981,097 (49%)	909,583 (45%)	2,014,249	D 71,514
Nor/Central Coast	6%	189,227 (39%)	261,190 (54%)	483,922	R 71,963
Cent. Valley Cities	13%	354,326 (32%)	714,649 (64%)	1,119,771	R 360,323
LA County	23%	967,149 (49%)	907,919 (46%)	1,971,076	D 59,230
South. Cal.	28%	726,307 (30%)	1,615,496 (66%)	2,455,346	R 889,189
Rural Cal.	7%	158,626 (25%)	441,320 (69%)	635,052	R 282,694
State	100%	3,376,732 (39%)	4,850,157 (56%)	8,679,416	R 1,473,425

Ethnic Breakdown /Social Group Voting

Group	D%	R%	% of State Voters
Asians	39%	60%	6%
Blacks	70%	27%	6%
Hispanics	59%	36%	15%
Whites	32%	63%	70%

White Sub-Groups:

White Liberals	51%	43%
Conservatives	24%	72%
Bay Area Suburbs	44%	50%
South Cal. Whites	21%	75%
Bay Area White Workers	52%	43%
LA County White Workers	41%	53%

Sources: The ethnic vote breakdowns come from averaging the LA Times and networks' consortium exit polls.

Year: 2006   Democrat: Dianne Feinstein
Election: US Senate   Republican: Richard Mountjoy

Geographic Breakdown:

Region	% of State	Dem (%)	Rep (%)	Total Votes	Margin
Bay Area	23%	1,444,905 (73%)	417,435 (21%)	1,991,185	D 1,027,470
Nor/Central Coast	6%	289,466 (61%)	143,463 (30%)	477,765	D 146,003
Cent. Valley Cities	13%	570,532 (52%)	472,191 (43%)	1,103,147	D 98,341
LA County	23%	1,298,820 (67%)	536,200 (28%)	1,934,666	D 762,620

South. Cal.	28%	1,192,181 (49%)	1,097,031 (46%)	2,408,741	D 95,150
Rural Cal.	7%	280,385 (45%)	324,502 (52%)	625,972	R 44,117
State	100%	5,076,289 (59%)	2,990,822 (35%)	8,541,476	D 2,085,467

Ethnic Breakdown /Social Group Voting

Group	D%	R%	% of State Voters
Asians	70%	26%	6%
Blacks	87%	10%	6%
Hispanics	71%	22%	15%
Whites	53%	41%	70%

White Sub-Groups:

White Liberals	76%	18%
Conservatives	45%	50%
Bay Area Suburbs	70%	25%
South Cal. Whites	41%	54%
Bay Area White Workers	74%	22%
LA County White Workers	60%	36%

Sources: The ethnic vote breakdowns come from the networks' consortium exit polls.

Year: 2008   Democrat: Barack Obama
Election: President   Republican: John McCain
Turnout: 79%
Geographic Breakdown:

Region	% of State	Dem (%)	Rep (%)	Total Votes	Margin
Bay Area	22%	2,222,528 (74%)	732,409 (24%)	3,011,588	D 1,504,121
Nor/Central Coast	5%	432,846 (64%)	228,082 (34%)	677,866	D 204,764
Cent. Valley Cities	13%	886,822 (52%)	781,266 (46%)	1,700,013	D 105,556
LA County	24%	2,295,853 (69%)	956,425 (29%)	3,318,248	D 1,339,428
South. Cal.	29%	2,044,477 (51%)	1,853,398 (47%)	3,978,167	D 191,079
Rural Cal.	7%	391,947 (46%)	460,201 (54%)	856,018	R 68,254
State	100%	8,274,473 (61%)	5,011,781 (37%)	13,561,900	D 3,262,692

Ethnic Breakdown /Social Group Voting

Group	D%	R%	% of State Voters
Asians	64%	35%	6%

Blacks	94%	5%	9%
Hispanics	74%	23%	18%
Whites	52%	46%	65%

White Sub-Groups:

White Liberals	76%	22%
Conservatives	46%	52%
Bay Area Suburbs	73%	25%
South Cal. Whites	39%	59%
Bay Area White Workers	73%	25%
LA County White Workers	58%	39%

Sources: The ethnic vote breakdowns come from the networks' consortium exit polls.

APPENDIX 3. KEY CALIFORNIA PROPOSITIONS, 1958 TO 2008

Note: All state, precinct, county, city and Assembly District figures taken from the California Secretary of State Archives. The designation "(#)" refers to each Proposition number in a given year.

Year: November, 1958   Yes, Institute Right-to-Work laws
Election: Right-to-Work (#18)   No
Turnout: 79%

Geographic Breakdown:

Region	% of State	Yes (%)	No (%)	Total Votes	Margin
Bay Area	25%	473,540 (36%)	817,185 (64%)	1,290,725	N 343,645
Nor/Central Coast	4%	93,589 (45%)	114,397 (55%)	207,986	N 20,808
Cent. Valley Cities	10%	207,205 (39%)	322,761 (61%)	529,966	N 115,556
LA County	41%	857,683 (40%)	1,264,835 (60%)	2,122,518	N 407,152
South. Cal.	15%	398,015 (47%)	398,015 (53%)	752,579	N 43,451
Rural Cal.	5%	93,394 (38%)	153,644 (62%)	247,038	N 60,250
State	100%	2,079,975 (40%)	3,070,837 (60%)	5,150,812	N 990,862

Ethnic Breakdown /Social Group Voting

Group	Yes %	No %	% of State Voters
Asians	33%	67%	1%
Blacks	9%	91%	5%
Hispanics	16%	84%	4%
Whites	43%	57%	90%

White Sub-Groups:

White Liberals	39%	61%
Conservatives	48%	52%
Bay Area Suburbs	39%	61%
South Cal. Whites	49%	51%
Bay Area White Workers	29%	71%
LA County White Workers	29%	71%

Sources: California Secretary of State Archives. Asians – Chinatown; Blacks – South Central Los Angeles; Hispanics – East Los Angeles.

Note: Proposition 18 would have repealed laws that required a "closed shop," meaning that union members could be replaced by non-members.

Year: November, 1964
Election: Fair Housing (#14)
Turnout: 88%

Yes: Repeal Fair Housing Act
No: Don't Repeal Fair Housing Act

Geographic Breakdown:

Region	% of State	Yes (%)	No (%)	Total Votes	Margin
Bay Area	24%	973,815 (58%)	696,860 (42%)	1,670.675	Y 276,955
Nor/Central Coast	4%	173,103 (60%)	114,595 (40%)	287,698	Y 58,508
Cent. Valley Cities	11%	479,905 (64%)	265,978 (36%)	745,883	Y 213,927
LA County	39%	1,802,620 (67%)	870,342 (33%)	2,672,962	Y 932,278
South. Cal.	18%	920,305 (72%)	350,491 (28%)	1,270,796	Y 569,814
Rural Cal.	4%	176,712 (64%)	97,481 (36%)	274,193	Y 79,231
State	100%	4,526,460 (65%)	2,395,747 (35%)	6,922,207	Y 2,130,713

Ethnic Breakdown /Social Group Voting

Group	Yes %	No %	% of State Voters
Asians	64%	36%	1%
Blacks	7%	93%	7%
Hispanics	33%	67%	5%
Whites	71%	29%	87%

White Sub-Groups:

White Liberals	49%	51%
Conservatives	78%	22%
Bay Area Suburbs	63%	37%
South Cal. Whites	75%	25%
Bay Area White Workers	71%	29%
LA County White Workers	77%	23%

Note: A "No" vote was pro-civil rights (to keep the Fair Housing Law).

Sources: California Secretary of State Archives. Asians – Chinatown; Blacks – South Central Los Angeles; Hispanics – East Los Angeles.

Year: November, 1972
Election: CA Coastal Comm. (#20)
Turnout: 82%

Yes: Create California Coastal Com.
No

Geographic Breakdown:

Region	% of State	Yes (%)	No (%)	Total Votes	Margin
Bay Area	25%	1,173,029 (60%)	771,070 (40%)	1,944,099	Y 401,959
Nor/Central Coast	5%	207,445 (54%)	175,096 (46%)	382,541	Y 32,349
Cent. Valley Cities	11%	453,710 (53%)	399,780 (47%)	853,490	Y 53,930
LA County	34%	1,469,186 (55%)	1,185,314 (45%)	2,654,500	Y 283,872
South. Cal.	22%	907,941 (52%)	849,392 (48%)	1,757,333	Y 58,549
Rural Cal.	4%	152,064 (48%)	167,528 (52%)	319,592	N 15,464
State	100%	4,363,375 (55%)	3,548,180 (45%)	7,911,555	Y 815,195

Ethnic Breakdown /Social Group Voting

Group	Yes %	No %	% of State Voters
Asians	57%	43%	1%
Blacks	60%	40%	7%
Hispanics	58%	42%	5%
Whites	54%	46%	87%

White Sub-Groups:

White Liberals	67%	33%
Conservatives	50%	50%
Bay Area Suburbs	57%	43%
South Cal. Whites	51%	49%
Bay Area White Workers	56%	44%
LA County White Workers	46%	54%

Sources: California Secretary of State Archives. Asians – Chinatown; Blacks – South Central Los Angeles; Hispanics – East Los Angeles.

Year: November, 1973   Yes
Election: Reagan tax cut (#1)   No
Turnout: 48%

Geographic Breakdown:

Region	% of State	Yes (%)	No (%)	Total Votes	Margin
Bay Area	25%	436,671 (42%)	608,835 (58%)	1,045,506	N 172,164
Nor/Central Coast	5%	90,083 (42%)	125,041 (58%)	215,124	N 34,958
Cent. Valley Cities	11%	180,514 (39%)	279,197 (61%)	459,711	N 98,683

LA County	33%	686,560 (48%)	734,132 (52%)	1,420,692	N 47,572
South. Cal.	22%	485,704 (52%)	452,210 (48%)	937,914	Y 33,494
Rural Cal.	4%	82,153 (44%)	103,611 (56%)	185,764	N 21,458
State	100%	1,961,685 (46%)	2,303,026 (54%)	4,264,711	N 341,341

Ethnic Breakdown /Social Group Voting

Group	Yes %	No %	% of State Voters
Asians	45%	55%	1%
Blacks	16%	84%	7%
Hispanics	37%	63%	5%
Whites	49%	51%	87%

White Sub-Groups:

White Liberals	35%	65%
Conservatives	59%	41%
Bay Area Suburbs	45%	55%
South Cal. Whites	52%	48%
Bay Area White Workers	40%	60%
LA County White Workers	50%	50%

Sources: California Secretary of State Archives. Asians – Chinatown; Blacks – South Central Los Angeles; Hispanics – East Los Angeles.

Note: Proposition 1 would have enacted a substantial cut in both property and income taxes.

Year: June, 1974   Yes
Election: Political Reform Act (#9)   No
Turnout: 54%

Geographic Breakdown:

Region	% of State	Yes (%)	No (%)	Total Votes	Margin
Bay Area	25%	848,021 (73%)	315,337 (27%)	1,163,358	Y 532,684
Nor/Central Coast	5%	173,608 (70%)	73,208 (30%)	246,816	Y 100,400
Cent. Valley Cities	11%	350,713 (69%)	160,670 (31%)	511,383	Y 190,043
LA County	32%	1,005,134 (69%)	459,687 (31%)	1,464,821	Y 545,447
South. Cal.	22%	701,144 (69%)	307,957 (31%)	1,009,101	Y 393,187
Rural Cal.	5%	146,145 (66%)	75,924 (34%)	222,069	Y 70,221
State	100%	3,224,765 (70%)	1,392,783 (30%)	4,617,548	Y 1,831,982

Ethnic Breakdown /Social Group Voting

Group	Yes %	No %	% of State Voters
Asians	74%	26%	1%
Blacks	74%	26%	7%
Hispanics	75%	25%	5%
Whites	69%	31%	87%

White Sub-Groups:

White Liberals	77%	23%
Conservatives	70%	30%
Bay Area Suburbs	71%	29%
South Cal. Whites	68%	32%
Bay Area White Workers	73%	27%
LA County White Workers	73%	27%

Sources: California Secretary of State Archives. The ethnic vote breakdowns came from the Field Poll.

Note: The May 29 Field Poll showed Proposition 9 with 69%. It actually received 70% a week later. Proposition 9 enacted strict rules on legislators and staff accepting gifts and contributions.

Year: June, 1978   Yes: Cut property taxes
Election: Proposition 13   No
Turnout: 69%

Geographic Breakdown:

Region	% of State	Yes (%)	No (%)	Total Votes	Margin
Bay Area	24%	991,207 (62%)	605,137 (38%)	1,596,344	Y 386,070
Nor/Central Coast	5%	226,519 (66%)	115,980 (34%)	342,499	Y 110,539
Cent. Valley Cities	11%	409,072 (57%)	306,759 (43%)	715,831	Y 102,313
LA County	31%	1,367,907 (67%)	662,817 (33%)	2,030,724	Y 705,090
South. Cal.	24%	1,059,256 (66%)	547,797 (34%)	1,607,053	Y 511,459
Rural Cal.	5%	226,728 (72%)	87,677 (28%)	314,405	Y 139,051
State	100%	4,280,689 (65%)	2,326,167 (35%)	6,606,856	Y 1,954,522

Ethnic Breakdown /Social Group Voting

Group	Yes %	No %	% of State Voters
Asians	61%	39%	1%
Blacks	18%	82%	7%

Hispanics	40%	60%	5%
Whites	64%	36%	87%

White Sub-Groups:

White Liberals	55%	45%
Conservatives	70%	30%
Bay Area Suburbs	68%	32%
South Cal. Whites	68%	32%
Bay Area White Workers	73%	27%
LA County White Workers	73%	27%

Sources: California Secretary of State Archives. The ethnic vote breakdowns came from the Field Poll. Note: Proposition 13 cut property by 50% and established a maximum 1% state property tax limit. (Local communities can still vote to raise their own tax rates).

Year: November, 1978   Yes
Election: Ban Gay Teachers (#6)   No
Turnout: 70%

Geographic Breakdown:

Region	% of State	Yes (%)	No (%)	Total Votes	Margin
Bay Area	24%	583,254 (36%)	1,052,710 (64%)	1,635,964	N 469,456
Nor/Central Coast	5%	130,479 (37%)	225,504 (63%)	355,886	N 94,928
Cent. Valley Cities	11%	357,825 (46%)	413,799 (54%)	771,624	N 55,974
LA County	29%	779,052 (39%)	1,214,423 (61%)	1,993,475	N 435,371
South. Cal.	26%	800,984 (46%)	933,595 (54%)	1,734,579	N 132,611
Rural Cal.	4%	171,699 (57%)	129,186 (43%)	300,885	Y 4 2,513
State	100%	2,823,293 (42%)	3,969,120 (58%)	6,792,413	N 1,145,827

Ethnic Breakdown /Social Group Voting

Group	Yes %	No %	% of State Voters
Asians	44%	56%	2%
Blacks	28%	72%	7%
Hispanics	39%	61%	5%
Whites	43%	57%	86%

White Sub-Groups:

White Liberals	24%	76%
Conservatives	46%	54%
Bay Area Suburbs	39%	61%

South Cal. Whites	47%	53%
Bay Area White Workers	43%	57%
LA County White Workers	46%	54%

Sources: California Secretary of State Archives. Asians and whites came from the Field Poll.
Black voters were sampled in South-Central Los Angeles County and Hispanics in East Los Angeles.
Note: Prop 6 would have allowed all school districts in California to ban or fire gay teachers.

Year: November, 1978   Yes
Election: Death Penalty (#7)   No
Turnout: 70%

Geographic Breakdown:

Region	% of State	Yes (%)	No (%)	Total Votes	Margin
Bay Area	24%	943,480 (62%)	583,740 (38%)	1,527,220	Y 359,740
Nor/Central Coast	5%	223,3-8 (67%)	109,122 (33%)	332,430	Y 114,186
Cent. Valley Cities	12%	552,580 (76%)	172,021 (24%)	724,601	Y 380,559
LA County	29%	1,278,639 (71%)	529,788 (29%)	1,808,427	Y 748,851
South. Cal.	25%	1,231,493 (78%)	346,729 (22%)	1,578,222	Y 884,764
Rural Cal.	5%	250,775 (77%)	76,957 (23%)	327,732	Y 173,818
State	100%	4,480,275 (71%)	1,818,357 (29%)	6,298,632	Y 2,661,918

Ethnic Breakdown /Social Group Voting

Group	Yes %	No %	% of State Voters
Asians	75%	25%	2%
Blacks	52%	48%	7%
Hispanics	66%	34%	5%
Whites	75%	25%	86%

White Sub-Groups:

White Liberals	55%	45%
Conservatives	77%	23%
Bay Area Suburbs	68%	32%
South Cal. Whites	78%	22%
Bay Area White Workers	71%	29%
LA County White Workers	73%	27%

Sources: California Secretary of State Archives. Asians and whites came from the Field Poll.
Black voters were sampled in South-Central Los Angeles County and Hispanics in East Los Angeles.

Note: Proposition 7 restored the death penalty option in first-degree murder cases.

Year: November, 1979   Yes
Election: Ban Busing (Prop. 1)   No
Turnout: 37%

Geographic Breakdown:

Region	% of State	Yes (%)	No (%)	Total Votes	Margin
Bay Area	24%	512,769 (60%)	347,357 (40%)	860,126	Y 165,412
Nor/Central Coast	5%	120,260 (63%)	69,802 (37%)	190,062	Y 504,458
Cent. Valley Cities	10%	252,633 (70%)	106,894 (30%)	359,527	Y 145,739
LA County	39%	775,838 (74%)	273,511 (26%)	1,049,349	Y 502,327
South. Cal.	25%	631,790 (71%)	257,950 (31%)	889,740	Y 373,840
Rural Cal.	6%	140,022 (71%)	57,409 (29%)	197,431	Y 82,613
State	100%	2,433,312 (69%)	1,112,923 (31%)	3,546,235	Y 1,320,389

Ethnic Breakdown /Social Group Voting

Group	Yes %	No %	% of State Voters
Asians	71%	29%	1%
Blacks	49%	51%	7%
Hispanics	61%	39%	5%
Whites	75%	25%	86%

White Sub-Groups:

White Liberals	61%	39%
Conservatives	78%	22%
Bay Area Suburbs	62%	38%
South Cal. Whites	72%	28%
Bay Area White Workers	67%	33%
LA County White Workers	74%	26%

Sources: California Secretary of State Archives. Asians and whites came from the Field Poll. Black voters were sampled in South-Central Los Angeles County and Hispanics in East Los Angeles.

Note: The August Field Poll showed Proposition 1 with 73%. It actually received 69% in November.

Year: November, 1979   Yes
Election: Gann Spending Limit (#4)   No
Turnout: 37%

Geographic Breakdown:

Region	% of State	Yes (%)	No (%)	Total Votes	Margin
Bay Area	25%	583,566 (69%)	267,083 (31%)	851,549	Y 315,583
Nor/Central Coast	5%	139,874 (74%)	48,718 (26%)	188,592	Y 91,156
Cent. Valley Cities	10%	247,828 (70%)	107,006 (30%)	354,834	Y 140,822
LA County	29%	763,826 (76%)	240,600 (24%)	1,004,426	Y 523,226
South. Cal.	25%	691,896 (79%)	182,305 (21%)	874,201	Y 509,591
Rural Cal.	6%	153,730 (78%)	44,545 (22%)	198,275	Y 109,185
State	100%	2,580,720 (74%)	891,157 (26%)	3,471,877	Y 1,689,563

Ethnic Breakdown /Social Group Voting

Group	Yes %	No %	% of State Voters
Asians	56%	44%	1%
Blacks	59%	41%	7%
Hispanics	68%	32%	5%
Whites	56%	44%	86%

White Sub-Groups:

White Liberals	68%	32%
Conservatives	82%	18%
Bay Area Suburbs	74%	26%
South Cal. Whites	81%	19%
Bay Area White Workers	74%	26%
LA County White Workers	77%	23%

Sources: California Secretary of State Archives. Asians and whites came from the Field Poll. Black voters were sampled in South-Central Los Angeles County and Hispanics in East Los Angeles.

Note: Prop 4 instituted a cap that limited the growth of state spending according to the cost of living and population growth.

Year: June, 1980   Yes
Election: Income tax cut (#9)   No
Turnout: 63%

Geographic Breakdown:

Region	% of State	Yes (%)	No (%)	Total Votes	Margin
Bay Area	24%	571,887 (37%)	993,139 (63%)	1,565,026	N 421,252

Nor/Central Coast	6%	131,689 (37%)	228,759 (63%)	360,448	N 97,070
Cent. Valley Cities	12%	234,986 (31%)	521,871 (69%)	756,857	N 286,885
LA County	28%	744,268 (41%)	1,062,544 (59%)	1,806,812	N 318,276
South. Cal.	25%	722,055 (44%)	914,660 (56%)	1,636,715	N 192,605
Rural Cal.	5%	133,782 (38%)	221,275 (62%)	355,057	N 87,493
State	100%	2,538,667 (39%)	3,942,248 (61%)	6,480,915	N 1,403,581

Ethnic Breakdown /Social Group Voting

Group	Yes %	No %	% of State Voters
Asians	42%	58%	2%
Blacks	23%	77%	7%
Hispanics	27%	73%	6%
Whites	41%	59%	84%

White Sub-Groups:

White Liberals	32%	68%
Conservatives	49%	51%
Bay Area Suburbs	38%	62%
South Cal. Whites	46%	54%
Bay Area White Workers	41%	59%
LA County White Workers	41%	59%

Sources: California Secretary of State Archives. Asians and whites came from the Field Poll. Black voters were sampled in South-Central Los Angeles County and Hispanics in East Los Angeles.

Note: Prop 9 would have enacted a 50% across-the-board income tax cut.

Year: June, 1982   Yes
Election: Crime Victims' Rights (#8)   No
Turnout: 53%

Geographic Breakdown:

Region	% of State	Yes (%)	No (%)	Total Votes	Margin
Bay Area	24%	691,484 (57%)	521,780 (43%)	1,213,264	Y 169,704
Nor/Central Coast	5%	144,903 (53%)	129,086 (47%)	273,989	Y 15,817
Cent. Valley Cities	12%	329,554 (54%)	283,389 (46%)	612,943	Y 46,165
LA County	27%	693,626 (51%)	673,519 (49%)	1,367,145	Y 20,107

South. Cal.	25%	784,348 (64%)	445,465 (36%)	1,229,813	Y 338,883
Rural Cal.	6%	182,166 (58%)	129,471 (42%)	311,637	Y 52,695
State	100%	2,826,081 (56%)	2,182,710 (44%)	5,008,791	Y 643,371

Ethnic Breakdown /Social Group Voting

Group	Yes %	No %	% of State Voters
Asians	70%	30%	2%
Blacks	34%	66%	8%
Hispanics	45%	55%	6%
Whites	59%	41%	83%

White Sub-Groups:

White Liberals	46%	54%
Conservatives	60%	40%
Bay Area Suburbs	61%	39%
South Cal. Whites	66%	34%
Bay Area White Workers	63%	37%
LA County White Workers	54%	46%

Sources: California Secretary of State Archives. Asians and whites came from the Field Poll. Black voters were sampled in South-Central Los Angeles County and Hispanics in East Los Angeles.

Note: Prop 8 allows crime victims the right to be notified of, to attend, and to state their views, at sentencing and parole hearings.

Year: June 1982   Yes
Election: Peripheral Canal (#9)   No
Turnout: 53%

Geographic Breakdown:

Region	% of State	Yes (%)	No (%)	Total Votes	Margin
Bay Area	25%	82,528 (6%)	1,275,618 (94%)	1,358,146	N 1,193,090
Nor/Central Coast	6%	55,444 (18%)	246,942 (82%)	302,386	N 191,498
Cent. Valley Cities	12%	121,516 (18%)	550,563 (82%)	672,079	N 429,047
LA County	27%	909,144 (61%)	582,010 (39%)	1,491,154	Y 327,134
South. Cal.	24%	844,547 (63%)	477,870 (37%)	1,322,417	Y 366,677
Rural Cal.	6%	35,863 (10%)	311,480 (90%)	347,343	N 275,617
State	100%	2,049,042 (37%)	3,444,483 (63%)	5,493,529	N 1,395,441

Ethnic Breakdown /Social Group Voting

Group	Yes %	No %	% of State Voters
Asians	36%	64%	2%
Blacks	59%	41%	8%
Hispanics	51%	49%	6%
Whites	30%	70%	83%

White Sub-Groups:

White Liberals	36%	64%
Conservatives	55%	45%
Bay Area suburbs	5%	95%
South Cal. Whites	63%	37%
Bay Area White Workers	6%	94%
LA County White Workers	60%	40%

Sources: California Secretary of State Archives. The ethnic breakdown came from the Field Poll.

Note: Prop 9 would have authorized the construction of a canal to send water from the Sacramento Delta to the southern part of the state.

Year: November, 1982   Yes
Election: Handgun Registration (#15)   No
Turnout: 70%

Geographic Breakdown:

Region	% of State	Yes (%)	No (%)	Total Votes	Margin
Bay Area	23%	812,795 (46%)	949,944 (54%)	1,762,739	N 137,149
Nor/Central Coast	5%	146,741 (36%)	259,180 (64%)	405,921	N 112,439
Cent. Valley Cities	12%	259,051 (28%)	679,284 (72%)	938,335	N 420,233
LA County	28%	899,424 (42%)	1,255,440 (58%)	2,154,864	N 356,016
South. Cal.	26%	641,344 (33%)	1,307,300 (67%)	1,948,644	N 665,956
Rural Cal.	6%	80,799 (19%)	348,438 (81%)	429,237	N 267,639
State	100%	2,840,154 (37%)	4,799,586 (63%)	7,639,740	N 1,959,432

Ethnic Breakdown /Social Group Voting

Group	Yes %	No %	% of State Voters
Asians	40%	60%	2%
Blacks	38%	62%	8%

Hispanics	45%	55%	6%
Whites	40%	60%	83%

White Sub-Groups:

White Liberals	61%	64%
Conservatives	34%	45%
Bay Area Suburbs	40%	95%
South Cal. Whites	32%	37%
Bay Area White Workers	35%	65%
LA County White Workers	33%	67%

Sources: California Secretary of State Archives. The ethnic vote breakdowns came from the CBS News exit poll. Note: Prop 15 would have required the registration of all handguns.

Year: November, 1986   Yes
Election: Toxic water treatment (#65)   No
Turnout: 59%

Geographic Breakdown:

Region	% of State	Yes (%)	No (%)	Total Votes	Margin
Bay Area	23%	1,109,735 (67%)	537,293 (33%)	1,647,028	Y 72,442
Nor/Central Coast	5%	225,943 (61%)	146,812 (39%)	372,755	Y 79,131
Cent. Valley Cities	12%	452,249 (52%)	423,814 (48%)	876,063	Y 28,435
LA County	27%	1,260,475 (66%)	649,358 (34%)	1,909,833	Y 611,117
South. Cal.	26%	1,142,726 (63%)	683,828 (37%)	1,826,554	Y 458,898
Rural Cal.	6%	209,343 (52%)	191,512 (48%)	400,855	Y 17,831
State	100%	4,400,471 (63%)	2,632,617 (37%)	7,033,088	Y 767,854

Ethnic Breakdown /Social Group Voting

Group	Yes %	No %	% of State Voters
Asians	60%	40%	2%
Blacks	74%	26%	8%
Hispanics	67%	33%	6%
Whites	67%	33%	83%

White Sub-Groups:

White Liberals	74%	26%
Conservatives	62%	38%

Bay Area Suburbs	65%	35%
South Cal. Whites	62%	38%
Bay Area White Workers	69%	31%
LA County White Workers	68%	32%

Sources: California Secretary of State Archives. The ethnic vote breakdowns came from the Los Angeles Times exit poll.

Note: Prop 65 established regulations to enhance water quality.

Year: November, 1986   Yes
Election: Confirm Rose Bird   No
Turnout: 59%

Geographic Breakdown:

Region	% of State	Yes (%)	No (%)	Total Votes	Margin
Bay Area	24%	739,582 (44%)	947,336 (56%)	1,686,918	N 207,754
Nor/Central Coast	5%	131,027 (35%)	243,583 (65%)	374,610	N 112,556
Cent. Valley Cities	12%	247,898 (28%)	627,612 (72%)	875,510	N 379,714
LA County	27%	752,676 (38%)	1,204,968 (62%)	1,957,644	N 452,292
South. Cal.	24%	536,918 (32%)	1,167,398 (68%)	1,704,396	N 630,400
Rural Cal.	6%	92,610 (22%)	310,747 (78%)	403,357	N 218,137
State	100%	2,417,877 (34%)	4,723,413 (66%)	7,141,290	N 2,305,536

Ethnic Breakdown /Social Group Voting

Group	Yes %	No %	% of State Voters
Asians	39%	61%	2%
Blacks	70%	30%	8%
Hispanics	51%	49%	6%
Whites	30%	70%	83%

White Sub-Groups:

White Liberals	52%	48%
Conservatives	22%	78%
Bay Area Suburbs	36%	64%
South Cal. Whites	31%	69%
Bay Area White Workers	35%	65%
LA County White Workers	43%	57%

Sources: California Secretary of State Archives. Asians and whites came from the Field Poll. Black voters were sampled in South-Central Los Angeles County and Hispanics in East Los Angeles.

Year: November, 1988
Election: 40% budget for schools (#98)
Turnout: 73%

Yes
No

Geographic Breakdown:

Region	% of State	Yes (%)	No (%)	Total Votes	Margin
Bay Area	23%	1,185,444 (56%)	932,255 (44%)	2,117,699	Y 253,189
Nor/Central Coast	5%	248,668 (50%)	249,252 (50%)	497,920	N 584
Cent. Valley Cities	12%	520,742 (48%)	575,086 (52%)	1,095,828	N 54,344
LA County	26%	1,315,549 (55%)	1,083,267 (45%)	2,398.816	Y 232,282
South. Cal.	27%	1,154,244 (46%)	1,349,774 (54%)	2,504,018	Y 195,530
Rural Cal.	6%	294,090 (40%)	310,869 (60%)	514,959	N 106,779
State	100%	4,628,737 (51%)	4,500,503 (49%)	9,129,240	Y 128,234

Ethnic Breakdown /Social Group Voting

Group	Yes %	No %	% of State Voters
Asians	67%	33%	2%
Blacks	75%	25%	8%
Hispanics	66%	34%	6%
Whites	47%	53%	83%

White Sub-Groups:

White Liberals	62%	38%
Conservatives	44%	56%
Bay Area Suburbs	51%	49%
South Cal. Whites	44%	56%
Bay Area	54%	46%
LA County	53%	47%

Sources: California Secretary of State Archives. Asians and whites came from the Field Poll. Black voters were sampled in South-Central Los Angeles County and Hispanics in East Los Angeles.

Note: Prop 98 guarantees that at least 40% of the State's General Fund spending will be reserved for education.

Year: November, 1988   Yes
Election: Insurance reform (#103)   No
Turnout: 73%

Geographic Breakdown:

Region	% of State	Yes (%)	No (%)	Total Votes	Margin
Bay Area	23%	1,180,955 (54%)	1,015,303 (46%)	2,196,258	Y 165,652
Nor/Central Coast	5%	220,773 (44%)	285,820 (56%)	506,593	N 65,047
Cent. Valley Cities	12%	426,514 (38%)	698,087 (62%)	1,124,601	N 271,573
LA County	26%	1,567,306 (63%)	934,596 (37%)	2,501,902	Y 632,710
South. Cal.	28%	1,248,760 (48%)	1,368,676 (52%)	2,617,436	N 119,916
Rural Cal.	6%	200,004 (38%)	328,270 (62%)	528,274	N 128,266
State	100%	4,844,312 (51%)	4,630,752 (49%)	9,475,064	Y 213,560

Ethnic Breakdown /Social Group Voting

Group	Yes %	No %	% of State Voters
Asians	68%	32%	2%
Blacks	75%	25%	8%
Hispanics	66%	34%	6%
Whites	47%	53%	82%

White Sub-Groups:

White Liberals	68%	32%
Conservatives	52%	48%
Bay Area Suburbs	49%	51%
South Cal. Whites	45%	55%
Bay Area White Workers	56%	44%
LA County White Workers	63%	37%

Sources: California Secretary of State Archives. Asians and whites came from the Field Poll. Black voters were sampled in South-Central Los Angeles County and Hispanics in East Los Angeles.

Note: Prop 103 established the state office of Insurance Commissioner.

Year: June, 1990   Yes
Election: Raise Gas Tax (#111)   No
Turnout: 41%

Geographic Breakdown:

Region	% of State	Yes (%)	No (%)	Total Votes	Margin
Bay Area	24%	676,217 (56%)	539,309 (44%)	1,215,526	Y 136,908
Nor/Central Coast	6%	151,182 (50%)	153,257 (50%)	304,439	N 2,075
Cent. Valley Cities	13%	323,992 (50%)	325,339 (50%)	649,331	N 1,347
LA County	24%	687,709 (59%)	487,352 (41%)	1,175,061	Y 200,357
South. Cal.	26%	647,058 (50%)	648,558 (50%)	1,295,616	N 1,500
Rural Cal.	7%	134,865 (38%)	224,214 (62%)	359,079	N 89,349
State	100%	2,621,023 (52%)	2,378,029 (48%)	4,999,052	Y 242,994

Ethnic Breakdown /Social Group Voting

Group	Yes %	No %	% of State Voters
Asians	71%	29%	2%
Blacks	68%	32%	8%
Hispanics	65%	35%	6%
Whites	49%	51%	82%

White Sub-Groups:

White Liberals	67%	33%
Conservatives	49%	51%
Bay Area Suburbs	54%	46%
South Cal. Whites	47%	53%
Bay Area White Workers	50%	50%
LA County White Workers	54%	46%

Sources: California Secretary of State Archives. Asians and whites came from the Field Poll. Black voters were sampled in South-Central Los Angeles County and Hispanics in East Los Angeles.

Year: November, 1990   Yes
Election: Big Green (#128)   No
Turnout: 59%

Geographic Breakdown:

Region	% of State	Yes (%)	No (%)	Total Votes	Margin
Bay Area	24%	754,287 (43%)	1,011,206 (57%)	1,765,493	N 256,919
Nor/Central Coast	6%	148,862 (35%)	272,189 (65%)	421,051	N 123,327

Cent. Valley Cities	13%	248,918 (27%)	680,521 (73%)	929,439	N 431,603
LA County	24%	746,633 (42%)	1,033,251 (58%)	1,779,884	N 286,618
South. Cal.	27%	626,365 (31%)	1,399,126 (69%)	2,025,491	N 772,761
Rural Cal.	6%	111,598 (23%)	373,729 (77%)	475,327	N 262,131
State	100%	2,636,663 (36%)	4,760,022 (64%)	7,396,685	N 2,123,359

Ethnic Breakdown /Social Group Voting

Group	Yes %	No %	% of State Voters
Asians	50%	50%	2%
Blacks	47%	53%	8%
Hispanics	55%	45%	6%
Whites	33%	67%	83%

White Sub-Groups:

White Liberals	56%	44%
Conservatives	30%	70%
Bay Area Suburbs	37%	63%
South Cal. Whites	30%	70%
Bay Area	38%	62%
LA County	39%	61%

Sources: California Secretary of State Archives. Asians and whites came from the Field Poll. Black voters were sampled in South-Central Los Angeles County and Hispanics in East Los Angeles.

Note: Prop 128, known as "Big Green," would have authorized far-ranging environmental regulations and provided financing for an office of "State Environmental Advocate."

Year: November, 1990   Yes
Election: Term limits (#140)   No

Geographic Breakdown:

Region	% of State	Yes (%)	No (%)	Total Votes	Margin
Bay Area	24%	854,678 (50%)	864,794 (50%)	1,719,472	N 10,116
Nor/Central Coast	6%	207,414 (51%)	201,250 (49%)	408,664	Y 6,164
Cent. Valley Cities	13%	475,379 (52%)	438,600 (48%)	913,979	Y 36,779
LA County	24%	818,984 (47%)	912,317 (53%)	1,731,301	N 93,333
South. Cal.	27%	1,112,356 (58%)	821,867 (42%)	1,934,223	Y 290,489
Rural Cal.	7%	275,636 (59%)	193,838 (41%)	469,474	Y 81,798

State	100%	3,744,447 (52%)	3,432,666 (48%)	7,177,113	Y 311,781

Ethnic Breakdown /Social Group Voting

Group	Yes %	No %	% of State Voters
Asians	65%	35%	2%
Blacks	30%	70%	8%
Hispanics	37%	63%	6%
Whites	54%	46%	83%

White Sub-Groups:

White Liberals	41%	59%
Conservatives	60%	40%
Bay Area Suburbs	54%	46%
South Cal. Whites	62%	38%
Bay Area White Workers	50%	50%
LA County White Workers	49%	51%

Sources: California Secretary of State Archives. The ethnic vote breakdowns came from the networks' exit poll.

Note: Prop 140 established term limits of six years for the State Assembly, 8 years for the State Senate and two terms for state constitutional offices.

Year: November, 1992   Yes
Election: Right-to-Die (#161) No
Turnout: 75%

Geographic Breakdown:

Region	% of State	Yes (%)	No (%)	Total Votes	Margin
Bay Area	23%	1,271,770 (51%)	1,215,464 (49%)	2,487,234	Y 56,306
Nor/Central Coast	6%	293,073 (50%)	292,413 (50%)	585,486	Y 660
Cent. Valley Cities	12%	531,436 (41%)	774,478 (59%)	1,305,914	N 243,042
LA County	25%	1,182,075 (45%)	1,433,894 (55%)	2,615,969	N 251,819
South. Cal.	28%	1,294,166 (44%)	1,671,010 (56%)	2,965,176	N 376,844
Rural Cal.	6%	290,958 (45%)	352,657 (55%)	643,615	N 61,699
State	100%	4,863,478 (46%)	5,739,916 (54%)	10,603,394	N 876,438

Ethnic Breakdown /Social Group Voting

Group	Yes %	No %	% of State Voters

Asians	35%	65%	4%
Blacks	39%	61%	6%
Hispanics	41%	59%	7%
Whites	48%	52%	82%

White Sub-Groups:

White Liberals	58%	42%
Conservatives	42%	58%
Bay Area Suburbs	49%	51%
South Cal. Whites	45%	55%
Bay Area White Workers	46%	54%
LA County White Workers	37%	63%

Sources: California Secretary of State Archives. The ethnic vote breakdowns came from the networks' exit poll.

Note: Prop 161 would have allowed patients and doctors to end the lives of terminally ill patients.

Year: November, 1992   Yes
Election: Wilson Welfare Cuts/Reform (#165)   No

Geographic Breakdown:

Region	% of State	Yes (%)	No (%)	Total Votes	Margin
Bay Area	23%	958,644 (39%)	1,488,476 (61%)	2,447,120	N 529,832
Nor/Central Coast	5%	254,359 (45%)	313,423 (55%)	567,782	N 59,064
Cent. Valley Cities	12%	617,648 (47%)	685,108 (53%)	1,302,756	N 67,460
LA County	25%	1,125,969 (44%)	1,454,875 (56%)	2,580,844	N 328,906
South. Cal.	28%	1,581,239 (54%)	1,330,387 (46%)	2,911,626	Y 250,852
Rural Cal.	6%	331,446 (52%)	304,790 (48%)	636,236	Y 26,656
State	100%	4,869,305 (47%)	5,577,059 (53%)	10,446,364	N 707,754

Ethnic Breakdown /Social Group Voting

Group	Yes %	No %	% of State Voters
Asians	46%	54%	4%
Blacks	37%	63%	6%
Hispanics	43%	57%	7%
Whites	48%	52%	82%

White Sub-Groups:

White Liberals	39%	61%
Conservatives	55%	45%
Bay Area Suburbs	43%	57%
South Cal. Whites	56%	44%
Bay Area White Workers	41%	59%
LA County White Workers	49%	51%

Sources: California Secretary of State Archives. The ethnic vote breakdowns came from the networks' exit poll.

Note: Prop 165 would have allowed the Governor to make unilateral spending cuts if the budget was late and out-of-balance and also would mandated immediate cuts in welfare spending.

Year: November, 1994   Yes
Election: 3-Strikes/Crime (#184)   No
Turnout:
Percent of Registered Voters Turning Out: 60%

Geographic Breakdown:

Region	% of State	Yes (%)	No (%)	Total Votes	Margin
Bay Area	23%	1,130,033 (59%)	771,015 (41%)	1,901,048	Y 350,018
Nor/Central Coast	6%	315,184 (67%)	155,474 (33%)	470,658	Y 159,710
Cent. Valley Cities	13%	805,619 (76%)	249,104 (24%)	1,054,623	Y 556,415
LA County	23%	1,407,499 (73%)	520,189 (27%)	1,927,688	Y 887,310
South. Cal.	28%	1,834,235 (79%)	491,097 (21%)	2,325,332	Y 1,343,138
Rural Cal.	7%	413,798 (76%)	127,669 (24%)	541,467	Y 286,129
State	100%	5,906,268 (72%)	2,314,548 (28%)	8,220,816	Y 3,591,720

Ethnic Breakdown /Social Group Voting

Group	Yes %	No %	% of State Voters
Asians	83%	17%	5%
Blacks	62%	38%	7%
Hispanics	74%	26%	9%
Whites	72%	28%	77%

White Sub-Groups:

White Liberals	59%	41%
Conservatives	79%	21%

Bay Area Suburbs	65%	35%
South Cal. Whites	80%	20%
Bay Area White Workers	71%	29%
LA County White Workers	81%	19%

Sources: California Secretary of State Archives. Ethnic vote breakdowns from the Los Angeles Times exit poll.

Note: Prop 184 established mandatory 20 years-to-life sentences for anyone convicted of any three felonies.

Year: Health Care Reform   Yes
Election: November, 1994 (#186)   No

Geographic Breakdown:

Region	% of State	Dem (%)	Rep (%)	Total Votes	Margin
Bay Area	23%	661,757 (34%)	1,271,762 (66%)	1,933,519	N 610,025
Nor/Central Coast	6%	144,413 (30%)	330,503 (70%)	474,916	N 186,090
Cent. Valley Cities	13%	219,174 (21%)	841,525 (79%)	1,060,699	N 622,351
LA County	24%	576,151 (29%)	1,388,059 (71%)	1,964,220	N 811,898
South. Cal.	28%	501,524 (21%)	1,848,202 (79%)	2,349,726	N 1,346,678
Rural Cal.	6%	109,662 (20%)	430,848 (80%)	540,510	N 321,186
State	100%	2,216,691 (27%)	6,110,899 (73%)	8,323,590	N 3,898,208

Ethnic Breakdown /Social Group Voting

Group	Yes %	No %	% of State Voters
Asians	33%	67%	5%
Blacks	33%	67%	7%
Hispanics	37%	63%	9%
Whites	24%	76%	77%

White Sub-Groups:

White Liberals	39%	61%
Conservatives	19%	81%
Bay Area Suburbs	28%	72%
South Cal. Whites	21%	79%
Bay Area White Workers	29%	71%
LA County White Workers	23%	77%

Sources: California Secretary of State Archives. The ethnic vote breakdowns came from the networks' exit poll.

Note: Prop 186 would have created a "single-payer" health care plan.

Year: November, 1994   Yes
Election: Prop. 187 – Immigration No

Geographic Breakdown:

Region	% of State	Yes (%)	No (%)	Total Votes	Margin
Bay Area	23%	900,455 (45%)	1,093,008 (55%)	1,993,463	N 192,553
Nor/Central Coast	6%	276,075 (57%)	210,621 (43%)	486,696	Y 65,454
Cent. Valley Cities	13%	705,550 (65%)	386,505 (35%)	1,092,055	Y 319,045
LA County	24%	1,145,622 (56%)	898,500 (44%)	2,044,122	Y 247,122
South. Cal.	28%	1,644,325 (68%)	780,286 (32%)	2,424,611	Y 846,039
Rural Cal.	6%	391,510 (71%)	160,512 (29%)	552,022	Y 230,998
State	100%	5,063,537 (59%)	3,529,432 (41%)	8,592,969	Y 1,534,105

Ethnic Breakdown /Social Group Voting

Group	Yes %	No %	% of State Voters
Asians	47%	53%	5%
Blacks	47%	53%	7%
Hispanics	23%	77%	9%
Whites	63%	37%	77%

White Sub-Groups:

White Liberals	43%	57%
Conservatives	67%	33%
Bay Area Suburbs	51%	49%
South Cal. Whites	70%	30%
Bay Area White Workers	51%	49%
LA County White Workers	66%	34%

Sources: California Secretary of State Archives. The ethnic vote breakdowns came from the Los Angeles Times exit poll.

Note: Prop 187 would have denied state services to all illegal immigrants and their families. (Some provisions were later overturned by federal courts).

Year: March, 1996   Yes
Election: Open Primary (#198)   No

Turnout: 42%

Geographic Breakdown:

Region	% of State	Yes (%)	No (%)	Total Votes	Margin
Bay Area	23%	764,278 (58%)	549,706 (42%)	1,313,844	Y 214,572
Nor/Central Coast	6%	213,308 (62%)	127,660 (38%)	340,968	Y 85,648
Cent. Valley Cities	14%	465,774 (61%)	297,565 (39%)	763,339	Y 168,209
LA County	22%	688,186 (56%)	534,426 (44%)	1,222,612	Y 153,760
South. Cal.	28%	938,318 (61%)	606,711 (39%)	1,545,029	Y 331,607
Rural Cal.	8%	270,778 (63%)	156,996 (37%)	427,774	Y 113,782
State	100%	3,340,642 (60%)	2,273,064 (40%)	5,613,706	Y 1,067,578

Ethnic Breakdown /Social Group Voting

Group	Yes %	No %	% of State Voters
Asians	67%	33%	4%
Blacks	67%	33%	6%
Hispanics	61%	39%	8%
Whites	60%	40%	81%

White Sub-Groups:

White Liberals	55%	45%
Conservatives	58%	42%
Bay Area Suburbs	62%	38%
South Cal. Whites	60%	40%
Bay Area White Workers	58%	42%
LA County White Workers	58%	42%

Sources: California Secretary of State Archives. The ethnic vote breakdowns came from the Los Angeles Times exit poll.

Note: Prop 198 created an "open primary" where voters could choose between candidates regardless of party registration or affiliation. (The US Supreme Court overturned it after the 2000 election).

Year: March, 1996   Yes
Election: No-fault insurance (#200)   No

Geographic Breakdown:

Region	% of State	Yes (%)	No (%)	Total Votes	Margin

Bay Area	24%	405,186 (30%)	949,193 (70%)	1,354,379	N 544,007
Nor/Central Coast	6%	116,638 (33%)	231,864 (67%)	348,502	N 115,223
Cent. Valley Cities	13%	291,001 (38%)	483,677 (62%)	774,678	N 192,676
LA County	22%	426,773 (34%)	835,992 (66%)	1,262,765	N 409,219
South. Cal.	27%	602,733 (38%)	977,720 (62%)	1,580,453	N 374,987
Rural Cal.	8%	160,436 (37%)	275,968 (63%)	436,404	N 115,532
State	100%	2,002,767 (35%)	3,754,414 (65%)	5,757,181	N 1,751,647

Ethnic Breakdown /Social Group Voting

Group	Yes %	No %	% of State Voters
Asians	39%	61%	4%
Blacks	29%	71%	6%
Hispanics	31%	69%	8%
Whites	38%	62%	81%

White Sub-Groups:

White Liberals	33%	67%
Conservatives	42%	58%
Bay Area Suburbs	32%	68%
South Cal. Whites	39%	61%
Bay Area White Workers	25%	75%
LA County White Workers	36%	64%

Sources: California Secretary of State Archives. The ethnic vote breakdowns came from the Los Angeles Times exit poll.

Note: Prop 200 would have established a "No-fault" insurance system and severely curtailed the ability of California drivers to sue for accidental damages.

Year: March, 1996   Yes
Election: Lawyers' fees (#202)   No

Geographic Breakdown:

Region	% of State	Yes (%)	No (%)	Total Votes	Margin
Bay Area	24%	554,501 (42%)	780,490 (58%)	1,334,991	N 225,989
Nor/Central Coast	6%	165,968 (49%)	173,653 (51%)	339,621	N 7,685

Cent. Valley Cities	13%	400,866 (53%)	358,641 (47%)	759,507	N 42,225
LA County	22%	566,108 (45%)	684,456 (55%)	1,250,564	N 118.348
South. Cal.	28%	853,468 (55%)	709,437 (45%)	1,562,905	Y 144,031
Rural Cal.	8%	228,552 (53%)	200,670 (47%)	429,225	Y 27,882
State	100%	2,769,466 (49%)	2,907,347 (51%)	5,676,813	N 137,881

Ethnic Breakdown /Social Group Voting

Group	Yes %	No %	% of State Voters
Asians	49%	51%	4%
Blacks	31%	69%	6%
Hispanics	42%	58%	8%
Whites	50%	50%	81%

White Sub-Groups:

White Liberals	40%	60%
Conservatives	56%	44%
Bay Area Suburbs	44%	56%
South Cal. Whites	56%	44%
Bay Area White Workers	38%	62%
LA County White Workers	51%	49%

Sources: California Secretary of State Archives. The ethnic vote breakdowns came from the Los Angeles Times exit poll.

Note: Prop 202 would have restricted legal fees in lawsuits settled without going to trial.

Year: November, 1996   Yes
Election: 209, Affirmative Action   No
Turnout: 66%

Geographic Breakdown:

Region	% of State	Yes (%)	No (%)	Total Votes	Margin
Bay Area	23%	1,037,238 (46%)	1,216,317 (54%)	2,253,555	N 179,079
Nor/Central Coast	6%	305,754 (56%)	236,985 (44%)	542,739	Y 68,769
Cent. Valley Cities	13%	740,005 (61%)	469,820 (39%)	1,209,825	Y 270,185
LA County	24%	1,073,016 (46%)	1,287,826 (54%)	2,360,842	N 214,810
South. Cal.	28%	1,689,234 (63%)	1,003,520 (37%)	2,692,754	Y 685,714

| Rural Cal. | 6% | 423,215 (71%) | 174,265 (29%) | 597,480 | Y 248,950 |
| State | 100% | 5,268,462 (55%) | 4,388,733 (45%) | 9,657,195 | Y 879,729 |

Ethnic Breakdown /Social Group Voting

Group	Yes %	No %	% of State Voters
Asians	42%	58%	5%
Blacks	26%	74%	7%
Hispanics	27%	73%	11%
Whites	62%	38%	74%

White Sub-Groups:

White Liberals	45%	55%
Conservatives	67%	33%
Bay Area Suburbs	52%	48%
South Cal. Whites	70%	30%
Bay Area White Workers	49%	51%
LA County White Workers	56%	44%

Sources: California Secretary of State Archives. The ethnic vote breakdowns came from averaging the Los Angeles Times and CNN exit poll results.

Note: A "Yes" vote for Proposition 209 would ban the use of affirmative action or racial preferences in all state government operations.

Year: November, 1996   Yes
Election: Medical Marijuana (#215)   No

Geographic Breakdown:

Region	% of State	Yes (%)	No (%)	Total Votes	Margin
Bay Area	23%	1,524,563 (68%)	725,630 (32%)	2,250,193	Y 798,933
Nor/Central Coast	6%	317,818 (58%)	227,982 (42%)	545,800	Y 89,836
Cent. Valley Cities	13%	571,900 (47%)	646,670 (52%)	1,219,570	N 74,770
LA County	24%	1,292,531 (56%)	1,028,957 (44%)	2,321,488	Y 63,574
South. Cal.	29%	1,390,638 (50%)	1,405,658 (50%)	2,796,296	N 15,020
Rural Cal.	6%	285,465 (52%)	267,063 (48%)	552,528	N 18,402
State	100%	5,382,915 (56%)	4,301,960 (44%)	9,684,875	Y 1,080,955

Ethnic Breakdown /Social Group Voting

Group	Yes %	No %	% of State Voters

Asians	49%	51%	5%
Blacks	70%	30%	7%
Hispanics	49%	51%	11%
Whites	56%	44%	74%

White Sub-Groups:

White Liberals	71%	29%
Conservatives	50%	50%
Bay Area Suburbs	64%	36%
South Cal. Whites	49%	51%
Bay Area White Workers	64%	36%
LA County White Workers	48%	52%

Sources: California Secretary of State Archives. The ethnic vote breakdowns came from the Los Angeles Times exit poll.

Note: Prop 215 authorizes the prescribing of marijuana for "medicinal" purposes.

Year: November, 1996   Yes
Election: HMO Reform, (#216)   No

Geographic Breakdown:

Region	% of State	Yes (%)	No (%)	Total Votes	Margin
Bay Area	23%	898,503 (43%)	1,194,389 (57%)	2,092,892	N 295,886
Nor/Central Coast	6%	218,310 (42%)	296,224 (58%)	514,534	N 77,914
Cent. Valley Cities	13%	390,422 (34%)	770,544 (66%)	1,160,966	N 380,122
LA County	24%	903,758 (41%)	1,287,528 (59%)	2,191,286	N 383,770
South. Cal.	28%	931,529 (36%)	1,646,374 (64%)	2,577,903	N 714,845
Rural Cal.	7%	198,323 (33%)	398,530 (67%)	596,853	N 200,207
State	100%	3,540,845 (39%)	5,593,589 (61%)	9,134,434	N 2,052,744

Ethnic Breakdown /Social Group Voting

Group	Yes %	No %	% of State Voters
Asians	45%	55%	5%
Blacks	47%	53%	7%
Hispanics	42%	58%	11%
Whites	35%	65%	74%

White Sub-Groups:

White Liberals	48%	52%
Conservatives	35%	65%
Bay Area Suburbs	41%	59%
South Cal. Whites	39%	61%
Bay Area White Workers	39%	61%
LA County White Workers	35%	69%

Sources: California Secretary of State Archives. The ethnic vote breakdowns came from the Los Angeles Times exit poll.

Note: Prop 216 would have created a more extensive "Patients' Bill of Rights."

Year: June, 1998   Yes
Election: Prop. 226/Union Dues   No
Turnout: 42%

Geographic Breakdown:

Region	% of State	Yes (%)	No (%)	Total Votes	Margin
Bay Area	24%	571,035 (41%)	818,279 (59%)	1,389,314	N 247,244
Nor/Central Coast	6%	162,157 (47%)	185,881 (53%)	348,038	N 23,724
Cent. Valley Cities	13%	381,966 (50%)	383,817 (50%)	765,783	N 1,851
LA County	23%	526,584 (40%)	801,066 (60%)	1,327,650	N 274,482
South. Cal.	27%	831,961 (54%)	707,380 (46%)	1,539,341	Y 124,581
Rural Cal.	8%	237,591 (54%)	199,977 (46%)	437,568	Y 37,614
State	100%	2,711,294 (47%)	3,096,400 (53%)	5,807,694	N 385,106

Ethnic Breakdown /Social Group Voting

Group	Yes %	No %	% of State Voters
Asians	48%	52%	3%
Blacks	31%	69%	14%
Hispanics	25%	75%	12%
Whites	55%	45%	69%

White Sub-Groups:

White Liberals	41%	59%
Conservatives	59%	41%
Bay Area Suburbs	44%	56%

South Cal. Whites	63%	37%
Bay Area White Workers	38%	62%
LA County White Workers	46%	54%

Sources: California Secretary of State Archives. The ethnic vote breakdowns came from the Los Angeles Times exit poll.

Note: Prop. 226 would have restricted the ability of labor unions to use members' dues for campaign purposes.

Year: June, 1998   Yes
Election: Bi-Lingual Ed (#227)   No

Geographic Breakdown:

Region	% of State	Yes (%)	No (%)	Total Votes	Margin
Bay Area	24%	742,200 (52%)	677,650 (48%)	1,419,850	Y 64,550
Nor/Central Coast	6%	223,349 (63%)	131,712 (37%)	355,061	Y 91,637
Cent. Valley Cities	13%	483,003 (62%)	290,444 (38%)	773,447	Y 192,559
LA County	23%	766,462 (56%)	593,991 (44%)	1,360,453	Y 172,471
South. Cal.	26%	1,073,634 (69%)	486,484 (31%)	1,560,118	Y 587,150
Rural Cal.	8%	310,664 (70%)	132,777 (30%)	443,441	Y 177,887
State	100%	3,599,312 (61%)	2,313,058 (39%)	5,912,370	Y 1,286,254

Ethnic Breakdown /Social Group Voting

Group	Yes %	No %	% of State Voters
Asians	57%	43%	3%
Blacks	48%	52%	14%
Hispanics	37%	63%	12%
Whites	67%	33%	69%

White Sub-Groups:

White Liberals	55%	45%
Conservatives	70%	30%
Bay Area Suburbs	58%	42%
South Cal. Whites	72%	28%
Bay Area White Workers	54%	46%
LA County White Workers	63%	37%

Sources: California Secretary of State Archives .The ethnic vote breakdowns came from the Los Angeles Times exit poll.

Note: Prop 227 ended the use of "bi-lingual" education in public schools.

Year: November, 1998   Yes
Election: Cigarette Tax (#10)   No
Turnout: 58%

Geographic Breakdown:

Region	% of State	Yes (%)	No (%)	Total Votes	Margin
Bay Area	23%	1,013,047 (55%)	835,133 (45%)	1,848,180	Y 77,914
Nor/Central Coast	6%	231,344 (51%)	221,708 (49%)	453,052	Y 9,636
Cent. Valley Cities	13%	459,243 (44%)	578,376 (56%)	1,037,619	N 19,133
LA County	23%	1,034,555 (55%)	836,830 (45%)	1,871,385	Y 197,725
South. Cal.	28%	1,090,123 (48%)	1,161,259 (52%)	2,251,382	N 71,136
Rural Cal.	7%	185,814 (39%)	330,702 (61%)	546,516	N 144,888
State	100%	4,044,126 (51%)	3,964,008 (49%)	8,008,134	Y 80,118

Ethnic Breakdown /Social Group Voting

Group	Yes %	No %	% of State Voters
Asians	54%	46%	5%
Blacks	60%	40%	7%
Hispanics	57%	43%	14%
Whites	48%	52%	72%

White Sub-Groups:

White Liberals	65%	35%
Conservatives	48%	52%
Bay Area Suburbs	51%	49%
South Cal. Whites	46%	54%
Bay Area White Workers	50%	50%
LA County White Workers	49%	51%

Sources: California Secretary of State Archives. Asians and whites came from the Field Poll. Black voters were sampled in South-Central Los Angeles County and Hispanics in East Los Angeles.

Note: Prop 10 increased the tax on tobacco products and uses the revenue to pay for early childhood education programs.

Year: March, 2000   Yes
Election: Ban Same-sex Marriage (#22)   No
Turnout: 54%

Geographic Breakdown:

Region	% of State	Yes (%)	No (%)	Total Votes	Margin
Bay Area	22%	815,423 (48%)	871,064 (52%)	1,686,547	N 55,581
Nor/Central Coast	6%	231,836 (54%)	195,374 (46%)	427,210	Y 36,462
Cent. Valley Cities	13%	702,771 (71%)	289,383 (29%)	992,154	Y 413,388
LA County	23%	1,005,686 (59%)	712,767 (41%)	1,718,453	Y 292,919
South. Cal.	29%	1,483,353 (68%)	693,069 (32%)	2,176,422	Y 790,284
Rural Cal.	7%	379,544 (72%)	147,663 (28%)	527,257	Y 231,881
State	100%	4,618,673 (61%)	2,909,370 (39%)	7,528,043	Y 1,709,303

Ethnic Breakdown /Social Group Voting

Group	Yes %	No %	% of State Voters
Asians	59%	41%	4%
Blacks	62%	38%	7%
Hispanics	65%	35%	7%
Whites	58%	42%	81%

White Sub-Groups:

White Liberals	36%	64%
Conservatives	69%	31%
Bay Area Suburbs	54%	46%
South Cal. Whites	70%	30%
Bay Area White Workers	59%	41%
LA County White Workers	72%	28%

Sources: California Secretary of State Archives. The ethnic vote breakdowns came from the Los Angeles Times exit poll.

Note: Prop 22 limits the recognition of marriage to opposite-sex couples.

Year: November, 2000   Yes
Election: Campaign Finance Reform (#34) No
Turnout: 71%

Geographic Breakdown:

Region	% of State	Yes (%)	No (%)	Total Votes	Margin
Bay Area	23%	1,331,645 (60%)	895,109 (40%)	2,226,754	Y 436,536

Nor/Central Coast	5%	331,023 (61%)	212,445 (39%)	543,468	Y 118,578
Cent. Valley Cities	13%	741,886 (59%)	512,203 (41%)	1,254,089	Y 229,683
LA County	24%	1,473,674 (62%)	916,753 (38%)	2,390,427	Y 556,921
South. Cal.	29%	1,679,229 (59%)	1,143,025 (41%)	2,822,254	Y 536,204
Rural Cal.	7%	376,646 (58%)	274,270 (42%)	650,916	Y 102,376
State	100%	5,934,103 (60%)	3,953,805 (40%)	9,887,908	Y 1,980,298

Ethnic Breakdown /Social Group Voting

Group	Yes %	No %	% of State Voters
Asians	66%	34%	6%
Blacks	70%	30%	6%
Hispanics	67%	33%	14%
Whites	59%	41%	71%

White Sub-Groups:

White Liberals	56%	44%
Conservatives	58%	42%
Bay Area Suburbs	60%	40%
North Coast	61%	39%
South Cal. Whites	58%	42%
Bay Area White Workers	65%	35%
LA County White Workers	59%	41%

Sources: California Secretary of State Archives. Asians and whites came from the Field Poll. Black voters were sampled in South-Central Los Angeles County and Hispanics in East Los Angeles.

Year: November, 2000   Yes
Election: Drug Treatment (#36)   No

Geographic Breakdown:

Region	% of State	Yes (%)	No (%)	Total Votes	Margin
Bay Area	22%	1,541,396 (68%)	727,556 (32%)	2,268,952	Y 813,840
Nor/Central Coast	5%	363,566 (65%)	196,888 (35%)	560,454	Y 166,678
Cent. Valley Cities	13%	657,366 (51%)	634,455 (49%)	1,291,821	Y 22,911
LA County	24%	1,627,382 (65%)	862,159 (35%)	2,489,541	Y 765,223
South. Cal.	29%	1,698,831 (58%)	1,225,823 (42%)	2,924,654	Y 473,008

| Rural Cal. | 7% | 344,881 (49%) | 362,627 (51%) | 707,508 | N 17,746 |
| State | 100% | 6,233,422 (61%) | 4,009,508 (39%) | 10,242,930 | Y 2,223,914 |

Ethnic Breakdown /Social Group Voting

Group	Yes %	No %	% of State Voters
Asians	66%	34%	6%
Blacks	79%	21%	6%
Hispanics	67%	33%	14%
Whites	59%	41%	71%

White Sub-Groups:

White Liberals	72%	28%
Conservatives	57%	43%
Bay Area Suburbs	63%	37%
South Cal. Whites	57%	43%
Bay Area White Workers	63%	37%
LA County White Workers	67%	33%

Sources: California Secretary of State Archives. Asians and whites came from the Field Poll. Black voters were sampled in South-Central Los Angeles County and Hispanics in East Los Angeles.

Note: Prop 36 authorizes courts to divert non-violent drug offenders to addiction-treatment programs.

Year: November, 2000   Yes
Election: Classify Fees as Taxes (#37)   No

Geographic Breakdown:

Region	% of State	Yes (%)	No (%)	Total Votes	Margin
Bay Area	22%	873,005 (41%)	1,263,505 (59%)	2,136,510	N 390,500
Nor/Central Coast	5%	241,778 (46%)	281,826 (54%)	523,604	N 40,048
Cent. Valley Cities	13%	625,265 (51%)	594,368 (49%)	1,219,633	Y 30,897
LA County	24%	1,061,234 (45%)	1,277,628 (55%)	2,338,862	N 216,394
South. Cal.	28%	1,461,592 (54%)	1,266,598 (46%)	2,728,190	Y 194,994
Rural Cal.	7%	330,532 (52%)	304,475 (48%)	635,057	Y 26,057
State	100%	4,593,406 (48%)	1,066,963 (52%)	9,581,956	N 395,044

Ethnic Breakdown /Social Group Voting

Group	Yes %	No %	% of State Voters

Asians	46%	54%	6%
Blacks	36%	64%	6%
Hispanics	46%	54%	14%
Whites	50%	50%	72%

White Sub-Groups:

White Liberals	37%	63%
Conservatives	55%	45%
Bay Area Suburbs	43%	57%
South Cal. Whites	55%	45%
Bay Area White Workers	48%	52%
LA County White Workers	50%	50%

Sources: California Secretary of State Archives. Asians and whites came from the Field Poll. Black voters were sampled in South-Central Los Angeles County and Hispanics in East Los Angeles.

Note: Prop 37 allows the rules for fees to be imposed by a simple majority vote instead of the 2/3 super-majority required for new taxes to stand. A "Yes" vote would have repealed this rule.

Year: November, 2000   Yes
Election: School Vouchers (#38) No

Geographic Breakdown:

Region	% of State	Yes (%)	No (%)	Total Votes	Margin
Bay Area	21%	587,623 (27%)	1,615,021 (73%)	2,202,644	N 1,027,398
Nor/Central Coast	5%	165,296 (29%)	406,632 (71%)	571,928	N 241,336
Cent. Valley Cities	12%	407,553 (31%)	903,224 (69%)	1,310,777	N 495,671
LA County	25%	697,656 (27%)	1,889,300 (73%)	2,586,956	N 1,191,644
South. Cal.	28%	1,011,329 (34%)	1,970,091 (66%)	2,988,420	N 965,762
Rural Cal.	8%	231,736 (27%)	630,769 (73%)	862,505	N 399,033
State	100%	3,101,193 (29%)	7,422,037 (71%)	10,523,230	N 4,320,844

Ethnic Breakdown /Social Group Voting

Group	Yes %	No %	% of State Voters
Asians	34%	66%	5%
Blacks	32%	68%	5%
Hispanics	23%	77%	13%
Whites	30%	70%	73%

White Sub-Groups:

White Liberals	24%	76%
Conservatives	35%	65%
Bay Area Suburbs	26%	74%
South Cal. Whites	35%	65%
Bay Area White Workers	26%	74%
LA County White Workers	31%	69%

Sources: California Secretary of State Archives. The ethnic vote breakdowns came from the Los Angeles Times exit poll.

Note: Prop 38 would have authorized the use of "vouchers" where students could attend the public school of their choice.

Year: November, 2000   Yes
Election: 55% on School Bonds (#39)   No

Geographic Breakdown:

Region	% of State	Yes (%)	No (%)	Total Votes	Margin
Bay Area	23%	1,347,009 (59%)	951,758 (41%)	2,298,767	Y 395,251
Nor/Central Coast	5%	309,057 (55%)	246,569 (45%)	555,626	Y 62,488
Cent. Valley Cities	13%	654,161 (51%)	623,528 (49%)	1,277,689	Y 30,633
LA County	25%	1,420,519 (57%)	1,079,185 (43%)	2,499,704	Y 341,334
South. Cal.	28%	1,403,882 (49%)	1,486,149 (51%)	2,890,031	N 82,267
Rural Cal.	7%	296,524 (44%)	373,122 (56%)	665,646	N 76,598
State	100%	5,431,152 (53%)	4,756,311 (47%)	10,187,403	Y 674,841

Ethnic Breakdown /Social Group Voting

Group	Yes %	No %	% of State Voters
Asians	57%	43%	5%
Blacks	60%	40%	5%
Hispanics	60%	40%	13%
Whites	50%	50%	73%

White Sub-Groups:

White Liberals	61%	39%
Conservatives	45%	55%
Bay Area Suburbs	54%	46%

South Cal. Whites	45%	55%
Bay Area White Workers	56%	44%
LA County White Workers	50%	50%

Sources: California Secretary of State Archives The ethnic vote breakdowns came from the Los Angeles Times exit poll.

Note: Prop 39 allows local districts to raise taxes with a vote of just 55% instead of a 2/3 vote.

Year: March, 2002   Yes
Election: Term Limits Reform (#45)   No
Turnout: 35%

Geographic Breakdown:

Region	% of State	Yes (%)	No (%)	Total Votes	Margin
Bay Area	23%	506,043 (45%)	614,892 (55%)	1,120,935	N 108,849
Nor/Central Coast	6%	128,111 (43%)	168,122 (57%)	296,233	N 40,011
Cent. Valley Cities	14%	259,707 (38%)	425,986 (62%)	685,693	N 166,279
LA County	20%	490,126 (51%)	463,438 (49%)	953,564	Y 26,688
South. Cal.	28%	535,834 (39%)	836,521 (61%)	1,372,355	N 300,687
Rural Cal.	8%	129,527 (32%)	281,194 (68%)	410,721	N 151,667
State	100%	2,049,348 (42%)	2,790,153 (58%)	4,839,501	N 740,805

Ethnic Breakdown /Social Group Voting

Group	Yes %	No %	% of State Voters
Asians	46%	54%	4%
Blacks	59%	41%	4%
Hispanics	57%	43%	10%
Whites	41%	59%	76%

White Sub-Groups:

White Liberals	54%	46%
Conservatives	34%	66%
Bay Area Suburbs	42%	58%
South Cal. Whites	35%	65%
Bay Area White Workers	41%	59%
LA County White Workers	45%	55%

Sources: California Secretary of State Archives. The ethnic vote breakdowns came from the Los Angeles Times exit poll.

Note: Prop 45 would have revised the term limits rule to extend legislators' tenure for an additional term.

Year: November, 2002   Yes
Election: After-school Programs (#49)   No
Turnout: 51%

Geographic Breakdown:

Region	% of State	Yes (%)	No (%)	Total Votes	Margin
Bay Area	23%	878,277 (54%)	748,142 (46%)	1,626,419	Y 130,135
Nor/Central Coast	6%	218,252 (52%)	197,986 (48%)	416,238	Y 20,266
Cent. Valley Cities	13%	531,702 (56%)	424,932 (44%)	956,634	Y 106,770
LA County	22%	983,163 (62%)	613,826 (38%)	1,596,989	Y 369,337
South. Cal.	28%	1,155,762 (58%)	835,803 (42%)	1,991,565	Y 319,959
Rural Cal.	7%	257,748 (49%)	263,433 (51%)	521,181	N 5,685
State	100%	4,024,904 (57%)	3,084,122 (43%)	7,109,026	Y 940,782

Ethnic Breakdown /Social Group Voting

Group	Yes %	No %	% of State Voters
Asians	62%	38%	6%
Blacks	67%	33%	4%
Hispanics	78%	22%	10%
Whites	53%	47%	76%

White Sub-Groups:

White Liberals	54%	46%
Conservatives	54%	46%
Bay Area Suburbs	55%	45%
South Cal. Whites	55%	45%
Bay Area White Workers	58%	42%
LA County White Workers	71%	29%

Sources: California Secretary of State Archives. The ethnic vote breakdowns came from the Los Angeles Times exit poll.

Note: Prop 49 authorizes the creation of state-sponsored after-school recreational and educational programs.

Year: November, 2002   Yes
Election: Election-day registration (#52)   No

Geographic Breakdown:

Region	% of State	Yes (%)	No (%)	Total Votes	Margin
Bay Area	23%	737,024 (45%)	897,441 (55%)	1,634,465	N 160,417
Nor/Central Coast	6%	189,239 (46%)	223,601 (54%)	412,840	N 34,362
Cent. Valley Cities	13%	344,258 (37%)	596,145 (63%)	940,403	N 251,887
LA County	23%	763,794 (47%)	846,544 (53%)	1,610,338	N 82,750
South. Cal.	28%	689,439 (35%)	1,277,948 (65%)	1,967,387	N 588,509
Rural Cal.	7%	164,453 (34%)	324,356 (66%)	488,809	N 159,903
State	100%	2,888,207 (41%)	4,166,035 (59%)	7,054,242	N 1,277,828

Ethnic Breakdown /Social Group Voting

Group	Yes %	No %	% of State Voters
Asians	51%	49%	6%
Blacks	53%	47%	4%
Hispanics	65%	35%	10%
Whites	35%	65%	76%

White Sub-Groups:

White Liberals	51%	49%
Conservatives	31%	69%
Bay Area Suburbs	42%	58%
South Cal. Whites	33%	67%
Bay Area White Workers	45%	55%
LA County White Workers	40%	60%

Sources: California Secretary of State Archives. The ethnic vote breakdowns came from the Los Angeles Times exit poll.

Note: Prop 52 would have allowed citizens to register to vote at any time, even on Election Day

Year: October, 2003   Yes
Election: End Collection of All Racial Data (#54)   No

Geographic Breakdown:

Region	% of State	Yes (%)	No (%)	Total Votes	Margin
Bay Area	23%	574,160 (29%)	1,391,530 (71%)	1,965,690	N 817,370
Nor/Central Coast	5%	177,058 (38%)	285,865 (62%)	462,923	N 108,807
Cent. Valley Cities	13%	476,456 (42%)	648,417 (58%)	1,124,873	N 171,961
LA County	23%	583,598 (29%)	1,404,968 (71%)	1,988,566	N 821,370
South. Cal.	29%	1,050,674 (41%)	1,493,377 (59%)	2,544,051	N 442,703
Rural Cal.	7%	282,199 (47%)	317,157 (53%)	599,356	N 34,958
State	100%	3,144,145 (36%)	5,541,314 (64%)	8,685,459	N 2,397,169

Ethnic Breakdown /Social Group Voting

Group	Yes%	No%	% of State Voters
Asians	28%	72%	6%
Blacks	13%	87%	5%
Hispanics	25%	75%	11%
Whites	38%	62%	73%

White Sub-Groups:

White Liberals	29%	71%
Conservatives	46%	54%
Bay Area Suburbs	34%	66%
South Cal. Whites	45%	55%
Bay Area White Workers	30%	79%
LA County White Workers	35%	65%

Sources: California Secretary of State Archives. The ethnic vote breakdowns came from the Los Angeles Times exit poll.

Note: Prop 54 would have banned the collection of all ethnic/racial data by the state.

Year: March, 2004   Yes
Election: Remove 2/3 budget rule (#56)   No
Turnout: 44%

Geographic Breakdown:

Region	% of State	Yes (%)	No (%)	Total Votes	Margin
Bay Area	24%	642,761 (42%)	881,351 (58%)	1,524,112	N 238,590
Nor/Central Coast	6%	161,363 (41%)	235,452 (59%)	396,815	N 74,089

Cent. Valley Cities	13%	307,906 (36%)	546,245 (64%)	854,151	N 238,339
LA County	20%	433,010 (31%)	846,384 (69%)	1,279,394	N 413,374
South. Cal.	28%	478,936 (26%)	1,335,039 (74%)	1,813,975	N 856,103
Rural Cal.	8%	161,892 (32%)	338,717 (68%)	500,609	N 176,825
State	100%	2,185,868 (34%)	4,183,188 (66%)	6,309,056	N 1,997,320

Ethnic Breakdown /Social Group Voting

Group	Yes %	No %	% of State Voters
Asians	35%	65%	5%
Blacks	41%	59%	5%
Hispanics	42%	58%	11%
Whites	33%	67%	76%

White Sub-Groups:

White Liberals	45%	55%
Conservatives	26%	74%
Bay Area Suburbs	38%	62%
South Cal. Whites	25%	75%
Bay Area White Workers	35%	65%
LA County White Workers	24%	76%

Sources: California Secretary of State Archives. The ethnic vote breakdowns came from the Los Angeles Times exit poll.

Note: Prop 56 would have removed the 2/3 required for the passage of the annual state budget.

Year: November, 2004   Yes
Election: Mental health programs/tax (#63) No
Turnout: 76%

Geographic Breakdown:

Region	% of State	Yes (%)	No (%)	Total Votes	Margin
Bay Area	22%	1,583,271 (62%)	979,783 (38%)	2,563,054	Y 603,488
Nor/Central Coast	5%	354,082 (57%)	261,774 (43%)	615,856	Y 92,308
Cent. Valley Cities	13%	700,061 (48%)	774,838 (52%)	1,444,899	Y 74,777
LA County	24%	1,624,214 (58%)	1,158,657 (42%)	2,782,871	Y 465,557
South. Cal.	29%	1,575,617 (47%)	1,772,370 (53%)	3,347,987	N 196,753

| Rural Cal. | 7% | 354,446 (46%) | 389,794 (54%) | 774,240 | N 35,348 |
| State | 100% | 6,191,691 (54%) | 5,337,216 (46%) | 11,528,907 | Y 854,475 |

Ethnic Breakdown /Social Group Voting

Group	Yes %	No %	% of State Voters
Asians	60%	40%	8%
Blacks	74%	26%	7%
Hispanics	64%	36%	14%
Whites	47%	53%	65%

White Sub-Groups:

White Liberals	61%	39%
Conservatives	42%	58%
Bay Area Suburbs	58%	42%
South Cal. Whites	47%	53%
Bay Area White Workers	61%	39%
LA County White Workers	54%	46%

Sources: California Secretary of State Archives. Asians and whites came from the Field Poll. Black voters were sampled in South-Central Los Angeles County and Hispanics in East Los Angeles.

Note: Prop 63 imposed a 1% surtax on millionaires to fund mental health programs.

Year: November, 2004   Yes
Election: Reform 3-strikes (#66)   No

Geographic Breakdown:

Region	% of State	Yes (%)	No (%)	Total Votes	Margin
Bay Area	22%	1,465,026 (56%)	1,158,988 (44%)	2,624,014	Y 306,038
Nor/Central Coast	5%	370,649 (59%)	258,376 (41%)	629,025	Y 112,273
Cent. Valley Cities	13%	624,499 (42%)	856,823 (58%)	1,481,322	N 232,324
LA County	24%	1,438,416 (50%)	1,418,231 (50%)	2,856,647	Y 20,185
South. Cal.	29%	1,370,029 (40%)	2,093,774 (60%)	3,463,803	N 723,745
Rural Cal.	7%	335,441 (43%)	451,868 (57%)	787,309	N 116,427
State	100%	5,604,060 (47%)	6,238,060 (53%)	11,842,120	N 634,000

Ethnic Breakdown /Social Group Voting

Group	Yes %	No %	% of State Voters

Asians	48%	52%	8%
Blacks	70%	30%	7%
Hispanics	55%	45%	16%
Whites	41%	59%	65%

White Sub-Groups:

White Liberals	58%	42%
Conservatives	37%	63%
Bay Area Suburbs	51%	49%
South Cal. Whites	38%	62%
Bay Area White Workers	57%	43%
LA County White Workers	41%	59%

Sources: California Secretary of State Archives. Asians and whites came from the Field Poll. Black voters were sampled in South-Central Los Angeles County and Hispanics in East Los Angeles.

Note: Prop 66 would have loosened the 3-Strikes law by mandating a life sentence only if the third strike was a violent offense.

Year: November, 2004   Yes
Election: Stem cell research (#71)   No

Geographic Breakdown:

Region	% of State	Yes (%)	No (%)	Total Votes	Margin
Bay Area	22%	1,766,248 (67%)	876,266 (33%)	2,642,514	Y 889,982
Nor/Central Coast	5%	387,511 (61%)	245,871 (39%)	633,514	Y 141,640
Cent. Valley Cities	12%	726,692 (49%)	749,748 (51%)	1,476,440	N 23,056
LA County	24%	1,848,313 (65%)	1,016,411 (35%)	2,864,724	Y 831,902
South. Cal.	29%	1,906,401 (55%)	1,569,140 (45%)	3,475,541	Y 337,261
Rural Cal.	7%	382,894 (48%)	409,654 (52%)	792,548	N 26,760
State	100%	7,018,059 (59%)	4,867,090 (41%)	11,885,149	Y 2,150,969

Ethnic Breakdown /Social Group Voting

Group	Yes %	No %	% of State Voters
Asians	72%	28%	9%
Blacks	68%	32%	7%
Hispanics	61%	39%	14%
Whites	56%	44%	65%

White Sub-Groups:

White Liberals	73%	27%
Conservatives	51%	49%
Bay Area Suburbs	66%	34%
South Cal. Whites	49%	51%
Bay Area White Workers	66%	34%
LA County White Workers	56%	44%

Sources: California Secretary of State Archives. The ethnic vote breakdowns came from the Los Angeles Times exit poll.

Note: Prop 71 passed state bonds to pay for stem cell medical research.

Year: November, 2004   Yes
Election: Health care mandate (#72)   No

Geographic Breakdown:

Region	% of State	Yes (%)	No (%)	Total Votes	Margin
Bay Area	22%	1,465,955 (57%)	1,102,821 (43%)	2,568,776	Y 363,134
Nor/Central Coast	5%	304,775 (49%)	311,491 (51%)	616,266	N 6,716
Cent. Valley Cities	13%	630,690 (43%)	822,926 (57%)	1,453,616	N 192.236
LA County	24%	1,585,681 (57%)	1,206,275 (43%)	2,791,956	Y 379,406
South. Cal.	29%	1,434,444 (42%)	1,955,728 (58%)	3,390,172	N 521,284
Rural Cal.	7%	287,955 (37%)	490,695 (63%)	778,650	N 202,740
State	100%	5,709,500 (49%)	5,889,936 (51%)	11,599,436	N 180,436

Ethnic Breakdown /Social Group Voting

Group	Yes %	No %	% of State Voters
Asians	59%	41%	9%
Blacks	75%	25%	7%
Hispanics	64%	36%	14%
Whites	42%	58%	65%

White Sub-Groups:

White Liberals	56%	44%
Conservatives	38%	62%
Bay Area Suburbs	53%	47%

South Cal. Whites	36%	64%
Bay Area White Workers	60%	40%
LA County White Workers	50%	50%

Sources: California Secretary of State Archives. The ethnic vote breakdowns came from the Los Angeles Times exit poll.

Note: Prop 72 repeals a state program that required businesses with more than 20 employees to provide health insurance. A Yes vote was to keep the program.

Year: October, 2005   Yes
Election: Teacher Tenure (#74)   No
Turnout: 50%

Geographic Breakdown:

Region	% of State	Yes (%)	No (%)	Total Votes	Margin
Bay Area	24%	628,945 (34%)	1,225,337 (66%)	1,854,502	N 596,612
Nor/Central Coast	6%	177,082 (41%)	256,829 (59%)	433,911	N 79,747
Cent. Valley Cities	13%	486,784 (48%)	520,040 (52%)	1,006,824	N 33,256
LA County	22%	672,269 (38%)	1,076,401 (62%)	1,748,670	N 404,132
South. Cal.	28%	1,237,883 (55%)	996,948 (45%)	2,234,831	Y 240,935
Rural Cal.	7%	313,108 (55%)	253,470 (45%)	566,358	Y 59,638
State	100%	3,516,071 (45%)	4,329,025 (55%)	7,845,096	N 812,954

Ethnic Breakdown /Social Group Voting

Group	Yes %	No %	% of State Voters
Asians	45%	55%	6%
Blacks	19%	81%	7%
Hispanics	25%	75%	15%
Whites	50%	50%	70%

White Sub-Groups:

White Liberals	36%	64%
Conservatives	62%	38%
Bay Area Suburbs	38%	62%
South Cal. Whites	57%	43%
Bay Area White Workers	32%	68%
LA County White Workers	46%	54%

Sources: California Secretary of State Archives. Asians and whites came from the Field Poll. Black voters were sampled in South-Central Los Angeles County and Hispanics in East Los Angeles.

Note: Prop 74 would have allowed school districts to raise the time requirement for teachers to earn tenure from 2 to 5 years.

Year: October, 2005   Yes
Election: Union dues (#75)   No

Geographic Breakdown:

Region	% of State	Yes (%)	No (%)	Total Votes	Margin
Bay Area	24%	662,978 (36%)	1,187,651 (64%)	1,850,629	N 524,673
Nor/Central Coast	6%	188,757 (44%)	244,396 (56%)	433,153	N 55,639
Cent. Valley Cities	13%	520,828 (52%)	485,951 (48%)	1,006,779	Y 34,877
LA County	23%	686,866 (38%)	1,078,194 (62%)	1,765,060	N 391,328
South. Cal.	29%	1,279,754 (57%)	953,396 (43%)	2,233,150	Y 326,358
Rural Cal.	7%	304,823 (56%)	240,824 (44%)	545,647	Y 63,999
State	100%	3,644,006 (47%)	4,190,412 (53%)	7,834,418	N 546,406

Ethnic Breakdown /Social Group Voting

Group	Yes %	No %	% of State Voters
Asians	40%	60%	6%
Blacks	19%	81%	7%
Hispanics	24%	76%	15%
Whites	54%	46%	70%

White Sub-Groups:

White Liberals	40%	60%
Conservatives	64%	36%
Bay Area Suburbs	40%	60%
South Cal. Whites	60%	40%
Bay Area White Workers	35%	65%
LA County White Workers	46%	54%

Sources: California Secretary of State Archives. Asians and whites came from the Field Poll. Black voters were sampled in South-Central Los Angeles County and Hispanics in East Los Angeles.

Note: Prop 75 would have restricted the ability of public employee unions to engage in political activities.

Year: November, 2006   Yes
Election: Highway bonds (#1B)   No
Turnout: 56%

Geographic Breakdown:

Region	% of State	Yes (%)	No (%)	Total Votes	Margin
Bay Area	23%	1,254,411 (64%)	690,490 (36%)	1,944,901	Y 563,921
Nor/Central Coast	6%	366,201 (58%)	196,267 (42%)	462,468	Y 69,934
Cent. Valley Cities	13%	652,614 (60%)	428,968 (40%)	1,081,582	Y 223,646
LA County	22%	1,219,112 (65%)	643,544 (35%)	1,862,656	Y 575,568
South. Cal.	28%	1,403,019 (59%)	963,250 (41%)	2,366,269	Y 439,769
Rural Cal.	7%	316,785 (52%)	296,138 (48%)	612,923	Y 20,647
State	100%	5,112,142 (61%)	3,218,657 (39%)	8,330,799	Y 1,893,485

Ethnic Breakdown /Social Group Voting

Group	Yes %	No %	% of State Voters
Asians	76%	24%	3%
Blacks	74%	26%	6%
Hispanics	71%	29%	12%
Whites	58%	42%	75%

White Sub-Groups:

White Liberals	68%	32%
Conservatives	55%	45%
Bay Area Suburbs	64%	36%
South Cal. Whites	55%	45%
Bay Area White Workers	66%	34%
LA County White Workers	62%	38%

Sources: California Secretary of State Archives. The ethnic vote breakdowns came from the Los Angeles Times exit poll.

Note: Prop 1B authorized the sale of bonds to pay for roads.

Year: November, 2006   Yes
Election: School Bonds (#1D)   No

Geographic Breakdown:

Region	% of State	Yes (%)	No (%)	Total Votes	Margin
Bay Area	23%	1,248,998 (64%)	698,688 (36%)	1,947,686	Y 550,310
Nor/Central Coast	6%	270,665 (59%)	192,748 (41%)	463,413	Y 77,917
Cent. Valley Cities	13%	606,325 (56%)	472,951 (44%)	1,079,276	Y 133,374
LA County	22%	1,142,754 (61%)	723,946 (39%)	1,866,700	Y 418,808
South. Cal.	28%	1,244,482 (53%)	1,121,394 (47%)	2,365,876	Y 123,088
Rural Cal.	7%	301,626 (49%)	311,328 (51%)	612,954	N 9,702
State	100%	4,814,850 (58%)	3,521,055 (42%)	8,335,905	Y 1,293,795

Ethnic Breakdown /Social Group Voting

Group	Yes %	No %	% of State Voters
Asians	70%	30%	3%
Blacks	78%	22%	6%
Hispanics	73%	27%	12%
Whites	54%	46%	75%

White Sub-Groups:

White Liberals	66%	34%
Conservatives	49%	51%
Bay Area Suburbs	62%	38%
South Cal. Whites	48%	52%
Bay Area White Workers	62%	38%
LA County White Workers	56%	44%

Sources: California Secretary of State Archives. Ethnic vote breakdowns from the Los Angeles Times exit poll.

Note: Prop 1D authorized the sale of bonds to pay for school facilities.

Year: February, 2008   Yes
Election: Reform Term Limits (#93)   No
Turnout: 58%

Geographic Breakdown:

Region	% of State	Yes (%)	No (%)	Total Votes	Margin
Bay Area	23%	974,478 (49%)	1,016,238 (51%)	1,990,716	N 41,760

Nor/Central Coast	5%	216,913 (49%)	229,032 (51%)	445,945	N 12,119
Cent. Valley Cities	13%	462,360 (43%)	605,471 (57%)	1,067,831	N 143,111
LA County	23%	969,358 (49%)	1,022,541 (51%)	1,991,899	N 53,183
South. Cal.	29%	1,094,839 (45%)	1,356,197 (55%)	2,451,036	N 261,358
Rural Cal.	7%	243,518 (41%)	345,347 (59%)	588,865	N 101,829
State	100%	3,961,466 (46%)	4,574,826 (54%)	8,536,292	N 613,360

Ethnic Breakdown /Social Group Voting

Group	Yes %	No %	% of State Voters
Asians	49%	51%	9%
Blacks	56%	44%	7%
Hispanics	54%	46%	20%
Whites	37%	63%	64%

White Sub-Groups:

White Liberals	51%	49%
Conservatives	42%	58%
Bay Area Suburbs	47%	53%
South Cal. Whites	44%	56%
Bay Area White Workers	50%	50%
LA County White Workers	44%	56%

Sources: California Secretary of State Archives. Asians and whites came from the Field Poll. Black voters were sampled in South-Central Los Angeles County and Hispanics in East Los Angeles.

Note: Prop 93 would have revised the term limits law to allow members to serve up to 12 years in a single house of the Legislature.

Year: June, 2008   Yes
Election: Restrict Eminent Domain (#99)   No
Turnout: 28%

Geographic Breakdown:

Region	% of State	Yes (%)	No (%)	Total Votes	Margin
Bay Area	26%	743,098 (67%)	370,086 (33%)	1,113,184	Y 373,012
Nor/Central Coast	7%	197,709 (67%)	97,396 (33%)	295,305	Y 100,313

Cent. Valley Cities	13%	334,931 (58%)	241,352 (42%)	576,283	Y 93,579
LA County	17%	475,379 (63%)	275,088 (37%)	750,467	Y 200,291
South. Cal.	28%	699,758 (58%)	501,192 (42%)	1,200,950	Y 198,566
Rural Cal.	9%	227,231 (59%)	159,395 (41%)	386,426	Y 67,836
State	100%	2,678,106 (62%)	1,644,509 (38%)	4,322,615	Y 1,033,597

Ethnic Breakdown /Social Group Voting

Group	Yes %	No %	% of State Voters
Asians	65%	35%	5%
Blacks	66%	34%	7%
Hispanics	62%	38%	12%
Whites	61%	39%	73%

White Sub-Groups:

White Liberals	68%	32%
Conservatives	55%	45%
Bay Area Suburbs	65%	35%
South Cal. Whites	57%	43%
Bay Area White Workers	64%	36%
LA County White Workers	56%	44%

Sources: All county, city and Assembly District figures taken from the California Secretary of State Archives.

Note: Prop 99 prohibited the use of "eminent domain" to take homes that have been owned for at least one year without the owner's permission.

Year: November, 2008   Yes
Election: Abortion – parents' consent (#4)   No
Turnout: 79%

Geographic Breakdown:

Region	% of State	Yes (%)	No (%)	Total Votes	Margin
Bay Area	22%	1,072,500 (37%)	1,803,212 (63%)	2,875,712	N 730,712
Nor/Central Coast	5%	256,589 (39%)	395,194 (61%)	651,873	N 138,605
Cent. Valley Cities	13%	908,759 (55%)	735,067 (45%)	1,643,826	Y 173,692
LA County	24%	1,437,830 (46%)	1,673,251 (54%)	3,111,081	N 235,421

South. Cal.	30%	2,104,761 (55%)	1,715,281 (45%)	3,829,042	Y 389,480
Rural Cal.	7%	440,034 (55%)	356,473 (45%)	796,507	Y 83,561
State	100%	6,220,473 (48%)	6,728,478 (52%)	12,948,951	N 508,005

Ethnic Breakdown /Social Group Voting

Group	Yes %	No %	% of State Voters
Asians	57%	43%	6%
Blacks	51%	49%	9%
Hispanics	53%	47%	19%
Whites	45%	55%	63%

White Sub-Groups:

White Liberals	25%	75%
Conservatives	53%	47%
Bay Area Suburbs	40%	60%
South Cal. Whites	55%	45%
Bay Area White Workers	48%	52%
LA County White Workers	56%	44%

Sources: California Secretary of State Archives. The ethnic vote breakdowns came from the CNN exit poll.

Note: Prop 4 would have prohibited an unemancipated minor from getting an abortion until at least 48 hours after her parents had been notified in writing.

Year: November, 2008   Yes
Election: Ban Same-Sex Marriage (#8)   No

Geographic Breakdown:

Region	% of State	Yes (%)	No (%)	Total Votes	Margin
Bay Area	22%	1,156,200 (39%)	1,815,642 (61%)	2,971,842	N 659,442
Nor/Central Coast	5%	291,438 (43%)	379,649 (57%)	671,087	N 88,211
Cent. Valley Cities	13%	1,077,269 (64%)	614,821 (36%)	1,692,090	Y 462,448
LA County	24%	1,624,672 (50%)	1,622,287 (50%)	3,246,959	Y 2,385
South. Cal.	29%	2,315,276 (59%)	1,638,024 (41%)	3,953,300	Y 677,252
Rural Cal.	6%	536,229 (62%)	331,059 (38%)	867,288	Y 205,170
State	100%	7,001,084 (52%)	6,401,482 (48%)	13,402,566	Y 599,602

Ethnic Breakdown /Social Group Voting

Group	Yes %	No %	% of State Voters
Asians	49%	51%	6%
Blacks	70%	30%	8%
Hispanics	53%	47%	18%
Whites	49%	51%	63%

White Sub-Groups:

White Liberals	25%	75%
Conservatives	59%	41%
Bay Area Suburbs	42%	58%
South Cal. Whites	59%	41%
Bay Area White Workers	51%	49%
LA County White Workers	62%	38%

Sources: California Secretary of State Archives. The ethnic vote breakdowns came from the CNN exit poll.

Note: Prop 22 from 2000 limited the recognition of marriage to opposite-sex couples. After the California Supreme Court struck down that law, voters amended the State Constitution to ban same-sex marriage.

Year: November, 2008   Yes
Election: Redistricting Reform (#11)   No

Geographic Breakdown:

Region	% of State	Yes (%)	No (%)	Total Votes	Margin
Bay Area	22%	1,295,748 (49%)	1,339,291 (51%)	2,635,039	N 43,543
Nor/Central Coast	5%	296,213 (49%)	308,483 (51%)	604,696	N 12,270
Cent. Valley Cities	13%	800,280 (52%)	737,390 (48%)	1,537,670	Y 62,890
LA County	24%	1,378,561 (48%)	1,513,159 (52%)	2,891,720	N 137,598
South. Cal.	29%	1,897,397 (54%)	1,634,433 (46%)	3,531,830	Y 262,964
Rural Cal.	7%	426,834 (54%)	364,899 (46%)	791,733	Y 61,935
State	100%	6,095,033 (51%)	5,899,655 (49%)	11,992,688	Y 197,378

Ethnic Breakdown /Social Group Voting

Group	Yes %	No %	% of State Voters
Asians	50%	50%	6%

303

Blacks	40%	60%	9%
Hispanics	45%	55%	18%
Whites	53%	47%	64%

White Sub-Groups:

White Liberals	50%	50%
Conservatives	57%	43%
Bay Area Suburbs	52%	48%
South Cal. Whites	55%	45%
Bay Area White Workers	46%	54%
LA County White Workers	49%	51%

Sources: California Secretary of State Archives. Asians and whites came from the Field Poll. Black voters were sampled in South-Central Los Angeles County and Hispanics in East Los Angeles.

Note: Prop 11 removed the ability of the State Legislature to draw state legislative lines and assigned this task to a "Citizens' Commission."

Year: May 2009 Special Election   Yes
Election: Prop 1A — Taxes   No
Turnout: 28%

Geographic Breakdown:

Region	% of State	Yes (%)	No (%)	Total Votes	Margin
Bay Area	25%	524,836 (44%)	665,392 (56%)	1,190,228	N 140,556
Nor/Central Coast	6%	111,855 (40%)	169,704 (60%)	281,559	N 57,849
Cent. Valley Cities	13%	232,207 (36%)	406,859 (64%)	639,066	N 174,652
LA County	18%	270,042 (32%)	576,999 (68%)	847,041	N 306,957
South. Cal.	38%	398,451 (27%)	1,057,558 (73%)	1,456,009	N 659,107
Rural Cal.	8%	130,825 (32%)	275,629 (68%)	406,454	N 144,804
State	100%	1,668,216 (35%)	3,152,141 (65%)	4,820,357	N 1,483,925

Ethnic Breakdown /Social Group Voting

Group	Yes %	No %	% of State Voters
Asians	30%	70%	8%
Blacks	41%	59%	6%
Hispanics	34%	66%	19%
Whites	31%	69%	65%

White Sub-Groups:

White Liberals	45%	55%
Conservatives	25%	75%
Bay Area Suburbs	41%	59%
South Cal. Whites	26%	74%
Bay Area White Workers	37%	63%
LA County White Workers	25%	75%

Sources: California Secretary of State Archives. The ethnic breakdowns come from a pre-election poll done by Survey-USA.

Note: Prop 1A would have authorized the two-year extension of a sales tax increase and required the creation of a "rainy day" budget fund.

Year: May 2009 Special Election   Yes
Election: Prop 1B – School Funds   No

Geographic Breakdown:

Region	% of State	Yes (%)	No (%)	Total Votes	Margin
Bay Area	25%	576,590 (49%)	611.248 (51%)	1,187,838	N 34,658
Nor/Central Coast	6%	118,372 (42%)	162,214 (58%)	280,586	N 43,842
Cent. Valley Cities	13%	244,042 (38%)	396,676 (62%)	640,718	N 152,634
LA County	18%	297,322 (35%)	548,378 (65%)	845,700	N 251,056
South. Cal.	30%	455,168 (31%)	995,619 (69%)	1,450,787	N 540,451
Rural Cal.	8%	142,748 (35%)	261,425 (65%)	404,173	N 118,677
State	100%	1,834,242 (38%)	2,975,560 (62%)	4,809,802	N 1,141,318

Ethnic Breakdown /Social Group Voting

Group	Yes %	No %	% of State Voters
Asians	38%	62%	8%
Blacks	53%	47%	6%
Hispanics	41%	59%	19%
Whites	34%	66%	65%

White Sub-Groups:

White Liberals	50%	50%
Conservatives	28%	72%
Bay Area Suburbs	45%	55%

South Cal. Whites	30%	70%
Bay Area White-Workers	41%	59%
LA County White Workers	28%	72%

Sources: California Secretary of State Archives. The ethnic breakdowns come from a pre-election poll done by Survey-USA.

Note: Prop 1B would have reserved over $9 billion in state spending for education.

Year: May 2009 Special Election   Yes
Election: Prop 1C – Lottery Loan   No

Geographic Breakdown:

Region	% of State	Yes (%)	No (%)	Total Votes	Margin
Bay Area	25%	498,221 (42%)	687,847 (58%)	1,186,068	N 189,626
Nor/Central Coast	6%	100,418 (36%)	179,482 (64%)	279,900	N 79,064
Cent. Valley Cities	13%	239,662 (38%)	396,682 (62%)	636,344	N 157,020
LA County	17%	295,448 (35%)	538,207 (65%)	833,655	N 242,759
South. Cal.	30%	442,220 (30%)	1,011,050 (70%)	1,453,270	N 568,830
Rural Cal.	8%	132,831 (33%)	271,870 (67%)	404,701	N 139,039
State	100%	1,708,800 (36%)	3,085,138 (64%)	4,793,938	N 1,376,338

Ethnic Breakdown /Social Group Voting

Group	Yes %	No %	% of State Voters
Asians	28%	72%	8%
Blacks	34%	66%	6%
Hispanics	26%	74%	19%
Whites	29%	71%	65%

White Sub-Groups:

White Liberals	40%	60%
Conservatives	26%	74%
Bay Area Suburbs	40%	60%
South Cal. Whites	30%	70%
Bay Area White Workers	35%	65%
LA County White Workers	26%	74%

Sources: All county, city and Assembly District figures taken from the California Secretary of State Archives. The ethnic breakdowns come from a pre-election poll done by Survey-USA.

Note: Prop 1C would have authorized the state borrowing against future lottery revenues.

Year: May 2009 Special Election   Yes
Election: Prop 1D – Children Services Funds   No

Geographic Breakdown:

Region	% of State	Yes (%)	No (%)	Total Votes	Margin
Bay Area	25%	463,344 (39%)	718,254 (61%)	1,181,598	N 254,910
Nor/Central Coast	6%	90,193 (32%)	188,913 (68%)	279,106	N 98,720
Cent. Valley Cities	13%	237,929 (37%)	398,809 (63%)	636,738	N 160,880
LA County	18%	281,540 (34%)	558,660 (66%)	840,200	N 277,120
South. Cal.	30%	423,892 (29%)	1,025,854 (71%)	1,449,746	N 601,962
Rural Cal.	8%	136,209 (34%)	267,190 (66%)	403,399	N 130,981
State	100%	1,633,107 (34%)	3,157,680 (66%)	4,790,787	N 1,524,573

Ethnic Breakdown /Social Group Voting

Group	Yes%	No%	% of State Voters
Asians	39%	61%	8%
Blacks	51%	49%	6%
Hispanics	38%	62%	19%
Whites	32%	68%	65%

White Sub-Groups:

White Liberals	39%	61%
Conservatives	27%	73%
Bay Area Suburbs	38%	62%
South Cal. Whites	28%	72%
Bay Area White Workers	33%	67%
LA County White Workers	26%	74%

Sources: All county, city and Assembly District figures taken from the California Secretary of State Archives. The ethnic breakdowns come from a pre-election poll done by Survey-USA.

Note: Prop 1D would have authorized the state to shift funds from tobacco taxes used for childhood programs (from Prop 10) to the General Fund.

Year: May 2009 Special Election   Yes
Election: Prop 1E – Mental Health Funds   No

Geographic Breakdown:

Region	% of State	Yes (%)	No (%)	Total Votes	Margin
Bay Area	25%	458,013 (39%)	711,545 (61%)	1,169,558	N 253,532
Nor/Central Coast	6%	90,150 (32%)	189,158 (68%)	279,308	N 99,008
Cent. Valley Cities	13%	230,041 (36%)	405,310 (64%)	635,351	N 175,269
LA County	18%	270,067 (32%)	564,262 (68%)	834,329	N 294,195
South. Cal.	30%	416,111 (29%)	1,030,140 (71%)	1,446,251	N 614,029
Rural Cal.	8%	133,525 (33%)	268,748 (67%)	402,273	N 135,223
State	100%	1,599,907 (34%)	3,169,163 (66%)	4,767,070	N 1,571,251

Ethnic Breakdown /Social Group Voting

Group	Yes %	No %	% of State Voters
Asians	37%	63%	8%
Blacks	38%	62%	6%
Hispanics	39%	59%	19%
Whites	50%	50%	65%

White Sub-Groups:

White Liberals	37%	63%
Conservatives	27%	73%
Bay Area Suburbs	38%	62%
South Cal. Whites	28%	72%
Bay Area White Workers	%	%
LA County White Workers	%	%

Sources: All county, city and Assembly District figures taken from the California Secretary of State Archives. The ethnic breakdowns come from a pre-election poll done by Survey-USA.

Note: Prop 1E would have authorized the state to shift funds from used for mental health programs (from Prop 63) to the General Fund.

Year: May 2009 Special Election   Yes
Election: Prop 1F – Legislative Salaries   No

Geographic Breakdown:

Region	% of State	Yes (%)	No (%)	Total Votes	Margin
Bay Area	25%	964,557 (82%)	218,199 (18%)	1,182,756	Y 746,358

Nor/Central Coast	6%	223,873 (80%)	57,615 (20%)	281,488	Y 166,258
Cent. Valley Cities	13%	487,298 (77%)	148,048 (23%)	635,346	Y 339,250
LA County	18%	586,556 (69%)	258,980 (31%)	845,536	Y 327,576
South. Cal.	30%	978,320 (67%)	474,541 (33%)	1,452,861	Y 504,779
Rural Cal.	8%	324,815 (80%)	80,311 (20%)	405,126	Y 244,504
State	100%	3,565,419 (74%)	1,237,694 (26%)	4,803,113	Y 2,327,725

Ethnic Breakdown /Social Group Voting

Group	Yes %	No %	% of State Voters
Asians	82%	18%	8%
Blacks	82%	18%	6%
Hispanics	74%	26%	19%
Whites	73%	27%	65%

White Sub-Groups:

White Liberals	81%	19%
Conservatives	66%	34%
Bay Area Suburbs	83%	17%
South Cal. Whites	65%	35%
Bay Area White Workers	78%	22%
LA County White Workers	75%	25%

Sources: All county, city and Assembly District figures taken from the California Secretary of State Archives. The ethnic breakdowns come from a precinct data.

Note: Prop 1F prohibits salary increases for state elected officials when there is a General Fund deficit.

BIBLIOGRAPHY

BOOKS

Barone, Michael and Richard E. Cohen, eds. *The Almanac of American Politics 2006*. Washington DC: The National Journal Group, 2005.

Bryce, James. *The American Commonwealth.*3 vols. 1888. Reprint, 2 vols., Indianapolis: Liberty Press, 1995.

Cain, Bruce E., Elizabeth R. Gerber and the University of California Berkeley Institute of Governmental Studies. *Voting at the Political Fault Line: California's Experiment in the Blanket Primary*. Berkeley and Los Angeles: University of California Press, 2002.

California Secretary of State. *A History of California Initiatives*. Sacramento, 2003. http://www.sos.ca.gov/elections/init_history.psdf.

———. *Statement of Vote2006 General Election*. http://www.sos.ca.gov/elections/sov/2006_general/measures.pdf.

Cannon, Lou. *Ronnie and Jesse: A Political Odyssey*. Garden City, New York: Doubleday, 1969.

Committee on Legislative Organization. *California Blue Book 1975*. (Sacramento, California: California Office of State Printing, 1975.

Cummings, Stephen D. *Red States, Blue States and the Coming Sharecropper Society*. New York: Algora Publishing, 2008.

Delmatier, Royce D, Clarence F. McIntosh and Earl G. Waters, eds. *The Rumble of California Politics 1848-1970*. New York: John Wiley and Sons, Ins., 1970.

Ed Source. *Potable School buildings: Scourge, Saving Grace, or Just Part of the Solution?* Palo Alto, California: Ed Source, April 1998

Green, Stephen, Editor. *California Political Almanac*. Sacramento: California Journal Press, 1989, 1991, 1993.

Gunther, John. *Inside USA*. New York: Harper and Brothers, 1947.

Hill, Gladwin. *Dancing Bear: An Inside Look at California Politics*. Cleveland: World Publishing Company, 1968.

Jacobs, John. *A Rage for Justice: The Passion and Politics of Phillip Burton*. Berkeley: University of California Press, 1995.

Kramer, Michael and Mark Levy, *The Ethnic Factor: How America's Minorities Decide Elections*. New York: Simon and Schuster, 1972.

Leigh, Wendy. *Arnold: An Unauthorized Biography*. Chicago: Congdon & Weed, 1990.

Lindert, Peter H. *Growing Public: Social Spending and Economic Growth Since the Eighteenth Century*. Cambridge: Cambridge University Press, 2004.

Lower, Richard Coke, *A Bloc of One: The Political Career of Hiram W. Johnson*, Stanford, California: Stanford University Press, 1993.

Mathews, Joe. *The People's Machine: Arnold Schwarzenegger and the Rise of Blockbuster Democracy*. New York: Public Affairs, 2006.

Matusow, Alan. *The Unraveling of America: A History of Liberalism in the 1960s*. New York: Harper and Row, 1984.

Miller Jim, *The Rolling Stone History of Rock and Roll* (New York: Random House), 1976.

McWilliams, Carey. *California: The Great Exception*. 1949 reprint, with a foreword by Lewis Lapham, Berkeley: University of California Press, 1999.

_____, *Southern California Country: An Island on the Land*. New York: Duell, Sloan, and Pearce, 1946; reprint Salt Lake City: Peregrine Smith books, 1988.

National Center for Public Policy and Higher Education. *Policy Alert: The Educational Pipeline: Big Investment, Big Returns*. San Jose, California: National Center for Public Policy and Higher Education, 2004.

National Education Association. *Rankings and Estimates, 2003-04*. Washington DC: National Education Association, 2004.

Pack, Robert, *Jerry Brown, the Philosopher Prince*. New York: Steiner and Day, 1978.

Pettigrew, Thomas and Denise Alston, *Tom Bradley's Campaign for Governor: The Dilemma of Race and Political Strategies*. Washington, DC: Joint Center for Political Studies, 1988.

Phillips, Kevin. *The Emerging Republican Majority*. New York: Arlington House, 1969.

Rarick, Ethan. *California Rising: The Life and Times of Pat Brown*. Berkeley and Los Angeles: University of California Press, 2005.

Rieff, David. *Los Angeles: Capital of the Third World*. New York: Simon and Schuster, 1991.

The Road Information Program. *Bumpy Roads Ahead: Cities with the Roughest Rides, and Strategies to Make Our roads Smoother*. Washington DC: The Road Information Program, April 2004.

Schrag, Peter, *California: America's High Stakes Experiment*. Berkeley and Los Angeles: University of California Press, 2006.

Schwarzenegger, Arnold and Douglas Hall. *Arnold: The Education of a Bodybuilder*. New York: Simon & Schuster, 1977.

Starr, Kevin. *California: A History*. New York: Random House, 2005.

Turner, Henry A and John A, Vieg. *The Government and Politics of California*. New York: McGraw-Hill. 3rd ed., 1967.

U.S. Congress. Joint Committee on Printing. *Congressional Directory 2007-2008, 110th Congress*. Washington DC: Government Printing Office, 2007.

California after Arnold

Weintraub, Daniel. *Party of One: Arnold Schwarzenegger and the Rise of the Independent Voter.* Sausalito, California: PoliPointPress, 2007.

Worthen, James. *Governor James Rolph and the Great Depression in California.* Jefferson, North Carolina: McFarland & Company, 2006.

Zubrini, Nancy. *A Travel guide to Basque America,* 2nd ed. Reno, Nevada: University of Nevada Press)

ARTICLES

Alesina, Alberto, Reza Baqir and William Easterly. "Public Goods and Ethnic division." *Quarterly Journal of Economics* 114, no.4 (November 1999).

Associated Press Writer. "AP NewsBreak: Proposed Deal for Calif. Inmate Care." *Sacramento Bee,* May 28, 2009. http://www.sacbee.com/state_wire/v-print/story/1900432.html.

———. "Calif. Unemployment Climbs to Record 11.5 Percent." *Sacramento Bee,* June 19, 2009. http://www.sacbee.com/state_wire/v-print/story/1960877.html.

"Biography of Antonio Villaraigosa, Mayor of Los Angeles." *Los Angeles Almanac.* http://www.laalmanac.com/government/gl12.htm

The Buzz. "The Buzz: California's GDP Grew in 2008, analyst Find." *sacbee.com,* June 9, 2009. http://www.sacbee.com/capitolandcalifornia/v-print/story/1930331.html.

———.. "IOUs Seem Tame Compared to Massachusetts' Solution." *sacbee.com,* July 14, 2009. http://www.sacbee.com/capitolandcalifornia/story/2023570.html.

California Department of Agriculture. *2006 Annual Report.*

California Department of Finance. *Governor's Budget Summary, 2004-05.* http://www.dof.ca.gov/HTML/BUD_DOCS/Bud_link.htm.

Cannon, Lou. "Jerry Brown: A Back to Basics." *Washington Post,* August 13, 1980.

Capitol Alert. "AM Alert: Feinstein, Whitman Atop Early 2010 Poll." *sacbee.com,* March 9, 2009.

———. "Bass Doles Out Committee Perks, Penalties." *sacbee.com,* March 3, 2009. http://www.sacbee.com/static/weblogs/capitolaltetlatest/020304.html.

———. "Brown Says Prop 1A Will Help 'Next Governor.'" *sacbee.com,* April 14, 2009. http://www.sacbee.com/static/weblogs/capitolaltertlatest/021519.html.

———. "AM Alert: Garamendi to Drop Gov. Bid and Run for Congress." *sacbee.com,* April22, 2009.

———. "Controller: State Cash Outlook 'Hammered' by Weak Retail Sales." *sacbee.com,* April 10, 2009. http://www.sacbee.com/static/weblogs/capitolaltertlatest/021447.html.

———. "McClintock Douses Conservative fire Over Gubernatorial Field." *sacbee.com,* May 4, 2009. http://www.sacbee.com/static/weblogs/capitolaltertlatest/022030.html.

———. "Newsom: I'm a Candidate for Governor." *sacbee.com,* April 21, 2009. http://www.sacbee.com/static/weblogs/capitolalertlatest/021685.html.

———. "Poizner Campaign mounts Attack Against Whitman." *sacbee.com,* April 16, 2009. http://www.sacbee.com/static/weblogs/capitolalertlatgest/021597.html.

———. "Poll; Feinstein Tops Dems field: GOP Race Tight in 2010." *sacbee.com,* February 6, 2009. http://www.sacbee.com/static/weblogs/capitolalertlatgest/019330.html.

———. "State Cash Hole Deepens." *sacbee.com*. http://www.sacbee.com/static/we-blogs/capitolalertlatgest/023001.html.

Chandra, Shobhana. "Joblessness Reaches 10% in Indiana; Jumps in Oregon (Update 3)." *Bloomberg.com*, April 17, 2009. http://www.bloomberg.com/apps/news?pid=2 0601087&sid=aAF9sIUABJQ7c.

Day, Brian. "Assemblyman Adams Served with Recall Papers." *pasadenastarnews.com*, April 8, 2009. http://www.pasadenastarnews.com/ci_12104064.

DiCamillo, Mark and Mervin Field. "While California Voters Prefer Spending Cuts to Tax Increases to Resolve the State Budget, Majorities Oppose Cutbacks in Ten of Twelve Spending Categories." *The Field Poll*, Release #2306, April 30, 2009. http://media.sacbee.com/smedia/2009/04/29/15/0429rls.souce.prod_affiliate.4.pdf.

Dowd, Maureen. "Win One for the Groper." *New York Times*, October 5, 2003

Editorial. "No Recall." *San Diego Union-Tribune*, February 18, 2003.

Farhi, Paul. "Lessons from 1929." *Washington Post National Weekly*. November 3-9, 2008.

Finnegan, Michael. "The Times Poll: As Vote Nears, Schwarzenegger Surges Ahead; Survey finds Republican governor leading Democratic challenger Angelides 50% to 33%. Most see incumbent as a stronger leader." *Los Angeles Times*, October 1, 2006.

———. "Whitman Unveils Conservative Positions." *Los Angeles Times*, February 11, 2009. http://articles.latimes.com/2009/feb/11/local/me-whitman11?page_type=article&exci=2009/02/11/local/me-whitman11&pg=1.

Goldenberg, Sally. "Wild-Fired by the Zoo." *New York Post*. April 24, 2009. http://www.nypost.com/php/pfriendly/print.php?url=http%3a%2f%2Fwww.nypost.com%2Fseven%2F04242009%2Fnews%2Fregional   news%2Fwild_fired_by_the_zoo_165956.htm.

Goldmacher, Shane. "Republican Whitman Launches 2010 Bid for Governor." *Sacramento Bee*, February 10, 2009. http"//www.sacbee.com/story/1612318.html.

Goldmacher, Shane and Eric Baily. "Legislative Panel Approves Oil and Tobacco Taxes." *Losw Angeles Times*, June 17, 2009. http://www.latimes.com/news/local/la-me-budget17-2009jun17,0,1715367.story.

Harman, Steven. "Heat Coming from All Sides as Leaders Work on Budget." *Contracostatimes.com*, February 5, 2009. http://www.contracostatimes.com/localnews/ci_11631255?nclick_chck=1.

Hecht, Peter. "L.A. Mayor's Star on the Rise Again as higher Office Beckons." *Sacramento Be*, February 2, 2009. http://www.sacbee.com/capitolandcalifornia/v-print/story/1632869.html.

———. "Field Poll: California Voters Oppose Five of Six May 19 Ballot Measures." *sacbee.com*, April 29, 2009. http://www. sacbee.com/politics/v-print/story/1818253.html.

———. "Poll: Californians Want Health Care Overhaul, but They're Divided on Taxes." *Sacramento Bee*, June 18, 2009. http://www.sacbee.com/state_wire/v-primary/story/1956233.html.

———. "Pollsters Evaluate California Special election Results." *Sacramento Bee*, June 17, 2009. http://www.sacbee.com/capitolandcalifornia/v-print/story/1952810.html.

———. "Q & A: Poizner Explains Views on California Budget." *Sacramento Bee*, February 18, 2009. http://www.sacbee.com/capitolandcalifornia/story/1590994-p2.html.

Howard, John, "Economy Trumps Education, Public Safety in New Poll." *Capitol Weekly*, June 4, 2009. http://www.capitolweekly.net/article-php?1&_c=y2gz9h3kg5titn&xid=y0zd934yqrllup&done=.y2gzfu5pu7ij7h#.

"In Comes the Wave." *The Economist*, June 18, 2005.

Kasler, Dale. "State, Local Jobless Rates Tops 11 Percent." *Sacbee.com*, April 17, 2009. http://www.sacbee.com/1089/story/1788481.html.

Kugler, Reuben Fred. *The California Democratic Council, Highlights in its Record of Achievements 1953-1972*. Ventura, California: CDC Archives, 1972.

———. *Volunteers in Politics: The Twenty-seven year History o the California Democratic Council 1953-1980*. 5th ed. Ventura, California: CDC Archives, 1980.

Marinucci, Carla. "Newsom Declares for governor in high-Tech Style." *San Francisco Chronicle*, April 22, 2009. http://www.sfgate.com/cgi-bin/article.cgi?f=/c/a/2009/04/21/MNJO176EKA.DTL.

McLaughlin, Ken. "Can Tom Campbell Upset Billionaires Running for California Governor?" *San Jose Mercury News*, June 20, 2009. http://www.mercurynews.com/fdcp?1245689984089.

"Meg Whitman 1956-." *Reference for Business-Business Biographies S-Z*. http://www.referenceforbusiness.com/biography/S-Z/Whitman-Meg-1956.html

Office of the Governor of the State of California. *Governor Delivers Speech on the Status of State Budget*, June 12, 2009. http://gov.ca.gov/index.php/print-version/speech/125520/.

——— *Governor Schwarzenegger's State of the State Address*, 01/05/2005. http://gov.ca.gov/speech/2408/.

———. *Governor Schwarzenegger's 2006 State of the State Address, Thursday, 01/05/2006 As Delivered*. http://gov.ca.gov/index.php?/print-version/speech/358/.

———. *Transcript of Governor Schwarzenegger's Second Inaugural Address*. 01/05/2007. http://gov.ca.gov/index.php?/press-release/5049/

———. *Transcript of Governor Arnold Schwarzenegger's State of the State Address*. 01/09/2007. http://ca.gov/indexphp?/press-release/5089/.

Quinn, Tony. "Arnold's Keystone Kops." *Sacramento Bee*, July 26, 2005.

———. *California Morning Report*, January 6, 2006.

———. "Davis Strategy." *Los Angeles Times*, September 2003.

Rau, Jordan and Evan Halper. "California budget Faces New $8 Billion Shortfall." *Los Angeles Times*, March 14, 2009. http://www.latimes.com/news/local/la-me-budget14-2009mar14,0,3882637.story.

Reddy, Patrick. "The Arnold Factor." *Buffalo News*, August 10, 2003.

———"Arnold's First 100 Days." *United Press International*, March 5, 2004.

———. "Arnold in Total Recall 2?" *United Press International*, July 28, 2003.

———. "California Recall Election Coming." *United Press International*, July 10, 2003.

———. "Cruz Bustamante's American Dream." *United Press International*, September 3, 2003.

———. Memo, June 1992.

———. "President Schwarzenegger/" *Buffalo News*, January 30, 2005.

———. "Wild and Crazy Candidates." *Buffalo News*, September 28, 2003.

———. "Will California Recall Governor Davis?" *United Press International*, May 6, 2003.

Roberts, Jerry and Phil Trounstine, "The Calbuzz Primary Starts Today," *Calbuzz*, June 8, 200-9. http://callbuzzer.blogspot.com/2009/06/calbuzz-primary-starts-today.html.

———.. "Jerry Brown: I'm Going to be an Apostle of Common Sense." *Calbuzz*, April 13, 2009. http://calbuzzer.blogspot.com/2009/04/jerry-brown-im-going-to-be-apostle-of.html.

———. "Why Rich Guys Don't Win Top Offices in California." *Calbuzz*, May 4, 2009, http://calbuzzer.blogspot.com/2009/05/why-rick-guys-don't-win-top-offices-in.html.

Rosenberg, Stan. "Moody's Downgrades California GO Debt To 'A2' Stable." *Wall Street Journal (WSJ.com)*, March 19, 2009. http://online.wsj.com/BT-CO-20090319-714047.html.

Sanchez, Rene and Dan Balz. "More than 125 File in Calif. Recall Election; Davis Criticizes Effort as a Dangerous Carnival." *Washington Post*, August 10, 2003.

Scammon, Richard and Ben Wattenberg. "Is It the End of an Era?" *Public Opinion*, October 1980.

Schickel, Richard. "A Delicate Beefcake Ballet." *Time*, January 24, 1977.

Schneider, William. "An Insiders' View of the Election." *Atlantic*, July 1988.

Silva, Fred. "California's Two-Thirds Legislative vote Requirement and its Role in the State Budget Process." *Western city Magazine*, November 2008. http:/www.cacities.org/index.jsp?zone=wcm&previewStory=27483.

Skelton, George. "Governor Has Reason to Worry Over Dump-Davis Effort." *Los Angeles Times*, March 13, 2003. http://8.12.42.31/2003/mar/13/me-cap13.

———. "Jerry Brown Wants to be a Back-to-Basics Governor." *Los Angeles Times*, April 20, 2009. http://www.latimes.com/news/local/la-me-cap20-2009apr20,0,2315392.column.

———. "Note to Budget Doctors: Don't Spare the Knife; Treasurer Bill Lockyer Tells Democratic Lawmakers That Voters Are Angry and Want Them to Solve the Fiscal Problems Now." *Los Angeles Times*, June 11, 2009. http://www.latimes.com/news/local/la-me-cap11-2009jun11,0,4963544,print.column.

South, Garry. "Meg Whitman: a Female Checci or Simon?" *Capitol Weekly*, May 7, 2009. http://capitolweekly.net/article.php?1&_c=xynb684e779dgp&xid=xyl4lnkv7fhkum&done=,xyn9ajv66gqu0j&_ce=1241720339.fc23d8db8503f2c45328fb2a5f9d68f8

Taub, Daniel. "California Home Prices Decline 41% on Foreclosures (Update 1)." *Bloomberg.com*, March 25, 2009. http://www.bloomberg.com/apps/news?pid=20601087$sid=aRhTT4MNBjM&refer=home.

"The Text of Gov. Arnold Schwarzenegger's Inaugural Address." *sfgate*, November 18, 2003. http://www.sfgate.com/cgi-bin/article.cgi?f=/c/a/2003/11/18/MNG-HA34EEM1.DTL.

Tugend, Tom and Brad A. Greenberg. "Villaraigosa Runs Hard for Second Term on Record, future." *JewishJournal.com*. February 25, 2009. http://www.jewishjournal.com/community/article/villaraigosa_runs_hard_for_2ⁿᵈ_term_on_record_future_20090225/.

Walsh, Danny. "U.S. Judge Won't Oust California Prison Medical Czar." *Sacbee.com*. March 25, 2009. http://www.sacbee.com/capitolandcalifornia/story/1726379.html.

Walters, Dan. "Dan Walters: California Ballot Message Was 'Don't Tax Me'" *Sacramento Bee*, June 17, 2009. http://www.sacbee.com/politics/v-print/story/1953095.html.

———. "Villaraigosa's Departure Boosts Brown." *Sacramento Bee*, June 23, 2009. http://www.sacbee.com/capitolandcalifornia/story/1968293.html.

———. "Villarigosa Says He Won't Run for Governor." *Sacramento Bee*, June 22, 2009. http://www.sacbee.com/1095/v-print/story/1967562.html.

White, Deborah. "Antonio Villariagosa: The Bumpy Road of a Rising Democratic Superstar." *About.com*. http://www.usliberals.about.com/od/peopleinthe news/a/Antonio.htm.

Wiegand, Steve. "California Asks Feds to Back its IOUs." *Sacbee.com*, April 15, 2009. http://www.sacbee.com/topstories/story/1781008.html.

———. "Dems Vow to Pass 'Share-the-Pain' Budget." *Sacramento Bee*, June 17, 2009. http://www.sacbee.com/topstories/v-print/story/1955307.html.

———. "Looming State Cash Crisis Seem by California Analyst." *sacbee.com*, May 8, 2009. http://www.sacbee.com/capitolandcalifornia/v-print/story/184200.html.

Willon, Phil. "Villaraigosa's Future, Once Bright, Looks Dimmer Now." *Los Angeles Times*, June 20, 2009. http://www.latimes.com/news/local/la-me-poll21-2009jun21,0,3001867.story.

Wilson, James Q. "A tour of Reagan country." *Commentary*, June 1967.

Woo, Stu. "Whitman Lays Out Plans to Solve California's Fiscal Woes." *The Wall Street Journal*, April 27, 2009. http://blogs.wsj.com/washwire/2009/04/27/Whitman-lays-out-plan-to-solve-californias-fiscal-woes/.

Yamamura, Kevin. "California GOP Leaders Reject All 6 Ballot Measures." *Sacbee.com*, April 19, 2008. http://www.sacbee.com/capitoland California/story/1791244.html.

———. "Fitch Cuts California' bond Rating, Now Worst in Nation." *Sacbee.com*, March 20, 2009. http://www.sacbee.com/politics/story/1714893.html.

———. "Governor Says $2.8 Billion More is Needed." *Sacramento Bee*, May 30, 2009. http://www.sacbee.com/capitolandcalifornia/v-print/story/1903769.html.

———. "Voters Take Dim View of Governor, Legislature." *sacbee.com*, May 1, 2009. http://www.sacbee.com/politics/v-print/story/1825240.html.

OTHER

Bass, California Speaker Karen and Senator Darrel Steinberg. Letter sent to California Democratic State Central Committee members. April 10, 2009.

Caddel, Patrick. Commentary, *MSNBC*, November 5, 2002.

California Association of Realtors. "May 2008 Sales and Price Report (June 25, 2008 press release)." *California Association of Realtors (CAR.org)*. http://www.car.org/newsstand/newsreleases/2008newreleases/0508salesandpricereport/.

Campbell, Tom. Candidate website. http://www.campbell.org.

Field Polls. Look under http://field.com/fieldpollonlione/subscribers/ ... for Mervin Field polls.

Hartgen, David T. "The Looming Highway Condition Crisis: Performance of State Highway Systems, 1984-2002. Manuscript, February 2002. http://www.john-lock.org/policy_reports/2004020943.html.

Internet Movie Data Base. Look under http://www.imdb.com for Arnold Schwarzenegger and his films.

Kennedy, Sen. Edward, Interview, *CNN*, August 2003.

Maslin & Tuchin. Press Release. August, 2003.

Newsom, Gavin. Candidate website. http://gavinnewsom.com

Poizner, Steve. Candidate website. http://www.stevepoizner.com.

Reddy, Patrick. Conversation with Bill Cavala in Speaker's Office.

————. Conversation with Bill Cavala and Trent Hager.

————. Conversation with Darry Sragow. Fall, 1998.

————. Conversation with Tony Quinn. Spring, 2003.

————. Interview of Bernd Schwiern. Fall, 2005.

————. Interview of Jim Alford. November, 2005.

————. Interview of Senate Budget Staffers.

"Schwarzenegger's List"(cartoon). *Spy*, February 1994.

Villaraigosa, Antonio. Assembly Democrats 1998 Blueprint for victory, Campaign Manual.

Whitman, Meg. Candidate website. http://www.megwhitman.com